Gibran, Rihani & Naimy

Gibran, Rihani & Naimy

East–West interactions in early
twentieth-century Arab literature

AIDA IMANGULIEVA

Translated from the Russian by Robin Thomson

INNER FARNE PRESS · OXFORD

Originally published in Russian as *Korifei novoarabskoy literatury: k probleme vzaimosvyazi literatur Vostoka i Zapada nachala XX veka*, by Elm, Baku, Azerbaijan, 1991

First published in English as *Gibran, Rihani & Naimy: East–West interactions in early twentieth-century Arab literature*, by Inner Farne Press, 2009
English edition © Afaq Khanum, 2009

Inner Farne Press is an imprint of Anqa Publishing
PO Box 1178
Oxford OX2 8YS, UK
www.ibn-arabi.com

British Library Cataloguing in Publication Data
A CIP catalogue record for this book is available from the British Library

ISBN   978 1 905937 27 1

Cover design by Anneke Germers

Our thanks to Bekir Shahin and the staff of the Bolge Yazmalar Kutuphanesi in Konya, Turkey, for permission to reproduce the ebru image

Printed in the USA by Worldcolor

Dedicated to the memory of my mother

Contents

Foreword by Dr Afag Asadova

A treasure of Azeri literary thought

In times of changing values and the emergence of new social relations, the societal norms and ethical and moral values that have so far provided a basis for the existence and functioning of society have, throughout history, found themselves striving to win the right to their continued existence. What values should be preserved in an evolving society, and what values can such a society be based on? In our present era is it possible for literature to serve as a criterion for the values on which we are to build our lives and our way of life? And will those values pass through the filter of literary artistic thought?

If one answers these questions in the negative, one may refute the significance of the perennial values that ensure the integrity and continuity of life, of society and of history. In such a case, the significance of human life and of humaneness in society would be lost in a society of permanent contradictions, in which good clashes with evil, light with darkness and life with death.

There is much discussion today over the role, position and responsibility of the Arts, both of the written word and of literary thought, which form the criteria of literature, literary criticism and literary studies. And criteria, like all things, are measured and selected. It is natural that different tendencies give rise to different ideas. Solutions to these issues are found in literary–critical works and in recent examples of literary thought – and even in many that are decades old but have not lost their scholarly and historical importance. It is true that historical upheavals or social and political crises can, during the period of turmoil, keep thinking minds at the level of basic survival. As time passes, however, the moral and aesthetic values that are the requirements of the soul, and which form the conditions for our common survival, together with examples of literary–critical thought that provide the criterion by which "the written word will be enriched" within the existence of a society, as well as works on literary study, all need to be found among the broader mass readership – and equally in the interest of each person who has at least some level of a given social culture.

Aida Imangulieva's book *Gibran, Rihani and Naimy* is a timeless example of literary–critical thinking, classical literary studies and first-class Oriental studies. Of immense academic importance, this work is that of a master and a great mind, a work of intensive criticism devoted to the problems of interaction between Eastern and Western literature in the early twentieth century. In her study of the reception and mutual influence of the English Romantic traditions, with which a considerable part of this study is concerned, together with that of the American Transcendentalists, and of the Critical Realism of the Russian tradition on the new Arab literature of

the time, Aida Imangulieva has examined many philosophical, literary and
sociopolitical systems of thought and currents of ideas, their origins and
importance, and the extent of research carried out on them. Along with
the general conclusions she reached, this forms an immense contribution
to Azeri and international literary studies. Like all spheres of scholarship
and culture, the study of Azeri literature was in a state of change and development in the twentieth century and had achieved substantial progress.
However, the fetters imposed by totalitarianism limited that development
to a certain degree – to the point, in fact, at which it began to pose a threat
to the existence of the regime. The primary goal and source of development for scholarly literary studies, as with other humanitarian and social
sciences, is to gradually give expression to universal values and ideals, at
the same time as developing a national consciousness. In the prevailing
historical conditions, it was only those literary scholars whose thought
did not fit within the ideological framework imposed by the regime who
were able to broaden the horizons of their thinking; in other words, only
those with the gifts and talent and an advanced scholarly and philosophical
world-view were able to preserve the essence, meaning, direction and goals
of that scholarship. Aida Imangulieva's book *Gibran, Rihani and Naimy* is
an achievement of scholarship that has been applied at a contemporary
and perfected level of a systematic approach gained during the course of
historical development; it also reflects the most recent level of development of Azeri literary studies and thereby gives rise to a new tendency and
a new school.

A century after the emergence of the questions that the book addresses,
and hand in hand with the positive aspects of political and economic growth
and globalisation that characterise the world at the start of the twenty-first
century, the far-sightedness and perspicacity of thinkers such as Aida Imangulieva are once again striking: unity, integration and globalisation must
occur to the same degree as cultural and literary development. Ms Imangulieva asserts that the national literature of every society is linked indissolubly
and inherently by its character to universal human achievement. Were the
unity of the national with the universal to be fractured, no literature could
develop; there would be no literary development in any upward direction.
Her scholarly achievement is not so much an affirmation of this established
fact as her own examination of the mechanism by which national literatures
influence one another, together with the points of contact between them,
and her identification of the links between the national and the universal. By
considering the effect of the smallest unit that links national literatures to
the individuals who created it, Ms Imangulieva reveals the complex threads
between the literatures of different peoples and shows, through a philosophical prism, the correlation of artistic thought to life, and that of literary
directions to historical periods.

Ms Imangulieva was supremely aware of the sociopolitical nature of her
time, and it was not simply through an accident of academic interests that

she arrived at these topics of research. Appealing to a diversified circle of interest that itself expresses the mutual influence of the idea-currents of East and West, which she studied in depth, she sought to raise the level of Azeri social consciousness to one that would embrace universal ideas and values, thus releasing it from the moral and ideological fetters prevalent at that time. With feelings of patriotism and social conscience, the author characterises the roles of the prominent Arab writers Kahlil Gibran, Ameen Rihani and Mikhail Naimy in the following way: "Their literary activity served, as it were, as the channel of communication that enabled Western and Eastern literatures to exchange their intellectual achievements." Using her research as an information channel, Ms Imangulieva enriched the flow with universal ideas to provide a continuity and longevity for the development of Azeri social consciousness and national self-consciousness. Not merely as a scholar and researcher but also as a deep-thinking philosopher and a fine writer, she expresses her own ideas through references to numerous writers and philosophers from the East and West. During the ban on free speech and thinking in her time, she managed to find a scholarly literary method of freely expressing her thoughts on ideas that have been the source of unbounded and endless speculation, ideas which have occupied humankind for millennia: God, Freedom, Beauty, Literature and so forth.

Gibran, Rihani and Naimy is a monumental work in terms of its theoretical importance, its richness of information, the breadth of scope of its topics, the depth of its ideas, the formulation of its questions, the systematic approach to its subject, and its stylistic and expressive qualities. The author presents the conditions that precipitated the emergence of a new literary school as a response to the "needs of an awakening people"; this was given the representational name of "Syro-American", and the activities of this school as a new historical phase that was being embarked upon. She further describes how, through the protagonists of this school, the national literature moved into a new developmental stage, drawing upon the achievements of Western culture and literature. This new movement embodied the ideas and forms of a new historical reality, creating various literary tendencies and methods as the literary process developed, each one being transformed and replaced by another and, parallel with this, how the literary genres evolved and were refined.

While it combines elements of both Oriental and literary studies, this book does not fit neatly into the usual mould in terms of its ideas or aims, nor does it express the sociopolitical views, ethical and moral opinions, or philosophical position of its author. As well as preserving its theoretical importance and immense scholarly value, the work also reveals traits of creative styles. It portrays the wealth and unlimited range of ideas and expressive possibilities that are the product of an innate talent, in addition to the author's intensive research. Ms Imangulieva has thoroughly assimilated models of both art and literature from many centuries in both East and West, along with their philosophical and ethical views and sociopolitical attitudes, and has studied the works of the various writers and thinkers in their original languages – Arabic, English and Russian.

The structure of the book is in conformity with its style and content. In the first chapter questions are addressed concerning the influence – general and specific – of both Arab literature (in the USA) and foreign literature on the writers of the Syro-American School. This is followed by a discussion of the historically existing sociopolitical conditions for Arab literature, the cross-influence of literatures, East–West cultural links and their history, the evolution of types of artistic thought and of literary tendencies – Enlightenment, Sentimentalism, Romanticism, Critical Realism – and the dynamics of their development. Each of the following three chapters is devoted to the works of one of the three principal exponents of the new Arab literature. These chapters are an attempt to comprehend the subject along with questions of literary theory; yet there is no duplication, as in each case these are seen differently, in terms both of each author's exposure to foreign literature and of an analysis of their tendencies and methods, forms and genres.

Chapter 2 examines the work of Kahlil Gibran, and outlines the writer's progression from Sentimentalism to Romanticism together with the basic characteristics of this artistic method, its stages of development, and application in specific examples and details. The principle, form and content of such genres as the poem, short story, essay and prose poem are analysed. The chapter also looks at the wider influence of English and American Romanticism on Arabic literature through the example of Gibran's work.

Chapter 3, whose theme is the role of Ameen Rihani in the formation of Arab Romanticism, examines the development of the ideas and conceptions of Romanticism as a full artistic method, as well as that of artistic thinking in Rihani's works. It also discusses how his world-view accords with the spiritual and intellectual foundations of American Transcendentalism. Using Rihani's work as its basis, the chapter analyses various poetic genres – poems, narrative poems, stories with multiple plots, and short prose genres.

The fourth and final chapter examines the mutual interactions of Arabic and Russian literatures, and the way in which Mikhail Naimy was influenced by leading exponents of Russian literature in the twentieth century: Vissarion Belinsky, Leo Tolstoy, Ivan Turgenev and Anton Chekhov. Interestingly, Ms Imangulieva explores this influence from the perspective of different literary genres to those referred to in earlier chapters: critical articles, plays, novels and stories.

As can be seen, each chapter possesses a completeness of form and content, a committed structure and a free subject. In addition, the cohesion of inner content and ideas, the logical integrity and affinity of the author's aims, in terms of covering all the literary tendencies and the forms and genres that were characteristic of the period under investigation, the philosophical schools, movements of ideas, and sociopolitical outlooks – all form part of an integral whole. Seeking to capture certain historical moments in the work of the three writers, and registering the spiritual values of literature that are one of the fundamental conditions for human existence, Imangulieva describes Gibran's *The Prophet* and Naimy's *The Book of Mirdad* as an ethical and moral credo in which the author's own philosophical and religious thoughts and ideas are gathered.

On the same basis, this book may likewise be referred to as both a philo-sophical–ethical and a moral–ethical credo that contains a valuable scholarly legacy. *Gibran, Rihani and Naimy* is the product of a lifetime's work. While preserving its complete originality, the author's personal approach and po-sition, and her unique qualities of analysis and expression, it also embraces its subject from a broad canvas down to the smallest details – but not before having "squeezed the juice from the fruit" and imbibed of the essence, sub-stance and spirit of hundreds of scholarly, literary, artistic and philosophical books, works of research, articles, and other documents. Ms Imangulieva is well aware of the responsibility she bears: in her scholarly activity she follows the words of Leo Tolstoy that she cites in the present book: "In order to find gold in art it is necessary to collect a lot of material and sift it through the sieve of criticism." Thus she selects the very essence, just as she makes her comparative analysis of Belinsky and Naimy and considers carefully the material, opinions and positions on the topic in question.

Aida Imangulieva is a scholar and an innovator. Her innovativeness con-sists not only in her choice of topic, the way she formulates questions and her original approach to the subject, but also in the academic method she develops in this book. In her systematic approach to research she generally uses comparative methods more than is strictly called for by the subject matter. After all, within the study of literature, a comparative study of the works of different writers and of national literatures within literary studies, and the analysis of literary connections, is a broad domain with a particular history. The use, influence and adoption of literary connections are, for Ms Imangulieva, not merely a literary event, but one of the methods for better disclosing the artistic characteristics of the subjects of the process of influ-ence and adoption. For her, the assimilation of other literatures in order to understand oneself through art is a perspective that reveals the comparison, mutual influences and connections between different writers and between the literatures of different peoples; the same applies to the artistic charac-ter of particular individual writers and, indeed, the more general, global questions of literature. In this way Ms Imangulieva was able to reconstruct the theoretical problems of literature, as well as the sociopolitical, cultural and philosophical substance and vista of one historical epoch that played a crucial role in the development of humanity.

As a research scholar the author bases her opinions, abstractions and con-clusions on the criteria of scientific nature, veracity and objectivity. She exposes causes and motives, recording both the general and the necessary. She boldly engages in polemics with other scholars, regardless of their authority or reputation, who file their claims on the basis of outer appear-ance or association. As an academic Ms Imangulieva seeks the triumph of facts, just as the aesthete seeks the triumph of beauty and the philosopher that of reality. Nevertheless, in comparisons between East and West one can detect a subtle Eastern bias, the result of her immense love of the East and of its history and literature, which is linked to the spiritual roots of her own people.

Gibran, Rihani and Naimy is a valuable example of a literary–philosophical work in twentieth-century Azeri social thought. This work is a treasure of scholarship that has not yet found due recognition in the history of social thought. A proper assessment of this work, and more broadly of Aida Imangulieva's achievements as a whole, may be given in other works that examine and analyse her scholarly and theoretical legacy in a comprehensive manner and from various theoretical perspectives. A study of her work is also valuable from the viewpoint of determining the level of the Azeri literary and philosophical world-view in the twentieth century.

This book offers a fresh view by a late twentieth-century scholar of the world existing at the end of the nineteenth and start of the twentieth centuries. Yet really this is a view of our own time, in that the basis of today's scientific world-view – along with many of our global problems – were established in the period covered by the book. In *Gibran, Rihani and Naimy*, Aida Imangulieva discusses the mutual influences and links of American and English cultures with Arab culture and the synthesis of Western and Eastern thinking; she also explores the thought of those geniuses who founded modern Arabic literature and who, at the start of the twentieth century, sought to modify Eastern thought in accordance with the demands of the modern world, thus throwing light equally onto modern perspectives and approaches to problems. As Ameen Rihani says in his bitingly ironic question:

> I am the East.
> I have philosophies and religions.
> Who would exchange them for aircraft?

And as Mikhail Naimy says, expressing the pain in his heart: "Many critics evade the truth by means of 'patriotic' phrases such as 'Our country is the cradle of inspiration and humanity and the homeland of the prophets.' 'Centuries passed, and still we knock our foreheads on the threshold of churches ... a thick layer of rust has covered our hearts and minds.'" And here, finally, is the sublime image of Gibran, who "embodied all epochs, ideals and great deeds, the undying voice of the ages": "The sight of the ruined city [of the Past] brings the poet to despair, but Life tells him he must depart and look instead for the City of the Future: Come, for only the coward tarries, and it is folly to look back on the City of the Past."

The many political, economic, social and ecological problems facing the world today dictate the necessity and importance of the works and activity of such intellectuals as Aida Imangulieva. The solution to all such problems lies in the transformation of the cultural values of the world's peoples, East and West, into universal values for all humanity.

Following the words of the Russian genius Dostoevsky, who declared in the nineteenth century that "Beauty will save the world", many great thinkers of the twentieth century have been of the same view. The American philosopher–poet Emerson, to whom Ms Imangulieva makes frequent reference, also believed that beauty is the "creator of the universe".

In researching links between American and Arabic literature, Ms Imangulieva remarks on how close Gibran's conceptions of the beauty that "saves the world" are to those of Emerson: "Beauty is literature that regards itself in the mirror." If indeed these great thinkers are correct in saying that beauty will save the world, then *Gibran, Rihani and Naimy* – as bestowed upon the treasury of universal thought by the prominent scholar, Orientalist, philosopher and thinker Aida Imangulieva – will portray literature as "the mirror of beauty".

Introduction

Historical background: new Arabic literature and the Syro-American School

There are periods in the history of every nation in which its achievements become a substantial component of world civilisation. Arab culture enjoyed such a flowering in the eighth to twelfth centuries, during which it made its distinctive contribution to the cultural ascent of the Renaissance. Then, for reasons determined by history, its development slowed sharply.

A new stage in the ascent of Arab sociopolitical and cultural life began at the close of the eighteenth century, following the French expedition to Egypt and Syria (1798–1801). This resulted, in particular, in considerably increased contact between the Arab world and the West.[1] From this time, and owing to a series of historical factors, Egypt emerged as the leading country of the Arab East. Egyptian literature moved into first place and became the most influential among the literatures closest to it in historical destiny: those of Syria and Lebanon. By the mid-nineteenth century, however, Syria and Lebanon, which at the time were a single country, began to excel alongside Egypt. The Orientalist Ignaty Yulianovich Krachkovsky wrote: "In Syria and Egypt in the nineteenth century there began a period of great revival that concentrated, in the main, on Lebanon with its centre at Beirut."[2]

By the beginning of the nineteenth century Beirut already stood out from other Arab cities for its developed trade, its blossoming in artisan and skilled crafts and its Europeanised appearance. This was frequently remarked upon by visiting European travellers. "Beirut can be briefly characterised thus: of all Asiatic cities it is the least Asiatic; of all cities of the East it is the most European",[3] the Italian-French writer Princess Cristina Belgioioso (1806–71) noted in her diary. There are also accounts by Europeans of Lebanon as a whole. In their reminiscences the French writer Alphonse de Lamartin, the Austrian Arabist Alfred von Kremer, the Russian consul Konstantin Bazili and others not only admired Lebanon's natural features and its favourable geographical position, but also remarked on the high level of culture among the inhabitants of Beirut in comparison with other Arab peoples.

Gradually Beirut became an outpost of Western culture in the East. The penetration of European missionary activity also increased, and although the primary aim of the missionaries was to build and disseminate the influence of the countries they represented in the economic and intellectual lives of the Arabs, pursuing this policy also facilitated the spreading of cultural enlightenment.

1

A number of literary, public and academic organisations were set up in Lebanon.[4] A new periodical press made its presence widely known and facilitated the appearance of journalism as a genre.[5] Journalism, with its topical content and social and political themes, then provided the basis on which a new imaginative literature could develop. Much interest was also being shown in translations from European languages at this time.

These social and cultural shifts, which took place over a number of decades, brought internal changes to the country and a growing national consciousness. Lebanon had become active in the forms of world trade and the financial relations that would lead to capitalism; new social strata emerged; and significant changes were taking place against the background of the country's general intellectual and cultural ascendancy. By the mid-nineteenth century Lebanon was ready to encounter the cultural values, including literature, of other peoples of the world.

However, such an enhanced cultural life in Lebanon, with its growth in national consciousness and the birth and development of an intelligentsia, was in stark contrast to the country's economic backwardness and political suppression under the totalitarian power of the Ottoman Empire. The situation was further complicated by the expansionism of the European powers. From the 1870s the economic position of Lebanon changed dramatically. With the opening of the Suez Canal in 1868 the port of Beirut lost its international importance. Trade in the country gradually dwindled, while the earlier supremacy in the arts and crafts fell into neglect and the peasantry was ruined. These circumstances were also partly the result of internecine religious conflicts.

Sociopolitical and economic conditions in Lebanon at the close of the nineteenth century were such that a considerable part of the population emigrated *en masse* to the USA, and this left its mark on the country's cultural life. To this migration of the Lebanese artistic intelligentsia to the USA, and in particular to New York, can also be attributed the germination of Arab émigré literature, which subsequently grew into the isolated and unique phenomenon known as the Syro-American School.* This would play a key role in the establishment of the new Arabic literature.

The Syro-American School produced a number of major figures in Arabic literature. In Arab studies, both in the Soviet Union† and abroad, the important contribution of its members to the overall development of Arabic

---

* The academically accepted term "Syro-American School" was first used by I.Yu. Krachkovsky. It refers to the group of writers from Syria and Lebanon who pursued literary activities in the USA. Krachkovsky used the term not only in a purely geographical sense to refer to the place of residence of these writers but also to highlight a specific synthesis of Arab and American literatures. See Krachkovsky, *Arabskaya literatura v XX veke*, pp.17–25.

† [Editor's note] This book was written and first published (in Russian) before the dissolution of the Soviet Union.

literature continues to be recognised. A study of the evolution of the works of the principal representatives of the School, Kahlil Gibran, Ameen Rihani and Mikhail Naimy – under the direct influences of Western Romanticism and Russian Critical Realism – is above all a study of the evolving interaction of the new Arabic literature with various movements and artistic methods in world literature. The objective importance of this subject arises from the part played by literary interactions in the formation of a new type of Arabic literature, based on different ideological and aesthetic principles to those of late Medieval literature.

In the late nineteenth and early twentieth centuries, during a period of cultural revival and development of the Enlightenment movement and Islamic reform, the conditions for developments in Arabic literature were comparatively favourable. Such a literary fermentation then naturally created conditions receptive to the experiments of foreign literatures. This was all the more the case since the historical events of this time encouraged the forming of literary contacts.

The role of rejuvenator of Arabic literature, by way of familiarising it with the practices of foreign literatures, fell to the leading members of the Syro-American School. Gibran and Rihani occupied themselves with Western Romanticism. However, these writers did not so much isolate its external traits or mechanically transpose its basic principles to Arabic literature as assimilate Romanticism as an artistic method, that is, as a new point of view that allowed them to express their relationship to the demands of Arab reality. The principles of Critical Realism, adopted by Naimy from the Russian classics, formed the basis of his first works, in which he as artist and realist reflected Arab life in its newly developed stage, with all its attendant features.

The influence of foreign literatures in the work of Gibran, Rihani and Naimy appears exactly as described by A. Dima, that is, "as a set of impulses thanks to which talents are awoken and the possibilities contained within them become a reality. Accordingly, the true purpose of such influences is to stimulate creativity."[6] The importance of the creative work of these writers is that they perceived and transformed the ethical and artistic values of European and American literatures in a new way, synthesising the achievements of those with the best of their own national traditions. The Syro-American School, as epitomised by its most talented artists, responded to those elements of foreign literatures that addressed the vital requirements for social development in the Arab countries. Thanks to the efforts of these writers, Arabic literature in the early twentieth century was able to overcome its former reticence – as relating to a regional community – to actively participate in the global literary process.

For all the uniqueness of what it achieved, the Syro-American School is a characteristic example of development through contact, and of the formation of a new literary practice under the influence of the literatures of other nations. Given that in each particular instance of similar interactions between two or more literary traditions the specific character of the synthesis is contingent on the source material of the tradition, then as a whole the entry of a national literature into the global literary process is inevitably accompanied by a stage of contact.

The works of the writers of the Syro-American School represent an uncommon situation. In their zone of contact there appeared three different traditions simultaneously: the English "Lake School", American Transcendentalism and the Critical Realism of Russian literature.

The description, comparative analysis and research into these literary facts both broadens the picture of how a new Arabic literature was formed, and reconstructs a typologically reliable map of the complex and contradictory forms of the historical development of the new literatures of the East. The result of the contact of the Syro-American School with these three movements was the formation within it of certain artistic methods: the Lake School and Transcendentalism served the emergence of a Romantic method in the works of Gibran and Rihani, while contact with Russian literature formed the Realism of Naimy.

Making general conclusions about how the Syro-American School evolved has a fundamental methodological value, insofar as they create the basis for building a typology of development through contact in modern Eastern literatures, and can demonstrate the process by which artistic methods and movements form within them.

The fundamental goal of this investigation is to identify and interpret the patterns that characterise the process by which the substance of the foreign literature is received by the literature that perceives it – in this case the Syro-American School, which was in fact already moving into a more advanced stage of development and creating a new artistic method for its national literary tradition. Subsequently the achievements of this School would become the achievement of all Arabic literature.

Here a series of interrelated questions arises: firstly, how Western and Eastern traditions were synthesised in the practice of the Syro-American School; secondly, what specific elements were received from the schools of Western European and American Romanticism and Russian Critical Realism; and finally, how these artistic methods were developed in their works.

The principle behind the selection of works for comparative analysis should be stated here. This has been determined by the task of representing in as clear a focus as possible the processes that were taking place in Arabic literature. Therefore priority [in selection of material] has been given to works that demonstrate the assimilation of the new processes rather than those that are already based upon them. In addition, preference has been given to works in which the results of the synthesis and evolution of the creative methods of Arab writers are most clearly visible.

Studies by Russian and Soviet scholars

The research in this study rests upon the work of the following Soviet Orientalists: A.A. Dolinina, V.N. Kirpichenko, I.Yu. Krachkovsky, A.E. Krymsky, A.B. Kudelin, Z.I. Levin, V.B. Lutsky, K.V. Ode-Vasil'eva, S.V. Prozhogina, N.K. Usmanov, I.M. Fil'shtinsky, E.P. Chelyshev, L.Ye. Cherkassky and B.Ya. Shidfar. Reference has been made in the study to literary–historical studies on English, American and Russian literature by A.I. Batyuto, G.P. Berdnikov, P.I. Biryukov, L.O. Blagovy, G.A. Byaly, T.N. Vasil'eva, T.D. Venediktova, I.A. Gurvich, N.Ya. D'yakonova, M.Ye. Yelizarova, A.A. Yelistratova, Ye.I. Kiyko, G.V. Kurlyanskaya, M.O. Mendelson, T.L. Motyleva, O.K. Rossiyanov, L.I. Startsev, D.M. Urnov, A.V. Fedorov, A.I. Shifman and others.

In examining questions of creative method and the interactions of literatures, I have relied on the investigations of the following theoretical literary critics: A.S. Bushmin, I.F. Volkov, A. Dima, D. Dyurishin, V.M. Zhirmunsky, N.I. Konrad, D.S. Likhachev, I.G. Neupokoeva, I.D. Nikiforova, L.I. Timofeev, U.R. Fokht, M.B. Khrapchenko and others.

Acknowledgement is due to the following Arab scholars for works consulted on the history of émigré literature and the lives and activities of émigré writers: A.K. Ashtar, A.I. Qindilchi, A. Jundi, J. Jabr, I. Qunsul, H. Mas'ud, M.Yu. Najm, I. Na'uri, Nadira Jamil Sarraj, J. Saydah, K.M. Talisi, G. Tomeh, M. Taymur, D. Anas, Philip Hitti, M. 'Abd al-Ghani Hasan, H. Jad Hasan, M.M. Haddara and others, and the Western European scholars Carl Brockelmann, Georg Kampffmeyer, Tahir Khemiri, Joseph Ghougassian, Adele Younis and others.

This monograph also makes use of the findings of Ph.D. dissertations by M.V. Kuteliya, H.K. Muminov, I.E. Bilyk, M.V. Nikolaeva, L.A. Tazetdinova and V.V. Markov, and material from various articles, forewords and afterwords to translations of Arabic works into Russian.

The first to realise the importance of the Syro-American School for the new Arab culture was the Academician Krachkovsky, who placed a high value on the contribution of its members to cultural development.[7] He sets out succinctly the history of Arab émigré literature in many of his works, concentrating on the USA.[8] In special works devoted to Rihani,[9] Gibran[10] and Naimy,[11] Krachkovsky identifies their place and role in the development of the new Arabic literature. Through his efforts many works by émigré writers were made available to a wider circle of readers than merely specialists in the field. Krachkovsky translated several works by Gibran, Rihani and Naimy into Russian.[12] The scholar's archive contains still-unpublished translations of works from the Syro-American School.[13]

Krachkovsky observes an accelerated rate of development in émigré literature and direct contacts with Western literature. He points out several times, for example, the influence of the Western Romantic school on Gibran and Rihani: "His [Rihani's] favourite forms are, on the one hand, small articles – sketches on the most diverse of topics – ethical, literary and political – and on the other, prose poetry, which appears here for the first time in any significant quantity and which was the result of the influence of Walt Whitman."[14] While not over-estimating this influence, in his article *Arabic literature in America (1895–1915)* Krachkovsky remarks:

> There is no doubt that the immigrants are far better acquainted with European literature than their brothers in the East, but this familiarity has a purely eclectic, mostly coincidental quality and is not specifically directed towards their new homeland. Of course they recognise individual representatives of it; without doubt, the influence of Walt Whitman comes through exposure to America: and yet it is also from the Americans that we [sic] first gained a closer knowledge of Voltaire and Goethe and Keats and Carlyle.[15]

Krachkovsky deserves further credit for being the first to reveal the close ideological and artistic links between certain members of the Syro-American School, in particular Naimy, and classical Russian literature.[16]

The basic ideas contained in Krachkovsky's works have been developed in many studies by Soviet Arabists. The sources on Arab émigré literature on which Krachkovsky based his work have since been considerably augmented. Nevertheless, the general methodological positions that he set out continue to be pivotal for research on the subject.

Certain works by Gibran, Rihani and Naimy have been included in an anthology of Arab writers compiled by Klaudia Viktorovna Ode-Vasil'eva.[17] She has also written prefaces to two anthologies, *Stories by Lebanese Writers*[18] and *Lebanese Short Stories*,[19] giving concise information about Arab émigré literature and its main figures.

The work of A.A. Dolinina[20] on the Syro-American School has also been fruitful. She has given particular attention in her research to developments in the main literary movements and individual genres of Arab émigré literature, and has pointed to the relationship of works by Gibran, Rihani and Naimy with Russian and Western literatures. Many prefaces and afterwords written by Dolinina to collections in Russian translation of Arabic writers are of interest despite their bulk, and helpful in the study of the works of the Syro-American School. It is to Dolinina, after Krachkovsky, that credit is due for introducing the artistic legacy of Gibran, Rihani and Naimy to Soviet readers.[21]

In recent times a series of works have appeared by authors who have set themselves the tasks of studying specific problems in relation to the Syro-American School.

The dissertation on Gibran by M.V. Kuteliya, *The World-View of Khalil Gibran*,[22] gives much space to the treatment of problems already known and studied. The main theme is examined in statistical terms and not linked to the creative evolution of the writer's method. While examining Gibran's world-view, Kuteliya does not even mention the way he was influenced by Western poets and writers, and merely sketches the influence of the philosophy of Nietzsche on his work without discussing this in depth.

The preface by V.V. Markov to a volume of selected works by Gibran in Russian translation[23] will be of some interest to scholars. He describes Gibran at once as a Romantic with a philosophical tendency.* He proposes that the basis of Gibran's Romantic world-view is the idea of the human being as the highest creation in nature, who strives incessantly towards completion. Markov supports this view with works by Gibran that include *Broken Wings, A Tear and a Smile, The Tempests* and *The Forerunner*. It is through these works that he traces the evolution of a single Romantic theme, which was to occupy Gibran throughout his creative life. Markov considers the writer's philosophical approach to be revolutionary in its very essence, founded as it is on the trinity of Love, Rebellion and Freedom. He supports his belief by referring to a book by Naimy on Gibran, whose main thesis is Gibran as revolutionary, as the rebel who moves humanity to a more perfected and moral state of life. The author correctly affirms the deep relationship of Gibran's style to the classical traditions of Arabic poetry.

A pamphlet by Z.I. Levin[24] examines the world-view of Rihani, but does not discuss his artistic output. In Levin's view the fundamental premise of Rihani's philosophy is the struggle to reconcile materialism with idealism. For him the origin of all existence is God, whom he identifies with nature, which embodies in itself Love, Truth and Mystery. Rihani proposes that the basis of historical social development is the perfection of the individual, which in turn leads to the improvement of morals in society itself. It is particularly important that individuals be allowed to develop freely, without being oppressed by racial, national or religious prejudices. Levin observes that for Rihani the social process therefore consists in the "humanising" of a human being. For him social relations come down to ethical relations. The main themes of Levin's pamphlet are also reflected in his book, *Principal Developments in Social and Political Thought in Syria and Egypt*.[25]

A further interesting work is the dissertation by L.A. Tazetdinova[26] on the poetry of Rihani. To a certain degree this work fills a gap in studies of the writer's creative output. Tazetdinova gives a general description of the Syro-American School and a biography of the writer, and deals with the sources of his system of imagery and the features of his versification technique; but the most interesting part of her work is the third chapter, which concentrates on the themes and images of Rihani's poetry. Tazetdinova divides Rihani's poetry into two periods: before and after the 1920s. For her the basis of

---

* The Preface by V. Volosatov to earlier publications of Gibran in translation contains brief notes on the history and work of the writer. It does not, however, deal with the author's methods. See Volosatov, V.A., 'Dzhebran Khalil Dzhebran', in *Slomannie krylya*, Moscow, 1962, pp.3–13; Volosatov, V.A., Preface to *Sleza i ulybka*, Moscow, 1976, pp.5–12.

this periodisation is the type of thematic material characteristic of each period. Before the 1920s the poet used predominantly universal human subjects, typical of a Romantic world perception. After the 1920s, however, the Romanticism in Rihani's poetry acquires a uniquely national colouring, expressed in the way he poses certain problems that are specific to an Eastern author and of a purely national character: the struggle for freedom of the Arab peoples, the aspiration to join the best features of Western culture to Arab culture, and so forth. We would argue, however, that such a strict period division of Rihani's poetry by thematic character is not entirely valid, since the principal Romantic themes and motifs remained in various forms in Rihani's work throughout his creative life. A new and interesting insight in Tazetdinova's dissertation is in the section on Rihani's style and system of versification, in which she discusses the poetry of Whitman and underlines his influence on the work of the Lebanese writer.

It may be stated, however, that of the various members of the Syro-American School, the greatest attention by Soviet Orientalists has been devoted to Mikhail Naimy.[27]

The dissertation by H.K. Muminov, based on a wealth of factual material, primarily examines the historical background and traces the development of critical thought in the Arab countries. Muminov's picture of Naimy's literary and critical thinking is drawn mostly from his book *The Sieve*. He finds that Naimy drew many of his ideas from those of the Russian critic Vissarion Belinsky. Correctly considering Naimy to be "the founder of a school of Realist literary criticism of a new kind", Muminov discusses, in our view rather simplistically and academically, the "class limitations of Naimy's world-view".[28] Nor can we agree with Muminov's view of the book by Naimy about Gibran (*Kahlil Gibran: his life and death and literary and artistic works*) as purely a work of criticism, when this book is an original artistic undertaking that reconstructs the complex person of the writer. Muminov furthermore omits to mention the view that several theoretical utterances by Naimy in this book develop and consolidate a Romantic position.

The dissertation by I.E. Bilyk, in which Naimy's work is considered within the unified context of the historical, social, political and cultural conditions in Lebanon, is certain to be of interest. In this study Naimy's work is divided into three periods: (1) 1910 to 1920 (early stories, including *Memoirs of a Vagrant Soul*); (2) 1930 to 1950 (the story "The Meeting" and the novel *The Book of Mirdad*); and (3) the mid-1950s to the 1960s (late stories and the novel *The Last Day*). The stream of different influences that transformed and implanted themselves – Russian, Western and classical Arabic literature – could not but leave their mark on Naimy's artistic method as a whole. His artistic method was also exposed to the non-Realist tendencies of the West: Existentialism and Surrealism, and in the religious dimension, Christianity and Sufism. Bilyk concludes that this is the cause of the ambiguity in Naimy's artistic method. And from this perspective she analyses all the works mentioned and reveals a variety of "methods" within them – Critical Realism, Romanticism, Enlightenment Realism and Sentimentalism – and sometimes even traces of Surrealism and Existentialism. All this is more or less true, but this constant small-scale assertion of "hints" of various different methods ultimately conceals and clouds any clear conclusion: so which method has the writer really used in one or another of his works?

In her conclusion Bilyk asserts that in the first of the three stages Naimy, abstracting himself from Arab traditions and responding to the achievements of world literature, "gains a basic mastery of both Romanticism and Critical Realism, with a partial 'imposition' on these methods of Enlightenment Realism and Sentimentalism."[29]

In his second creative period Naimy's work shows a preference for Enlightenment Realism, and continues to develop the Romantic line "with a partial mastery of Surrealism". The last period is characterised as the pinnacle of his development of "Critical Realism, but also of Surrealism with a layer of Romantic elements", that is to say, with the development of non-Realist methods.

From this one may gain the impression that it is possible to see in Naimy any method one cares to find – be it Enlightenment Realism, Critical Realism, Romanticism, Surrealism or Existentialism – and that his artistic method is a conglomeration of all possible artistic systems. However, such a point of view is unacceptable to us. An artistic method is a comprehensive whole by which the world is perceived. It is common knowledge that in his first creative period Naimy produced a number of Realist stories and the play *Fathers and Sons* in the spirit of Critical Realism. Over time Naimy moved steadily away from this towards Romanticism in his creative works, whereas the Realist method predominates in his essays and in the late collections of stories.

It is also difficult to agree with the conclusion that Naimy's story "The Barren Woman" was written under the influence of Aleksandr Ostrovsky's *The Storm*. Not one similar situation, not one identical motif can be seen between these two works: in Ostrovsky's play, Katerina has a freedom-loving nature, but suffers a strong oppression from without, her feelings and desires suppressed. The heroine of "The Barren Woman" chooses suicide after disappointment in her beloved, while Katerina perishes, haunted, defamed, and having lost all connection with life.

We also object to the idea that Naimy's stories "The Donkey's Tail" and "The Gift" "do not reflect concrete reality". In our view, these stories realistically recreate the specific features of life in Lebanon at that time.

Studies in the Arabic-speaking world

In the Arab countries themselves, particular attention is devoted to the history of émigré literature and the works of its individual representatives; a very large number of works by Arab researchers have been devoted to this subject. These may be divided notionally into three groups:
1. Literary–historical works that examine Arab émigré literature.[30]
2. Studies of the development and formation of individual genres.[31]
3. Monographs on the life and work of the prominent exponents of émigré literature: Gibran,[32] Rihani[33] and Naimy.[34]

Works concerning the history of émigré literature tend to be constructed more or less monotonously: they usually contain extensive information and factual material about the mass emigration from Syria and Lebanon to America and give an overview of the émigré press, the activities of various social and literary organisations and the lives and works of individual persons in the émigré literature. As a rule they also examine general questions of the character and peculiarities of émigré literature, especially of poetry. A lot of space in such books is given over to descriptions of the content of the émigré writers' works.

There is no doubt that each of these works has its own scholarly value, and taken as a group they complement one another and facilitate a deeper and more complex understanding of the literature of the émigré Arabs. Despite their extensive academic and factual material, however, the works enumerated share a common shortcoming, which arises from their authors' methodology. This is above all evident in their mainly informative, descriptive, survey-like character, which replaces any analysis of the facts they purport to convey. For the most part the authors of these works show little interest in the patterns that define the essence of this literary school and its role in the development of the new Arabic literature.

From among the works mentioned, the monograph by two well-known Arab literary critics, Muhammad Yusuf Najm and Ihsan 'Abbas, entitled *Arabic Poetry in Exile*,[35] stands out. In this work the authors seek to establish the patterns of social processes and the currents of ideas that to a large extent predetermined the aesthetic and philosophical programme of the Syro-American School.

Najm and 'Abbas give primary importance to the subjective factor, considering that in his psychological constitution Gibran was an innate Romantic. As a result, in their view, Gibran was able to first of all "come unaided to that to which earlier representatives of Romanticism had come".[36] It is true that the authors do not deny the influence of William Blake on Gibran's world-view: "If we were to say that Gibran was not subjected to the influence of other Romantics, but came to Romanticism through his own innate talent, then the question of the effect on his work of William Blake would remain open."[37] They see Blake's influence above all in the identical approach of both poets to the cardinal philosophical problem of

understanding the essence of the human "I". Both Blake and Gibran reject
the binary and dualistic consideration of the human person and do not split
it into the material and spiritual, or into body and soul, but rather see it as
an inviolable unity both with the world (God) and with itself. The authors
conclude: "And this does not rule out the possibility that on this question
Gibran came under the influence of Blake."[38]

'Abbas and Najm point out that the influence of European Romanticism
on the writers of the Syro-American School came through the American
Romantics Emerson, Thoreau and Whitman, whose works, in the
considered opinion of the authors, Gibran knew well. They write: "This
youth [Gibran] heard or read about Emerson's philosophy, about the
'great teacher's' relationship to nature, or about Thoreau's 'Forest'. He
probably also somehow came across the voice of the poet Whitman, who
considered that a man can reach freedom by freeing his mind and body
through democracy, his soul through love and his spirit through religion."[39]
Krachkovsky also remarked that America served as an intermediary between
the Arabs and Europe.[40]

Gibran's reverence towards nature and his worship of it is linked by
Najm and 'Abbas to the pantheism of European and American Romantics:
"For Gibran the Forest is that Nature that was deified by Wordsworth,
Coleridge, Blake, Rousseau and Thoreau."[41]

In passing the authors also note the effect of Russian literature on Mikhail
Naimy and on Nasib 'Arida.[42] They even find a consonance between the
poetry of Alexander Pushkin and that of the well-known émigré poet
Iliya Abu Madi (or Elia D. Madey, 1889–1957), and make a comparative
analysis of Pushkin's poem "A Winter's Evening" with Abu Madi's poem
"Evening".[43]

However, 'Abbas and Najm do not attempt to uncover the foundations
of Gibran's Romantic inclination or of Naimy's relationship to Russian
Realism, limiting themselves solely to a statement of facts.

Other Arab academic works characterise the works of Gibran, Rihani and
Naimy only in general terms. Even the specialist monographs that examine
these writers with regard to the evolution and development of artistic
methods give no consideration whatsoever to the possible influences of
Western Romantic or Russian classical works on the émigré writers.

Two monographs may also be added to the list of works by Arab literary
specialists, published in English in Beirut. Their authors are Khalil Hawi,[44]
a professor at the American University in Beirut, and Nadeem Naimy.[45]

Hawi examines the work of Gibran in terms of the evolution of his
philosophical ideas. He notes that Gibran's personality and world-view
were formed under the influence of both Western and Eastern cultures. To a
considerable degree this explains the contradictions in his inner world, torn
as it was between the contemplative way of the East with its prioritisation
of the spiritual principle, and the rationalistic and sociological ideas of the
West. He believes that the poet's main teacher of ideas was Jean-Jacques

Rousseau: "There is, then, nothing in Gibran's idea of Nature which cannot be traced back to Rousseau. The same is true of his attitude to society: like Rousseau, he also wept over it and denounced it, and pitied the poor for their sufferings under it."[46] In Hawi's view, the influence of other writers and Romantics was largely determined by the extent to which they themselves perceived the ideas and stylistic particularities of Rousseau's work. His book also includes a detailed stylistic examination of Gibran's poetry.

The study by Nadeem Naimy, nephew of Mikhail Naimy, is also a work of substance. He is the first to give a systematic overview of the writer's legacy, concentrating individually on his best-known works, and he analyses the factors that influenced the formation of his world-view. Nadeem concludes that Mikhail's outlook was influenced by the Bible, in particular the Gospels, but also by the ethical homilies of Leo Tolstoy.[*] In his view, a distinctive philosophical conception was already present in the writer's early works, combining Taoism, Buddhism, Platonism and Christianity.[47]

Studies by Western and other scholars

No specialist studies have been made in Western European Arabic studies of either the Syro-American School or its leading exponents. Isolated mentions are found only within general works and in histories of Arabic literature. A small section of the famous work by Carl Brockelmann on Arabic literature is devoted to the émigré authors, in which he describes the appearance of émigré literature and gives brief biographical information on the members of the New York Pen League.[48]

The research by Georg Kampffmeyer[49] is of a general and descriptive character. In a special book compiled jointly with Tahir Khemiri,[50] the authors introduce examples of work by writers of the Syro-American School to European readers and give brief biographical details about the writers. In the section on Gibran the authors underline the influence of the Arabic translation of the Bible and also of works by Rabindranath Tagore on the writer's style. However, they do not argue their ideas particularly convincingly. Some information can be found about the émigré writers in the work of the English Arabist H.A.R. Gibb.[51]

Islamic Literature, published in New York, gives some space to the works of the émigré Arab writers.[52] A number of specialist works[53] were published in the USA, most interesting of which is the book by Joseph P. Ghougassian, an assistant lecturer in the Department of Comparative and Arabic Philosophy at the University of San Diego,[†] entitled *Kahlil Gibran:*

---

* Certain proposals for the influence of Tolstoy on Naimy are treated subjectively by Nadeem Naimy. We shall discuss these in the appropriate chapter (4) of this monograph.

† [Editor's note] Joseph Ghougassian is presently (April 2009) deputy senior

wings of thought – the people's philosopher, dedicated to Gibran. Its main focus is an analysis of Gibran's philosophical outlooks as reflected in his creative works. The author concludes that Gibran's world-view is deeply idealistic, since the basic premise on which his philosophical conception is built is that life is primarily the life of the soul. Ghougassian considers the closeness of this to the philosophical views of Blake.[54] "Both Blake and Gibran believed that the poet should have an apocalyptic vision of the world, should seek the links between the transcendental phenomena and the essence of God and fulfil the role of the prophet, who returns humanity to truth."[55] In the author's view, all of Gibran's philosophical interests are therefore concentrated in the examining of ethical and moral laws and aesthetic and theological questions. This is the source of his acutely critical attitude to official religion and those who minister it, to social norms and rules, and to society in general.

Kahlil Gibran: his life and world[56] – written by Jean and Kahlil Gibran, the writer's sister and cousin, respectively – is also of some interest. It contains a detailed biography of Gibran based on the reminiscences of members of his family, acquaintances and friends. Considerable factual material was drawn from Gibran's correspondence and from the press, and many documents and photographs were published in this book for the first time.

The above survey of philological works by Soviet and foreign scholars demonstrates that many scholars of Arabic literature have thrown light, to a greater or lesser extent, on the formation and development of Arab émigré literature, on some of its exponents and on the emergence of various genres, etc. Attention has been given to the relationships between the Syro-American School and Russian and Western literatures. However, these works have not considered adequately the sources, essence and character of those relationships, nor have they ascertained the role and significance of reception in the way the method of the school's leading representatives were formed. This subject, it should be added, is of great scholarly interest.

The pressing need in contemporary Arabic studies for research into these matters has determined the set of questions that will be examined in this monograph and the form of its structure.

adviser to the Iraq Ministry of Higher Education & Scientific Research (MHESR) and former US ambassador to Iraq and Qatar.

Chapter 1

Arab émigré literature in the USA: origins and influences

Social and political life in Lebanon in the late nineteenth and early twentieth centuries and the origins of Arab émigré literature

Lebanon's early contact with European countries played an important part in its cultural ascent, and this can be explained by the country's history. The geographical location of this small country put it at the centre of constant interactions among various civilisations: the East of antiquity, the classical world, Arab Islamic culture and Christianity. The establishment of Byzantine supremacy in Lebanon (and in Syria) in the fourth century AD founded a root of Orthodox Christianity, in which the Church was governed entirely from Greece. From the Middle Ages Beirut was important as a convenient seaport on the trade route from the Mediterranean Sea to the Persian Gulf. For many centuries, therefore, Lebanon was drawn into direct contact with the countries of the Mediterranean and Christian Europe.[1]

Contact between Lebanon and European countries began to strengthen after the sixteenth century, when interest in the lands of the East began to grow in the West. In 1584 a special school for Lebanese Maronites was opened in Rome. During the rule of King Louis XIV Maronites studied in French educational institutions, and in 1608 the Emir of Lebanon, Fakhr ad-Din II (1585–1635), concluded a trade agreement with the Duke of Tuscany. European scholars were invited to Lebanon, and Western countries, particularly England and France, embarked on active economic development there. Raw materials – silk, wool, tobacco, olive oil and citrus fruits – were exported westwards, while various textile and manufactured goods were imported from Europe. Pursuing their own interests, the Western trading companies applied no little effort in turning Beirut into a modern city. A new port and seafronts were built, a gasworks was set up for street lighting, water pipes were laid, a number of large public and administrative buildings were constructed and a highway was laid between Beirut and Damascus.

From the beginning of the nineteenth century the history of Lebanon had been closely linked to the activities of Western missionaries. Lebanon was one of the first Eastern countries to become an arena for their work.[2] Missionaries were quick to establish themselves there: Catholics from France, Protestants from England, Presbyterians from America and

15

Orthodox from Russia. In part this was to do with the geographical location of the country, but also with the availability of good ports and natural resources. A further important element was that a large portion of the Lebanese population were historically Christian. Naturally, the missionaries pursued political interests in addition to religious ones, but "while directing the influence of the colonial powers in the East, the missionaries nevertheless brought literacy to the local Christians and spread European languages; sometimes they were the facilitators of cultural initiatives, and in particular created in the Arab countries an Enlightenment society."[3]

British, American, French and Russian missionaries built schools, colleges, higher educational establishments and libraries, and published periodicals. New educational programmes were established, and well-known Arab writers and journalists such as Sheikh Nasif Yaziji (1800–71) and Butrus Bustani (1819–83) participated in their preparation. The importance of the missionary schools was immense: some graduates continued their education in Western Europe and Russia, and on returning home pursued active lives in literature and society.

The establishment of the universities was an important cultural development. The American University[4] was founded in Beirut in 1866, as was the University of Saint Joseph, and in 1874 the French Catholic University opened. The universities had well-equipped libraries with literature in Arabic and foreign languages, allowing scholarly work on ancient manuscripts to be carried out, and the compilation of an Arabic–French dictionary.

Local printing presses were also established, which broadened the publishing base, and the expansion of translation activity was closely linked to this. Even though most of the works being translated in Egypt at this time were of a scientific and technical nature, in Syria and Lebanon many translations were made of imaginative literature by European writers, especially the French, since French influence on the country was particularly strong.[5]

Changes in the social and political situation in Lebanon led naturally to considerable shifts in its intellectual life, and to the growth and formation of a collective self-consciousness.[6] Lebanon was the first Arab country in which an Enlightenment movement appeared[7] and a national intelligentsia was formed. Gradually this Enlightenment ripened and developed, with the awakening of public consciousness resulting initially from the ideological activities of the Lebanese "enlighteners". Nasif Yaziji, Butrus Bustani, Marun Naqqash (1817–55), Ahmad Faris Shidyak (1805–87) and others, the leading representatives of the emerging national bourgeoisie, publicly opposed feudal backwardness and political stagnation. The Enlightenment was to make a fundamental impression on not only the social and political but also the cultural life of the Arab countries.

During the Enlightenment period a new Arabic literature gradually began to form. The ideas and ideals of the Enlightenment movement started to influence the social consciousness of the Arabs and required literature to address the problem of the individual; they also posed acute questions of social inequality, national freedom, the emancipation of women and so on. The "desire to turn the faceless mass of subjects under the power of feudal rulers into a union of individuals living by their wits and not by the instructions of the authorities"[8] was a completely new proposal for Arab society and became the foundation and motivation for all the actions of the Arab enlighteners – individuals such as Rifa'a Tahtawi (1801–73), Butrus Bustani, 'Abd al-Rahman al-Kawakibi (1849–1903), Nasif Yaziji, Ahmad Faris Shidyak, Adib Ishaq (1856–85), Qasim Amin (1865–1908), Mustafa Kamil (1874–1908), Jurji Zaydan (1861–1914), Ya'qub Sarruf (1874–1908) and others. These writers brought variety to the narrative genre, and enriched Arabic literature with literary essay-writing and with a vivid oratorical style. The enlighteners widened the possibilities for imaginative literature. Arabic poetry was torn, as it were, from the clutches of the Middle Ages and took on a social and political dimension.[9] Gifted poets such as Mahmud Sami al-Barudi (1839–1904), Ismail Sabri (1854–1923), Ahmad Shawqi (1868–1932), Hafiz Ibrahim (1871–1932), Khalil Mutran (1871–1949) and others succeeded in combining traditional forms in their works with topical subject matter. Muhammad Muwaylihi (1858–1930), Aisha Taymuriya (1840–1902), Muhammad Lutfi Jum'a and others experimented within the classical forms of *maqam* (didactic stories or harangues) and with *saj'* (rhymed prose) to faithfully reflect life in its most typical manifestations.[10]

"An important part was played in the spreading of the Enlightenment and in the development of Arab culture in the latter half of the nineteenth century by various scientific, political and literary circles and societies."[11] The Syrian Society [of Arts and Sciences] was formed in Beirut in 1847, followed by the Oriental Society (1850, established by the Catholic Jesuits), the Syrian Scientific Society (1857, organised by Butrus Bustani and Nasif Yaziji), the Society of Learning (or Refinement, organised by Muhammad Arslan) and the Oriental Scientific Academy (1882). The first National School was founded in 1863.[12] Bustani and Yaziji prepared a Great Explanatory Dictionary of the Arabic language (*Muhit al-muhit*, 1867) and a seven-volume Arabic encyclopaedia (*Da'iratu-l ma'arif*, 1887).

In the second half of the nineteenth century a periodical press appeared in Lebanon; prior to this the Lebanese read only newspapers and magazines.[13] Enlightenment traditions were cultivated in the new publications, to the extent that the censor permitted; ideas of democracy and freedom were propagated, and a call for unity and struggle against foreign interference was sounded.

Despite the persecution and harsh repression by the Turkish powers, social and political life in Lebanon in the late nineteenth and early twentieth centuries became noticeably more active. This was particularly evident following the Russian bourgeois-democratic revolution of 1905–07. Under the influence of this revolution there was a powerful upsurge in national liberation movements in the Arab countries, particularly Lebanon.[14]

The downfall in Turkey of Abdul Hamid II's regime following the Young Turks revolution (1908) gave the Arabs new hopes of independence,[15] but in 1909 the democratic movement was crushed by the Turkish powers. At the insistence of France the treaties were revised in 1912, with the result that Lebanon's rights were considerably increased.[16] New and progressive social organisations were also formed in Lebanon at this time: the Beirut Reform League, the Lebanese Revival and others.

In September 1918 the British, together with the army of the Emir Faisal al-Hashimi, went on the offensive in Palestine, routed the Turkish army, and then moved rapidly northwards into Lebanon and Syria. Beirut was occupied by the British on 8 October. Having now completely collapsed, Turkey was forced to sign the Armistice of Mudros. In an agreement between Britain and France signed in London on 30 September 1918, Lebanon and western Syria passed into French administration, headed by the High Commission. Thus, having been liberated from centuries of Ottoman rule, the Lebanese now found themselves the subjects of a French–British colonial regime.

As European powers had begun to expand, particularly Britain and France in the mid-nineteenth century, Lebanon experienced a growing religious animosity between its two main population groups, the Maronites and the Druze, accompanied by bloody clashes and internecine fratricidal struggle.[17] Even Karl Marx commented on the political battle that extended to the coast of Syria'.[18] All this weakened the economic condition of the country and led to a stagnation in its spiritual and cultural life.

Occupation, political repression and persecution, religious strife, devastation of the country and economic crisis, together with the missionaries' propaganda that promised a free and prosperous life in the West, meant that as early as the end of the nineteenth century not only the Lebanese intelligentsia but also ordinary people were awoken to the possibility of emigration. The first country to which the leading Lebanese intelligentsia made its way was Egypt, with its comparatively relaxed political regime and censorship. In Cairo, the leading cultural centre of the Arab Orient of that time, Lebanese emigrants found highly favourable conditions for their activities. Before long many of them, including Adib Ishaq, Salim Naqqash, Nudra Haddad, Jurji Zaydan, Farah Antun, Labiba Hashim and Khalil Mutran occupied leading positions there in literature and journalism, and exerted a strong influence on the development of the periodical press in Egypt.[19] Then, having concentrated practically the entire periodical press in their hands, they, together with the progressive Egyptian intelligentsia, played an exclusive role in founding the idea of national liberation within the Enlightenment movement and in popularising European learning and culture. The role of the Lebanese in this country was so great that the work of many of them – Ishaq, Mutran, Haddad and Zaydan – became an inseparable part of literary life in Egypt. Thanks to this energetic activity by members of the Lebanese and Syrian intelligentsia, in Egypt "at the beginning of the twentieth century the period of enlightening and popularisation came to a close. A sustainable reading public had been created, and there was a demand for new literary forms that had previously not existed."[20]

The Lebanese also emigrated to European countries, but their attempts to create hotbeds of national culture in the major European centres did not meet with success. By the end of the nineteenth century, mass emigration had begun to the Americas, and in particular to the USA.[21] Among the emigrants were many highly educated people, who spoke Russian and European languages and had been exposed to progressive Western European ideas. Their activities in exile were an organic response to the demands of an emerging nation as it moved into a new stage of historical development. Above all, they felt the necessity for the closest acquaintance with Western culture and literature, which could provide the new ideas and forms so necessary for Arab writers for the renewal of national literary traditions. "The destiny of the new Arabic literature is entirely linked to emigration and marches under its flag",[22] wrote Krachkovsky.

Social and political instability in other Arab countries also encouraged emigration. Not only Syrians and Lebanese emigrated to America, but also groups from Jordan, Iraq, Egypt and Morocco.[23] The first Arab immigrants settled in New York, where initially they were known as "Asiatic Turks". Not until the end of the nineteenth century were the Arab immigrants referred to as "Syrians".[24] According to statistics presented by the researcher Amir Ibrahim Qindilchi, 20,695 Arabs emigrated to the USA in 1898. By 1924 there were more than 105,000 – and this did not include those Arabs who were born in the USA.[25]

Krachkovsky writes:

> The Arabs in America: for many people this combination of words may call up the same suggestion as "Kafirs in Berlin" or "Zulus in Paris". The reader involuntarily thinks of some kind of exotic troupe that has appeared unexpectedly in an ethnographical exhibition or at the circus. Even an intelligent person reacts with disbelief when people talk about the Arabic publishing house in São Paulo, the Arab theatrical society in Rio de Janeiro or Arabic newspapers and magazines in New York and Chicago. Meanwhile the Arab colony has been culturally active in the New World for about half a century now, and this work is reflected in the general intellectual development of its mother countries ... of Syria and Egypt, two important hives of cultural activity among the Arab race.[26]

For many, America seemed to be the Promised Land, in its way a kind of goldmine. "I imagine America to be a country beyond the horizon, where people take handfuls of earth and it turns into gold",[27] wrote the young Naimy in his diary. However, on reaching the New World the Arabs often found themselves facing hardship. They were forced to live in poor districts of Washington and New York and to work night and day. Many of them were disillusioned and tried to return to their homeland.

Those Arab immigrants who succeeded in establishing themselves in America took a keen interest in the life of the homeland they had forsaken, and strove to preserve their national traditions and language. In order to unite still more closely in this foreign land the Arabs joined together in various clubs and societies and started newspapers and magazines. This explains the appearance in the USA of a range of Arab societies, religious, charitable and literary. Examples include *Jam'iyyat al-Suriyyin al-Muttahida* (United Syrian Society, New York, 1907); *al-Muntadi al-Suri al-Amriki* (Syrian American Club, New York, 1908); *al-Jam'iyya al-Thaqafiyya al-Tahdhibiyya al-Suriyya* (Syrian Education Society, New York, 1916); *Jam'iyyat al-Ikhwan al-Dimashqi* (The Damascus Fraternity, New York, 1917); *Mahfilun Dimashqi al-Masuni* (Damascus Masonic Lodge, 1917); *Jam'iyyat al-Shabab al-Muslimin* (Society of Muslim Youth, 1924); and others. In New York and Washington organisations that had a political character appeared, including *Jam'iyyat al-nahda al-Lubnaniyya* (Society for Lebanese Revival, New York, 1911) and *Lajnatu Tahrir Suriya wa Lubnan* (Freedom Committee of Syria and Lebanon, New York, 1917).[28] Many of these organisations had their own printed publications, the pages of which resounded with the call for struggle for national independence and Arab unity.

The literary and political forces of the émigré Arabs gathered round the periodical press. The editorial offices of newspapers and magazines became centres where émigré men of letters gathered, and served as their spiritual citadels. Émigré publishing in a foreign country was extremely difficult; there was felt to be a lack of educated contributors, and the financial base for publication was small and inconstant. It was not without reason that the émigré poet Ilyas Qunsul describes the journalistic activities of the Arabs in exile as heroic.[29]

The first Arabic periodical in the USA was the newspaper *Kawkab Amrika* (*Star of America*, New York, 1892–1909, ed. Najib Arbili).[30] The best-known émigré Arab newspapers in the USA included *al-Ayyam* (*The Days*, 1897, ed. Yusuf Ma'aluf); *al-Huda/Hoda* (*The Guidance*, 1898, ed. Nahum Mukarzil); *Mir'at al-Gharb* (The *Mirror of the West*, 1899, ed. Najib Musa Diyab); *al-Muhajir* (*The Émigré*, 1903, ed. Amin al-Ghurayyib); *al-Sa'ih/Sayeh* (*The Traveler*, 1912, ed. 'Abd al-Masih Haddad); *al-'Alam al-Jadid* (*The New World*, 1918, ed. Sallum Mukarzil), and others. Magazines included *al-Funun/Funoon* (*The Arts*, 1913, ed. Nasib 'Arida) and *al-Samir/Sameer* (*The Companion*, 1927, ed. Iliya Abu Madi). This is far from a complete list of Arabic publications in the USA. Newspapers and magazines were published in various cities – New York, Boston, Washington, Detroit – and were often in two languages, Arabic and English.

The Arabic press in the USA covered events of the day as they related to social and political life in the Arab countries. Much space was devoted to creative writing, to articles that bravely criticised the stagnation in Arabic literature and to reviews of new works by Arab authors. Moreover, the periodical press fulfilled a propagandistic and educational role for the émigrés and facilitated the awakening among them of a national consciousness. "The newspapers and magazines published by the émigrés served the function of a comprehensive school", wrote George Tomeh, "they awakened patriotic feelings among the émigré Arabs and summoned them to the struggle for high ideals".[31]

In addition to its basic social purpose – of uniting the Arabs, awakening national self-consciousness, and influencing their spiritual and cultural lives and feelings of patriotism – the press functioned for the émigré writers as a true school. This was where many writers and poets first saw themselves in print, and it was from here that Arab readers came to know their names. The *qasida* verse of Iliya Abu Madi, Sha'ir al-Qarawi, the Maalouf brothers, I. Farhad and Nasib 'Arida, the poems and prose of Rihani and Gibran, and the stories and articles of Naimy, 'Abd al-Masih Haddad and others, were first published in émigré newspapers and magazines. Tomeh writes: "Re-reading old issues of émigré publications, you see how beautiful they are and how deep their content. The high artistic content and quality of thinking in these publications makes them still attractive today. Often they can be rated higher than the magazines and newspapers of today."[32] This periodical press further served to introduce a wider circle of American and European readers to Arab culture and the issues of modern Arab life.

The periodical press prepared the ground for the formation of a single literary society that would be able to unite and rally the efforts of émigré writers towards more fruitful and more specifically targeted activities. In New York in 1920 the Pen League (*al-Rabita al-Qalamiyya*, 1920–31) was formed.[33] Its members were talented and socially active émigré writers. Kahlil Gibran was elected chairman and the secretary was Mikhail Naimy. The Association became a social and cultural centre in which the ideas and principles of the new Arabic literature were formed. During the years of its existence the Association had the character of a pioneering and experimental school, and its activities gave a new creative impulse to many Arab writers.

The conditions for the emergence of a special émigré literary school, and one that had acquired the name "Syro-American", were undoubtedly the needs of the awakening nation and its new period of historical development. The émigré writers felt it necessary to become as closely acquainted as possible with the achievements of Western culture and literature, which brought with them the new ideas and new forms that Arab writers needed if they were to reflect that historical reality with which they were engaging. This naturally led them also to seek new artistic means and methods. As this process continued, émigré literature transcended the remnants of Enlightenment didacticism and Sentimentalism and achieved a poetics of Romanticism and Critical Realism.

In parallel to this a renewal of literary genres was taking place. Development was strongest in the small forms – the sketch, essay, article, short story – which were best suited to quickly echoing the demands of the time. At the same time, the medium-sized genres – longer stories and plays – were also being reworked.

A particular place in the work of the émigré writers is occupied by the genre of prose poetry (poetry in prose, *al-shi'r al-mansur*), which was important to the period under consideration. The appearance of this genre in one form or another has been observed in many Eastern literatures as one of the typological indications of a rearrangement in the genre system at the moment of formation of a new type of literature.* Before Rihani and Gibran the prose poem did not exist in Arabic literature. As Krachkovsky wrote:

> Curiously enough, before the present time this form was entirely unknown to the Arabs. The explanation, in this case, must be sought not only in the development of Arabic poetry itself, which is extremely conservative in regard to form, but in the very language or way of thinking, for which the understanding of verse is indissolubly linked to the understanding of metre.[34]

The prose poems of Rihani and Gibran are the first examples of *al-shi'r al-mansur* in Arabic literature. A further innovation of these writers is that they brought to this non-traditional genre a new, socially orientated content, and the result was thus a new genre in Arabic literature. In the words of Krachkovsky, the subject of Gibran's prose poems may be considered universally human.[35] This feature of Gibran's prose poems was noted by the critic Nadira Jamil Sarraj: "The content of his poems is always linked to reality. He described a simple life, calling for goodness and justice. The poetry of Gibran is **a revolution in Arabic literature**."[36]

The prose poems of Gibran have characteristics that distinguish them from those of Rihani. Dolinina comments that "for Gibran it is lyrical miniatures, poetic in their imagery and language, but without strict rhythmic organisation and without rhyme ... In Rihani, works of this genre possess a clearly accented rhythm, they rhyme and have refrains."[37] We would add that a high emotional charge is characteristic of both, and that their systems of imagery and groups of motifs and ideas are close to one another.

In the wake of Rihani and Gibran this genre gained wide popularity in the Arab East and became highly developed, in particular in the works of well-known poets such as Mayy Ziyada (or Ziadeh, 1895–1941, Lebanon), Muhammad Mahdi al-Jawahiri (1903–97, Iraq) and Abu al-Qasim al-Shabbi (1909–34, Tunisia). Many Arab Romantics wrote in this genre, and the Egyptian modernists were also attracted to it. The form was also adopted by writers in other languages.[38]

---

* See for example Klyatoshorina, V.B., *"Novaya poezia" v Irane*, Moscow, 1975; Gerasimova, A.G., *Literatura Afganistana* (in Pashto), Moscow, 1986; Milikov, T.D., *Nazym Hikmet i novaya poezia Turtsii*, Moscow, 1987.

The émigré writers created a new literary style. So far as was possible, they freed it of archaisms, from ponderous syntactical constructions and from swathes of artificial ornamentations of diverse kinds. In so doing they set an example of conserving the values of classical Arabic literature.

Harith Taha Rawi, author of the article *The revolution of ideas in the literature of emigration*, writes:

> The émigré poets and writers were not supporters of the idea of "art for art's sake" or indeed of "literature for the sake of literature"; rather, they proclaimed the slogan "literature for life". They did not rest on their laurels, realising that any stagnation would necessarily lead to decay in literature. Despite the physical separation, they always remained with their own people.[39]

The activities of the Syro-American School were also highly praised by other Arab researchers, in particular Muhammad Yusuf Najm[40] and 'Isa Nawri.[41]

The influence of this School has also been recognised by many Arab writers closer to our own time. As Mahmud Taymur writes:

> The American school, which was created by our Lebanese and Syrian brothers in exile, has spread its influence across Egyptian literature. I was gripped by the works of this school ... it went beyond the boundaries of tradition and drew inspiration in the West. It created a new style. This unusual, elegant style was to our liking ... We should not deny the service that this school has rendered: new blood flowed in the veins of our conservative literature, it was penetrated by new life.[42]

On this point, Krachkovsky also remarks: "The influence of the Syro-American School on contemporary Arabic literature was great ... its effects had impacts even in countries such as Hijaz and Tunisia."[43]

Despite the fact that Arab émigré literature is only a small episode in the overall history of Arabic literature, the writers of the Syro-American School gained wide popularity in both the Arab East and the West, and it is impossible to imagine the full picture of the development of the new Arabic literature without their work.

The influence of foreign literature on the Syro-American School

Links between the Arab world and the West have a long history. During the Middle Ages, between the eighth and thirteenth centuries, the enormous territory that lay under the hegemony of the Islamic caliphate, and which contained dozens of tribes and states, underwent a complex historical process in which borders were eroded and old cultural regions lost, and new commonalities emerged. The result was the formation of a new cultural region: the Islamic world. Arab Muslim culture became its foundation, having absorbed the achievements of many pre-Islamic civilisations, particularly those of the peoples of Iran, Greece, Spain, Asia Minor and Central Asia, and the newly formed Islamic world continued to develop on this basis.

Medieval culture began to flourish earlier in the East than it did in the West. The science and literature of the East gained particular importance and exerted an influence on the development of world civilisation. Medieval literature from the Near and Middle East shows traits of a love of freedom and humanism. The literature of the Near East, writes Yeliazar Meletinsky, "owing to its earlier comprehension of the cultural traditions of antiquity, to the influence of heretical tendencies and philosophical freethinking, became imbued far earlier with humanistic ideas, and approached the formulation of such issues as became accessible to the West only as late as the Renaissance."[44] And the process of mutual cultural enrichment between East and West began in the Middle Ages.

"In every historical period," Yevgeny Chelyshev noted, "the leading actors in culture and scholarship in the West discovered the enduring ideological and aesthetic importance of the cultural legacy of the peoples of the East and linked this to the foremost achievements of Western culture."[45] A direct cultural exchange also took place. The customs and ceremonies of Muslim courts and highborn Arabs became known in the capitals of Christian kingdoms. Eastern music and the imitation of Muslim court etiquette and clothing were absorbed into the daily life of wealthy Christians. Celebrations in European palaces, like those in the Islamic world, included singers, poets, musicians and dancers.

The interaction of literatures occurred both within one or another region and between regions:

> Border regions were particularly important in the development of literary connections in the Middle Ages, that is to say, "junctions", places where literatures touched. Sometimes there would form in such places a distinctive "border" literature that bore the marks of both neighbouring literatures. The most vivid example of this is Andalusian literature of the period from the eighth to the fifteenth centuries.[46]

The role of Andalusian literature was significant as a mediator between Western Europe and the East. Through Andalusia and into Europe flowed the cultural traditions that the Arabs had assimilated – of antiquity, of the ancient East and of the Islamic Arab world. Andalusian literature was closely related to early Provençal poetry, and through this to the European culture of the time.

Developments in the cultural links between Arab countries (in particular Egypt, Syria and Lebanon) and the West were particularly intense in the early twentieth century, and the last barriers that kept remote places isolated from the world were finally removed. This was the "age of intensive and ever-growing mutual exchange between cultures and literatures on the ground of universal familiarisation with the problems of the contemporary world".[47]

The Arab lands, and in particular Egypt, Syria and Lebanon, were participants in the general system of world capitalism. The results of this process could hardly not have had an impact on social, political and cultural life in these countries, nor could it have left Arabic literature untouched, ready as this was to actively embrace the accomplishments of foreign literatures. "The national literary system is not a self-sufficient organism. Genetically, typologically and by contact it is intimately and inextricably linked to the common advance of world literature."[48]

Thanks to the interconnections between different regions of the world, the achievements of each national literature also become the achievements of the others, even of those that are physically distant. The literature of any people, for all its national character, is inseparably joined to universal human achievement. None of the world's literatures would have been able to develop without that unity of the national with the international, nor would there have been any movement of culture in an upward direction.

Of course, any cultural borrowing is conditioned by social factors. "This conditionality is determined by the internal patterns inherent in the national development that preceded it, both social and literary."[49] A writer who adopts the achievements of an artist from another country essentially satisfies the deeply necessary and historically patterned need of his own people in their search for self-expression and for the possibility of speaking out about the things that arise, burn and become ingrained in their consciousness. Neupokoeva writes:

> It must be underlined that the process of the mutual enrichment of literatures does not boil down merely to an influence that can be mechanically reflected on another national literature as though this were some kind of static "screen". … It also includes a creative perception that is always actively selective and is always the result of a struggle in the artistic development of the author or in the development of one or another national literature and of other forces and tendencies.[50]

Familiarity with Western literature among Arab writers began in earnest in the second half of the nineteenth century, when signs of new ways of seeing the surrounding reality began to appear within the ideology and world-view of the feudal society. The historical epoch itself, with those characteristic processes that accompanied a change in social structures, facilitated an acceleration in literary development. Progressive Arab thinkers and artists, like all the leading national intelligentsia of the countries of the East, turned to the values of Western culture in their search for ways to renew and revive, and assimilated its achievements.[51] At this time, however, ordinary Arab people perceived that culture with hostility, regarding it as colonial.

In essence, the influence of foreign literature on the Arabic began long before the appearance of the Syro-American School. In the mid-nineteenth century Arabic literature was already being enriched by translations, adaptations and arrangements of literature from European languages. Contact also became established thanks to individual people; for example, certain prominent translators of foreign literature (notably Sulayman Bustani, Rifaʻa Tahtawi and Farah Antun) visited Europe and America. The imitation of Western forms and part-borrowings of subjects, images, ideas and forms could also be observed.[52] Meanwhile European literature did much for the adoption of the literatures of the Arab East.

With the development of philo-Orientalism* in Western literatures, beginning in the eighteenth century, many European artists also turned to Arab themes. For example, certain French writers frequently used motifs from *The Thousand and One Nights*. Among those to make use of Arab motifs were Pierre Corneille, Molière and Jean Racine. The renowned German poet Friedrich Rückert (1788–1866) was the first to start translating classical Arabic literature from the original, beginning with the *maqam*s of al-Hariri of Basra (1054–1122).[53] An artistic interest in the Arabic classics, that is, in their themes, motifs and subjects also appeared in English literature. Examples include works by Samuel Johnson and Oliver Goldsmith.

Oriental literary traditions played a defining role in the formation of the Western Romantic world-view. Many Western poets turned specifically to the East for inspiration for their Romantic fantasy. In the early nineteenth century Goethe indicated a route of pilgrimage to Romantic poets:

> North and West and South up-breaking!
> Thrones are shattering, Empires quaking;
> Fly thou to the untroubled East,
> There the patriarchs' air to taste!
> What with love and wine and song
> Chiser's fount will make thee young.
>
> Goethe, *Hejira*[54] (translated by Edward Dowden)

Viktors Ivbulis remarked that the German interest in India "served as a powerful catalyst that promoted the rapid spread of a Romantic disposition not only to literature and the visual arts but also to the performing arts, philosophy, history and even religion."[55]

In England, interest in the traditions of the East went hand in hand with the search for a Romantic method. "We do not find one among the important English Romantic poets in whose work there is not reflected, in one or another form, a general infatuation with the East."[56] In the works of the "Lake School" poets, in particular those of William Wordsworth

---

* Lit. "love of the East", a tendency in Western literatures in which many European writers, philosophers and translators were involved. See for example Braginsky, I.S., "Zapadno-vostochny sintez v 'Divane' Gete", in Gete [Goethe], Zapadno-vostochny divan 'Moganni-nameh' [West-östlicher Diwan: "The book of the singer"], Moscow, 1988, p.572. See also Kassel', L.M., Gete i "Zapadno-vostochny" divan, Moscow, 1973, pp.36–97.

(1770–1850), Samuel Taylor Coleridge (1772–1834) and Robert Southey (1774–1843), the Oriental themes found a new resonance and became an organic part of their Romantic poetry. For,

> if previously a Western author could easily borrow any individual element from an Oriental work, such as a theme or motif, and insert it into his own artistic system, then the Romantics perceived each element as part of a more complex whole and considered that simply disembodying and using it to their own ends would not bear fruit. The problems of borrowing were, for the Romantic poets, similar to those of the interaction of one's own national traditions with those of another culture.[57]

On this matter it is interesting to consider Robert Southey's poem "Thalaba the Destroyer", in which he used motifs from Arab fairytales, Coleridge's poem "Kubla Khan" and the famous fragment "Mahomet", and Wordsworth's poem "The Prelude". The Lake Poets were among the first in English literature to open up the immensely rich world of the East, in particular that of Arab culture, which they found in deep consonance with their own aesthetic searching.

It is well known that the process of development of the new Arabic literature was severely held up by historical conditions. The Arab countries' "situation as colonies, semi-colonies or dependencies retarded the collapse of feudalism and made the development of capitalist relations slow, restricted and contorted".[58] All this, of course, was also reflected in the way that literature developed. "The later a particular national literature appeared and formed, the later it was absorbed into the general literary process, and the more important to it was the influence of other, more developed foreign literatures",[59] writes A.S. Bushmin.

At the start of the twentieth century the Arab East was ready to draw on foreign literature and, in the words of Taha Husayn, Arab writers did not see "any harm in borrowing the ideas and methods of the Europeans".[60] The influence of European literature, and in particular the works of Sir Walter Scott and Alexandre Dumas, could already be felt in Syrian Enlightenment prose and in the historical novels of Jurji Zaydan and Ya'qub Sarruf. Arab writers often made free translations of Western works of literature. A typical exponent of this practice was Mustafa Lutfi al-Manfaluti (1876–1924). He produced Arabic adaptations of, among others, *Pour la Couronne* by François Coppée, *Cyrano de Bergerac* by Edmond Rostand, *Sous les tilleuls* by Alphonse Karr, *Paul et Virginie* by Bernadin de Saint-Pierre, *La Dame aux Camélias* by Alexandre Dumas and *Atala* by François-René de Chateaubriand.[61] A new literary school began in Egypt in the early twentieth century (the poets of the "Diwan" group, 1921) that looked to European, and particularly French and English, aesthetic thinking.[62]

It is true that the lessons of Western literature, for the writers discussed here and their contemporaries, were still not sufficiently productive; their meeting with Western literature did not have the character of deep understanding and active and selective perception, in the full sense of the word. These were the first steps of Arabic literature towards a familiarisation with the values of the artistic culture of a different people, and the first signs of interaction between two types of culture. In this respect the Syro-American School represents an entirely new stage in this process, as do the results of its assimilation of foreign literary experience. And here it would seem significant that the writers of the Syro-American School encountered the works of Western literature not in translation but in their original languages and directly in the setting in which they were created. Furthermore, there is little doubt that literary contacts and a better perception of the artistic discoveries and ideas of the Western schools were facilitated by the fact that all three Arab writers belonged to the Christian community of Syrian immigrants in the United States. For them there did not exist, to the same degree as for Muslim writers, the difficulties of overcoming the barrier of ideological rejection of Western cultural values; it was easier for them to find an appropriate means of asserting those values within their own culture on the basis of those universal and humanistic ideals that had been primordially associated with the culture of the peoples of the East. At the same time it should never be forgotten that these writers were surrounded by an émigré environment, one that preserved the language and customs of its homeland. As a result of this they proved to be bearers of two cultural traditions: the East and the West.

The period in which the Syro-American School flourished was that in which Western literature was turning away from Romanticism towards such movements as Symbolism, neo-Romanticism and neo-Classicism. However, for various ideological and psychological reasons, and also typologically, Arab émigré writers found themselves closer to the chronologically more distant Romanticism. Social and artistic thought in their homelands was not yet ready for Realism.

"Romantic art is a highly original phenomenon in the history of artistic culture, and so important that without its essence and its place in the history of world art a circumstantial examination of the patterns of artistic development would be more or less impossible overall, and for the nineteenth and twentieth centuries in particular",[63] writes Ivan Fyodorovich Volkov. As a type of artistic thinking, Romanticism preceded Realism, prepared the ground for the latter and equipped it with its achievements. In defining the basic principles of Realism, N.I. Konrad remarks that "Realist literature could not have become what it did without the preceding stage of a fully-fledged and developed Romantic literature."[64]

Romanticism, which was conceived at the end of the eighteenth and beginning of the nineteenth centuries, constitutes an entire period of artistic thought. Many attempts have been made to give a definition of this method. The most authoritative definitions are given in Volkov's book *Creative Methods and Artistic Systems*. Here A.N. Veselovsky defines Romanticism as "liberalism", I.I. Zamotin as "idealism"; V.V. Sipovsky, P.S. Kogan and G.A.

Gukovsky see in Romanticism "individualism" and "subjectivism", while P.N. Sakulin considers it "the suspension of actual reality", B.S. Meylakh "a dream", N.K. Gey "the affirmation of the ideal" and A.M. Gurevich "the absolute character of ideals together with the recognition of the impossibility of their realisation in actual reality".[65] Ivbulis understands the most defining characteristic of Romanticism as "the response of art to the time of collapse of the feudal structures and of the formation of the bourgeois system in some countries, and disappointment in the capitalist order in others; and a protest against the regulation of the artistic process and of normative aesthetics".[66]

As can be seen, practically none of these definitions really detracts from or contradicts the others. There are, however, also many other important signs that characterise Romantic narrative. These are, in particular, the search for harmony in the world, in which the most important and active element is the human being. This explains the exclusive interest in the individual and in the understanding of the place occupied by the person in this view of the world. The main achievement of the Romantic method was the discovery in art of the individual as the centre of the surrounding world, as an inimitable individuality that has the right to free self-expression and to be independent of its social setting and conditions of life. Other important factors that are invariably present in the works of the Romantics include the interrelationship of the self and society, the opposing of a grand past to an insignificant present and a chasm between the ideal and the actual. Romanticism is also characterised by a mutinous protest against established social relations, by subjectivism and a pessimistic mood, a tendency towards confession and prophesying, and elements of didacticism. And always there is a heightened emotional state – anger, denial, rapture, approval, love, hate or compassion.

As A.S. Dmitriev writes:

> The main reason why this problem remains current for scholars, indeed of increasing importance, is the degree to which Romanticism, now remote from us in time, continues to exert its aesthetic, ideological and philosophical influence up to the present day. Again and again not only readers but also many of our modern-day authors are turning to the legacy of the Romantics, interpreting, and also in some way also taking in the experience of the Romantic writers.[67]

It is currently thought that for Western literature Romanticism "was a response to the French Revolution and its immediate aftermath".[68] It should be borne in mind, however, that "the literature of every country had its preconditions, which determined both the origins of Romanticism and its specifics".[69] It is well known that in the period of the collapse of feudalism and the emergence of bourgeois relations, Oriental literature "began moving forward with increased speed, absorbing various layers of historically conditioned artistic thought simultaneously. Alongside the medieval traditionalism that the literature had preserved, there now appeared Renaissance and Enlightenment traits, which in several literatures Romanticism was already hurrying to replace."[70] In Arabic literature, assimilation of the Renaissance and its main ideas – humanism and democracy, freedom from the indisputable authority of religion, and hatred of violence and slavery – were of great importance.[71] Nevertheless, having still not completely absorbed the achievements of Renaissance Realism into artistic practice, Arabic literature soon turned to Sentimentalism and Romanticism, since the understanding of the new and highly complex problems into which certain Arab countries (Egypt, Syria and Lebanon) had run in the early twentieth century could no longer be contained within the ideology of Renaissance Realism. And so, at the beginning, the Enlightenment and Romanticism appeared, as it were, syncretically.

"In the order of events, Romanticism comes exactly at the time of the formation of modern national literatures, appearing either as the final stage (after the Enlightenment) or as a tendency that is typical of any time of national revival, interwoven with other ideas and with artistic searches of other kinds."[72] This position also applies to the case of Arabic literature, where, in the words of Dolinina, "the boundaries between Romanticism and literary Enlightenment appear much less stable than in European literatures",[73] and we may add that they practically followed one after the other in time. Therefore, from among the various characteristics that determined the national specifics of Arab Romanticism one should particularly single out its organic link with the literature of the Enlightenment.*

One can begin to trace the origins of Romantic tendencies in the works of, for example, Adib Ishaq, Mustafa Kamil and Wali al-Din Yekun at the end of the nineteenth century. However, the socio-political journalism and dry didacticism of the Enlightenment gave way only gradually to Romantic fantasy. At the same time the succeeding generation of Arab writers preserved and developed the social ideals of those enlighteners who did not succeed in exhausting their artistic potential.

In Arabic literature Romanticism first appeared distinctly in Egyptian poetry and prose. The work of al-Manfaluti, for example, is notable for a combination of Enlightenment values and a Romanticism that carries traces of Sentimentalism, testifying to the typological pattern of appearance of a Romantic perception of the world among Arab writers.

The Romantic inclination was more widespread in Egyptian poetry. It was initiated by the well-known poet Khalil Mutran, a Lebanese by birth. "He was one of the first Arab Romantic poets who was in a position to adopt the new subject matter, vivid imagery, style, figures of speech and poetical

---

* In certain Eastern literatures Romanticism is considered a movement within the Enlightenment. See Ayzenshteyn, N.A., "K voprosu o prosvetitel'stve v Turtsii", in *Prosvetitel'stvo v literaturakh Vostoka*, Moscow, 1973, p.27; Paevskaya, Ye.V., *Razvitie bengal'skoy literatury*, Moscow, 1979, pp.183–4.

forms, while also mastering the language, rhetoric and forms of conventional poetry",[74] wrote the French researcher Shmuel Moreh. For Mutran the most important thing in poetry was a subjective view of the world. This was also the basis of his method of building an image of reality. Comprehending the subjectivity of artistic representation was, however, also characteristic of Romantics of other countries and particularly of Russian Romantic poetry. "Starting from the earliest moves by the Romantics in connection with the aesthetic self-determination of a new literary movement, the most significant departure of the latter from earlier inclinations was seen by the Romantics themselves as the subjective character of their art, focusing on the individual, its emotional experiences and its apprehending of its surroundings."[75]

However, Mutran's Romanticism was also endowed with traits of Sentimentalism. The basic hero of his Romantic works (*A Story of Two Lovers, A Tragedy in a Joke, A Wedding, or a Funeral, Christmas, To a Dying Youth* and others) is a lonely, misunderstood person who is alienated from life and stands before an aura of tragedy. The influence of French Romanticism can be found in Mutran's poetry. In his lyric poems he made a distinct step towards a new type of poetic art. His followers included Ahmad Zaki Abu Shadi, Ibrahim Naji, Muhtar Wakil and Ali Mahmud Taha.[76]

As already discussed, Arab Romanticism was subjected, for the most part indirectly, to foreign influences due to contacts between Arabic and foreign literatures. This is also apparent in the work of the poets of the "Diwan" group: 'Abbas Mahmud 'Aqqad (1889–1964), Ibrahim 'Abd al-Qadir Mazini (1880–1949) and 'Abd al-Rahman Shukri (1886–1958). These poets drew on the experiences of the English Romantics. However, the Romanticism of these poets tended to be lyrical and intimate rather than deal with public and social themes. The importance of the Diwan poets is that their "poetry of feeling" was the first attempt in Arabic literature to lay bare the internal world of the human. The assimilation of foreign influences was not greatly productive in their work, and their artistic legacy did not make a significant mark on Egyptian poetry.[77] Thus, although the Arab Romantics made an initial foray into the problem of the human self, this did not go beyond sentimental descriptions of emotional experience.

Romanticism in Arabic literature at the start of the twentieth century made further timid and hesitant steps; meanwhile "among Arab writers living in the other hemisphere the Romantic school had already formed".[78] This reference is to the Syro-American School, that is to say, to Kahlil Gibran and Ameen Rihani. It was no coincidence that the leading members of the Syro-American School had studied the English Lake Poets of the first decade of the nineteenth century and also representatives of the American Romantics of the mid-nineteenth century – Emerson, Thoreau and Whitman.

English and American Romanticism was a powerful echo of the acute cataclysms of the century that had shaken the European and American continents, above all the French Revolution (1789–94), the Napoleonic Wars that redrew the map of Europe and the tumult of other European revolutions.

The spirit of English Romanticism also had deep repercussions among Arab émigré writers. The interpretation of a wide range of social questions through the prism of the Romantic conflict of the individual and society, and the pathos of feeling and intuition, was in stark contrast to the straightforwardness and rationalism of Enlightenment in addressing questions of world vision. The depth and restlessness of passion among the English Romantics of the Lake School could not have been closer to the expectations and artistic demands of Gibran and Rihani in their ideas for the liberation of their homeland, its enlightenment and its renewal. Following the achievements of the Romantic method, these writers exalted the individual as the centre of the universe, as a unique being possessing the right to free self-expression.

Such was the important influence on Gibran and Rihani of the American Romantic Transcendentalists, in particular Ralph Waldo Emerson (1803–82), Walt Whitman (1819–92) and Henry David Thoreau (1817–62), who strove to adapt Puritan philosophy and morals to the new tasks of bourgeois democracy in the mid-nineteenth century and criticised the false moral values of capitalist society, yet in resolving conflicts in society gave primary importance to the spiritual self-perfection of the individual. "The Transcendentalists opposed the hypocritical morals of bourgeois society … with the conscience of a separate individual and the transcendentalist notion of an innate sense of justice that must be the highest law and criterion of being human."[79]

In Emerson's philosophical theory the human being is the spiritual centre of the universe. The human commands the same spiritual strength as does the cosmos since he can encompass the whole world, know it and be joined with it. And the individual realises his identity with the soul of the world and with nature. From here also arises the pantheistic approach to nature of the Transcendentalists, which always purifies the human from interests of "vulgar materialism".

It should be pointed out that in their interpretation of nature Gibran and Rihani acknowledged elements both of American Transcendentalism and European Romanticism. If they, like the Transcendentalists, understood nature as the deep meaning of the universe, in which the human is regarded as an inalienable part, then they also saw in nature, like the Romantics, the ideals of freedom, harmony, beauty and naturalness.

In the view of the Transcendentalists, "intuition and imagination are a truer way of apprehending the truth than abstract logic or scientific method".[80] Hence the specific notion among them of the role of the poet, who is called to reveal the deep and true principle of the universe. The poet becomes the carrier of the highest moral values, which brings him close to God; he is an orator, a soothsayer, who reveals the truth to the people.

The Arab writers sensed in the American Romantics the idea of a moral principle and the self-perfection of the individual, understood as an abstract, extra-societal phenomenon. Interest in Western Romanticism by Gibran and Rihani was not only the result of the peculiarities of their individual apperceptions, but also of objective factors such as the particular historical and aesthetic preconditions which formed this "perceiving" consciousness. As V.M. Zhirmunsky notes,

> an influence is not a coincidence, a mechanical impulse from outside; nor is it an empirical fact of the individual biography of a writer or group of writers, nor is it the result of reading a new book ... For the phenomenon to become possible, there must exist the need for such an ideological import; and the existence is necessary of analogous tendencies of development, more or less formed, in the given society and in the given literature.[81]

From one collection to the next of Gibran's and Rihani's work their creative potential increases, thanks to their assimilation of the lessons of Western Romanticism, which raises these writers to pose the widest global and universal questions, and in the final analysis makes them, on the one hand, equal participants in the world literary process and, on the other, the heralds of new artistic values. Gibran and Rihani were the first to demolish the narrow framework of the Enlightenment and make the breakthrough to Romanticism.

This is not the place for expounding in detail which of the Western Romantics were preferred by the Arab writers. What is significant is the overall effect of the sum of the ideas, moods, motifs and thoughts that they carried between them. As Khalil Hawi puts it, "as a late Romantic, Gibran inherited the traditions of that epoch-making movement, taking them from a plurality of sources and imbibing from the very atmosphere of the period. It is therefore unnecessary, and indeed impossible, to establish who in particular of the Romantic writers exerted the greatest influence".[82]

Both Arab writers raise such themes, widespread among the Romantics, as hatred of violence, the grandeur of man as the summit of the universe and the pantheistic deification of nature; they acknowledge the pre-eminence of intuition, feeling and instinctual understanding of the essence of life and of God over rational and logical principles. Also connected to this is the matter of the predestination of the poet, and much else.

An important proof of the fact that Gibran and Rihani had a sufficiently thorough knowledge of European and American literature can be found in evidence from the writers themselves. In an article devoted to a *qasida* by Ibn Sina,[83] Gibran demonstrates the influence of the ideas and outlook of Ibn Sina on many important Western writers – Shakespeare, Goethe, Shelley, Dante, Heine and others. Gibran does not merely state this position, but juxtaposes a number of thoughts and ideas from Eastern classicism with corresponding extracts of poetry by the European writers, in which he finds similar ideas and motifs.[84] In another article,[85] in which he is expounding his ideas on the importance of dialects in the development of the literary Arabic language, he makes references to works by Ovid, Dante and Petrarch. These facts lead one to the natural conclusion that Gibran had more than a passing acquaintance with the works of the authors mentioned. As the epigraph to his article "Letters in Flames"[86] Gibran took several lines of John Keats, whose works he not only knew but loved and valued, having found in them a certain resonance with his own thoughts and moods.

Rihani also spoke of how well he knew the works of Western writers, and in particular in his book *Arab Monarchs* he writes: "I did not adopt American customs in the way that certain Syrians living in America did. This was thanks to the great American philosopher Emerson, whose works were my first guide."[87]

The work of the writers of the Syro-American School was not, however, shaped exclusively by Western Romanticism. Some of them were also influenced by the Russian classics of the nineteenth century. Naimy, 'Abd al-Masih Haddad (1881–1950) and Nasib 'Arida (1887–1946) were fostered by Russian missionary schools, so they knew the Russian language well and were familiar with Russian literature. The influence of classical Russian literature on the work of Naimy was particularly great: in his first creative years he produced a series of works in which he emphasises incisive social themes and problems and acts as a pioneer for Realism.

The penetration of Russian cultural influence into the Arab East started in the late nineteenth century, when the Russian spiritual mission began its activities in Syria and Palestine.[88] The support of Orthodoxy in the Near East by the Russian state reached its full embodiment in the creation of the Imperial Orthodox Palestinian Society (1882–1914),[89] whose activities were propagated "in the spirit of Russian official Orthodoxy among the Orthodox section of the Arab population of Palestine and then also of Syria".[90] The Russian mission was headed by the consul general of Russia in Beirut, Konstantin Mikhaylovich Bazili, together with the learned archimandrite Porfiry Uspensky (1804–85). The names of the great Russian academic Orientalists of the period were closely associated with the activities of the Palestinian Society: the professor N.A. Mednikov and the members of the Russian Academy of Sciences, Ignaty Yulianovich Krachkovsky, Pavel Konstantinovich Kokovtsov, Nicoghayos Marr, Fyodor Ivanovich Uspensky and Nikodim Pavlovich Kondakov.

The first Russian missionary school was opened in 1882 in the village of Madjal, near Nazareth. The first elementary girls' school was opened in 1885 in Nazareth. Another important moment was the opening in Nazareth of a male teachers' seminary (1886). In the years that followed, missionary schools were created in Damascus, Beirut, Tripoli and Jerusalem, and not only in these major cities but also on the periphery.[91] Krachkovsky wrote about his impressions of these schools during his time in Syria thus:

The importance of these schools, which were often only poorly furnished, was great. Through the teachers' seminary of the Palestine Society the great legacies of Pirogov and Ushinsky* with their high ideals penetrated from Russia even here ... The power of the book manifested itself with all its might. And it is no coincidence that so many contemporary writers of the older generation, not only translators from Russian but also creative artists who have spoken their words in the name of the entire Arab world, came from the schools of the Palestinian Society.[92]

These schools taught not only theological but also secular subjects. Khalil Baydas (Beidas), who formerly studied at the Russian teachers' seminary in Nazareth and subsequently became a well-known translator of Russian classical literature into Arabic, valued the Russian missionary schools highly: "In those distant days Russian schools in Palestine were, without a doubt, the best."[93] Naimy also writes on this: "Russia surpassed its rivals [the missions of France and England], because it ran schools that were free of charge ... and these schools, in their curricula and organisation, met the latest standards."[94]

The main language spoken in the schools was Arabic, but much importance was also attached to the study of Russian: "The Russian language had to serve for them [the Arabs] as the main and truest medium in their further ... development",[95] wrote A.A. Dmitrievsky, a professor at the Kiev Spiritual Academy. The Russian schools, especially the Nazareth teachers' seminary, rendered a great service in spreading Russian culture in Arab lands.[96]

The new educational institutions were well equipped with libraries and held public lectures, readings and exhibitions of books and pictures. Printing houses were built and publishing increased year by year, as did translation activity. Ahatanhel Krymsky wrote: "Syria at the time of the Palestine Society ... made the acquaintance of fine Russian literature (Pushkin, Gogol, Turgenev and other classics) primarily through education, on the school benches of the Palestine Society institutions and at the same time through the libraries set up by the Russian–Palestinian schools, which were well stocked with Russian books."[97]

Before the first half of the nineteenth century there had been no translations from Russian into Arabic, and the Arabs were almost entirely unacquainted with Russian literature. "The first article on Russian literature, based on English materials, appeared in an Arabic encyclopaedia of the 1870s published in Beirut."[98] A direct encounter by the Arabs with Russian literature did not begin until the turn of the twentieth century.[99]

* [Editor's note] Nikolay Ivanovich Pirogov, a Ukrainian field doctor who served at Sevastopol and was involved in the introduction of anaesthetics, was a writer/practitioner on teacher training, especially for teaching Russian subjects abroad. Konstantin Dmitrievich Ushinsky, a Russian teacher and writer, was said to be the founder of scientific pedagogy in Russia.

The translators from Russian were usually Arabs, graduates of the Nazareth teachers' seminary or of middle or higher educational institutions in Russia, where they had come to love Russian culture, and "when they returned to their homeland already carried a direct acquaintance with Russian literature, above all, of course, with the classics".[100]

The first well-known translator of the Russian classics was Khalil Baydas. He translated *Resurrection* by Leo Tolstoy, *Crime and Punishment* by Fyodor Dostoevsky, *Taras Bulba* by Nikolai Gogol, *Prince Silver* by A.K. Tolstoy and various short stories by Anton Chekhov. Many Russian writers were translated, in particular Leo Tolstoy, by Salim Qubʿayn. In 1901 Qubʿayn published his book *The Teachings of Count L.N. Tolstoy* in Cairo, after which he translated the *Gospel* and the *Kreutzer Sonata* (1904).

Following the Russian revolution of 1905 Arab interest in Russia grew still further. Translators started to look at the works of Maxim Gorky. A publication appeared in Cairo in 1907 containing four pieces by Gorky: "The king who holds his banner high", "One of the kings of the republic" and "Beautiful France" [from the collection *My Interview*], and [the pamphlet] *On the Jews*, translated by Qubʿayn. The work of Anton Ballan, another graduate of the Nazareth seminary, was also significant. His translations of Chekhov, Tolstoy, Leskov and Gorky appeared periodically in the journal *Hims*.

Thus by the beginning of the twentieth century the Arab East was well acquainted with the best examples of Russian classical literature, and the sources of translation and popularisation of Russian literature in these countries were the graduates of the schools of the Russian Palestinian Society.

"The turning to Russian and Soviet literature was caused and conditioned by the appearance of Realist methods in the literatures of the countries of the East",[101] wrote L.Ye. Cherkassky. Indeed, in the first decades of the twentieth century, in the Arab countries and in particular in Egypt, an evolutionary process in artistic consciousness and the formation of a new literary system began, with the appearance of writers whose works prioritised a realistic portrayal of contemporary life in their country. V.N. Kirpichenko described this period as the first time of change, the first change of direction in Arabic literature. In this researcher's own view, the basic substance of the new literature "consisted in the 'discovery' by it of reality as an object of aesthetic assimilation".[102] Among the innovators one may mention the Taymur brothers Muhammad (1892–1921) and Mahmud (1894–1973), Muhammad Husayn Haykal (1892–1921), Taha Husayn (1889–1973), Tawfiq al-Hakim (1898–1978), ʿIsa ʿUbayd (1877–1922) and his brother Shihata (d.1961), Mahmud Tahir Lashin (1894–1954) and others, in whose works could be observed the marks of a Realist world perception. However, despite the fact that "the formation of Realism as an artistic method was based in many respects on the rejection of the artistic principles of Romanticism",[103] there remained in the prose of these writers the poetic manner and style of Romanticism and Sentimentalism. This was a familiar pattern in all Oriental literatures. N.I. Konrad pointed out that "literature in the countries of the East at this stage of their history was, as it were, in a hurry. Scarcely – and completely true to form! – had it embarked on the path of Romanticism than, not having succeeded in this to the necessary degree, it was already rushing beyond, towards Realism."[104]

The work of the Realist authors forms an important landmark in the history of the new Arabic literature. At the same time as the first steps were being taken in Egyptian literature (from the beginning of the First World War to the 1920s) towards a faithful and natural representation of the realities of national life, in the USA Naimy was working on his Realist stories.

While asserting the powerful influence of Russian literature on this writer, in particular during his first years of writing, we would point out that this was not only due to the objective requirements of his nation in its revival, with its new economic, political and cultural path, nor was it entirely due to the fact that Naimy had spent a number of years in Russia and become well acquainted with Russian literature. To a certain degree, rather, it may be attributed to the personality of Naimy himself. An impressionable person, he had been sensitive from his youth to the beautiful and to deep self-analysis. He was troubled by moral questions, and Realist Russian literature, in which there predominates "the depth of moral substance, great hopes, great ideas and great thoughts of the future",[105] left an indelible impression on him. He grasped many of the characteristics of nineteenth-century Realism, and Naimy's familiarity with the Russian classics was clearly discernible in his early works, in which he set out as a writer who followed the principles of Critical Realism.

Having comprehended in his own unique way some of the accomplishments of classical Russian literature and responded artistically to what he had perceived in it, Naimy applied this organically to his own work, forming a distinctive reflection of life in Lebanese society at a certain point in its historical development. This, however, gives no grounds for suggesting that his work is imitative; on the contrary, the keen insight of this writer is a sign of the complexity and inner richness of his person, for

> the creative perception of impulses and artistic values ... is not evidence of a lack of imagination on the part of the author but speaks rather of the writer's inner possibilities ... it is an expression of his organic sensitivity to diverse artistic impulses. It is one of the aspects of the multiple meanings of artistic creation and one of the indicators of its wealth and richness of content.[106]

The distinctive and original work of Naimy once again demonstrates the argument that

> to recognise the fact of an influence is in no way to disparage the uniqueness of the literature that comes under that influence. On the contrary, an interest

in those artistic accomplishments of another people that could be of use to the literature of the country concerned testifies to the breadth of thinking and outlook of the writer and his ability not to become closed within a national exclusivity and to see the development of his country's literature not from a perspective of isolation from the global literary process but rather from one of organic connection with it.[107]

In examining such an important literary phenomenon as the Syro-American School, attention must be paid to the entire complex of factors that called it into being. Of particular importance in this case are the specific national characteristics and the problem of literary interactions. To expose the character of the defining literary influences is to take stock of one of the most important factors in the literary development of this school. Of no less significance are the artistic contacts and conditions of development and formation of the person of the artist himself. This has obliged us to explore the specific historical reasons why Gibran and Rihani adopted the legacy of Western Romanticism and Naimy that of Russian Critical Realism, and of the particular manner in which these methods were received and assimilated by the Arab authors. Thus we can make an assessment from a position of historical method and comparative typological analysis, and from the perspective of the interrelations of literatures of this phenomenon within the general development of Arabic literature.

Chapter 2

Kahlil Gibran: the development of the Romantic method

Introduction

Kahlil Gibran (1883–1931) was one of the leading members of the Syro-American School, and an organiser, leader and active member of the Pen League.[1] Lebanese by birth, Christian by creed, he was the inheritor and bearer of two cultures: Western and Arab. A man of many gifts, both refined and emotional, a painter and a musician, he was, however, most famed as a major figure of literature. He penned short stories, parables, prose poems, essays, fables, poetry and criticism. His first publications were the book *al-Musiqa* (*Music*, 1905), and two collections of stories, *'Ara'is al-Muruj* (*Nymphs of the Valley*, 1907) and *al-Arwah al-Mutamarrida* (*Spirits Rebellious*, 1908). His only further large-scale works in Arabic were the story *al-Ajniha al-Mutakassira* (*Broken Wings*, 1912), the poetical diwan *al-Mawakib* (*The Processions*, 1919), the collection of articles and prose poems *Dam'a wa ibtisama* (*A Tear and a Smile*, 1914), *al-'Awasif* (*The Tempests*, 1920) and *al-Bada'i' wa al-Tara'if* (*The New and the Marvellous*, 1923). The remainder of his output was written in English: *The Madman* (1918), *The Forerunner* (1920), *The Prophet* (1923), *Sand and Foam* (1926), *Jesus the Son of Man* (1928), *The Earth Gods* (1931), *The Wanderer* (1932), *The Garden of the Prophet* (1933) and others. All these works were translated into Arabic and published in various editions in the Middle East.

Notwithstanding his sharply expressed individuality, Gibran's fate and his world-view bear the characteristic marks of the Arab creative intelligentsia in exile. He is filled with democratic aspirations, he is troubled about the destiny of the ordinary working man, the situation of Arab women (e.g. "Marta al-Baniyah", "The Cry of the Graves", "The Bride's Bed", *Broken Wings*) and social injustice in Lebanese life (e.g. "The Cry of the Graves", "The Palace and the Hut", "A Tear and a Smile"). He realises that society is divided into the haves and have-nots, and that the latter toil by the sweat of their brow yet live in poverty, subjected to exploitation not only by the rich but also by the ministers of religion (e.g. "John [Yuhanna] the Madman", "Khalil the Heretic").

Some Arab scholars, including Yamni al-Ida, consider that "Gibran was unable to go deeply into the existing social and economic situation, and paid no attention to the working class".[2] It should be remembered, however, that Gibran's works only describe life in Lebanon, where capitalism had not yet become fully formed. Recognising the liberation movement of the peasants as a significant force, the writer became a kind of apologist for a "peasant revolution" ("Khalil the Heretic"). Gibran was sure that a better future can only be had by struggle, that freedom is obtained by fighting, not by dreaming:

> They tell me: If you see a slave sleeping, do not wake him lest he be dreaming of freedom.
>
> I tell them: If you see a slave sleeping, wake him and explain to him freedom.
>
> "Handful of Beach Sand"[3]

A man must not be satisfied with the mere present; he must strive for a better future, because – in the author's deep conviction – "only the coward tarries, and it is folly to look back on the City of the Past".[4]

In tracing the development of Gibran's work, we shall try to show that as he progressed towards artistic maturity his creative method underwent significant changes. For this it is necessary to examine his relationship to the English Lake School and the American Transcendentalists, and to trace the evolution of his outlook and poetic language and the changes in the image of the Romantic hero in his works. To examine the artistic development and legacy of Gibran it would seem expedient to single out his most characteristic works.

Sentimentalism in Gibran's early works

Gibran's creative method underwent significant changes as he progressed towards artistic maturity. The evolution in his comprehension of the world is reflected in the transition from the Sentimentalism of his early prose, which was then the natural stage of his artistry, to Romanticism.

Sentimentalism as a literary tendency was a reaction to Enlightenment Rationalism. Belinsky paid tribute to the role of Sentimentalism in the development of Russian literature thus: "The purpose of Sentimentalism, which was introduced to Russian literature by Karamzin, was to arouse society and prepare it for a life of the heart and of feeling."[5]

In Arabic literature, as also in that of Western Europe and Russia, Sentimentalism was closely connected to Enlightenment Classicism. It was a transitional period between Enlightenment and Romanticism, and represented a step forward in the development of the new Arabic literature. The work of a number of Arab writers developed along the Sentimentalist path, among them Mustafa Lutfi al-Manfaluti and Muhammad Husayn Haykal.[6]

Naimy gives an original and poetic description of how Sentimentalism came to Arabic literature:

As a tendency, Sentimentalism acted out its role on the boards of the theatre of Western literature and then disappeared behind the curtain; not one of the spectators applauded with so much as a clap of the hands ... One gains the impression that having thus failed in the West, Sentimentalism then set out in search of pastures new, and by chance stumbled upon the little East. Finding here many tearful eyes, and still more who suffered the pains of the heart, it pitched its pavilions in Egypt and Syria and became with its retinue and servants a dear and esteemed guest.[7]

Of course, one should not agree completely with Naimy's simplistic, half-jesting appraisal, in which the attributes of Sentimentalism are merely excessive sensitivity, tearfulness and artificiality.

In turn, Belinsky also wrote with irony about these attributes of Sentimentalism: "Sensitive souls went in crowds to stroll at Liza's pond: Erasts, Leons, Leonids, Melodors, Filarets, Ninas, Lizas, Emilies and Julias, multiplied to extremes. Their sighs made the calmest of days windy, and their tears flowed in rivers."[8]

Sentimentalism was also a natural stage in the development of Gibran's artistic method. Dolinina writes: "Gibran's early works ... are permeated with sentimental motifs, with searches for harmony in the world, whose origin are necessarily love and beauty, poured into nature; they are full of sadness for the lot of the 'humble and insulted'."[9] Some Arab and Western scholars of Gibran have claimed that the writer was influenced by Rousseau through certain works of his that he knew.[10] We can concur with this opinion, while not forgetting that Gibran's Sentimentalist style is likely to owe more to the storytelling tradition of his upbringing in classical Arabic literature.

Krachkovsky considers that the excessive sensitivity and high-flown tone, which sounds deliberate and affected, is not in fact merely the style of a few Arab writers but rather characteristic of the general psychology and behaviour of the Arabs as a nation:

And if we compare the style of Gibran with the style of, say, contemporary Arab life, we will no longer see that artificiality that struck us at first sight. That is the way life is, and not just the literature that reflects it. The roots of this style are to be found in the spiritual nature itself, not only of the individual writer but of the entire life out of which he grew.[11]

In Gibran's works the qualities of Sentimentalism and Romanticism co-existed, as it were, in parallel for a considerable time. The works contained in the collection *A Tear and a Smile* (1914), written in the period 1903–08, the collections *Nymphs of the Valley* (1907) and *Spirits Rebellious* (1908), and in particular the story *Broken Wings* (1912), are evidence of a particular national variety of early Romanticism, in which traits that are intrinsic to Arabic literature, such as a disposition towards sensitivity and a quality of moralising, can be seen.

In a number of short stories, for example "Marta al-Baniyah",[12] "Warda al-Hani"[13] and the longer story *Broken Wings*,[14] the characteristics of Sentimentalism are predominant.

Significantly, in all these works the author addresses the topic of the emancipation of the Oriental woman, regarding it not from a social perspective but rather in terms of defending the feelings of women and their rights within the sphere of the family. Such an approach to women's emancipation was characteristic of Arab Enlighteners, in particular Qasim Amin, who believed that the rebirth of a nation and the struggle for progress must begin with changes in the conditions of women's lives and a reorganisation of the family.[15]

The theme of woman particularly occupied Gibran. In one of his letters to the Syrian writer Maryam Ziyada ("Mayy") he wrote:

> I am indebted for all that I call "I" to women ever since I was an infant. Women opened the windows of my eyes and the doors of my spirit. Had it not been for the woman-mother, the woman-sister and the woman-friend, I would have been sleeping among those who disturb the serenity of the world with their snores.[16]

Gibran's approach to women in the stories "Warda al-Hani" and "Marta al-Baniyah", like that of many other Arab writers and Enlighteners, emphasises the subject of love. In the Arab East in those years the women's question was not yet one of political rights as in Europe, but a question of family and love, of the right of women to love and happiness. It was necessary for literature to show that women were also "capable of love".[17]

Both stories are highly melodramatic and the author's entire attention is concentrated on the tortuous inner life of the heroes. Almost all of the substance boils down to the sensitive monologues of the heroines, in which they speak of their unhappy lives, while the author listens and shows sympathy with them.

"Marta al-Baniyah" is the story of a young village girl tempted by a rich city-dweller who is passing through. Having enjoyed himself with her for a certain time, he drops her and her young child. To avoid starvation, Marta is forced to sell her body. Exhausted both morally and physically, she soon dies, leaving her young son to the will of fate.

The stylistic mode of the story betrays its tendency to Sentimentalism. Marta's life in the village of her birth had been difficult:

> From her mother she inherited only tears of grief and her orphan state. ... Each morning she walked barefooted in a tattered dress behind a milch cow to a part of the valley where the pasture was rich, and sat in the shade of a tree. She sang with the birds and wept with the brook while she envied the cow its abundance of food. She looked at the flowers and watched the fluttering butterflies.[18]

Here, it would seem, are all the accessories of Sentimentalism. The mass of "sensitive" collisions continues throughout the story: the unbearable suffering of rejection, the painful illness, her passionate awaiting of death and so on. Here is the last supplication as she dies: "O Justice who are hidden, concealed behind these terrifying images, you, and you alone, hear the cry of my departing spirit and the call of my neglected heart."[19] These words naturally do not come across as the speech of an illiterate village girl forced to become a prostitute; they contain too much of the voice of the author, filled with sentimental sadness for the fallen woman.

Traces of Sentimentalism can also be found in the story "Warda al-Hani" ("Madame Rose Hanie"). The subject here is remarkable: a young woman, realising that she does not love her distinguished and wealthy husband, leaves him for a poor youth she does love. The step she thus takes, without fearing the blame placed on her by society, is practically unheard of for an Arab woman. In this story Gibran tells of the extremely common situation in the East in which girls are married for reasons other than love. Warda recounts to the narrator a series of distressing stories of women who were married at the will of their parents. With these specific examples the heroine underlines the naturalness of her brave deed, which yet appears to those around her to be so immoral and shameful.

The story contains many high-flown images, expressions and turns of speech. It is not only in the long monologues of Warda, or her husband Rashid Bey, in which they speak of their feelings and intimate experiences, that the signs of Sentimentalism appear, but also in the speech of the narrator himself. Here is how the teller describes his state on hearing the sorrowful complaints of the abandoned husband: "I rose with tears in my eyes and mercy in my heart, and silently bade him [my friend] goodbye; my words had no power to console his wounded heart, and my knowledge had no torch to illuminate his gloomy self."

"Marta al-Baniyah" and "Warda al-Hani" are generally artistically poor. There is little lyrical digression by the author and the images of Marta and Warda are simplistic: the characters are revealed only to the degree necessary to expose the ideas contained in them.

Gibran's Sentimentalism finds its fullest expression in *Broken Wings*, the story of the tragic fate of a woman forced to marry a man she does not love. (It is to a certain extent autobiographical: as confirmed by various biographers, Gibran suffered a tragic love affair in his youth, which ended in the death of his beloved, who had been promised to another man.)[20] It is a typically melodramatic story, narrated by the person of the author. The plot is limited to revealing the internal world of the heroes and their elevated feelings and experiences.

The outline of the story is as follows: the narrator, himself a character in the work, goes to visit a friend whose father has died. There he meets the daughter of the household, Selma. Love between the two young people flourishes instantly, but is short-lived and ends unhappily. It emerges that Selma has been promised to the nephew of the archbishop, and owing to the latter's high position her father does not dare to refuse him. The end of the story is tragic: the father dies of grief, realising that he has made his daughter unhappy, and in giving birth to the archbishop's child, both Selma and the newborn die.

The tale consists of a lyrical prologue and ten short chapters, each of which has a title corresponding to its position in the development of the plot. This indicates the author's attempt to mark out a chain of events. The events themselves – acquaintance, rendezvous, marriage, separation and so on – are what effectively move the story forward. Many events appear to take place, yet these are merely starting points, a kind of code that allows the author to begin and continue an uninterrupted lyrical monologue in which he reveals the world of his feelings and emotional experiences. There is no real action in the detailed development of the work. The sequence of events indicated in the chapter headings serves merely as a framework for extended discourses by the heroes and the author, and not for developing the action of the narrative. No sooner has the first meeting with Selma at the opening of the story been mentioned than there follows a whole stream of reasoning and declarations – of beauty and its essence, of love, of Selma's interior world, of the sublimity and refinement of her form, of the soul seized by grief, of the charm of her silent sorrow:

> Selma sat by the window, looking on with sorrowful eyes and not speaking, although beauty has its own heavenly language, loftier than the voices of tongues and lips. It is a timeless language, common to all humanity, a calm lake that attracts the singing rivulets to its depth and makes them silent.
>
> Only our spirits can understand beauty, or live and grow with it. It puzzles our minds; we are unable to describe it in words; it is a sensation that our eyes cannot see, derived from both the one who observes and the one who is looked upon. Real beauty is a ray which emanates from the holy of holies of the spirit, and illuminates the body, as life comes from the depths of the earth and gives colour and scent to a flower.
>
> Real beauty lies in the spiritual accord that is called love which can exist between a man and a woman.
>
> *Broken Wings*[21]

Other chapters also contain little by way of narrative. Despite the fact that the story involves various characters, in essence the entire piece is solely a monologue by the author. In these outpourings, moreover, the narrator barely touches on social or public questions. For the most part he is occupied with ethical questions, philosophy and the life of the heart and the soul. The exception to this is his reflection on the theme of the clergy and on the role of the woman in the family.

A further characteristic of the story is the inertness of its heroes and their submissiveness to circumstances. There is not the slightest protest: no murmur, no attempt to change their lot, no hint of a struggle. The substance of the story amounts to a description of sensations and emotions: comparison clings to comparison, metaphor to metaphor, image to image. The melodramatic outcome in the destinies of the heroes – sadness, dejection, submissiveness to fate and bitter disappointment, with no storms of despair, cursing or anger – are explicit signs of the Sentimentalist method. The mood of the heroes is characterised by a sensitiveness that constantly borders on tears. There are also scenes of great contrast: the jolly feast held by Selma's husband, the death of the child, the sobbing of the doctor and Selma's cries of despair, all of which are portrayed on this single canvas.

A feature of Sentimentalism in both Western European and Russian literature – for example in the works of Samuel Richardson, Laurence Stern, Jean-Jacques Rousseau and Nikolay Karamzin – is an interest in everyday life, the world of things and the details of daily living. Here for example is Karamzin's description of Liza's actions when Erast asks her for a glass of milk: "She ran to the cellar, brought a clean earthenware pot covered with a clean wooden disc, took a glass, washed it and wiped it with a white towel, filled it and served it at the window."[22] In Gibran's *Broken Wings* the tokens of everyday life are reduced solely to the statement of individual specific facts. The author is almost never distracted into describing any kind of realia such as situations, portraits or the setting. The details of the portrait, given in the form of brief epithets – "slender", "slim", "golden hair", "sorrowful look" – descend into lengthy, verbose digressions. Here is an example:

Selma Karamy had bodily and spiritual beauty, but how can I describe her to one who never knew her? Can a dead man remember the singing of a nightingale and the fragrance of a rose and the sigh of a brook? Can a prisoner who is heavily loaded with shackles follow the breeze of the dawn? Is not silence more painful than death? Does pride prevent me from describing Selma in plain words since I cannot draw her truthfully with luminous colors? A hungry man in a desert will not refuse to eat dry bread if Heaven does not shower him with manna and quails.

The beauty of Selma's face was not classic; it was like a dream of revelation which cannot be measured or bound or copied by the brush of a painter or the chisel of a sculptor. Selma's beauty was not in her golden hair, but in the virtue of purity which surrounded it; not in her large eyes, but in the light which emanated from them; not in her red lips, but in the sweetness of her words; not in her ivory neck, but in its slight bow to the front. Nor was it in her perfect figure, but in the nobility of her spirit, burning like a white torch between earth and sky. Her beauty was like a gift of poetry. But poets are unhappy people, for, no matter how high their spirits reach, they will still be enclosed in an envelope of tears.[23]

And so on. The dialogue, which usually helps to move a plot forward, is also weak in this story.

The attention given to landscape description is also fitting to the Sentimentalist method, whereby the natural setting reflects the psychological and emotional state of the heroes and underlines the soft lyricism of the work:

The scent of flowers mingled with the breeze as we came into the garden and sat silently on a bench near a jasmine tree, listening to the breathing of sleeping nature, while in the blue sky the eyes of heaven witnessed our drama.

The moon came out from behind Mount Sannin and shone over the coast, hills, and mountains; and we could see the villages fringing the valley like apparitions which have suddenly been conjured from nothing. We could see the beauty of Lebanon under the silver rays of the moon.

Broken Wings [24]

This entire extract is characterised by the special selection of words and expressions that bring into the world an exalted ideal beauty. The landscape sketch could not be better suited to the forthcoming event – the first meeting of the lovers.

A moralising tendency can be seen in the style of the story. At every opportunity the author draws on a supply of morality elements. In speaking, for example, of the hypocrisy and predatoriness of the clergy and the evil that they bring upon the people, the author-narrator resorts to an adage: "However, the people of Oriental nations place trust in such as they – wolves and butchers who ruin their country through covetousness and crush their neighbors with an iron hand." [25] Or on wealth, "In some countries, the parent's wealth is a source of misery for the children ... The Almighty Dinar which the people worship becomes a demon which punishes the spirit and deadens the heart", [26] or "our days are perishing like the leaves of autumn", "The mother is everything – she is our consolation in sorrow, our hope in misery, and our strength in weakness", [27] and so on. Sometimes these adages acquire the character of aphorisms: "Will a hungry man give his bread to another hungry man?", [28] "A bird with broken wings cannot fly in the spacious sky", [29] "The cup does not entice our lips unless the wine's color is seen through the transparent crystal", [30] for example. The entire story is filled with these aphorisms, adages, moralising generalisations and brief philosophical conclusions.

The lyricism and confessional nature of *Broken Wings* and its monologue quality demand a constant appeal to the personal experience of the author-narrator. Even when the subject is the thoughts and feelings of other people, such as Selma and her father, it is as though the narrator steps out from behind their names in order to complete the story in his individual way. Here, in essence, we encounter one of the basic principles of Romanticism: the investing of the entire surrounding world with one's own human passions. The confessional-lyrical, exclusively monological style of *Broken Wings* is also evidence of early shoots of a Romantic outlook within this work, whose basic method is still Sentimentalist.

Dolinina comments on these characteristics and defines the style of the story as "Romantic Sentimentalism", [31] and in fact the traits of Romanticism can already be seen in it. Particularly Romantic is the heroine Selma, with her exceptional nature that strives towards her wishes and freedom.

Elements of Romanticism appear in the hyperbolising of feelings and descriptions and in the landscape sketches that are sometimes secret and symbolic. Nevertheless, *Broken Wings* remains an example of a Sentimentalist work. It contains no challenge to fate, to people or to God; no rebellion or proud solitude, such as is so manifest in Gibran's subsequent works. However, *Broken Wings* set the tone, to a certain extent, for the way in which Romanticism started to emerge in the new Arabic literature, where restlessness or hints of active protest against contemporary social norms were still alien, but interest in the psychology of the characters began to appear. "Romanticism", wrote Belinsky, "is the interior world of man, the world of the soul and heart, a world of sensations and beliefs, a world of impulses toward the infinite, a world of secret visions and contemplation, a world of divine ideals".[32]

Apart from the fact that in *Broken Wings* Gibran anticipated the development of the Romantic method in Arabic literature, he secured for it two important topics: the theme of women and that of anticlericalism. The question of women's freedom is given a wider treatment in the story than merely the personal drama of one woman: "Thus destiny seized Selma and led her like a humiliated slave in the procession of miserable oriental woman."[33] Nonetheless, the writer examines the lot of women not in terms of rights and society, but only in the sphere of family and conjugal relations. Gibran believes that in future women will have a full place in society, but does not give so much as a hint as to when or under what circumstances this might happen: "Will the day ever come when beauty and knowledge, ingenuity and virtue, and weakness of body and strength of spirit will be united in a woman? I am one of those who believe that spiritual progress is a rule of human life, but the approach to perfection is slow and painful" ("Before the Throne of Death").[34]

On the problem of marriage, Gibran writes: "Marriage these days is a mockery whose management is in the hands of young men and parents. In most countries the young men win while the parents lose. The woman is looked upon as a commodity, purchased and delivered from one house to another."[35]

He equates the oppressed woman to an oppressed nation, so that her suffering, lack of rights and ignominy become the suffering, lack of rights and indignity of the whole nation: "But my dear readers, don't you think that such a woman is like a nation that is oppressed by priests and rulers? Don't you believe that thwarted love which leads a woman to the grave is like the despair which pervades the people of the earth?"[36]

Anticlerical motifs are also prominent in the story. On learning that the archbishop has promised his dissolute nephew to Selma, the narrator gives himself up to extensive reflections:

> The heads of religion in the East are not satisfied with their own munificence, but they must strive to make all members of their families superiors and oppressors.

The glory of a prince goes to his eldest son by inheritance, but the exaltation of a religious head is contagious among his brothers and nephews. Thus the Christian bishop and the Moslem imam and the Brahman priest become like sea reptiles who clutch their prey with many tentacles and suck their blood with numerous mouths.

"Lake of Fire"[37]

The author's criticism of the dependent position of Eastern women and his exposure of clericalism and the dissolute life of members of the aristocracy, together with other topical issues of his day, lend the story a certain social sharpness and reveal the author's relationship to contemporary life. Nonetheless, these moments of revelation in the story are not emphasised or highlighted, nor are they commented on by the heroes or the author.

To summarise, *Broken Wings* is a Sentimentalist work that contains certain Romantic elements. Its content and purpose are confined solely to revealing the interior world of the heroes and their elevated feelings and experiences. Naturally, this arrangement leads the author to a large stock of moral generalisations and lends the work a philosophical character. The very landscape is in sympathy with the moods of the characters. Yet with *Broken Wings* Gibran broke out of the conventions of Sentimentalism. The entire spirit of the story and the development of its plot are subordinated to its principal function: that of the author–narrator's self-expression, which takes the form of an unbroken interior confessional monologue that also includes a story about the feelings and experiences of the other characters. The whole story is cemented by the personality of the author, and this is the realisation of one of the basic principles of the Romantic form.

Broken Wings thus combines motifs of Enlightenment Humanism and Sentimentalism. At the same time, Gibran's Sentimentalism shows a clear development towards Romanticism.

The formation of Gibran's Romantic world-view and his assimilation of English and American methods

If there was a predominance of Sentimentalism in Gibran's narrative prose, then the genres included in the collection *A Tear and a Smile*[38] – essays and prose poems – could not hint more distinctly at Romantic stylistics. *A Tear and a Smile* shows the way in which Gibran began to master Romanticism. It contains works published over several years (1903–08) in émigré publications, particularly in the newspaper *al-Muhajir* (*The Émigré*). Gibran had now taken up the genre of prose poetry, short essays that capture assorted impressions and thoughts of the author and his philosophical reflections. They are elegant and musical, their language refined and often aphoristic.

The range of topics touched by Gibran in his book is broad: the position of the individual in society, his relationship to nature, the meaning of human existence, the poet and poetry, love and beauty. Many of the pieces in the collection are imbued with Sentimentalist motifs and regarded with extreme sensitivity, intense lyricism and a tendency towards moralising and homily. The style of the work is expressive, and in Gibran a special role is played by rhetorical questions and exclamations ("A Visit from Wisdom", "O Wind", "The Secret Conversation" and others):

> Who am I, Wisdom, and how came I to this frightening place? What manner of things are these mighty hopes and these many books and strange patterns? What are these thoughts that pass as doves in flight? And these words composed by desire and sung by delight, what are they? What are these conclusions, grievous and joyous, that embrace my spirit and envelop my heart? And those eyes which look at me seeing into my depths and fleeing from my sorrows? ... What is this world that leads me whither I know not, standing with me in despising? ... O Wisdom, what manner of things are these?
>
> "A Visit from Wisdom"[39]

The poems are filled with such perplexity and with tragic exclamations that reflect the complex and poignant interior world of the poet.

Regarding *A Tear and a Smile*, I.Yu. Krachkovsky wrote that Gibran's Sentimentalism

> does not bring a smile, because it meets with an echo in the soul of every Arab, whether he live in New York or be still in his Lebanese village beside the hills of cedars. Those same speeches that seem to us to be unnatural and stilted will be heard at any gathering where only an Arab feels at home and among his own kind, although the reason that caused them will also seem to us to be strangely unfitting to the extremely elevated and passionate tone of the words.[40]

The recognition of the human dignity of the poor and sympathy towards them, contrasted with censure of the moral deafness and iniquitous way of life of the wealthy, is a typical theme in Sentimentalism and strongly evident in this book. However, Gibran does not emphasise the social demarcation of the problem of wealth and poverty. His protest is a protest by humanity "in general" against injustice "in general". Examples include his prose poems "The Palace and the Hut", "The Criminal", "The Dumb Beast" and "A Tear and a Smile". The first of these[41] is a highly contrasted picture of the lives of the wealthy and the labourers:

> Night was falling and the lights in the mansion of the rich man shone brightly. The servants, clad in velvet, with buttons gleaming on their breasts, stood awaiting the guests. Music played and the lords and ladies descended on that palace from all parts, drawn in their carriages by fine horses. There they entered, dressed in gorgeous raiment and decorated with jewels.
>
> Then the men rose from their places and took the ladies to dance. And that hall became a garden through which the breezes of melody passed, and its flowers inclined in awe and wonder.

Soon midnight approached and the table was laid with the choicest of fruits and the finest of foods. Cups were passed from one to another and wine played with the senses of all those there until they in turn took to play. And when morning was near they dispersed, for they were tired with merrymaking and bemused by wine and wearied of dancing and revelry. And everyone betook himself to his bed.

"The Palace and the Hut"[42]

And here is the picture for the poor:

As the sun sank low beyond the horizon, a man dressed in the garb of a labourer stood at the door of a mean house and knocked thereon. It opened to him and he entered, greeting those within with a cheerful countenance, and sat down in the midst of his children by the fire. [...]

At dawn's approach that poor man rose from his bed and partook of a little bread and milk with his wife and little ones. Then he kissed them and went away with a heavy spade over his shoulder to the field, to water it with his sweat and make it fruitful that it might feed those mighty ones who yestereve made merry.

"The Palace and the Hut"[43]

The work ends with an adage characteristic of the Sentimentalists: "So is man's burden: a tragedy played on the stage of time. Many are the spectators that applaud; few are they that comprehend and know."[44]

The ending is typically calm, as though merely stating a fact. The picture that the poem has painted seems too abstract and non-specific. This is not Lebanon, nor Egypt, nor any other country in particular. It is simply the eternal and natural order of things, which causes the author a feeling of sadness, but one to which he seems to submit.

The method of contrast noted in "The Palace and the Hut" appears most distinctly in the prose poem "A Smile and a Tear",[45] in which it is less concerned with revealing social contrasts than in contrasting experiences and feelings: happiness and calmness are juxtaposed with tragedy and hopelessness.

The story "The Criminal"[46] also treats the social theme in an abstract manner. A hungry youth, unable to find work, begs for charity. But his appearance does not arouse compassion and, to avoid dying of starvation, he is forced to turn to crime: "Many years passed and that youth severed necks for the sake of their adornment, and destroyed bodies to satisfy his appetite. He increased in riches and was renowned for his strength and violence. He was beloved among the plunderers of the people and feared by the law-abiding."[47] The prose poem ends with the following adage: "Thus do men in their greed make of the wretched criminals, and with their harshness drive the child of peace to kill."[48] Gibran does not so much as hint at any kind of class patterns in this story. A poor man, it turns out, became a criminal because of the miserliness and hard-heartedness of the people around him. In the end, however, the former pauper grows rich by plundering and becomes the ruler. Gibran condemns the nature of the man who is cruel to good, but poor and needy, people but who fawns on unjustly obtained wealth.

"The Dumb Beast"[49] is the tale of a pitiful homeless dog. In effect the author recreates its thoughts and feelings and its fear of existence, which is so joyless and difficult for it. This little story has much tenderness and sympathy, but far more tragedy, as the parallel theme arises of the fate of many people whose lot is similar to the dog's: "I, human being, am a helpless animal, but I find a like thing between me and many of your brothers in kind when they are no longer strong enough to gain their sustenance".[50]

The examples given above are characteristic of the Sentimentalist depiction of reality, in which society is forever divided into rich and poor. The author relates to the former with condescending admonition and to the latter with profound pity and sympathy. In essence, however, human relations, like those of society, do not interest Gibran. People are understood as being either good or bad, righteous or evil, etc. There is [thus] much that is highly sensitised, and sometimes also dramatic, since the author, in analysing reality, sees no alternative and points only to evil.

The same works also reveal another of the traits of Sentimentalism: the special role of the landscape. Gibran's landscapes frequently depict conciliation and radiant beauty, be it the hot rays of the sun or the soft light of the moon, aromatic flowers, the peaceful blue sky, the charming song of the birds, the gentle wafts of the breeze and so forth. Generally the landscape evokes a description of equally serene feelings: the reconciliation and gratitude of life for the fact of its being as it is:

> The sun gathered up its garments from over those verdant gardens, and the moon rose from beyond the horizon and spilled its soft light over all. I sat there beneath the tree watching the changing shades of everything. I looked beyond the boughs to the stars scattered like coins upon a carpet of blue colour, and I heard from afar the gentle murmur of streams in the valley.
>
> "A Smile and a Tear"[51]

In *A Tear and a Smile* a number of typically Romantic themes can be traced that had not been articulated so distinctly in Arabic literature prior to Gibran: the poet and his role in society, the grandeur and omnipotence of the human self, love and beauty, nature and its close relationship to man. Gibran's experience of the English and American Romantics can be discerned in both the theme and the stylistic aspects of many of his works. V. Markov is entirely correct in remarking that the book "represents to a certain degree the sum of Gibran's searching in his early years, when the themes begin to appear that will occupy a pre-eminent position in the outlook of his mature period."[52]

One of the most important themes in the collection is that of the poet ("The Poet's Death is his Life", "The Poet", "Night", "A Poet's Voice"

and others), and this is clear evidence of the influence of the Western
Romantics on Gibran. Many English and American Romantics associate
the artistic realisation of this theme with problems of the self and of the
intuitive knowledge of its truth. The essence of the heavenly and earthly
soul is incomprehensible to the rational mind and is not subject to everyday
experience. Emerson, therefore, considers that the principal instrument of
cognition must be the imagination and insight of which only the poet is
capable. It follows that the destiny of the poet is the mission of the visionary,
the announcer of truth, the prophet.

Coleridge considered the poet to be a chosen one of God. Whitman
called him a "prophet". Wordsworth remarked that "the Poet binds together by passion and knowledge the vast empire of human society".[53] For
Emerson, the poet is greater than the theologian, and "stands among partial
man for the complete man ... who sees and handles that which others dream
of, traverses the whole scale of experience, and is representative of man, in
virtue of being the largest power to receive and impart."[54]

An analogous understanding of the poet's function, summoned into the
world to bring love, truth and beauty into the life of mankind, is also found
in Gibran. The poet, by his definition, is "a noble soul, sent by the Goddess
of Understanding".[55] Further,

> A Link
> between this world and the hereafter;
> a pool of sweet water for the thirsty; [...]
>
> An angel
> Sent by the gods to teach man the ways of gods.
> A shining light unconquered by the dark,
> Unhidden by the bushel
> Astarte did fill with oil;
> And lighted by Apollo. [...]
>
> Alone,
> He is closed in simplicity
> And nourished by tenderness;
> He sits in Nature's lap learning to create,
> And is awake in the stillness of night
> In wait of the spirit's descent.
> A husbandman who sows the seeds of his
>   heart in the garden of feeling,
> Where they bring forth yield
> To sustain those that garner. [...]
>
> And you, O Poets,
> Life of this life:
> You have conquered the ages
> Despite their tyranny,

> And gained for you a laurel crown
> In the face of delusion's thorns.
> You are sovereign over hearts,
> And your kingdom is without end.   ("The Poet"[56])

It is difficult to deny that Gibran's understanding of the poet's calling is largely in agreement with the ideas of the Western Romantics.

In Shelley's view, poets see clearly not only the present, but also the future in the present. The same definition of the poet can be found in Gibran's words: "That which alone I do today shall be proclaimed before the people in days to come. And what I now say with one tongue, tomorrow will say with many."[57]

The theme of the poet continues without significant changes throughout Gibran's works. Sometimes the image of the poet takes on cosmic dimensions and the microcosm of the self becomes proportioned to the cosmos and harmonised to it. In the poem *Night* the poet writes of himself:

> I too am a night, vast and calm, yet fettered and rebellious.
> There is no beginning to my darkness and no end to my depths ...[58]

The poet does not set out as an artisan, working with the medieval yardstick and the ordinary tools of his trade (the *lafz* and the *ma'na*, the word and the poetic motif), but rather as poetry itself in the flesh. There is no need to separate the poet's works from the person himself, or to distinguish the form and content in his poetry:

> Poetry is not an opinion expressed. It is a song that rises from a bleeding
>   wound or a smiling mouth.[59]
> A poet is a dethroned king

Yet here the poet's greatness is the greatness of the fallen angel, that of the sovereign stripped of power. The origins of these images in the Satanism of Romantic poetry are hardly characteristic of the traditional concept of creativity in classical Arabic literature.

> Poetry is wisdom that enchants the heart.
> Wisdom is poetry that sings in the mind.
>
> A great singer is he who sings our silences.   ("Sand and Foam"[60])

These and other utterances highlight the special attribute of poetry as a mediatrix between two worlds – the secret and the evident, the ineffable and the commonplace.

If the influence of Emerson's Transcendentalist philosophy led Gibran to seek a divine origin in the poet, then thanks to Walt Whitman he learned also to see in the poet an earthly person who reflects upon the good of humanity and strives for its future. Maurice Mendelson remarks that, for Whitman, the poet "is not only a composer of verse but also a prophet, paving the ways to the future".[61] Whitman himself speaks of this more than once in his works, in particular in his "Song of Myself":

> I celebrate myself, and sing myself,
> And what I assume you shall assume ...[62]

It is true that for Gibran the poet remains primarily the high priest of beauty and truth (see below), but it is the poet, in his view, who is chosen to give people a guiding thread in everyday life and to maintain the ideal of harmonious existence. In his prose poem "A Poet's Voice"[63] he writes:

> Strength sows within the depths of my heart and I harvest and gather
>   ears of corn and give it in sheaves to the hungry.
> The spirit revives this small vine and I press its grapes and give the
>   thirsty to drink.
> Heaven fills this lamp with oil and I kindle it and place it by the window
>   of my house for those that pass by night.[64]

However, the poet's life only becomes meaningful when he feels himself understood, loved and valued. "The proof of a poet is that his country absorbs him as affectionately as he has absorbed it",[65] wrote Whitman in his preface to *Leaves of Grass* in 1855. He also expresses this in "By Blue Ontario's Shore":

> I am willing to wait to be understood by the growth of the taste
>   of myself,
> Rejecting none, permitting all.[66]

Gibran shows a view in common with Whitman in the following:

> Would that I were a well, dry and parched, and men throwing stones
>   into me;
> For this were better and easier to be borne than to be a spring of
>   living water
> When men pass by and will not drink.
> Would that I were a reed trodden underfoot,
> For that were better than to be a lyre of silvery strings
> In a house whose lord has no fingers
> And whose children are deaf.
>   "My soul is heavy laden with its fruits"[67]

One may also agree with the American scholar Joseph Ghougassian, who found a consonance between the views of Gibran and William Blake as regards the mission of the poet: "The poet – considered Blake and Gibran – is a man who ... has a messianic mission in leading the people back to Truth."[68]

For Gibran the theme of the poet is indissolubly related to the feeling of loneliness. He repeatedly comments on the contrast between the poet and the reality that surrounds him. In his play *Sulban* he writes: "The artist

– I mean a creative person who makes new forms for the expression of his thoughts and feelings – is always a stranger to his family and friends, a stranger in his homeland and generally a stranger in this world."[69]

The same idea is also clearly sketched in his prose poem "The poet's death is his life".[70] A young and talented poet lives alone in a pitiful hovel, dying of hunger, for, as he says, "men have rejected me and cast me into the corners of forgetfulness".

> The ages passed, and the people of that city remained in the stupor of ignorance and folly. When they awoke therefrom and their eyes beheld the dawn of knowledge, they set up in the centre of the town a great statue of the poet, and at an appointed time each year they held a festival in his honour.
> How foolish are men!

In Gibran the theme of the poet is always accompanied by a disclosure of the author's ethical and moral principles and his views on the world, humanity and society. To a large extent these views overlap with the views and convictions of the Romantics.

The theme of love and beauty, which occupies an important place in *A Tear and a Smile* (for example, in the poems "The Life of Love", "Before the Throne of Beauty", "The Queen of Fantasy", "Secrets of the Heart" and "Song of Beauty"), is closely connected to the theme of the poet, and the two complement each other.

The ideal of beauty and humaneness was always also the ideal of the Romantic artist. The English Romantic poet John Keats (1795–1821) said in his "Ode to a Grecian Urn":

> "Beauty is truth, truth beauty," – that is all
> Ye know on earth, and all ye need to know.[71]

For the Romantics, art and beauty are synonyms. Art is counterposed to evil, deception and baseness. Shelley writes of this in his "Hymn to Apollo":

> The sunbeams are my shafts, with which I kill Deceit,
> that loves the night and fears the day;
> All men who do or even imagine ill
> Fly me, and from the glory of my ray
> Good minds and open actions take new might,
> Until diminished by the reign of Night.
> [...]
> I am the eye with which the Universe
> Beholds itself, and knows it is divine;
> All harmony of instrument or verse,
> All prophecy, all medicine, is mine.[72]

In contradistinction to the Enlighteners, the Romantic poet links reason with intuition and feeling, that is, he copes with the world "artistically", by means of inspiration, and breaks away from the commonplace outward appearance of existence, beneath which beauty hides.

Like the English Romantics, Gibran considered beauty as something general and ideal; like nature, so man is also suffused with beauty. Beauty is not the privilege of the noble or the wealthy, but "the sacred property of all humanity". In "Song of Beauty" he writes:

> I am the abode of happiness
> And the source of joy.
> I am the beginning of repose.
> [...]
> I am the poet's imagination
> And the artist's guide.
> I am teacher to the music-maker.
> I am the glance in the eye of a child
> Beheld by a tender mother.
> [...]
> I am a Truth, O people, yea, a Truth.[73]

The poem "Beauty" is also devoted to this idea:

> O you, who perish in the night of contradictions and drown in the depths of conjecture! For in beauty is truth, which denounces suspicion, drives away doubt and shines with a light that protects you from the darkness of untruth.[74]

For Gibran beauty is the kernel, the essence of living, a high and eternal truth. He considers nature to be the embodiment and symbol of beauty: "Beauty is all of nature". The appreciation of beauty is as natural as is the charm of nature. "Watch for the awakening of spring and the breaking of the morning, for beauty is the destiny of those who watch! Listen for the song of birds, the rustle of branches and the murmur of streams, for beauty is the portion of those who listen."[75] Beauty is inseparable from the moral understandings of love and kindness: "Dedicate your body, like a temple, to beauty and dedicate your heart, like the altar, to love, for beauty is the worshippers' reward."[76] The perception of beauty elevates and ennobles the man and brings him to goodness and unselfishness.

For the Romantics, love and beauty are that light of spirituality that illuminates the heart and imagination of the poet. Emerson writes that the poet is an Aeolian harp that "trembles to the cosmic breath",[77] that gives things their names and acts as beauty's representative. People who are distracted by everyday concerns frequently pass beauty by. The task of the poet is to halt their attention in front of it, for it is the prototype of truth ("The Queen of Fantasy").[78] Accordingly, beauty is allotted a high position in the system of spiritual values.

A further aspect of the theme of the poet in Gibran's poetry is the exhortation of the Romantic self on Earth, its purpose in life and belief in it. Ivan Fyodorovich Volkov writes: "It was Romanticism that opened for literature the self as such – intrinsic in value not only in the sense of the uniqueness of its individual characteristics, but also in the profound content of his character, and this brought art considerably closer to real human life."[79]

Gibran makes reference to the self with its Romantic understanding of the world in various prose poems, among them these from *A Tear and a Smile*: "The City of the Past", "The Blind Force", "Under the Sun", "Song of Happiness" and "The Hymn of Man".

In "The Blind Force" the elements of nature break free and descend on mankind, which is helpless in the face of it, wantonly destroying everything man had made with his own hands.

> And so it was, the while the grieving spirit looked on from afar, sorrowing and reflecting. It pondered upon the limited night of men before unseen forces, and sorrowed with the fleeing victims of fire and ruin. [...]
>
> Yet did I find among these wrongs and misfortunes the divinity of man standing upright as a giant mocking earth's foolishness and the anger of the elements. And ... it sang a hymn of immortality, saying: "Let the Earth then take what is to it; **for I am without end.**"[80]

The poet proudly acknowledges the strength of man, the invincible strength of his spirit that defies all the elements. This resonates with examples from Blake, Shelley and Whitman, such as this extract from Whitman's "Song of Myself":

> This day before dawn I ascended a hill and look'd at the crowded heaven,
> And I said to my spirit When we become the enfolders of those orbs,
> and the pleasure and knowledge of every thing in them, shall we
> be fill'd and satisfied then?
> And my spirit said *No, we but level that lift to pass and continue beyond.*[81]

In the prose poem "Under the Sun"[82] Gibran takes for an epigraph the biblical saying "all is vanity". The words of King Solomon, "I have seen all the works that are done under the sun; and, behold, all is vanity and vexation of spirit"[83] seem to him to be "born of weakness and despair", for life has a purpose, while impassivity is akin to indifference. But people understand beauty in the beautiful, wisdom in the wise and virtue in the just, and the poet considers that Solomon should repent of his efforts to deprive people of belief in their own power.

The Romantic belief that all in nature is in steady forward progress towards truth and beauty is expressed in the argument between the lyrical subject of the poem and the wise man of the Bible:

> Now it is known to you that life is not as a vexation of spirit, nor that
> all under the sun is in vain; but rather that all things were and
> are ever marching towards truth.
> [...] Well do you know that the spirit is going toward the light in face
> of the obstacles of life ...[84]

The forward movement of man is a path of unending learning, struggles and victories. And this requires that man overcome his past experience, which in Gibran is symbolised by the remains of a ruined city: "The City of the Past". In this city the poet sees

> places of work sitting like great giants beneath the wings of slumber. And sanctuaries of words around which hovered souls crying out in despair – and singing in hope. I beheld temples of religion set up by faith and destroyed by doubting, ... meeting-places of knowledge illumined by wisdom and darkened by folly.
>   The sight of the ruined city brings the poet to despair, but Life tells him he must depart and look instead for the City of the Future: Come, for only the coward tarries, and it is folly to look back on the City of the Past.[85]

The image of man stubbornly moving forward towards unending knowledge and to the "City of the Future" and the "Society of the Future", and the theme of his eternal striving for physical and moral perfection, accord with the poetry of the Western Romantics, in particular of Blake and Whitman. Blake's "The Everlasting Gospel" includes these lines:

> God wants not Man to humble himself: [...]
>
> If thou humblest thyself, thou humblest me;
> Thou also dwell'st in eternity.
> Thou art a Man, God is no more,
> Thy own humanity learn to adore ...[86]

The same proud idea of the essence of Man can be found in Whitman:

> Long I was hugg'd close – long and long.
> Immense have been the preparations for me,
> Faithful and friendly the arms that have help'd me.
> Cycles ferried my cradle, rowing and rowing like cheerful boatmen,
> For room to me stars kept aside in their own rings,
> They sent influences to look after what was to hold me.[87]

In speaking about this trait in Romanticism, Oleg Rossianov remarks that

> seeing man as the crown of creation and art and literature as the highest form of activity, the Romantics divined and affirmed the participation of the self and of literature in the great macrocosm and the small creative universe – and in the universe of the entire soul of man and of very being. It was the aesthetic experience of this co-belonging and co-involvement in society that was the source of the particular intensity of the Romantic perception of the world.[88]

This statement may be fairly applied to the work of all Romantics, and to Gibran in particular. His "Hymn of Man" opens and closes with the lines:

> I was,
> And I am.

So shall I be to the end of time,
For I am without end.[89]

The notion of the value of human existence – in unending striving "forward and upward" – is constant in Gibran's work. Even many years later, in his book *Sand and Foam* (1926), it can be found in the form of aphorisms:

> The significance of man is not in what he attains, but rather in what
>   he longs to attain.[90]
> Humanity is a river of light running from ex-eternity to eternity.[91]

In his poem "Gods" Whitman names Man as God directly:

> Thou, thou, the Ideal Man,
> Fair, able, beautiful, content, and loving,
> Complete in body and dilate in spirit,
> Be thou my God.[92]

For Gibran also, Man is the "cornerstone of creation", despite the tragic loneliness and misunderstanding he constantly feels. His lyrical hero passionately loves people, grieves over their fates and feels himself joined to them by blood. In *My Birthday*: "I have loved all people – much I have loved them. In my sight people are of three kinds. One curses life; one blesses it; one observes it. I have loved the first for his despair; the second for his tolerance; the third for his understanding."[93]

A sincere hymn of love for mankind can also be found in several pieces in his later book *The Forerunner* (1920):

> My friends and my neighbours and you who daily pass my gate, I would speak
> to you in your sleep ...
>   I love the one among you as though he were all, and all as if you were one.
> And in the spring of my heart I sang in your gardens, and in the summer of my
> heart I watched at your threshing-floors.
>   Yea, I love you all, the giant and the pygmy, the leper and the anointed, and
> him who gropes in the dark even as him who dances his days upon the mountains.
>   "The Last Watch"[94]

All Romantics are united in the struggle for the violated dignity of the human, for his spiritual and social freedom. "As if organically, Blake's entire work is permeated by the tragic theme of the physical and spiritual enslavement of the person",[95] writes N.Ya. D'yakonova. The same may be said of Shelley, although there are exceptions, such as his poem *Prometheus Unbound*, the principal theme of which is protest, defying all the dark forces that seek to belittle the free human spirit that will not be subordinated.

The Romantics saw the future as a society of free, happy people with equal rights. This is a characteristic and enduring theme in their poetry. One gains the impression that Gibran is in agreement with their poetry, and in particular with Whitman's "The Song of the Broadaxe". In the great city of the future "where the slave ceases and the master of slaves ceases", women have equal rights to men; those who are active in politics are the servants of the people. This is the city of "the faithfulest friends". Here a world of natural citizens prevails, "where outside authority enters always after the precedence of inside authority". In his utopia "A Glimpse into the Future"[96] Gibran also depicts an ideal world where equality, brotherhood, friendship and justice prevail; a society in which man attains his dignity. He has been "lifted above smallness and raised above little things". A similar happy future for mankind appears in Shelley's poem "Queen Mab". This golden age of a happy, free and harmoniously developed state of man is also described by other Romantics.

There is not one work by Gibran that is not also a hymn to nature. In his approach to nature Gibran appears as an innovator. Nature does not serve in his works as a mere background but rather is invested with a persona of its own, as if to see, hear and comprehend all things by itself. The theme of nature is one of the fundamental elements in *A Tear and a Smile*. The collection includes a cycle of songs about nature – the song of the wind, of the wave, of the rain, of the flower and of the seasons – in which the phenomenon of nature becomes animated and speaks. The wave sings a song:

> I and the shore are lovers:
> the wind unites us and separates us.
>
> I come from beyond the twilight
> to merge the silver of my foam with the gold of its sand;
> and I cool its burning heart with my moisture.
>
> Comes the ebb and I embrace my love;
> It flows, and I am fallen at his feet.
>   "Song of the Wave"[97]

The song is echoed by the torrents of rain:

> I am the silver threads
> The gods cast down from the heights,
> And Nature takes me to adorn the valleys.
>
> I am the precious pearls
> Scattered from Astarte's crown,
> And the daughter of morning stole me to
>   beautify the fields.
>
> I weep and the hillocks smile;
> I am abased and the flowers are lifted.
>
> I rise from the lake's heart
> And glide upon wings of air

Until I am a verdant garden.
Thereon I descend
And kiss the lips of its flowers
And embrace its boughs.

In the stillness, with my gentle fingers,
I tap upon window panes:
The sound thereof is a song known to feeling spirits.

I am the sigh of the ocean
And heaven's tear
And the smile of the field.   ("Song of the Rain"[98])

For Gibran nature is a sanctuary for lovers, a world of desired being, where the treasure house of the human spirit may be disclosed. Close to nature, man feels a kinship or oneness with it and finds gratification for his restless and lonely soul, and nature resonates to his interior world:

> One heavy day I ran away from the grim face of society and the dizzying cla-mour of the city and directed my weary steps to the spacious valley. I pursued the beckoning course of the rivulet and the musical sounds of the birds, until I reached a lonely spot where the flowing branches of the trees prevented the sun from touching the earth. I stood there, and it was entertaining to my soul – my thirsty soul who had seen naught but the mirage of life instead if its sweetness.
> "Before the Throne of Beauty"[99]

For Gibran the sky is the "source of spiritual peace", and all nature is the "haven of rest and tranquillity". Here he is close to Emerson. "Where do we find ourselves?", asks the American poet in his essay "Experience", and answers: "Nature causes each man's peculiarity to abound".[100]

Gibran does not oppose "high nature to miserable humanity", but rather sings the idea of a harmonious union of nature and man. The Arab scholar Ashtar writes: "In their works they [Gibran and Rihani] ... brought us closer to nature, to the point of merging with it."[101]

Gibran strove, as it were, to plunge into the secret of nature and to merge with it in a single impulse. Like many Romantics he was a pantheist and considered man to be an organic part of nature; nature was the pledge for the eternal life of the spirit. Together with Emerson, Shelley and Coleridge, he highlights the kinship of the rule of nature and that of mankind and their common basis. The closeness and indivisibility of the ideas of "nature" and "man" is particularly revealed in Gibran's poem "O Earth":

> Who are you, O Earth, and what are you?
> You are "I", O Earth!
> You are my sight and my discernment.
> You are my knowledge and dream.
> You are my hunger and my thirst.

You are my sorrow and my joy.
You are my inadvertence and my wakefulness.
You are the beauty that lives in my eyes,
the longing in my heart, the everlasting life in my soul.
You are "I", O Earth.
Had it not been for my being,
you would not have been.[102]

A similar understanding of the unity of nature and human spirit is inherent in the English Romantics. Irina Neupokoeva writes: "The pantheistic world perception which is characteristic of all Shelley's work is linked to the poet's striving to overcome the rupture between philosophical materialism and idealistic dialectics. It is from pantheism that Shelley's attempt to animate matter and to see enclosed in it some kind of special 'living', 'acting' force arises".[103]

In his poem "Song of Prosperine" Shelley emphasises the kinship of the dominion of nature and that of man with their common basis – Mother Earth:

Sacred Goddess, Mother Earth,
Thou from whose immortal bosom
Gods and men and beasts have birth,
Leaf and blade, and bud and blossom ...[104]

A similar idea appears in Coleridge's "Hymn to the Earth":

Earth! thou mother of numberless children, the nurse and the mother,
Hail! O Goddess, thrice hail! Blest be thou! and, blessing, I hymn thee![105]

For Whitman, man also merges with nature and plunges into its secrets:

We are Nature – long have we been absent, but now we return;
We become plants, leaves, foliage, roots, bark;
We are bedded in the ground – we are rocks;
We are oaks – we grow in the openings side by side...
              "We two – how long we were fooled"[106]

Gibran's poem "O Wind"[107] is permeated with belief in the inevitability and necessity of the unceasing renewal of life:

Now singing and rejoicing, now weeping and lamenting.
We hear, but behold you not; we feel your presence yet do not see you.
You were as a sea of love submerging our spirits, yet not drowning us ...

You bear the breath of illness from city streets, and from the heights the
        spirit of a flower; ...
Here do you tarry; there do you hasten. Thither you run, but you abide
        not. ...

Are you fickle as the ages ...?

You pass in anger across deserts and trample underfoot the caravans and
bury them in graves of sand. ...

You fall upon the seas in assault and disturb the peace of their depths ...[108]

"O Wind", in its mood, thematic content and even to a degree its compositional form, is reminiscent of the well-known "Ode to the West Wind"[109]
by Shelley, in which the poet emphasises the dialectic of destruction and
creation. For both poets the symbol of this is the wind:

O wild West Wind, thou breath of Autumn's being,
Thou, from whose unseen presence the leaves dead
Are driven, like ghosts from an enchanter fleeing,

Yellow, and black, and pale, and hectic red,
Pestilence-stricken multitudes: O thou,
Who chariotest to their dark wintry bed

The winged seeds, where they lie cold and low,
Each like a corpse within its grave, until
Thine azure sister of the Spring shall blow

Her clarion o'er the dreaming earth, and fill
(Driving sweet buds like flocks to feed in air)
With living hues and odours plain and hill:

Wild Spirit, which art moving everywhere;
Destroyer and preserver; hear, oh, hear!

The idea of the unending and incessant renewal of life in nature can also
be seen in "The Life of Love", a prose poem in which Gibran describes the
changes of the seasons and likens them to the poet's love. Spring marks the
flowering of love, summer the ripeness of nature and the maturing of love,
and autumn the presentiment of silence and the end of happiness:

... for the leaves of the trees are become yellow ...

... for the birds have taken flight to the seashore ...

... for the brooks have ceased their flowing and the springs are no more,
for the tears of their joy are dried up; and the hillocks have cast
aside their fine garments.

... For nature is overcome by sleep ...[110]

The arrival of winter and the spectacle of nature cheerless saddens the heart of the poet and he addresses his beloved with the words:

> Ah, my beloved one, how deep is the ocean of sleep! How distant the morning ... in this night![111]

The sad tone of this work distinguishes it from Shelley's "Dirge for the Year"; it lacks the feeling of bright hope that runs through the latter:

> January gray is here,
> Like a sexton by her grave;
> February bears the bier,
> March with grief doth howl and rave,
> And April weeps – but, O ye Hours!
> Follow with May's fairest flowers.[112]

While singing the beauty and greatness of nature, the Romantics were the first to touch on the negative role of urbanism and bourgeois civilisation in human life. Dmitry Urnov writes: "The Romantics were the first to discern, and highly perspicaciously, the disfigurement of the rapidly growing cities and the cost of bourgeois progress. Everything that has come to be a problem in the contemporary era was first pointed out by the Romantics."[113]

Of course these characteristics appeared uniquely and individually for each Romantic poet or writer. If Shelley and Byron ignored the patriarchal idyll, then for Wordsworth Romanticism was rural peace and quiet, a particularly joyful and quiet love of nature and an unhurried reflection on it. "Nobody from among his contemporaries ... advocated so insistently and passionately ... that poetical union with nature that elevates and ennobles the soul."[114]

Wordsworth contrasted the capitalistic and industrialising world to the peasants with their naturalness and morals. He wrote of how to ennoble the soul in a letter to John Wilson in 1802: "by stripping our hearts naked and looking out of ourselves to men who lead the simplest lives and most according to nature, who have never known the false refinements, wayward and artificial desires, false criticisms, effeminate habits of thinking and feeling, or who, having known these things, have outgrown them".[115]

As a matter of fact, the aesthetic of city life was alien to all Romantics, and they contrasted it with the lives of simple people close to nature. Gibran's anti-urbanism also carries an expression of characteristically Romantic dissatisfaction with the changes in human life that accompanied industrial development. Even in his early works Gibran hints at the idea of returning to nature. For example, in the story "Marta al-Baniyah" discussed above, the city represents the source of evil temptation and the false values of culture and civilisation, opposed to which is the village, embodying the naturalness of being:

Those of us who have spent the greater part of our existence in crowded cities know little of the life of the inhabitants of the villages and hamlets tucked away in Lebanon. We are carried along on the current of modern civilisation. We have forgotten – or so we tell ourselves – the philosophy of that beautiful and simple life of purity and spiritual cleanliness. If we turned and looked we would see it smiling in the spring; drowsing with the summer sun; harvesting in the autumn, and in the winter at rest; like our mother Nature in all her moods. We are richer in material wealth than those villagers; but their spirit is a nobler spirit than ours. We sow much but reap nothing. But what they sow they also reap. We are the slaves of our appetites; they, the children of their contentment. We drink the cup of life, a liquid clouded with bitterness, despair, fear, weariness. They drink of it clear.[116]

Other works devoted to this theme include "History and the Nation", "Lament of the Field" and "The Abode of Happiness". In the allegorical prose poem "History and the Nation"[117] the incursions of Western civilisation in the East are associated with the ruin of nature and misery for the labourers. A shepherdess (a metaphor for one of the Eastern countries) addresses History, an old wandering man who represents progress in the Western sense:

"What do you wish of me, History?" Then she pointed to her sheep. "This is the remnant of a healthy flock that once filled this valley. This is all that your covetousness has left me. Have you come now to sate your greed on that? These plains that were once so fertile have been trodden to barren dust by your trampling feet. My cattle that once grazed upon flowers and produced rich milk, now gnaw thistles that leave them gaunt and dry."[118]

In *A Tear and a Smile* nature is almost always soft, tender and kind to ordinary people, who in turn love her and live in harmony with her. For Gibran nature symbolises the wholeness of the world, the meaning of life and the path to beauty, love and physical and moral perfection. In this his work resonates with that of the Western Romantics.

We have already noted that individual depictions of nature in *A Tear and a Smile* are Romantic, with shades of Sentimentalism. Nevertheless, certain landscape sketches in the book reveal accuracy and rigour of vision. A similar co-existence of elements from different methods was also encountered in considering other themes in the collection.

The works included in *A Tear and a Smile* reveal the closeness of the Sentimentalist and Romantic principles in Gibran's work, along with the Romantic world outlook of the writer. An analysis of the book reveals his familiarity with the works of English and American Romantics, which is reflected in both the style and subject matter of his works. The glorification of mankind, the exaltation and pantheistic view of nature, the admiration of beauty and the recognition of the special function of the poet and his role in society are all typical Romantic themes. There is, however, no distinct expression of social orientation; there is no passionate call to arms to change the social ills that are described, or the radical resolution of them, that is so characteristic of the English Romantics. Gibran, as a true Arab writer, is mostly concerned with spiritual problems.

Romanticism as the fundamental method in Gibran's work

Towards the end of the 1920s and in the early part of the 1930s, Romanticism was established as the principal method in Gibran's work. This phase of his creative life is represented in his book *al-'Awasif* (*The Tempests*, 1920). Two more of his works from this period, *The Madman* (1918) and *The Forerunner* (1920), both written in English, are similar in subject matter and style to the first; we have nevertheless selected *The Tempests* because it most clearly demonstrates the signs of Romanticism, and because it became the best-known of the three among Arab readers.

Almost all the pieces in this collection are adorned with Romantic sentiments: motifs of rebellion, disdain for the world, a thirst for solitude, a deep disappointment in the life of civilised society, a passionate hunger for nature, the rejection of the Church and its rites, a proud challenge to God and so on. The book also contains a variety of genres – essays, stories and prose poems – in which some items are more extended in length. The ideas in this collection and the motifs of most of its works make it clear that not only did Gibran know the works of the English Romantics well but that he was also imbued with their ideas and attitudes.

Most representative of the collection as a whole is the story "The Storm",[119] whose basis is the characteristically Romantic problem of the relationship between the self and society, the conflict of the freedom-loving hero with the surrounding world that he finds unsatisfactory. "At the centre of Romantic art is the lonely individual who finds himself in conflict with his environment" (A. Anikst);[120] "the Romantic hero is always alone" (B. Suchkov).[121]

The intrinsic value of the self is what sets Romanticism apart from other world-views. This distinction is confirmed by other scholars, in particular A. Izergina: "This was the first artistic movement of the nineteenth century in which the creative individual appeared distinctly as the subject. In this sense Romanticism contradicts not only Classicism but also every preceding Western European movement. This is the first feature of Romanticism, its authentic and principal innovation."[122] Furthermore, "in addressing the problem of the self and society the Romantics shifted the emphasis onto the first component of this correlation, believing that the disclosure and affirmation of the human self and its perfection in all aspects will lead ultimately to the strengthening of the highest social and civic ideals."[123]

It should be noted that in "The Storm" and a number of other works, Gibran's Romantic hero appears as a dreamer who has withdrawn into his interior world, and not as a fighter who dedicates himself to great deeds. His individualism does not take the form of rebellion; secluded in dignified solitude, he opposes reality.

The story is extended in length, which affects its form: the author himself divides it into small chapters. Only one image is given: that of Yusuf al-Fakhri, a rejectionist who has run away from people, the city and civilisation to the bosom of wild nature. This immediately summons analogies with the character images of Romantic heroes who, rejecting the reality that surrounds them, strive to escape from it. These would include Byron's Childe Harold and characters created by Victor Hugo, wrenched and outcast from their homeland, those heroes of Chateaubriand that cannot find their place in life, and indeed those of Shelley, thrown into worlds that are foreign to them. Such heroes either remain tragically lonely dreamers, or else their individualism takes the form of rebelliousness. The latter is particularly characteristic of Byron's heroes:

> He did not follow what they all pursued,
> With hope still baffled, still to be renew'd;
> Nor shadowy honour, nor substantial gain,
> Nor beauty's preference, and the rival's pain:
> Around him some mysterious circle thrown
> Repell'd approach, and showed him still alone...   ("Lara"[124])

The main hero in "The Storm" rejects the reality around him, the society and the people and their morals: "In the thirtieth year of his life Yusuf al-Fakhri abandoned the world and all that is in it to live as a silent, ascetic hermit in that solitary cell at the edge of the Qadisha Valley on the north side of Mount Lebanon."[125]

Yusuf is entirely unknown to his neighbours, who do not know who he is, where he is from or why he lives in seclusion. His life is enveloped in mysteries and riddles as befits a Romantic hero. One inclement, rainy autumn day the narrator succeeds in meeting Yusuf. Despite the evident resistance and lack of hospitality on the part of Yusuf, the narrator succeeds in entering his hovel. In his first sentences the hermit convinces his guest to follow his example: "Now if you believe in the truth of what you say, abandon men with their corrupt customs and their worthless laws. Live in a remote place and follow no law but the law of earth and sky!"[126]

Yusuf then expresses his deep disappointment in people and their lives, and launches into a diatribe against them: "I fled from men because my character was not compatible with their characters, my dreams did not agree with their dreams. I abandoned men because I found myself a wheel turning to the right among many wheels turning to the left."[127] He left the city, the sight of which appeared to him hopeless and monstrous: "I left the city because I found it a diseased tree, ancient and strong, with roots deep in the darkness of the earth and branches rising beyond the clouds, but whose flowers were ambition, evil and crime, whose fruits were care, affliction and woe."[128]

These words of Yusuf express practically the entire substance of the anti-urbanist theory of the Romantics. Yusuf seeks solitude not out of asceticism, not in service to God or by way of prayer. Rather, he is repulsed by a human society dominated by hypocrisy, sanctimony and ignorance, where arrogant rich men and politicians "play games with the hopes of nations and leave gold dust in their eyes and fill their ears with the echoes of words", and where the clergy "exhorted men with counsels that they themselves did not follow, asking others what they did not expect of themselves". He has therefore chosen to leave "that great and awful palace called civilisation, that building with its fine architecture standing upon a hill of human skulls".

In his striving to escape to nature, to be far from people, in whose souls he sees only the darkest features, Gibran's Romantic hero is close to the heroes of Byron – Lara, the Corsair and especially Childe Harold, who said:

> To sit on rocks, to muse o'er flood and fell,
> To slowly trace the forest shady scene,
> Where things that own not man's dominion dwell,
> And mortal foot hath ne'er or rarely been;
> To climb the trackless mountain all unseen,
> With the wild flock that never needs a fold;
> Alone o'er steeps and foaming falls to lean,
> This is not solitude; 'tis but to hold
> Converse with Nature's charms, and view her
>   stores unroll'd.
>   "Childe Harold's Pilgrimage"[129]

It is true that the English poet was expressing another transitional period, in which the dream of a future era of freedom and equality, which had been nurtured by the best minds of humanity, was discarded for a long time to come. Immense was the heat of Byronic disappointment in that age, in the impressions and experiences of being, as the poet writes:

> Kingdoms and empires in my little day
> I have outlived, and yet I am not old;
> And when I look on this, the petty spray
> Of my own years of trouble, which have rolled
> Like a wild bay of breakers, melts away.
>   "Epistle to Augusta"[130]

This explains his rejection of the social milieu that was his birthright; hence also the scepticism of his Romantic heroes and his turning to nature:

> Fortune! take back these cultured lands,
> Take back this name of splendid sound!
> I hate the touch of servile hands,
> I hate the slaves that cringe around.
> Place me among the rocks I love,

> Which sound to Ocean's wildest roar;
> I ask but this – again to rove
> Through scenes my youth hath known before.
>   "I would I were a careless child"[131]

These traits are absent from Gibran. His Romantic hero goes to nature primarily because that is where he finds "a life of spirit and thought, of heart, of heart and body", where his soul is revealed with its concealed depths; and from this comes knowledge of the world, for that is equivalent to self-knowledge. Advocacy of a "life of the spirit" was a typical mark of Transcendentalism. Under the rule of nature Yusuf gives himself up to wakefulness, takes pleasure in reflection and undergoes a spiritual awakening. Yusuf considers the achievements of civilisation to be wholly useless, and calls Western progress yet another "manifestation of empty delusion". He asks, "What are these inventions and discoveries except vices by which the mind distracts itself in moments of boredom and discontent?"[132]

We can see that none of the European Romantics opposes the industrial achievements of the contemporary world. Even Wordsworth, who leaned towards the idyll of the patriarchal past, never spoke out directly against the technical progress of his time. And Gibran, unlike his hero, takes more realistic positions, closer to the people and their lives. He reasons as follows: "Yes, spiritual wakefulness is befitting to man – indeed, it is the goal of being – but is not civilisation, with its obscurities and ambiguities, one of the causes of spiritual awakening? I wonder how we are able to deny an existent thing when its very existence is evidence for the truth of its right?"[133] This reflection indicates that the author is able to reconcile "spiritual awakening" with the acceptance of the achievements of civilisation.

It is nevertheless interesting that Yusuf, while despising and rejecting progress and its achievements, does not deny certain of the benefits and pleasures that this progress brings. In his wretched hovel can be found good wine, fragrant coffee, aromatic cigarettes and delicious victuals. Despite the insistent appeals to his visitor to "follow no law but the law of earth and sky", his way of life is far from ascetic.

Undoubtedly "The Storm" is a Romantic work; the individualism of its hero expresses a rejection of the surrounding world and the denial of accepted norms. The particular relationship of Gibran to his Romantic hero should, however, be noted. Most importantly, the author does not himself intend to fully reject human society and does not express his evident antipathies to it, as do the Western European Romantics, especially Byron. Gibran does not reconstruct the Byronic experience in its entirety, with its complete rupturing of the hero from society and his unending disillusionment with it. And in solving the problem of the self and society, the Arab writer steps back from the extremes of the subjectivist anthropocentrism of the Western European Romantics.

In comparing Gibran to the English Romantics, we frequently note that his Romantic pathos and the intensity of his feeling, hate and passion appear in a somewhat softened form. One possible exception to this is Gibran's anticlerical motifs, which appear in his works with great sharpness and emotional charge.

In the story "Satan",[134] which deals with the philosophical problem of the necessary and inevitable eternal coexistence and struggle of the two absolute principles of good and evil, the author's criticism is directed sharply at the Christian Church. The story goes as follows: out in the fields one day the theologian and clergyman Samaan encounters a creature lying naked, dying of wounds. It turns out to be Satan, who has just been beaten by the archangels. When Satan confesses to Samaan who he is, the latter recoils in revulsion, fearful of defiling himself by touching an unclean spirit. But Satan reminds the clergyman that the prosperity and livelihood of the servants of the Church depend on the existence of an unclean force:

> As a clergyman, do you not realize that Satan's existence alone has created his enemy, the Church? That ancient conflict is the secret hand which removes the gold and silver from the faithful's pocket and deposits it forever into the pouch of the preacher and the missionary. How can you permit me to die here, when you know it will surely cause you to lose your prestige, your church, your home and your livelihood?[135]

Satan also opens the clergyman's eyes to a further truth: that Satan and the force of a struggle against God are necessary to people, since this struggle is that which arouses activity, enterprise and energy – in a word, everything that promotes the development of the material and spiritual life of the people.

> In every city under the sun my name was the axis of the educational circle of religion, arts, and philosophy. Had it not been for me, no temples would have been built, no towers or palaces would have been erected. I am the courage that creates resolution in man. I am the source that provokes originality of thought. I am the hand that moves man's hands.[136]

The devil goes on to assert that he is necessary "for the preservation of mankind": "If I cease to exist, fear and enjoyment will be abolished from the world, and through their disappearance, desires and hopes will cease to exist in the human heart. Life will become empty and cold, like a harp with broken strings.[137]

In the subtext of the story is the image of a God estranged from man, who exists in the form of an indisputable truth and eternal force that requires submission and obedience, and thereby imprisons the freedom-loving and creative spirit of man. All the English Romantics are permeated by this same idea. For them man himself is divine, the centre of the universe; and all his activity is directed towards the knowledge of the universe and its subjugation. Blake writes of this with particular strength and purpose in his "Everlasting Gospel":

> Thou art a Man: God is no more:
> Thy own Humanity learn to adore...[138]

A.A. Elistratova suggests that "The subtext of his 'Prophecy' is the destiny of a humanity humbled, enslaved but yearning for freedom and happiness."[139]

A further observation can be made from this story. In "The Storm" Gibran sharply criticises the rites and ceremonies of the Church. For Gibran the Church is a symbol of weakness in man: it appeared when the world seemed to humanity to be hostile and full of secrets, so that man himself felt vulnerable. Exploiting the ignorance of the people, the Church set itself up as mediator between them and the unknown forces of nature. Anticlericalism is a distinguishing feature of almost all émigré literature that developed under the influence of the ideas of the Enlightenment and Romanticism. This characteristic forms the typological kinship of the Syro-American School with the Romantic schools of Western literature, and simultaneously demonstrates the point of contact that existed between them.

Neupokoeva comments that Shelley described religion as "a code of absurd superstitions upheld everywhere by the ruling class for the purposes of maintaining their power".[140] A similar attitude to religion can also be found in Gibran. Even in his early stories "John the Madman" and "Khalil the Heretic" the author angrily refutes the sanctimony and self-interest of religion. John, the hero of the first story,[141] is an honest and devout young man who discovers the greed and hypocrisy of the "servants of God" and their flouting of the sacred commandments when he allows his herd of calves accidentally to wander onto monastery land. He tries to explain this to his parents, simple peasants, but they do not believe him and think that he has gone mad. The young man is put into confinement in the monastery – thus do the clerics make short work of him. John cries out fervently: "You are numerous and I am alone. You may do unto me what you wish. The wolves prey upon the lamb in the darkness of the night, but the blood stains remain upon the stones in the valley until the dawn comes, and the sun reveals the crime to all."[142] The word "mad", applied to John in the story mostly because of his "unusual" desires, can be understood in the sense of a synonym for independence from received norms of behaviour.

"Khalil the Heretic"[143] continues the theme of "John the Madman". The hero, Khalil, is raised from an early age in a monastery. There he is mercilessly exploited, subjected to beating and made to go hungry. Gradually, however, his awareness awakens and he begins to understand that the monks tell lies, that they do not believe in God, that they live by labour and are later made destitute. Once Khalil begins to berate those around him with the truth, he is thrown out of the monastery in the middle of winter, naked and hungry and doomed to certain death. By chance he is found by two poor women, Rachel and Miriam, a mother and daughter. In the village where they live, the priest and the shaykh have deprived them of their human dignity. Khalil, who remains in the village, then makes an inflammatory speech in front of the inhabitants, calling on them to rise up against the shaykh and the priest and to gain a new life for themselves.

> Do you realize that this land you are working like slaves was taken from your fathers when the law was written on the sharp edge of the sword? That the monks deceived your ancestors and took all their fields and vineyards when the religious rules were written on the lips of the priests? Which man or woman is not influenced by the lord of the fields to do according to the will of the priests?[144]

The peasants rise up and drive the shaykh and the priest out of the village. We have to assume that afterwards the land that had been taken away by the clerics is returned to them, and that the peasants begin to live happily and free of oppression and violence. The Romantic ending of the story is like a hymn to justice and a call to rebellion and disobedience.

In discussing the influence on Gibran of the English Romantics we have already mentioned that one of the Romantic motifs – the intensity of feeling, hate and passion – is subdued in Gibran; he is less radical and less emotional. This does not apply, however, in the case of anticlericalism, which he expresses in his works with fullness and passion. This is no coincidence, since Gibran is a native of Lebanon, in which religious hostility held sway. The pressure exerted by the Christian Church on society was strong.

Some stories and essays from the collection *The Tempests* (including "The Gravedigger", "Slavery" and "The Captive Ruler") would seem to contain the quintessence of the Romantic world-view. In some cases (for example "The Gravedigger") their symbolism is complex. On the whole, the tone of these works is of desperation, hopelessness and sadness; they express one of the aspects of Gibran's Romanticism – his conviction that man has the calling of a spiritual life and strives for moral perfection. This brings him close to the Transcendentalists. Let us consider the brief story "The Gravedigger".[145] The narrator describes how he walks at night along the "valley of life", scattered with bones and skulls. On the bank of the "river of blood" he sees a terrible spectre that advises him to give up his literary pursuits and become a gravedigger. Then he would be able to rid "the few living of the corpses heaped about", for they have been dead since they were born and there were none who would bury them. When asked how to distinguish the living from the dead, the spectre replies: "Your illusioned eyes see the people quivering before the tempest of life and you believe them to be alive ... dead creatures who tremble with the storm and never walk with it."[146] Therefore, the most necessary and useful occupation for those still alive is to be a gravedigger, to bury the "living dead" and in this way to purify the earth.

There is, however, no concrete explanation in the story of what one should understand by the term "tempest of life". One would assume that this is primarily spirituality and self-knowledge, rather than the gratification of base carnal interests when, in the opinion of the author, the primordial purpose of man – reaching union with God – is forgotten. It is no coincidence that the spectre repeats: "we genii are the only possessors of reality". The story expresses an aspect of Gibran's Romanticism: his belief in the spiritual purpose of human life, for the life of man is the life of the spirit – the unending striving for perfection and awakening and the thirst for the new. The symbolism of the story is Romantic: life is an unending storm or struggle, in movement, an "obstacle race". Calm, satisfaction and the absence of spiritual movement, on the other hand, are tantamount to death.

The same deeply pessimistic attitude to the life of human society can be found in the essay "Slavery",[147] in which the author fully denies the possibility of free manifestation of the human self. This brief essay is a sharp criticism of slavery, which permeates all spheres of life and all interpersonal relations. The work thus begins: "Men are but slaves of life".[148] Slavery accompanies man from the moment of his birth, known for "seven thousand years"; it is "inherited from the fathers by the sons as they inherit the breath of life". In the author's view all people are slaves, regardless of their social status, intellectual development or worldly position. Slavery prevails in all countries: "from Babylon to Paris, from Nineveh to New York".[149] By slavery Gibran understands the worship of God, idols, science or property; or an admiration for laws, traditions, force or power, or the following of the tastes of the masses:

> They fought and killed for it and called it "patriotism". They submitted to its will and called it the "shadow of God on earth". Then they burned their houses and razed their buildings at its will, and called it "fraternity" and "equality". They strove then and made every effort for it, calling it "wealth" and "trade".[150]

The entire work consists of a pessimistic monologue permeated with despair. Humanity, Gibran considers, has known only two true "sons of Liberty", but "One died crucified, one died mad".[151] Undoubtedly Gibran is referring here to Jesus Christ and Nietzsche. "And none other was born", he continues. Dolinina believes that if by this "son of Liberty" Gibran does not mean himself, then he considers himself all the same to be his forerunner.[152]

These stories, and also the story "The Storm", have led certain scholars, both Soviet and Arab, to speak of Gibran's receptivity at this stage to the philosophy of Nietzsche.[153] The philosophy of Nietzsche exerted an influence on many writers and thinkers in the late nineteenth and early twentieth centuries, both in Europe and the East, for example, the great Indian poet and philosopher Muhammad Iqbal (1877–1938).[154] There is no doubt that Gibran was also influenced. To some degree Nietzsche's conservative and Romantic views, as expressed in early essays such as "Morgenröte" (= "Daybreak"), "Die fröhliche Wissenschaft" ("The Gay Science") and "Jenseits von Gut und Böse"("Beyond Good and Evil"), and his cult of a powerful self whose individualism overcomes the banality of bourgeois consciousness and the Romantic idea of a "man of the future" who has left the present age with its vices and falsehood far behind, would have been close to his own outlook. Gibran undoubtedly took on certain features of the German philosopher's prophetic and messianic style. Nietzsche's view on the Church and social institutions also turned out to be close to his own. Here we may draw on the research of Joseph Ghougassian: "From Nietzsche Gibran learned how to convey his ideas in a messianic overtone, while at the same time using a flammatory style for criticizing the organized religion and the social establishment."[155] A little later Ghougassian quotes the words of Gibran himself: "His [Nietzsche's] form [style] always was soothing to me. But I thought his philosophy was terrible and all wrong. I was a worshipper of beauty – and beauty was to me the loveliness of things."[156]

However, S.F. Oduev comments that Nietzsche's main characteristic is his advocacy of strength and the strong individual, who possesses the right to exploit the weak and even to eradicate them for the sake of consolidating his strength.[157] Nietzsche believed that war cleanses humanity of the impurity of weakness and doubt and leads to the triumph of strength and the preservation of nature. What is particularly alien in Nietzsche for the Eastern Romantics, however, is his contempt and hatred for the "crowd", and the opposition of "the crowd" to the "selected individual" and "the masses" to the "Superman" that is typical of bourgeois individualist consciousness. Also foreign to Gibran is the glorification of the strong individual who stands mercilessly and triumphantly on the throat of his victim. If Gibran also allows himself animosity and cruelty, as in "The Gravedigger", then this is only intended to challenge the inertness of his compatriots, their fatalism and their indifference to the vices of society. Indeed, on the whole certain of his works ("The Storm", "The Gravedigger" and "Slavery") have a mood of hopelessness and sadness. Even when he shows open contempt for people and their civilisation, one can feel a longing for people and an immense pity for them, which changes into a fathomless despair and an unbearable sorrow. Gibran passionately loves and pities mankind. In the individualism and strong-man of the author is concealed his pain and suffering for humanity and his thoughts on it.

Overall, Gibran's path was complex. Ultimately his form of rebellion had a specific character that differed from that of the Romantics in Western literature. This difference is most evident in the less-than-complete splitting of the Romantic person from society, in his conceptions of the prophetic role of the poet in the Arab tradition, and in the philosophical thought of Gibran himself. It should be noted here that certain of his works (such as "Defeat", "The Eye", "The Ambitious Violet", "The Captive Ruler" and "O Sons of my Mother") as it were refute the idea that the theme of the hero's complete break with society and the feeling of superiority over the crowd is not characteristic of Gibran. Certainly, the parable "The Eye"[158] can be interpreted as a hymn to Romantic rebellion, while "The Ambitious Violet"[159] glorifies self-sacrifice for the sake of self-perfection in order to become "like God".

A violet sees a rose, is astonished by its beauty and wants to become a rose herself. She addresses nature in a prayer, asking to be changed into a rose. Nature replies to her with a word of caution: "You know not what you are seeking; you are unaware of the concealed disaster behind your blind ambition. If you were a rose you would be sorry, and repentance would avail you but naught."[160] However, the violet gets her way and becomes a rose. Later a storm blows up and the violet that has become a rose is destroyed and her petals are scattered through the mud. The other violets, which have survived the storm because they grow low to the ground, begin to reproach her in an arrogant and facetious manner. But the violet replies to them: "I shall die now, for my soul has attained its goal. I have finally extended my knowledge to a world beyond the narrow cavern of my birth. This is the design of Life ... This is the secret of Existence."[161] One can detect notes in this story of a later neo-Romanticism and a Nietzschean enthusiasm.

The collection *The Tempests* is entirely devoid of the marks of Sentimentalism. Gibran's work, influenced by the Western Romantics, has finally taken on the garb of the Romantic method. And this can be seen not so much in the individual motifs and themes as in the overall rebellious, protesting spirit of the collection as a whole. In terms of Romanticism it presents a problem of the relationship of the individual to society, re-evaluates the role of civilisation, glorifies the individual and harshly criticises the Christian Church and its rites. While underlining the closeness of Gibran's Romantic hero to those of Western Romantics, we should point out their areas of difference: the degree of rebelliousness and rejection in Gibran's heroes comes over in a far more subdued manner, as though clad in the dress of pacification. His Romantic hero is more lyrical and inclines towards abstracts. The link between the Romanticism of *The Tempests* and the traditions of classical Arabic literature can also be traced in such elements as complex symbolism, an exalted style, the richness of metaphor and the presence of didactic elements.

The Prophet: a new stage in Gibran's work

From among Gibran's later works we have selected his book *The Prophet* (*al-Nabi*), because this work signifies the final stage in the development of his creative method. Its theme is one of the most widespread in world literature. A prophet is frequently understood to be someone with a high calling, a poet or tribune who proclaims elevated and eternal truths. One may point here to John Milton and Blake in English literature, Ernest Renan in French, and Alexander Pushkin and Mikhail Lermontov in Russian. Genealogically speaking, the motif derives from the Old Testament legends of the prophets and from the Koranic account of the Prophet Muhammad.

The Prophet was written in English and published in New York in 1923. Not until after Gibran's death was it translated into Arabic, by the

Archimandrite of Damascus, Antonius Bashir. In the Preface to his translation Bashir writes:

> If we confined ourselves to merely the external appearance of religion, then one
> could call Gibran an atheist, and in that case I would be mistaken in translating
> this book into Arabic. But this translator is not an atheist, and he examines the
> essence of the religion and not merely its exterior. If we approach Gibran and
> his works in this way, then it becomes clear that he stands at the head of the most
> faithful, but at the same time seeks the eternal truth without fear or delusion
> and without the bustle and vanity of the world.[162]

Bashir goes on to represent Gibran as a talented writer and innovator
who was able to liberate himself from "blind imitation" and from "the eyes
of the past". Here he quotes extracts from statements by Western cultural
figures about Gibran, in which they speak with admiration and love for
his person and his artistic mastery: "In years, Gibran is still a youth, but in
his intelligence and artistry he is an elder"; "in Gibran's work there is not
a trace of imitation or stagnation. He is not an optimist but neither is he
a pessimist. He is not a minister of religion, but nor is he an atheist. He is
simply a prophet and clairvoyant, one who sings the hymn of eternal art.
With the eyes of an Easterner he was able to see what we, inhabitants of the
West, were unable to see"; "All of Gibran's books urge the reader to deep
reflection"; "We are certain that the work of Gibran is immortal"; "Gibran
has come close to the West, but there remains on his lips the lovely smile
of the East". Also quoted are the words spoken by Auguste Rodin after
visiting an exhibition of Gibran's pictures in Paris: "The world may expect
much of this exceptional figure from Lebanon, from the William Blake of
the twentieth century."[163]

In 1955 Mikhail Naimy, who after many years of close contact with
Gibran knew him well, produced a second translation of *The Prophet* that
came closer to the original.[164] This allowed him to assert that "*The Prophet* is
Gibran's moral and ethical credo". Naimy avoided a literal translation, and
sought forms of expression that matched the spirit of the original.

The idea for *The Prophet* came to Gibran early on. Work on the book
began in 1918 and continued for more than four years. It contains the quintessence of the writer's world-view: his thoughts on life and death, on the
essence and meaning of human existence, and on good and evil. The author
embraces human life in all its complexities and depths, unified with, and
mutually permeated by, the unending stream of life and by the unity of
existence. In a letter to Mayy Ziyada, Gibran writes about *The Prophet* as
follows:

> As for *The Prophet* – this is a book which I thought of writing a thousand years
> ago, but I did not get any of its chapters down on paper until the end of last year.
> What can I tell you about this prophet? He is my rebirth and my first baptism,
> the only thought in me that will make me worthy to stand in the light of the

sun. For this prophet had already "written" me before I attempted to "write" him, had created me before I created him.[165]

In *The Prophet* the author strives to move out of his individualism and to understand and express the thoughts and hopes of ordinary people. Everything that they feel and experience, the hero must feel and experience. In another letter to Mayy he wrote: "This book is only a small part of what I have seen and what I see every day, a small part only of the many things yearning for expression in the silent hearts of men and in their souls."[166]

Gibran's mature and settled philosophical conception in *The Prophet* is matched by the completeness of the composition and the refinement of the language. It is difficult to give this work an unequivocal definition of genre. It is at once a confession, a framed narrative and a philosophical essay in the form of a prose poem.

The structural harmony and completeness of composition of *The Prophet* form a counterpoint to the simplicity, naturalness and compactness of the narrative. The content of the work can be summarised as follows: al-Mustafa, who has lived in the city of Orphalese for 12 years, awaits the ship that is to take him back to his homeland. Before the ship arrives, a crowd of men and women hurry towards him to see him off and ask him to speak to them before he departs. Al-Mustafa then leads them to the great square in front of the temple in the city, and addresses the people with his words of farewell. These form the entire body of the work.

Addressing the people of Orphalese, al-Mustafa is aware of a sense of immense responsibility towards them and also towards himself. It is necessary for him to speak about everything that he has comprehended in his depths and achieved, for the sake of the people. He asks himself, "Shall the day of parting be the day of gathering? And shall it be said that my eve was in truth my dawn?" He begins to speak about love and marriage, about children, about houses, about clothing and eating and drinking, about work, about buying and selling, crime and punishment, friendship, good and evil, pain and pleasure, beauty, sorrow and joy; he speaks on religion and prayer, life and death, teaching and self-knowledge and other matters. Then evening comes and the ship draws near. "Farewell to you and the youth I have spent with you", he says to the people of Orphalese, and then "he made a signal to the seamen, and straight away they weighed anchor and cast the ship loose from its moorings, and they moved eastward."[167]

We should first remark that the image of al-Mustafa the Prophet, the teacher and visionary, corresponds precisely to Gibran's Romantic understanding of the Poet. His Prophet, just as the Poet of the Romantics and Transcendentalists, is called to express all that which other people experience intuitively but cannot utter. As Emerson says: "The sign and credentials of the poet are, that he announces that which no man foretold. He is the true and only doctor; he knows and tells; he is the only teller of news, for he was present and privy to the appearance which he describes."[168]

The same is true of Gibran's Prophet. Addressing the people, he says: "Ay, I knew your joy and your pain, and in your sleep your dreams were my dreams. And oftentimes I was among you a lake among the mountains. I mirrored the summits in you and the bending slopes, and even the passing flocks of your thoughts and your desires."[169]

In one of his letters to Mayy, Gibran wrote of the agonising struggle he underwent within himself in realising subconsciously that the poet can only become realised as such when he becomes the voice and mouthpiece of the people, the one who expresses thoughts and feelings:

> *The Prophet*, Mayy, is only the first letter of a single word ... in the past I was under the impression that this word was mine, in me and derived from me; for that reason I was unable to pronounce the first letter of that word. My inability to do so was because of my illness, indeed the cause of my soul's pain and suffering. After that God willed that my eyes be opened so that I could see the light, and God willed that my ears be opened so that I could hear other people pronounce this first letter, and God willed that I should open my lips and repeat that letter. I repeated it with joy and delight because for the first time I recognised that other people are everything and that I with my separate self am nothing.[170]

Gibran's Prophet cannot remain detached; it is only by merging with the people that his significance as a unique figure is realised.

A number of questions vital for man's world-view are posed in *The Prophet*: freedom, life and death, good and evil and the essence and meaning of human existence. They are treated very briefly and with remarkable simplicity, when one considers the abstract character of the problems posed. They are all treated from a deeply humanist perspective and in the spirit of high Romantic pathos, which calls man to a path of knowledge and perfection. In seeking to penetrate these problems Gibran starts out from the certainty that the human is the highest achievement of the creation, that his nature is deeply moral and that he has the potential to overcome the forces of evil. On his approach to complete freedom man must above all overcome all that is false, which would detract from the principal aims of perfection and knowledge. And in order to become free, it is necessary to liberate oneself from base needs and wants. The Prophet says:

> You shall be free indeed not when your days are without a care nor
>   your nights without a want and a grief,
>
> But rather when these things girdle your life and yet you rise above
>   them naked and unbound.[171]

In his discussion of man, his destiny and completion, Gibran, like the Transcendentalist poets, does not indicate a specific individual belonging to a particular race, religion or social group, but speaks rather of a kind of universal, a person free of any specific circumstances or conditions.

Hope in the possibility of improving human nature and belief in spiritual development are reflected in moral principles, the requirement of unconditional integrity and the necessity of work. Speaking of work, the Prophet expresses a thought dear to the writer: that life is work, and to love life is to love work:

> And in keeping yourself with labour you are in truth loving life,
> And to love life through labour is to be intimate with life's
>   inmost secret.[172]

Man's primary calling is to knowledge of life and the essence of being. But this is impossible without work: "And all knowledge is vain save where there is work".[173] Gibran's understanding of the necessity of work was an organic element among the progressive Romantics. We can point specifically to Thoreau in his book *Walden*, in which he declares work to be the basis of life, and to numerous verses and poems by Whitman ("Song of the Broadaxe", etc.).

The basic premises of the Prophet coincide almost completely with those of the Transcendentalists, in the treatment of global questions relating to the existence of man and exalting him as the centre of the creation:

> Like the ocean is your god-self;
> It remains for ever undefiled.
> And like the ether it lifts but the winged.
> Even like the sun is your god-self ...[174]

We may recall Emerson's statement: "Man carries the world in his head, the whole astronomy and chemistry suspended in a thought. Because the history of nature is charactered in his brain, therefore is he the prophet and discoverer of her secrets."[175] Like Emerson, Gibran considers man to be the most important part of nature: "That which is you dwells above the mountains and roves with the wind."[176] Or "But you who are born of the mountains and the forests and the seas can find their prayer in your heart".[177]

Gibran's representation of the human is in permanent agitation, striving upwards, towards spirituality and the heights of unlimited knowledge: "But you, children of space, you restless in rest, you shall not be trapped and tamed. ... For that which is boundless in you abides in the mansion of the sky, whose door is the morning mist, and whose windows are the songs and the silences of night."[178]

Religion in the book is not confined to the limits of Christianity, Islam or any other religion. In his preaching, al-Mustafa not only does not recognise religion with its external attributes, rites and priesthood, but also makes no reference to the independent existence of God. For him, religion and God are life itself; religion is found in the thoughts and deeds of people. Asked by the crowd what is religion, he replies: "Your daily life is your temple and your religion."[179]

The question of beauty and its essence, a favourite among the Romantics, is also examined in *The Prophet*. Understanding beauty as inspiration,
intuition and an instinctive comprehending of the truth, Gibran gives an
aphoristic definition: "Beauty is not a need but an ecstasy." He repudiates
all external attributes of beauty and regards it as the essence of life itself,
from which the outer covering is shorn away: "Beauty is eternity gazing at
itself in a mirror."[180] Here again Gibran is close to Emerson, who considered
beauty to be "the creator of the universe".

The Prophet also talks about everyday life, simple concerns: food and
drink, housing and clothing, buying and selling, pain, joy and sorrow,
giving and so on. In doing this he draws on the common experience, honed
over centuries, and on profoundly moral traditional ideas. For example, he
preaches moderation in eating and drinking and in clothes:

> And though you seek in garments freedom and privacy you may find in
> them a harness and a chain.
> Would that you could meet the sun and the wind with more of your
> skin and less of your raiment ...[181]

When asked about buying and selling, al-Mustafa replies:

> And suffer not the barren-handed to take part in your transactions,
> who would sell their words for your labour.[182]

On the question of giving, the Prophet again gives a purely folk conception of "charity": giving in response to the call of the heart, without expect-
ing either gratitude or a reward in heaven: "It is when you give of yourself
that you truly give."[183] One's attention is drawn here to the refined aphoristic character and specificity of aim of the Prophet's speech.

The addresses of al-Mustafa, his sermons and his desires contain not only
the Romantic contemplation of the world of the Transcendentalists, which
draws man into the sphere of abstract moral ideas, but also the concrete
aspiration to share those things that are borne and suffered by the hero
himself. The entire tone of al-Mustafa's preaching is imbued with a deep
respect for and goodwill towards people, for they have no menace, anger,
coercion or intimidation.

What is unique about Gibran the Romantic is that his hero appears
much closer to the people than do the classic Romantic heroes. With his
love for the common people and his proximity to them, his understanding
of their everyday life and their needs, al-Mustafa is not only contrasted
with the "crowd", but also, as it were, merges with it. While the principal
theme in Romanticism is that of the self and the crowd, and is formed out
of sharp opposition and conflict, the Prophet expresses the thoughts and
feelings of the crowd and is always ready to come to its aid like a wise and
devoted friend. The attitude of the people to the Prophet is in accordance
with this: he is always surrounded by an atmosphere of kindness, love and
respect.

In his farewell speech al-Mustafa speaks of his deep commonality with all people: "And your heartbeats were in my heart, and your breath was upon my face, and I knew you all."[184]

The confessionary character of the poet's address to the people is uncharacteristic of Romantic literature. Furthermore, in *The Prophet* Gibran acknowledges that he is called not only to devote himself to the people and to teach them, but also, necessarily, to learn from them wisdom, optimism and patience: "I came to take of your wisdom ... it is a flaming spirit in you ever gathering more of itself ... You have given me my deeper thirsting after life."[185]

It may seem at first sight that the image of al-Mustafa might to some degree resonate with that of the prophet from Nietzsche's book *Also Sprach Zarathustra*. We would point out at once that the humanistic and democratic pathos of the Arab writer's work differs sharply from the nihilistic and all-destroying tenor of Nietzsche's book, and we can find nothing in common between these two characters whatsoever. The teachings of al-Mustafa are not in any way contiguous with those of Zarathustra. The positive side of the latter's message is his blistering criticism of the Church and the foundations of bourgeois culture, which are absent in Gibran's work. Gibran's positive hero, meanwhile, liberated of anything supernatural, has nothing in common with the "Superman" of the German philosopher.

Something in common can be seen between the image of al-Mustafa and that of Christ in Ernest Renan's *Vie de Jésus* (*The Life of Jesus*). This is expressed primarily in the attempts by both writers to reach a moral ideal. Renan found this ideal in Jesus Christ, in his idea of love, all-forgiveness and belief in the principle of the basic good of the human person. Gibran also took these moral principles as the basis for his hero, the Prophet. Into the mouth of al-Mustafa he puts the idea of selfless love, which can bring people together:

> Like sheaves of corn he gathers you unto himself.
> He threshes you to make you naked.
> He sifts you to free you from your husks.
> He grinds you to whiteness.
> He kneads you until you are pliant;
> And then he assigns you to his sacred fire, that you may
>   become sacred bread for God's sacred feast.[186]

It should be noted that there was a certain period during which the image of Christ occupied Gibran's creative imagination in a number of his works, such as "Eventide of the Feast",[187] "The Crucified"[188] and *Jesus the Son of Man* (1928).[189] Gibran embodied in Christ his belief in the ideal that was intended to become the symbol of "truth and freedom".

A number of Arab scholars of Gibran believe that he would not have become an artist had he lost his belief in this ideal. In particular, 'Abd al-Karim Ashtar writes: "His belief in Christ prevented Gibran from

completely rejecting religion and becoming an atheist. And had he lost
that belief and those convictions ... his rebelliousness and extremism would
be without aim and his activities would end in spiritual ruin, as occurred
with Nietzsche. And, like Nietzsche, he would have created for himself an
abstract Superman."[190]

In Gibran's works Christ is a real person, a martyr and a rebel, who
struggles for the high ideals of goodness and love. "The Crucified" is for
him the herald of high justice and true humanity.

Gibran's Christ "never lived a life of fear, nor did He die suffering or
complaining",[191] but rather "He lived as a leader; He was crucified as a
crusader; He died with a heroism that frightened His killers and tormen-
tors".[192] The author represents him not as "a bird with broken wings";
rather, "He was a raging tempest who broke all crooked wings";[193] he came

> to send forth upon this earth a new spirit, with power to crumble the foundation
> of any monarchy built upon human bones and skulls. ... He came to demolish
> the majestic palaces, constructed upon the graves of the weak, and crush the
> idols, erected upon the bodies of the poor. ... He came to make the human heart
> a temple, and the soul an altar, and the mind a priest.[194]

The Prophet should not be understood as something unusual that is out
of line with the general principles and logical development of Gibran's
previous work, but rather as the concluding phase in his natural and
logical movement. In *The Prophet* the Romantic conception of belief in
the human being is joined to the conviction of the possibility of his moral
resurrection.

Gibran's Prophet is an exceptional individual whose intrinsic self-value is
interior, but this does not place him in opposition to the surrounding world.
The purpose of his teaching is not "to humiliate the people and elevate
himself", but instead to reveal to them the deepest truths. There is no divid-
ing wall between him and the people; he does not consider himself superior
to the "crowd" and has no disdain for anybody. The essence of the image of
the Prophet is what Volkov called "the profound meaning of the character
of the individual", who lives not merely as the life of the soul and heart, but
also in the life of the people around him. This determines the evolution of
Gibran's Romantic creativity towards actual reality and characterises his
inclination to simplicity and clarity. Our observation on the complexity of
Gibran's approach to the problem of the hero versus the crowd, which is
fully revealed in *The Prophet*, can also be justified in relation to later developments in Oriental Romanticism.

The demand in Gibran for complete human liberation, his hatred of
slavery, his idea of the interdependence and interlinking of the phenomena
of life and human actions, and his ideas of love and belief and the principle
that goodness and justice are inherent in man, bring the writer's position
close to the philosophical ideas and principles of the Romanticism of the
Transcendentalists, in particular Emerson.

In terms of subject matter *The Prophet* is continued to a degree in the later *The Garden of the Prophet* (1933, published posthumously).[195] This book describes the arrival of al-Mustafa on his native island and his reception by its inhabitants. For forty days he retreats to the garden where his house is situated and where his ancestors are buried. After this, students and inhabitants of the island come to see him, and he addresses them with homilies and guidance.

The Garden of the Prophet is closer to a philosophical treatise; its discussions are more abstract and cover general philosophical questions – the essence of matter, of forms and of existence, etc. Rarely in this book does al-Mustafa directly address the people, and he almost never touches on their worldly everyday needs. His preaching is in fact closer to a self-absorbed confession. However, both works are imbued with the idea of the unity of the prophet and the people.

In philosophical terms *The Garden of the Prophet* reaffirms and develops the same optimistic conception as does *The Prophet*: the life of the universe is eternal, and man is its most important manifestation, whose grandeur is unfathomable. The self of man is that "which is for ever the deep calling upon the deep". Later in the work he adds: "I teach you your larger self, which contains all men".[196] The idea is also further developed that the essence of the being of an individual self consists in the knowledge and degree of completion of that self.

The common subject matter and philosophical basis of the two *Prophet* books also gives rises to a number of repeating symbolic images. For example, in both works the universe is likened to the ocean, and the life of each person to a stream or river that is finally united with that ocean. The image of the mist and the crystal also recurs, symbolising the infinity of matter and the image of endlessly unfolding life, represented in the seeds of plants and the human generations. Both works carry the motif of the unity of man and nature.

Something of a departure from *The Prophet* is the development of the theme of "being". Here, "being" is considered not solely from a philosophical perspective but also in terms of human life and the relations between the various lines of work: thus, "to be" is to be a weaver, a builder, a ploughman or a fisherman, etc.

In *The Garden of the Prophet* Gibran also touches on issues that concern the life of the Arab nation in general. These are his Romanticised understandings of various principles attributed to the East and the West. On the one hand, he blames the West for its exploitation of the East, and on the other hand, he blames the East for its failure to act, its submissiveness and its humility.

Generally speaking, *The Garden of the Prophet* continues the ideas of love and goodness and of mutual understanding and tolerance. This work not only maintains the principle of moral didactics of *The Prophet*, but also introduces new clements. From an artistic point of view, however, in our opinion – in terms of the completeness of the subject, the belief in, and valuing of real life, and the clarity and precision of the language – *The Prophet* is clearly superior to the second book.

Gibran's creative method formed unusually quickly. Beginning with Sentimentalism, and mastering many of its achievements, he made his contribution towards the establishment of Sentimentalism within Arabic literature. His story *Broken Wings* and several short stories (such as "Marta al-Baniyah" and "Warda al-Hani") possessed, in addition to their intimate and contemplative subject matter, a social relevance, and in artistic and stylistic terms were to a certain degree enriched by Romantic tendencies and elements.

The transition from Sentimentalism to Romanticism did not involve, in Gibran's case, a long incubation period. This would seem to be explained by the fact that throughout his creative life there were no great changes in the subject matter and problematics of his works. The themes of freedom, beauty, love and the value of the individual and of nature permeate all the author's works.

After 1914, Gibran's work runs along a Romantic course (*A Tear and a Smile*). In the early twentieth century Gibran became one of the leading Romantics of Arab émigré literature (*The Tempests*, 1920, *The Prophet*, 1923). The legacy of the Western Romantics, and in particular of the Lake School and the American Transcendentalists, was one of the primary sources for Gibran, and his assimilation of this legacy enabled him to establish and develop the Romantic method in his own works.

Chapter 3

Ameen Rihani and his role in the formation of Arab Romanticism

Introduction

Alongside Kahlil Gibran and Mikhail Naimy, Ameen Rihani (1876–1940) was instrumental in the development of the new Arabic literature, bringing it closer to real life and everyday concerns. His activities, which were influenced by the ideas of the Arab Enlightenment and which developed under the influence of Western Romanticism, were entirely consonant with the new Arabic literature.

In the modern history of every literature there have been writers to whom it fell to familiarise their national literature with the most progressive ideas of world culture. The Academician N.I. Konrad described these figures thus:

> The appearance of such writers depended upon there forming, in the countries of the East that were making contact with the leading countries of Europe, a group of intellectuals who were wholly Europeanised, fully familiar with the science, literature and societies of the leading countries of Europe and fluent in the languages of those countries. It was few in number, this group; its development surpassed the general level of culture of the bourgeoisie to whom this intelligentsia belonged; thus the writers who belonged to this set acted as heralds or founders of a literary movement. That movement took shape and acquired a corresponding social significance only later.[1]

Such was Ameen Rihani, one of the classic writers of Arabic literature and a co-founder of Arab Romanticism, who in his creative development took the lead in the literature of his time. The extraordinary destiny of this writer, split between the bustling major centres of Western civilisation and the idyllic, peaceful valley of Frayki (Freiki, al-Fureiki), was as it were impregnated with all the vacillations of the new Arabic literature.

Ameen Rihani was born in one of the most picturesque places in Lebanon, the village of Frayki. There he attended a French missionary school. In 1888, as an adolescent, he travelled with relatives to the USA, where, once he had learnt English, he attended an evening school and later became a student at Columbia University. Through all these years Rihani pursued a steady course of self-education. While in America, he became familiar with the history of Arab culture from works by American and British writers. Several times Rihani returned from America to his homeland, and after the First World War he finally settled in Lebanon,

85

from where he made a number of journeys to the Arab countries. According to Krachkovsky,

> Ameen Rihani's fate was cruelly cast. After Syria came Paris, London, America and then Beirut, in the period of blossoming hopes that followed the Turkish revolution of 1908–09. Then back to England and America, but already with broken hopes, and then, like a long nightmarish finale, came the world war which left his long-suffering homeland in tatters. Neither journalism nor political activity nor theatre, in all of which Rihani had been active, brought peace to his soul.[2]

The very way of life of the writer, with his travels in the cities of Europe and America and the countries of the East, predisposed him to a wide circle of learning, interests and creative exploration.

Rihani worked in a variety of genres: he was a poet, essayist, prose writer, author of political articles, critic, historian and translator, and his writing career lasted almost four decades. Four volumes of his works were published in his lifetime. Volumes 1 and 2 had the title *al-Rihaniyyat: Majmu'at maqalat wa khutab wa shi'r mansur* (Beirut, 1910). These volumes contained articles, essays and prose poems. In 1923–24 Volumes 3 and 4 of *al-Rihaniyyat* appeared. In addition, Rihani published travel notes and books about his journeys: *Muluk al-'Arab* (*Kings of the Arabs*, Beirut, 1924), *Qalb Lubnan* (*The Heart of Lebanon*, Beirut, 1928), *Qalb al-'Iraq* (*The Heart of Iraq*, Beirut, 1935), and *Maghrib al-aqsa* (*The Far Morocco*, Beirut, 1938). He was also the author of several historical works: *Mu'jaz ta'rikh Nubda fi al-thawra al-Faransiyya* (*A Short History of the French Revolution*, New York, 1902), *al-Nakabat: khulasat ta'rikh Suriya* (*Misfortunes: a short history of Syria*, Beirut, 1928), *Ta'rikh Najd al-hadith wa mulhaqatihi* (*The Modern History of Najd*, Beirut, 1928), *Faysal al-awwal* (*Faysal the First*, Beirut, 1933) and others. He also produced collections containing his articles on social and political issues, including *al-Qawmiyyat* (*Essays on Nationalism*, Vols. 1 and 2, Beirut, 1924) and *al-Tatarruf wa al-islah* (*Extremism and Reform*, Beirut, 1928).

The main literary critical articles that were not included in *al-Rihaniyyat* appeared in the collection *Adab wa fann* (*Literature and Art*, Beirut, 1956) and *Antum al-Shu'ara'* (*You the Poets*, Beirut, 1934); two stories were also published separately: *The Lily of Ghore* (*Zanbaqat al-ghawr*, New York, 1910) and *Outside the Harem* (*Kharij al-harim*, also called *Jahan*, New York, 1917), as was his collection of poems, *Hutaf al-awdiya* (*Hymns of the Valleys*, Beirut, 1955) and others.

The themes and problems central to Rihani's work were typical of many progressive figures in Arab society in the latter half of the nineteenth century and the early twentieth century, such as Muhammad 'Abduh, Qasim Amin and 'Abd al-Rahman al-Kawakibi; these writers and thinkers "raised the problems of the society and politics of Arab life of the day, striving to resolve them in the interests of progress, which was of great educational importance in Arab society".[3]

Nor did Rihani confine himself simply to the narrow sphere of literary activity; he took an active part in public life.

It is possible that in the literature of European peoples a writer such as Rihani might not have gained a recognition that was out of the ordinary; but for the new Arabic literature he was a significant phenomenon, and in the history of literature his name will always be associated with a certain movement. Rihani's role may be characterised as widening the scope of the usual material in contemporary Arabic literature to the point of bordering on global questions, such as the attempt to unite the two opposites that in the current conceptual framework are the East and the West.[4]

Although he was brought up with the idea of a chasm between the West and the East, Rihani felt that he belonged to both. He called upon the Arabs to adopt the innovations of the West in regard to economic and cultural progress. Yet, like many thinkers and artists of the East, Rihani held the deep conviction that cultural achievements and technical progress were in themselves not enough for a morally and socially just rebirth of the human, any more than the spiritual life and a deep philosophical understanding alone were enough for the perfection of life in the East. "And Rihani took upon himself the mission of bringing the knowledge of the West to the East, while taking to the West the philosophy and poetry of the East."[5] And this gave rise in Rihani to a particular mental state of dualism. On this point Krachkovsky emphasises that "it was this aspect of his personality, this split and dualism, that did not always make him comprehensible to the contemporary Arab world".[6]

The contradictions in the writer's world-view[7] were discernibly reflected in his artistic work. Rihani reduced all his demands to the necessity for reform and for moral self-perfection. "This opponent of official church religiosity, who hated the spirit of mercantilism that pervaded bourgeois society, celebrates the ideals of freedom, equality and the brotherhood of all people, and dreams of the unity of man with God-nature."[8] And for Rihani nature itself has a "social function": its task was to bring an element of pacification and purification to society.

It is not our aim, in examining the literature on Rihani's work, to give a detailed and comprehensive review. Within the framework of the present study we are concerned with the following questions: to what extent was Rihani the artist influenced by Western Romanticism, American in particular, and how did the ideas and concepts of Romanticism develop in his work? The ideas and spiritual foundation of American Transcendentalism – humanism and democracy, spiritual freedom, self-perfection and closeness to nature – resonated deeply with Rihani's temperament and his view of the world.

Innovative artists appear at pivotal moments in the history of a society, at times of major historical change. The Arab peoples, who were acutely aware of their backwardness and of the need for change without delay, experienced

such a period at the end of the nineteenth century and the beginning of the
twentieth. In that same period Arabic literature, as though trying to make
up for lost time, quickly mastered the achievements of foreign literature –
Enlightenment, Sentimentalism and Romanticism. It seems to us that this
process is reflected in the work of Rihani. Being a Romantic artist by his
very nature, Rihani did not dwell on his artistic development. The Romanticism in his works grew steadily more polished, bringing him close to a
realistic vision of the world.

Rihani's Romantic apprehension of reality and his experience of the American Romantics

The themes and motifs of Rihani's Romantic work are manifold, and include
nature, the poet and society, the idealisation of the nation's past, philosophical understandings of reality and the rejection of many of society's
institutions.

Rihani's artistic efforts were inclined less towards the Romanticism of
the Europeans, which was closely linked to the social and political practices of the period and which emphasised the human individual with his
social problems, than towards that of the American Transcendentalists,
whose priority was the spiritual significance of man as the sole reality. This
is why the American Transcendentalist poets Ralph Waldo Emerson, Walt
Whitman and Henry David Thoreau laid such particular emphasis on the
perfection of the human self rather than of society. The moral perfection
of the self always appears for these writers as the basis for a better life. The
Transcendentalists treated the interrelationship of nature and man likewise
in abstracto: as a unity, an absolute unification. Nature is in itself the embodiment of all spiritual and moral principles of existence, in which man alone
is involved.

The theme of nature occupies an important place in Rihani's poetry. "My
misfortune arises in the very nature from which I spring, and in which and
for which I exist",[9] he wrote. Krachkovsky also remarked that Rihani's relationship to nature was altogether different from that of other Arab literary
men, both classical and modern, whose writing about nature was meagre
and dry, devoid of any lyrical emotive content:

> Rihani has a rapturous love of nature. I do not know another Arab writer whose
> feeling for nature was so well developed. Sometimes he rises to the point of
> pantheism. It is surely strange that the Arabs, a people that always lived close
> to nature, had such an undeveloped feeling for nature. In all Arabic poetry
> we sometimes find a highly detailed, even photographic representation of the
> surrounding world, but never a real perception of nature.[10]

Many of Rihani's works are dedicated to the theme of nature, for example
"The Valley of Frayki, or a return to nature", "At the Cot of Spring",

"The Call of the Valleys", "My Temple in the Valley", "They Deserted it", "Return to the Valley", "Hymns of the Valleys" ("Goddess of the Valley! Heal me!") and "Nightingale of Life and Death". And in his other works, concerned with freedom and homeland or philosophical or religious ideas, there is at the same time almost always a depiction of nature.

Indeed the appeal to nature is common to all Romantics, but in most cases it carries the individual stamp of the author. For Rousseau, the return to nature is the return to naturalness and wisdom that teaches people to live in accordance with the principles laid down by Mother Nature. For Shelley it is the eternal source and example of renewal, rebirth, mutability and progress. This is the source of his optimism and belief that harmony will ultimately prevail in human society. For Wordsworth, nature is a call to the patriarchal way of life and to calm and peaceful enjoyment, a refuge from the troubles of civilisation. The American Transcendentalists advocated a cult of nature, seeking the commonality of man and nature, and contrasting nature and moral simplicity with the levelling effects of capitalism. As for Rihani, not only is nature for him the source of beauty and inspiration and the embodiment of truth; it also directly influences the relationship between man and society. He sees in nature a curative and morally purifying principle. As a follower of Transcendentalism, Rihani singled out in his perception of nature the idea of the union of Man, God and Nature. This trinity is the constant and indivisible Being that wholly embodies in itself the meaning of existence. This idea is expressed as follows in his poem "My Temple in the Valley":[11]

> Today in my heart dwells a part
> Of my neighbour's heart.
> And in the heart of the woods
> Dwells a part of mine.
> My heart is in the mind of this peasant,
> And his mind dwells in my heart. [...]
>
> And among the terebinth
> And under the lofty pine and oak trees,
> I build my home,
> The Temple of Faith,
> Where Nature and God live and roam ...[12]

The same idea can be clearly heard in Emerson, for whom the soul of man (the "I") is interrelated with nature:

> Sea, earth, air, sound, silence,
> Plant, quadruped, bird,
> By one music enchanted
> One deity stirred ...   ("The Sphinx"[13])

Both Rihani and Emerson affirm not only the abstract identity of man, God and nature, but also the interrelationship between them. Man comprehends God in the contemplation of nature. The stars, the flowers, the animals and the mountains – all this reflects the wisdom of His [God's] best hours.[14] Recognising "the vision of true and eternal beauty", man thereby understands "the divine principle of the universe". This philosophical postulate of Emerson is embodied by Rihani in his artistic work:

> I descended into the valley and stopped on the rock that rises above the river, and observed the traces of the storm and rain of the night. Last night the god of winter had gone to his bride, nature. The water in the river and streams was red like blood. I stopped in admiration and felt my soul depart from my body and soar high over the wet trees, over the rocks that are grey in summer and black after the rains.[15]

A.S. Dmitriev comments that the "endeavour to comprehend phenomena in their interrelationships and universality"[16] is a notable feature of Romantic thought in Western European literature. Walt Whitman's "On the Beach at Night, Alone" serves to illustrate this point:

> A vast similitude interlocks all,
> All spheres, grown, ungrown, small, large, suns, moons, planets,
>   comets, asteroids,
> All the substances of the same, and all that is spiritual upon the same,
> All distances of place, however wide,
> All distances of time – all inanimate forms,
> All Souls – all living bodies, though they be ever so different, or in
>   different worlds,
> All gaseous, watery, vegetable, mineral processes – the fishes, the brutes,
> All men and women – me also;
> All nations, colors, barbarisms, civilizations, languages;
> All identities that have existed, or may exist, on this globe, or any globe;
> All lives and deaths – all of the past, present, future;
> This vast similitude spans them, and always has spann'd, and shall forever
>   span them, and compactly hold them, and enclose them.[17]

This characteristic of Western Romanticism can also be attributed to many of Rihani's works dedicated to nature. Let us consider his essay "The Valley of Frayki, or the return to nature",[18] in which "the problems of the interrelationship of matter and spirit, of falsehood and truth, and of civilisation and nature, are intertwined in a single knot".[19] The author describes a day spent in the valley of Frayki, which for him was a symbol of the importance and greatness of nature. Here he feels himself to be the son of nature and, as it were, dissolves into her, recognising his unity with her: "I felt the spirit of the valley embody itself in me, and my soul went into the valley. Thus both I and the valley are one and the same: in my soul are the same shadows, apparitions and caves, in my soul are the same proud rocks, frightening descents, tumultuous waterfalls and flowing rivers."[20]

In these verses Rihani expresses the idea of the unity and universality of all that exists: "This is clear to all who have reached that stage in their spiritual development, in which the unity of the human spirit with the all-embracing spirit of nature can be understood ... for all nature belongs to them and in her they have no end."[21] In the same extract an element of Rihani's philosophical outlook can be discerned: his sense of the boundlessness of nature and also of the human soul that faces it.

For Rihani nature is "the altar of life and belief", in which there is joy and sadness, confusion and reconciliation. However, nature "does not threaten" man, does not spurn him; rather, "infusing in me of thy ruggedness and strength", it renews and refines him:

> O mother, eternal, divine, satanic, ...
> I have come to thee,
> I prostrate my face before thee ...
> O touch me with thy wand divine again;
> Stir me once more in thy mysterious alembics;
> Remake me to suit the majestic silence of thy hills ...[22]

Emerson's conviction that "The laws of moral nature answer to those of matter as face to face in a glass" and nature co-operates in the aims of man,[23] and his belief in man's closeness to nature, correspond to Rihani's ideas. Rihani speaks with passion about the health-giving and morally purifying action of nature upon man:

> Rejoice in every manifestation of nature, and draw goodness from it, if you have a grain of wisdom. Look at the tree and the broad shadow it casts, and turn your thoughts or your heart to what it is that you are seeing, and you will not be the loser ... learn from her [nature] steadfastness and sincerity, borrow from her strength and grandeur.[24]

A similar extract can be found in Thoreau's *Walden*: "We need the tonic of wildness ... We can never have enough of nature. We must be refreshed by the sight of inexhaustible vigor, vast and titanic features ... We need to witness our own limits transgressed, and some life pasturing freely where we never wander."[25]

There is, however, a significant divergence between Rihani's manner of appreciating nature and Thoreau's. For Thoreau, the love of nature has a famously utilitarian character – not only is she the source of aesthetic pleasure, but also of material well-being. Nature for Rihani, however, is primarily a spiritual delight. He appeals to the bosom of nature not to labour but rather to be inspired by the spiritual principle, in order subsequently to convey this charge of cheer, beauty and purity to other people. "When I am amongst nature I recall only spiritual joy", he writes.[26]

In creating civilisation, man has wilfully separated himself from nature and striven to master her by force, to put her at his service, and so it is unsurprising that he finds himself in the power of false values. So now, in order to find the unity of nature, in the words of Rihani, he must "tread on the thorns of prejudices, walk through the briars of tradition and the valleys of false conceptions and swim across the streams of untrue love ... to come to the bushes of the powerful, the thickets of the rulers and the ditches of the laws".[27]

Thoreau believed that nature embodies "the transcendental ideal, purity, beauty and chastity". Rihani's relationship to nature is similar. Dolinina notes: "Linked to Rihani's view of God-Nature is the concept of happiness. That happiness is 'to live in complete harmony with nature and her laws'."[28] Immersed in nature, it is with revulsion that man recalls the world of falsehood, hypocrisy, artificiality and oppression. In nature alone, from "the humble grass, the little spider and the gnat", to "the life of the magnificent pine, luxuriant flowers and grand animals", every detail is filled with meaning, beauty and harmony. And man in the bosom of nature feels liberated, equal in rights and happy:

> And nature's son walks in the grove among bushes, under trees and shrubs; he is animated by the aroma of pine and intoxicated by the fragrance of the sweet earth, mingled with the scents of sage, pine needles and laurel. He steps out of his mother's house filled with energy, resolve and joy, particularly when he has seen her in a moment of agitation. He leaves with the consciousness that he is entitled to the relationship of nature to him as an equal, or rather, as one of her members, an equal before the eternal and universal law that does not stop before the wealthy and is not repealed for emperors and princes.[29]

Whitman enjoyed the same elevated relationship to nature; for him the "most joyful song", his "A Song of Joys", embodies all the beauty and fullness of the life of nature:

> O to make the most jubilant song!
> Full of music – full of manhood, womanhood, infancy!
> Full of common employments – full of grain and trees.
> O for the voices of animals – O for the swiftness and balance of fishes
> O for the dropping of raindrops in a song!
> O for the sunshine and motion of waves in a song![30]

Sometimes Rihani's verses have an almost religious quality of devotion to the inexhaustible spiritual force of nature:

> Goddess of the valley! Heal me!
> Goddess of the woods! Feel me!
> Goddess of the prairies! Cure me!
> Goddess of chanting! Aid me! [31]

The emotions with which this prose poem, "Hymns of the Valleys", is filled – love, tenderness, languor and comfort – are addressed to nature. As Rihani writes: "We are children of nature and to her we return."[32]

Rihani's descriptions of nature frequently contain a philosophical subtext and express important aspects of the author's own world-view. Even his little landscape sketches preserve the sense of the wholeness of existence and the connectedness of life and death. In his poem "The Bulbul and the Gale", the onset of night is portrayed as the death of the day:

> The forehead of Sannin frowns,
> And its bright colours are now like bits of the night
> Scattering the perfume of daisies in the sky
> Beyond the dark clouds.
> Thus the sparkling city disappears,
> The dancing brides leave,
> The silvery islands sink in the oceans,
> The golden ponds turn grey,
> And the night pours its darkness,
> Which is sipped by Death, over the Day,
> Which is confined in a grave of water,
> Wrapped with the lights woven by the night.
>
> In his cage the *bulbul* stops singing,
> And in the valleys the gale stops wailing.[33]

A typical example of Rihani's lyrical landscape poetry is "At the Cot of Spring",[34] which consists of a series of nature sketches from the Frayki valley. The entire poem has an elegiac quality, like a sad and tender melody:

> I have known you even before the mountains
> Wove for your towers
> Carpets of daisy and saffron flowers, ...
>
> I have known you before the last winter gust
> Constructed in your honour a victory bust
> Made of its tears, breath and blood,
> Before the wailing clouds departed,
> And over Sannin the smiling silver clouds faded,
> Before the morning sun with the rays
> Of love and tenderness attended to your days,
> And before it erected above your cot
> A dome made of its flaming spot.
> I have known you even before your face they veiled
> To conceal for a moment God's face
> Which in your face prevailed.[35]

This poem employs a distinctive compositional principle: a stringing together of individual pictures, visual images or brief descriptions of scenes from nature, with no obvious link or progression. The technique is reminiscent of Whitman, and particularly of his poem "Song of Myself", which is formed of 52 fragments, each containing an entirely new and independent turn of thought.

The Romantic conception of nature in Rihani, as with Gibran, is set against the theme of loneliness. In this both poets are clearly following the Transcendentalists, for whom the loneliness of the Romantic self is closely tied to the experience of "union with nature" (Thoreau). In Rihani we also encounter images of nature hostile to man, which symbolise society's incomprehension and the futility of all the lyric hero's efforts to act on his surroundings. In the poem "A Branch of Roses"[36] the lyric hero is the embodiment of love of his people and concern for them. He devotes all his spiritual powers and action, his thought and his desire, to serving the people:

> My love, in the fields of foreign lands, I planted;
> It bloomed before nature commanded.
> My love I planted in a fresh soil,
> But the roses around it mourned its soul.
> I spread my seeds generously all in all
> And sprinkled my seeds in the fields of liberty ...[37]

But the people do not understand and do not accept either his love or his good intentions. The poem describes the poet's bitter disappointment: the seeds of his love and tenderness have perished "in the swamps of hypocrisy and slander":

> My love, in the land of culture, I planted,
> But by thorns was deeply wounded
> And choked by the bramble,
> To whose poisoned roots my love surrendered.
> I planted it in the land of friends and beloved,
> But in the swamps of hypocrisy and slander it faded.[38]

The poet's mission is in the service of his people, and in the impulses of his soul and the intensity of his living he reflects the people's nobler characteristics, of which they are scarcely aware in their everyday lives:

> I am the pipe of the shepherds, your worshipper;
> I am the lyre of the lovers, your seekers;
> I am the music of your ball dancers;
> and I am the organ of your homeless slaves ...
> I am your voice, which was framed by ages, passing by;
> I am the spirit of Veda for the day of the resurrection ...
>
> In your lyre, I am a melody in bondage bound
> And by ignorance in the Pyramids ordained.
> I am a night song over the years maintained ...[39]

Not only is the poet filled with the voices and lives of the people around him, but his soul also keenly perceives the higher orders of human existence such as philosophy, art and poetry:

> With a drink from your lips, refresh my soul,
> And sing me melodies I can't recall;

> Those were the tunes
> I sang in the halls of Babel and Greece. ...
>
> I am, in your lute, the Phoenix's spirit
> Which under the cinders of death merit.
> I am the spirit of Orpheus,
> Which above the waves of Arts confess ...[40]

The American academic Henry Seidel Canby, speaking of the influence of Transcendentalism on Whitman, remarked that it manifested itself specifically in Whitman's poem "Song of Myself", where Whitman appears in the name of all people, and all qualities that are present in him he communicates as the "divine commonplace". In this "celebration of himself" can also be seen his closeness to Transcendentalism, and particularly to Emerson.[41] Throughout "Song of Myself" runs the golden thread of the poet's "I", which speaks for all humanity:

> I am of old and young, of the foolish as much as the wise,
> Regardless of others, ever regardful of others,
> Maternal as well as paternal, a child as well as a man ...
>
> I am the poet of the Body and I am the poet of the Soul,
> The pleasures of heaven are with me and the pains of hell
>   are with me ...[42]

The duty of the poet, Whitman maintains, is to be a leader among people and to make known the dreams of man.[43]

Rihani shares this view of the person of the poet. The "I" of his poems is a lyric persona that strives to express the thoughts of all humanity, and to embody in his spiritual activity its unlimited creative possibilities. He thus uses the image of the poet to personify his social and civic ideals.

The themes of good and evil, existence and death, time and space, and the essence of God and of religion were always central to Rihani's artistic and philosophical thinking. And this is natural, for "characteristic of the majority of the Romantics ... was deep philosophical enquiry, direct or subconscious ... The principles of artistic knowledge and reflection of reality by the Romantics cannot be comprehended separately from their philosophical content."[44]

The global problems of the essence of human existence, the purpose of man in this life, his relationship to God and many other questions are also continually touched upon in the work of the Transcendentalist poets since, in the words of A.S. Dmitriev, they understand poetry as a "field of philosophising". Concise formulations were alien to their idealistic philosophical system, which drew on all intuitive, unconscious and *a priori* experience from beyond the limits of the senses.

An affinity is created between Rihani and the Transcendentalist Romantics by their conception of the quintessence of life, such as love and mercy – the way to which is through moral improvement:

Help me, O God,
To sustain my spiritual, intellectual and corporeal strength
For the sake of Truth, Love and Wisdom![45]

In the poem "The Simoom Wind"[46] Rihani clearly states his moral creed:

Brother! There will come a time
When all that is in the world will vanish
Except for those monuments of spiritual solemnity,
Moments of glorious human souls and tranquillity.[47]

Rihani the Romantic understood progress primarily as the detailed development of individual persons and their moral improvement. This is also the basis of the Romantic individualism of his philosophy, since if the perfection of society is founded upon the moral enhancement of individual persons, rather than the improving of social institutions, it is necessary to concentrate attention on the individual, who stands at the centre of all things. Rihani's conviction of the importance of moral improvement is close to the basic premises of Emerson, who considered that with the moral principle it would be possible to resolve all contradictions[48] and believed in "the perpetual openness of the human mind to new influx of light and power".[49]

The understanding of the problem of morals is linked in Rihani to that of religion as a "moral feeling", in particular of love and mercy, and to the conception of God as a higher moral law. Like many Romantics, Rihani is a pantheist. Z.I. Levin writes: "God for Rihani ... is not an absolute spirit that is worshipped by subjective idealists, nor is it from among the human beings. It is 'love' and 'truth', it is 'the secret' contained within nature."[50]

In Rihani's view, "God is something that exists in all things",[51] "God is, in the worlds and the things",[52] "the visible world is nothing other than a symbol of the hidden being, and the hidden being is God".[53]

The most distinctive of Rihani's poems in regard to the understanding of God is "The Naj'wa",[54] which suggests that man is a particle of God and his eternal striving for the ideal. In effect, God for Rihani is the totality of mankind's own ethical conceptions. The poem is constructed as an internal dialogue between two voices: man, seeking the truth, and God, who responds to him. Man demands of God and God answers:

I counsel thee, man;
I set thy hands loose;
And I give thee my endowments.[55]

This opening to the dialogue immediately establishes a confidential and close relationship between God and man. Man requests of God:

O Everlasting Spring!
The lights of Love emanate from You
And flow into the waters of life and health. ...

> Do not deny me the grace of Your rectitude,
> And do not keep me away from Your springs.[56]

God reveals to man that he is present in all things: in nature, in people, in their thoughts and deeds, in the stars, the fields and the flowers, in the aroma of love and in beauty, and it is there that man must seek him.

> My springs burst amongst the stars;
> They tie the stars to one another
> And fortify their welfare and power.
>
> My springs burst in the fields,
> And flow among their flowers
> And their scents of beauty and love. ...
> All this, You can behold;
> All this, I place in your hand. ...
>
> In thee, I am the heartbeat of Life,
> The spirit of Love and the light of Wisdom.
> Guard these as they are
> Images of divine creed and certainty.[57]

Man sees in God all that is most elevated, while man is, for God, an imprescriptible particle of his being. Together, God and man form a unity. It can be seen from God's words that he lives in man, for man is the embodiment of the essence of life, of love, truth, wisdom and so on, which are the essence of God. In other words, apart from man, save in nature, God does not exist.

At the end of the poem Rihani puts into the very mouth of God the following address to man: *Anta ilahi wa la ilaha li illaka* ("You are My divinity; and for Me there is no divinity but you"), thus significantly altering the basis of the *shahada* formula of religious belief: *La ilaha illa-llah* ... ("There is no god but God ...").

The theme of the recognition of the divine principle in every man and the commonality of man and God, transpierced with the spirit of love, is a distinctive element of Rihani's philosophical lyric poetry. According to A.S. Dmitriev, "From the human commonality they [the Romantics] singled out certain individuals, each of whom, they believed, contained in themselves the entire universe. It was indeed by the development in all aspects of individuals, in their view, that the path led to a harmonious, all-embracing universal whole."[58] In the work of the Romantics this universalism could also be seen "in their utopian dreams of the triumph of the ideals of harmony in all human society".[59]

Linked with the spiritual perfection of the individual is Rihani's utopian dream of the ideal society of the future. This idea is also revealed in "The Simoom Wind".[60] The "simoom" is the unceasing movement of time that on the one hand takes all things away, but on the other is all-creating.

At the start of the poem the poet lists the conquests of mankind's con-
structive labour: "palaces with grandiose green gardens", "bridges, over
the waters, suspending / Glorious islands", "dams, firm and solid", "buildings of floors twenty", "lighted tunnels dug under rivers", "battleships
the waves of the seas breaking" and so forth. Conclusion: all this is only
seeming existence, merely appearance; it is perishable, transient, insub-
stantial. Only "Man's Toil, Gratitude, / Generosity and Goodwill" are
eternal. For Rihani, only spiritual achievements, and only the perfection
of the individual and the spirit, are true reality; all else is mirage and
illusion. The entire poem is another utopia of the Romantic world-view.
That is, Rihani sees the perfection of society in the perfection of the individual, when a person gains his spiritual freedom and becomes a "glorious
human soul" – strong, courageous – when "all that is in the world will
vanish", and

> Arrogant tyrants will shudder,
> And the strong winds will blow all over.[61]

This philosophical conception reveals the closeness of the ideas of the
Arab poet to those of the Transcendentalists, who also placed their hopes
above all on the "correction of morals". Whitman's idea that political ide-
ologies can be transformed not by means of politics itself, but great moral
spiritual forces[62] are close to Rihani's constant thesis that "in the perfection
of the individual is the perfection of society".[63]

A common theme among all Romantics is the belief in social progress
and the conviction that this movement is constant and that its advance does
not halt for a moment. Yet the historical reality and situation in which they
were situated did not instil realistic hopes for the present or the near future.
Disillusionment with the outcomes of the French Revolution of 1789 and
disbelief that its ideals would be realised, the social contradictions taking
place in Europe, the stormy shocks of war and social and political upheaval,
and the beginning of the emergence of capitalism all gave the Western Romantics on the one hand a more realistic vision of real life, but on the other
hand led them to create an indeterminate utopia based on a distant and
beautiful future. As I.A. Terteryan insightfully noted, "Romanticism created
grandiose and multiple utopias: the utopia of the ideal revolution, the utopia
of individual activity ... the utopia of national unity, the utopia of beauty and
the utopia of man and nature."[64]

For the Romantics this dream of a beautiful future always had an indistinct and blurred character and did not question specifically what actions
would lead to it. Let us give the example of a poem by Whitman in which
he sings of great hopes:

> Come, I will make the continent indissoluble,
> I will make the most splendid race the sun ever shone upon,

I will make divine magnetic lands,
With the love of comrades,
With the life-long love of comrades.

I will plant companionship thick as trees along all the rivers of America,
and along the shores of the great lakes, and all over the prairies,
I will make inseparable cities with their arms about each other's necks ...[65]

Similar ideas are to be found in the poem "The Harvest of Time"[66] by the American poet Harold T. Pulsifer. Rihani was given a collection of Pulsifer's work in Lebanon in 1933, and translated this one poem from it into Arabic. The utopically indeterminate ideas of the American poet about the perfected society of the future seem to have resonated with those of the translator. In addition to the translation, Rihani wrote a poem by way of reciprocation, entitled "Resurrection".[67] The basic idea of the translated poem can be seen from the following lines:

Time winnows beauty with a fiery wind,
Driving the dead chaff from the living grain.
Some day there will be golden sheaves to bind;
There will be wonder in the world again.
There will be lonely phrases born to power,
There will be words immortal and profound ...
Beauty endures though towering empires die.
O, speed the blown chaff down the smoking sky![68]

From Rihani's poem of reciprocation:

O my Western brother, truly your exposition is magically charming,
It blows joy into the mountain cedars ...
And the morning star will rise in this East.
Hurry to that happy day, hurry to salvation.[69]

The notion of a "radiant future" necessarily also involved the notion of freedom. For the Romantics this is a recurring theme, whereby freedom is understood in the broadest of senses. It encompasses freedom of the individual, artistic freedom, freedom of the people from oppression, political freedom and so on. "The ideal of the Romantic hero is freedom in the deepest sense – from social and political freedom to artistic freedom."[70]

The concept of freedom became an important feature of artistic consciousness in the canon of Romantic symbolism. This can be clearly seen in Rihani's lyric poetry. He speaks continually about "freedom", though almost never directing his argument to specific historical or social circumstances. This is freedom in general. In his article "Near to Freedom"[71] and many other works the concept of freedom tends to be vague, indistinct and generalised.

The theme of freedom appeared in Rihani's work as early as 1907, in "The Revolution".[72] Krachkovsky suggests that this poem was Rihani's direct response to the events of the Russian Revolution of 1905: "As usual, one can see in it echoes of the French Revolution, yet certain elements indicate that the direct stimulus for the work were the Russian events of 1904–1905."[73] In this poem, revolution is presented as an act of brutal violence, accompanied by bloodshed, the downfall of tyrants and the triumph of the avengers:

> It is a nervy and grimy day;
> Its night is lit with a startling ray,
> While its fading star alertly gazes.
> It is a day of fearful, turmoil noises,
> Of screams, clamour and moaning,
> Of roar, dispatch and groaning. [74]

Each stanza of "The Revolution" ends with a changing refrain whose common slogan is "Woe then to the oppressors!" The author enumerates the attributes of a popular uprising: the crimson flags, the echoing of horns and drums. The poem recalls revolutionary uprisings in Rome, Paris and England. In the author's view, a revolution is perpetrated by "manly and ferocious lads committed", "strong and haughty men entrusted" and "women with rage ornamented". Rihani gives his blessing here to both the revolution and its perpetrators, justifying their anger and thirst for revenge:

> When the oppressed the sword of the oppressor gains,
> And inflicts the corrupted with torturing pains.[75]

But for the sake of what do all these tragic events take place? In Rihani's view, they anticipate the creation of the "new world", that time when the "goodly spirit" will be liberated. The poet is unable to give a more specific suggestion than this: the "new world" is that vague "radiant future" where the "goodly spirit" triumphs.

Such a hazy understanding of the means and the ends for whose sake revolutions occur was generally typical among the leading Arabs. As Z.I. Levin remarked: "Before the Great October Revolution, the East knew virtually nothing not only of Lenin but also of Marx and Engels. Its notions of scientific socialism were incomplete and distorted."[76] Rihani's views on revolution, freedom and the means of attaining social justice are set out clearly in a speech he gave before the first performance of the play "The Prisoners, or Abdul Hamid in Athens":

> The truth is, gentlemen, that people do not now have true equality. After long suffering and persistent endeavour along the path of progress we may, perhaps, reach a situation in which every person will know their place and every person will be recompensed for their labour. And this, in my view, is real equality. Let each person be rewarded for their actions with complete fairness, and I guarantee that people will not then dream of equality.[77]

Deeply dissatisfied with the way of life in both the West and the East, with the situation of the individual in society and with social injustice,

Rihani sees the way out of this unjust state of affairs not in violent revolutions but in reform and education, rather as Thoreau foresees the future following a "peaceable revolution" (*Civil Disobedience*, 1849).

In the poem "The Stones of Paris"[78] (1925), which continues the theme of revolution, the revolutionary image is considerably softened, removed from scenes of terror, raging violence, vengeance, blood and flames. The French Revolution is portrayed subjectively: bloodless, for in the author's opinion it was defended with only "stones", not "bullets":

> Paris! Your stones and not your bullets,
> Your lights and not your fires,
> Were built to reclaim Freedom.
> They were raised as barracks to defend Freedom.
> They were constructed as fences to protect Freedom.
> And they were used to erect arches for victory of Freedom.[79]

The closing idea of the work, as frequently recurs in Rihani's writings, is that the chief enemy of freedom is ignorance:

> Our real enemy is ignorance.
> Ignorance here and there is our real enemy, Paris.
> Look, judge, execute, and do not hesitate, Paris.
> Tell the Druzes and Alawites,
> The Christians and the Muslims,
> That religion is for God
> But the nation is for all.[80]

In other works by Rihani, his ideas of the means of achieving freedom are more specific. These are the perfecting of morals, wide reforms and mass education; he does not admit violent struggle, since this might infringe on the freedom of individuals. In this agenda an exceptional role is usually allotted to the individual: "For the Romantics, belief in the unlimited possibilities of the human individual and in its sovereign right to the realisation of these possibilities was the philosophical transformation of the political idea of freedom."[81]

In the poem "Freedom: My Companion"[82] (1922), which eulogises the ideal of freedom, the author makes a direct appeal to imams, princes, kings and sultans – that is, to 'individuals' – calling on them to preserve freedom and bestow it on the people. In this poem Rihani also conforms to the individualistic system of Transcendentalism, which links the perfection of society with the perfection of the individual. The "Imams", "princes", "kings" and "sultans" have already achieved, in Rihani's view, the highest echelons. It is therefore up to them to convey their knowledge of life, freedom, morality and duty to the people, who remain in the morass of their ignorance and darkness:

You imams, princes, kings and sultans!
You are the guardians of a treasure,
A great heritage given to you by God. ...

You hold in your hand a nation
Which is not aware of its true interest. ...

You kings, sultans, princes and imams!
In your unified word lies the life of the nation.
This word is yours; would you not utter it?[83]

And here again Rihani indicates how to preserve freedom on the basis of knowledge, education and reform:

Are you willing to strive for unity?
Are you ready to promote the honour of the nation,
Which can prosper only through proper education?
Are you willing to build institutions of proper education?
Freedom addresses you, Arab world!

She is my travelling companion.
She is the subject and predicate of my life.[84]

Rihani considered his artistic work as being in service to society. It is also no coincidence that his works frequently include themes and ideas concerned with his longing for the renewal of his homeland and with the ways of nurturing that renewal.

The idealisation of the national past, which called for the renewal and unification of the nation, was a theme of importance in Enlightenment literature and was adopted and developed by Rihani. He sought in the past a harmonious and free individual; his Romantic pathos, like that of Whitman, is associated both with ideas of national traditions in the struggle for independence and with the cult of enlightenment. This was a further facet of his Romantic outlook. "The task of reconstructing the national past and of seeking and asserting a national character was inalienable and inherent in Romanticism in all its national variants."[85] L.Ye. Cherkassky notes, for example, in the case of China, that "a typical feature of Romantic art ... was resorting to the past in search of an ideal".[86]

The idealisation of the Arab past, which Rihani presents as a community of interests, is dependent on a national character and gives his Romanticism originality and a particular colouring. Neither struggle, conflict, oppression nor social demarcation are taken into account; he speaks of the nation as a whole, one that in the past experienced a period of prosperity and greatness. This idea is particularly evident in "The Arabian Eagle"[87] (1933), a poem that describes the natural and free life of the eagle, which symbolises the Arab people in the past:

The Arabian Eagle has as his airstrip the plains
And as his wings' whetstone the Prophet's mountains.
He is the beloved of *al-Haram ash-Shareef*
And the stepson of the desert, his milk-mother.
His refuge is the pavilion,
And his bed and his youth yard
Are the sands of the deserts.
The Arabian Eagle the haven of Freedom enjoys.[88]

Rihani sees one of the paths towards national revival as a unification of the best achievements of the West with those of the East. His poem "I am the East"[89] (1922) contains the idea of the past greatness of the East, and turns the East into a symbol: the place where the sun rises, the origin of life, the origin of man's procession on the Earth. The work begins in this vein:

I am the East.
I am the corner stone in the first temple of God ...
I am the bridge of the Sun ...[90]

Humanity is in constant motion; this is not a stopping caravan, whether one be in Liverpool or Samarkand, on the banks of the Nile or in New York.

Rihani places great value on the peaks of the spiritual life – wisdom, philosophy and the understanding of God – that were achieved by the East, regarding them as the highest moral laws. He calls on the young people of the West to adopt Eastern values:

I am the East!
I approached you, son of the West, as a companion ...

I have what may cool and refresh your confused soul
And what may cure your heart from the ills of civilisation.
I have that which stimulates in you with justice beyond your contempt
And control beyond that which is sanctified by others.
I have what may chain your feet and hands so you may rest
And watch the planets, as your mind roams freely,
And your heart rests comfortably,
While you contemplate the secrets of existence.[91]

The next section of this long poem criticises the contemporary East, sunken in the darkness of prejudice and fanatical adherence to external religious rites. Ignorance and prejudice turn the East away from all the achievements of Western civilisation. His advice in "I am the East" has an ironic tinge:

Bear in mind the foreign adversary
Though he holds his Bible.
Do not fear him though he may hold a machine gun.
Do not deal with him though he may have free merchandise.[92]

The poem ends with a bitter and ironic question:

> I am the East.
> I have philosophies and religions.
> Who would exchange them for aircraft?[93]

The notion of the possibility of uniting the best of what created the two civilisations is also revealed in the poem "Return to the Valley".[94] When Rihani's native valley of Frayki asks the poet what he has brought back from his long years abroad, he replies that he united in himself the best of all that was given him by the East and the West. The East gave him the best national traits:

> I brought you the contentment and honour,
> The freedom and the valour,
> And the independence and security of the Bedouin.

[A second voice continues:]

> I brought you the Arabian pride and veneration;
> I brought you the Arabian honour and devotion,
> And the Arabian simplicity of life and hospitality.
> I brought you the Arabian bravery
> And valour in times of hostility or tranquillity.[95]

From the West, meanwhile, he gained "the freedom / of the Frenchmen in their revolution", "the vigour of the Americans in their work" and "the Faith of the free men / In Life and in Man".

While in Lebanon in 1931, Rihani wrote his poem "To Gibran".[96] A new element in this poem is his attempt to approach the details of his life more realistically, while also celebrating in Gibran and his circle those qualities that somehow brought his image close to the people.

The principal idea of the poem is Gibran's purpose in life, expressed in his creative work which, in the author's view, had awoken the national consciousness of the Arab people. "In Lebanon, his spirit blows again", Rihani exclaims at several points. After a long and fruitless night, "life" can begin. Rihani wrote the poem in a classically Romantic vein, which is particularly evident in the image of Gibran himself. He is shown as a typical Romantic hero who embodies all that is extraordinary and exceptional. This is not merely an individual with a specific uniqueness but an elevated and inspiring person who gives himself wholly to artistic creation. Gibran is given the generic image of the poet who, in the mind of Rihani the Romantic, embodies the eternal aspiration to the ideals of beauty and love that permeate the essence of life through and through, in the very depths of the mysteries and in the meaning of human life. Gibran embodied all epochs, ideals and great deeds, the undying voices of the ages:

> And like the radio catches the voice waves,
> The immortal voices Gibran caught;
> Those voices echoed
> The history, literature and doctrines of the East.
> Indeed, he listened, awakened and learned.[97]

The hero of the poem is endowed with supernatural qualities, a "creator" or "maker", who lives on inspiration and elevated feelings; he feels the sinful earth beneath his feet "except in moments of consummation and dreams". Such a person inevitably soars above ordinary people, who constantly learn "his wisdom" and seek to attain to the "cradle of wisdom".

However, as already mentioned, "To Gibran" also reveals another aspect of Rihani's Romanticism: his efforts to penetrate more deeply into reality. The author builds a subtle and aesthetic image of Gibran, using rigorously selected strokes to portray the setting with which the philosopher–poet surrounded himself:

> There in this humble hermitage, dim and bright,
> There in the cradle of compassion and encounter,
> And amidst statues, pictures, books and paper,
> Amidst the wreckage of pages,
> Where thought and wisdom competed,
> Amidst small pearls by thorns supported,
> And pictures upon which his brush wandered,
> Amidst sacred toys,
> Church candles and symbolical drawings,
> There, this hermitage was overflowing
> With artefacts, literature and spiritual schemes,
> Lived Gibran for twenty years.[98]

Rihani convincingly and elegantly recreates the image of the ascetic toiler, surrounded by modest but refined beauty and immersed in noble creative work. The description of Gibran's lodgings agrees almost completely with Gibran's own description in his correspondence with Mayy Ziyada:

> My studio is my temple, my friend, my museum, my heaven and my hell ... In this studio of mine there are many things which I keep and cherish. I am [particularly] fond of the antique objects. In the corners of the studio is a small collection of rare and precious things from past ages, such as statues and slates from Egypt, Greece and Rome; Phoenician glass; Persian pottery; ancient books and French and Italian paintings; and musical instruments which speak even in their silence.[99]

Concisely, accurately and with a degree of generalisation Rihani sketches an urban landscape, the background against which Gibran lived the greater part of his conscious life. This is not only a portrayal of that centre of world industry that was New York, but also the image of the immense internal

conflict that existed between the poet and the city, in which everybody
"weighs, measures and counts", where there is no freedom for the ardent
heart or for the imagination:

> There, amidst the frightful and deafening noises,
> Where slaughtered are humble voices,
> Where even great passions become breathless
> In the heart of the current restless,
> Which enslaves the business moguls
> In the shades of skyscrapers.
> A city where electricity the sun replaces.
> There, in the city of iron and gold,
> In the city where man wears time and a scale holds,
> In the city which enumerates and measures all,
> There in New York lived he who could not compute;
> The measurements and scales, would refute.[100]

This sharp contrasting of two images is a poetic description of the spiritual estrangement of the creative individual from the bourgeois world so
alien to him.

Rihani's tendency towards a lapidary style is significant. He recreates
Gibran's patriotism and his yearning for his homeland in one and the same
image:

> The clanging of church bells in Lebanon he adored,
> And the melodies of the *oud* and of the pipes he devoured.
> In the valleys and the Cedar shade his imagination roamed; ...
>
> He left, but he did not depart.
> His country, he carried in his heart. [101]

It may be noted that this laconism appears to particular advantage when
compared with the poetry of other Arab émigré poets, in particular with
the likes of Nasib 'Arida and Iliya Abu Madi, which generally concentrated
on the theme of separation from the homeland and featured great pathos.

Also unusual in this poem is Rihani's treatment of nature. On the one
hand he portrays her in the manner of a typical Romantic pantheist, giving
intimations of her secrets, perceiving her through subtle poetic images and
investing her with the most elevated spiritual feelings. Here is the excerpt in
which Rihani depicts the joy, ecstasy and celebration of nature at the birth
of Gibran:

> And at the cradle of prophecies,
> Around the pilgrims' sanctuaries,
> Where rests the sacred valley
> Beneath the Cedar's boughs,
> Where days, hymns of praise, chanted,

Time stood, with reverence thrilled,
While poetry's brides from incensed valleys
Advanced with cups of ivory
Teeming Time's distilled potion;
And the brides of imagination
Came from the moistened prairies
Wearing thornless crowns of roses
And blackberries in coral clusters.[102]

This passage is marked by grandiloquent turns of phrase, such as "the cradle
of prophecies", "the pilgrims' sanctuaries", "the brides of imagination" and
"poetry's brides", and an element of exaggeration, as in "teeming Time's
distilled potion", "time stood, with reverence thrilled" and so forth. Sometimes, however, nature is described with great simplicity and economy, in
clear-cut detail:

Blackberries under a high rock,
All over spread their coral hue;
And at its foot, the laurel grew,
Terebinth and inula viscosa crowded,
And the crimson tulip sparkled;[103]

As can be seen, there is no exaggeration and no metaphorical complication
here: just specific detail.

Frequently Rihani resorts to extensive metaphor. A typical example is
Gibran's belonging to two cultures and his bilingualism; he is given the
image of a warrior fighting with two sabres simultaneously. In New York
he entered into single-handed combat with elements that tore each other
apart within him:

His spirit, reason and heart contested;
His armour was two swords:
One from the East
And another from the West;
He gave one what his heart offered,
And the other with his mind and spirit coloured.
Both Arabic and English he encountered
And tamed them to express his mind and imagination.[104]

In fact the entire poem can be seen as an extended metaphor: the birth
of Gibran heralded the awakening of Lebanon. It is a Romantic poem; it
contains much that is pure symbol, such as the image of three women, in
white, black and red, who symbolise art, passion and imagination.

The theme of the finale of the poem is the untimely death of the great
man, who left an indelible mark on the lives of his people. Gibran's aim of
uniting the achievements of two cultures into one was close to the heart
of Rihani. After all, both men lived the same dream and fulfilled the same
mission – to change and renew Arab society:

Whatever the message we carried to the East and to the West,
Time will ever acknowledge our best.
And whatever literature for our fellow men we created,
The future will give us justice ...[105]

Overall, "To Gibran" is wholly Romantic in its outlook and its methods. It contains much agitation and tension of feeling, and its hero is a singular individual who stands above the people. Creativity is portrayed as an unfathomable, intuitive and secret process. In the Romantic spirit, this elevated individual is juxtaposed with the capitalistic city. At the same time, however, we sense that in this poem Rihani is also looking for new means by which to reflect reality: there are many specific and lifelike details as well as typical generalisations; the concrete details include the recreation of the conditions in which the poet lived. The Romantic landscape cohabits with the realistic one. All this entitles us to speak of a certain tendency in Rihani's Romantic method towards Realism, simplicity and clarity. In these attempts in "To Gibran" to find new methods of reflecting life in its detail, Rihani enriched Arab Romanticism with new features.

Romanticism in Rihani's story *Jahan* and short prose genres

With his many interests and thoughts, Rihani found himself at the centre of the sociopolitical and spiritual life of his people. He was sorely dissatisfied with both the life he saw in his homeland and that which he experienced in the West. He had no extensive programme of action, and only knew – indisputably and firmly – that he hated the oppression of the individual, as well as brute materialism, reductionism, religious fanaticism, obscure prejudice and the unjust distribution of social wealth.

Rihani inherited many positive ideas from the legacy of the Arab Enlightenment. He was himself a successor to one of the cardinal Enlightenment themes: the emancipation of the Oriental woman from centuries-old oppression. The first to address this theme had been the champion of women's rights, Qasim Amin (1865–1908). Rihani first broached the subject of women's emancipation back in 1910 with his story *Zanbaqat al-ghawr* (*The Lily of Ghore*), but returned to the theme in more detail, more persuasively and more completely in the long story *Jahan*,[106] an artistically powerful, emotionally saturated work that captivates the reader with the brilliance of its images, the acuteness and modernity of the problems it deals with, and the complexity of its plot. It may be mentioned here that the conflict between the ideas of humanism and of Nietzschean permissiveness is of equal importance in this story.

The story was written in 1917 and its substance is as follows. The action is set in the Turkish capital of Istanbul, at the palace of the retired Turkish nobleman Reza Pasha. A complex relationship forms between his daughter

Jahan and the German military consul General von Wallenstein, who wants Jahan to become his wife or his lover. Although she has feelings of love towards this man Jahan shuns physical intimacy with him, since von Wallenstein belongs to the oppressors of her country.

Everything in the story, the principal idea, the plot, the method of outlining the main heroes, the characteristics of portraiture, the landscape sketches, and the style all reveal Rihani as a Romantic in the full sense of the word. The main theme is the struggle of woman for freedom from the power of the ignorant prejudices that humiliate her as a person and trample on her human dignity.

Jahan is the image of an exceptional woman, elevated above all around her, endowed with strong feelings and passions, alone, alienated from everybody and torn by internal conflicts between duty and love, between the thirst for revenge and patriotic feeling. The principal motivation for all Jahan's actions is her striving for freedom:

> The goal Jahan sought to attain, her new dream, appeared again and again before her, permeating the very depths of her ardent soul. Jahan longed for it with all her being. She directed her prayers to this focus of her intentions and spiritual searching, to the realisation of the martyr's paradise she had found and to this joyfully stirring symbol of hope. In wakefulness and in sleep this goal shone before her vision, and she constantly repeated the word that was precious to her.[107]

The character of Jahan is portrayed with psychological insight; the author reveals both her strengths and weaknesses, in all their contradictions. The heroine's actions are motivated by interior impulses, but these are not always clear, even to her. "The internal dividedness in which Jahan found herself had inevitably to lead to a crisis. The young woman's thoughts flowed first in one direction and then in another, and her attempts to resist their flow were in vain as she tried to understand what it was that she had to strive for."[108]

Everything about Jahan sharply sets her apart from other people: her unusual beauty, high breeding and totally independent social position; her wealth, superb education, and unique character; and her immense powers of will, resolve and courage. Not only is her goal Romantic, but likewise the fundamental conflict of the story – the struggle of opposing feelings in her soul. She loves a man who is responsible for the death of her father and brother, and who humiliates and torments her homeland. Should she avenge them? Kill him? Or submit to her love and bear him a son? The Romantics always choose conflict situations of this kind, which reveal with the greatest power, acuteness and clarity the extraordinary passion and emotions of their heroes and their capacity to accomplish heroic deeds, to resolve with death the tragic conflicts of life. "In artistic realism attention is drawn to other aspects of human life ... in all its psychological fullness. The Romantic artist concentrates primarily on the dramatic, the exceptional and the outstanding, revealing the human impulse at the moment of greatest internal stress and vividly and colourfully drawing out these driving aspects of life."[109]

A particular characteristic of Romantic heroes is their solitude. They are pushed to the fore of, and placed above, society. Because of the exclusiveness of their natures, ideals and aims, they hardly ever find companions on their path and invariably act single-handedly, although their strivings are for society's benefit. This speaks of the individualism of the Romantic hero, an individualism that is a protest and challenge to the ordinary, the prosaic; in it "the poetic and Romantic dream is realised that does not wish to be resigned to the spiritually impoverished and brutal prose of life".[110] And such is the heroine of Rihani's story: she fights for the emancipation of women and undertakes "social" actions, writes articles, appears in the newspapers and translates Nietzsche – yet all this makes absolutely no impression on her life, surroundings or human relationships: she is always alone. She is not capable of growing fond of anybody from among her people: "Would there be a person from among the sons of her country who would travel the same path as her? ... who would comprehend the height of her endeavour and would not subject her sacred dreams to derision!"[111]

Even her beloved father, of whom she is the only daughter, is not close to her. Jahan keeps her interior closed to him, isolated by her pride, reticence and estrangement. She is even separated from her people, condemning their prejudices, submissiveness and humbleness: "Is this really that spirit of Islam I summoned to help me? And is this that people whose support I need in the struggle for freedom and justice? No, no. They do not understand me, they cannot understand! Between me and them is an ominous abyss that grows wider by the day."[112]

The opposition of the Romantic hero to society and their mutual incomprehension is the most general indicator of their relationship – and this is understandable. Ordinary heroes after all lead ordinary lives: they are multifaceted, corporeal and complex. The hero of the Romantics is quite different; his life consists solely in elevated aims and ideals. For him everyday life does not exist, and therefore the Romantic artist does not portray it. G.N. Pospelov remarks that "All the Romantics sought their Romantic ideal beyond the boundaries of the reality around them. All of them, in one way or another, opposed the 'despicable "here"' to an 'indeterminate, secret "there"'."[113]

The plot of *Jahan* also unfolds according to the rules of Romanticism. It contains no sketches of everyday life, no fixed situations or settings. There are no incidental situations, distractions, descriptions of other figures close to the heroine, reminiscences of the past or tokens of ordinary life. Everything is concentrated on the principal heroine, Jahan: her endeavours, her experiences, her conflicts, her actions; all else is mere background, a mere reflection of her vital activity. Even the image of the man with whom she comes into lethal combat, her beloved and enemy, General von Wallenstein, is only roughly sketched, without any mention of his interior state. He is portrayed only from that perspective which most fully exposes the reason for his encounter with Jahan.

Von Wallenstein is depicted in the story as a "strong, blond-haired rogue" who always pushes his way through, sowing death and violence in his wake. The author's idea of his psychology is primitive: to subordinate all people to his power, and to eliminate all impediments to this purpose. He is constantly overwhelmed by feelings of extreme superiority over other people; he is self-assured and unshakeable in his persistence. On arriving in Turkey, von Wallenstein imagines that if "his long-cherished dream of ruling over this great power, from Bursa to Baghdad, finally becomes reality ... then he, General von Wallenstein, will have far surpassed in power the ancient Germanic kings".[114]

Rihani also sketches the outward appearance of von Wallenstein: "a manly face, burnt brick-red by the sun, in which deep blue eyes can be discerned".[115] What moves him first and foremost is his thirst for power. In sum, he is a typical exponent of Nietzschean philosophy, which was profoundly alien and loathsome to the writer.

The name of Nietzsche appears several times in the story. Jahan is translating his book *Also sprach Zarathustra* into Turkish; Reza Pasha speaks of this author with disgust, disapproving of his daughter's actions; von Wallenstein selects works by Nietzsche when going to meet with Jahan. And von Wallenstein often stands before Jahan herself in the manner of the "blond-haired beast", whom she must destroy in order to avenge all the evil he has caused.

Rihani has von Wallenstein candidly express thoughts and ideas of a Nietzschean persuasion. Here, for example, are the general's reflections on sensing that Jahan will not submit to him:

> "Is it really so that my greatness is exterior, affected and transient?", he asked himself. "Is there really not within it something of absolute will, primordial, that turns on its own axis? ... Surely the power of an individual, his ability to subordinate others to himself, manifests only in ruling over the fates of other people, in his capacity to turn them into slaves? Surely she does not also have powers over human abilities and souls?"[116]

It is no coincidence that the author makes von Wallenstein a follower of Nietzsche's philosophy, since at that time this theory enjoyed a certain popularity in the East. Many from among the Arab intelligentsia supposed that the problems of their country were due to a lack of engagement and single-mindedness in the people. However, Rihani does not recognise Nietzsche's thought in any of its aspects, and the story presents Nietzschean theory squarely in its primary idea – the power of the strong over the weak – with all its inhumanity and brutality.

To a certain extent, for Rihani, von Wallenstein represents Western military–industrial capital and the mercantilism of the bourgeois way of life, with its forfeiture of spirituality. And the image of Jahan, with her spirituality and aloofness from all that is petty or mercenary, to a certain degree opposes everything that von Wallenstein symbolises.

The Romantic structure of the plot concludes with the most Romantic of finales: at a rendezvous with von Wallenstein, Jahan kills him, and then ends her own life. It should be noted, however, that when *Jahan* was republished in 1933 Rihani had altered the ending. Jahan saves herself and moves far from Istanbul, devotes herself to journalism and raises the son she bore from her dead lover–enemy. This alteration was significant. The new ending to a certain degree reduced the exclusivity and exceptional nature of the heroine, bringing her fate closer to those of ordinary people and making her portrayal more realistic. The change was motivated by various elements of the narrative. In fact the author is trying to link the extravagance and exclusivity of her character to the objective "circumstances" of her life. Her bravery, determination and confidence in the omnipotence of her charms and her special destiny, for example, were all to a certain degree motivated by the conditions of her life. For all of it was given to her in the highest degree: exceptional beauty, the highest position in her family and society, and brilliant upbringing and education.

One may consider the most important objective "circumstance" to be the fact that Jahan, a Muslim, obliged to wear the veil, who was brought up in Europe "in the hands of a French governess", gained knowledge of European languages and a fine education that notably included an acquaintance with Nietzsche's philosophy. Yet this singular individual was required to live among "brutal customs and traditions"! This is the cause of her internal split between love of her country and protest against its backwardness and savagery: "This legacy of her forebears conflicted with her brave efforts and broke the logic of understanding dictated by a European education."[117]

Dolinina considers it no coincidence that of all the Oriental nationalities, Rihani selected a Turkish woman for his champion of women's rights. This reflects the reality of the time, since Turkish women did then enjoy the most favourable conditions among all the Islamic nations.[118]

An attempt to reflect the fullness of life and to address the most pressing issues of the time are characteristic of Romanticism. In making freedom the principal theme of the story, Rihani does not deviate from this tendency. The concept of freedom unites the idea of the free individual with freedom from the colonial yoke. But Rihani describes the period of the story with greater accuracy than is common for Romantic artists: the second decade of the twentieth century, the First World War, when Turkey was occupied by Germany and leading Turkish figures were engaged in a struggle against the foreign ruler.

A further Romantic element of *Jahan* is an intense lyricism, normally found mainly in poetry, with its free expression of a lyrical authorial element. For the Romantic, the objectively existing world is less important than the inner life and the revealing of the inimitable "I". In the story this takes the form of frequent lyrical interludes by the author, who comments on both the actions of the heroine and her inner experiences. Everything that affects the heroine arouses ardent involvement, overt admiration and sympathy in the author. Even Jahan's innermost spiritual experience is communicated through what is primarily the author's own "voice":

> She was concerned with the problems of the spirit – those longings that she had pledged to bring to fulfilment for her own sake and for that of her country ... [The] longings that stood before her again on that bright morning with the clarity of a divine revelation. Her thoughts soared with ease to the cloudless heights of the spirit.[119]

Rihani is almost always enraptured by his heroine: "Jahan stood, her head bowed joyfully before the eternal face of the sun ... She was herself like the sun that played on the domes of Istanbul: the same light illuminated her heart."[120] Sometimes the author's comments about the image of the heroine rise to the tone of Romantic political journalism, with its high style and emotive agitation:

> May the day be blessed that aroused the mind and soul of the Eastern woman, the dawn whose light filled her heart: that heart of the whole nation that is now being revived! Is this not a herald of victory for her sisters who yearn for freedom and light, and her brothers who now defend their belief and their fatherland?[121]

Some of the author's digressions are concerned with abstract subjects that have only a peripheral bearing on the plot. For example, he turns abruptly to the thought that has occurred to Jahan on the relationship between men and women: "O, how whimsical are women! Unsteady and inconstant, always new, they are the same reality as the heart that beats in her heart or the mouth with which she speaks; they are like the flowers by the side of the road that flourish in the dawn and then wilt in the heat of noontide."[122]

The lyrical quality of the story is heightened by the way in which the heroine is portrayed, so that what is most important is not specific detail but rather a certain general idea of her exclusiveness and uniqueness:

> But her eyes ... it seemed that they drank in the whole depth of the azure southern sky; in the lustre of her golden hair that fell over her bare shoulders could be seen the reflected light of the sunset ... Anybody fortunate enough to have seen her at that moment would have been convinced that they had seen a goddess.[123]

Not only does Rihani describe her appearance, which is striking in its spirituality, but he also details her unusual clothing:

> Then she put on a loose, translucent dress in green, the hem of which trailed lightly on the floor ... Over the dress she put on a light green mantle embroidered in gold, and bound it tight with a wide sash ... The shoes she chose were of the same delicate green silk as the mantle and also embroidered in gold. Above them gleamed gold bangles subtly encrusted with precious stones.
>
> In her dress Jahan was like a fairytale Oriental princess. No; rather, she was like a houri descended from paradise to the earth.[124]

Many of the landscapes in the story are also lyrically Romantic and resonate with the mood of the heroine. Thus, after her quarrel with her father
Jahan looks out her window at the view that unfolds before her:

> In the distance, in the bay of the Golden Horn, the waves were slightly ruffled
> and like silvery spiders' webs stretched between the sombre shores. The moon,
> breaking through the thin clouds for a moment, threw its soft light onto the
> minaret of the Eyüp Sultan mosque; the black silhouettes of cypress trees in
> the cemetery beside it seemed like clusters of mysterious darkness akin to that
> which stifles the light of hope.[125]

However, next morning Jahan perceives the same landscape entirely differently, when her soul has recovered its hope:

> In the rays of the sun the domes of Eyüp Sultan dazzled with their brightness. A
> little further away the cypresses had lost their formless night-time guise and now
> bowed to one side with the gusts of the morning breeze; the sight was cheering to
> behold and [Jahan] could breathe happily and easily. The pale blue waves of the
> bay dissolved into a rippling silvery haze, pierced with golden threads of light.[126]

The Romanticism of *Jahan* is evident not only in the emotively portrayed
love of freedom and social protest, the immersion in the inner life of the
heroine, and Jahan's exceptional nature, loftiness and elation, but also in
the principle by which the plot unfolds, whereby the entire chain of events
and all situational conflicts are concentrated solely on the heroine; all else
is mere background, serving only to highlight her specialness and lack of
similarity to other people.

The Romantic nature of the work is also clearly to be seen in a certain
lyrical element that pervades it. Apart from the lyrical digressions and
romanticised sociopolitical discourses already mentioned, Rihani's heroine
is constructed for the most part not from her actions and deeds but rather
"by the author", on the basis of his views and his attitude to what takes
place. Also, this lyrically subjective and descriptive portrait-like building
of her character and the landscape in both cases actively helps to reveal the
heroine's inner world and experiences.

The very style of the story is also Romantic: elevated, agitated and deeply
emotional: "Freedom! This your name shines like gold in the dark heavens,
it is inscribed in blood in the abyss of darkness ... it sparkles in the mirror
of human souls ... Freedom! Be the clothes for mourning, the warriors in
armour, the victors in purple."[127] And similarly: "May the day be blessed
that aroused the mind and soul of the Eastern woman, the dawn whose light
filled her heart: that heart of the whole nation that is now being revived!"[128]
Mysterious and strange images are piled together:

> Monstrous phantoms flashed past her eyes, each more awful than the previous
> ... and now a powerful arm – she could not tell whether it was a man's or that
> of a devil or of an angel – seized her and dragged her to the spectral gates of

happiness ... A werewolf, a huge insensate beast, bared its fangs, its eyes burned in the darkness and its claws gleamed in the moonlight.[129]

The story contains many typically Romantic similes: "Her feet in their green shoes were like the petals of a river lily, filled with the fresh breath of life; her pale face, framed by her golden tresses, resembled in its colour the silver surface of the sea",[130] and there are frequent extended metaphors: "For the soul is like a turbulent river; when the winter wind becomes too severe, the river suddenly stops in its tracks, ceases to flow and turns to ice.[131]

Jahan is evidence that by now Rihani had mastered many of the accomplishments of Romanticism, and the work also demonstrates the author's interest in real, everyday life, which "is proved in all his subsequent work, in which the Romantic tendencies gradually fade, while more and more space is given to documentary prose".[132]

Ameen Rihani always felt himself to be, as well as a writer, a fighter for patriotism. This explains his natural affinity with political journalism. At certain periods in his life journalism predominated over artistic creativity. This fact is also recognised by Naimy in his article "Rihani in the world of poetry": "His journalism is stronger than his prose and poetry, for in him the conceptual prevails over feeling and logic dominates over fantasy".[133] Thus it would seem no coincidence that Rihani's path to Romanticism was not by way of Sentimentalism, as with Gibran, but rather via Enlightenment Realism.

Rihani's short stories, pamphlets, essays and sketches are all filled with journalistic pathos. Their figurative artistic elements are closely interwoven with straight journalistic writing. Moreover, of all his creative writings only *Jahan* can be considered a purely artistic work, with a developed and finished plot. In other cases the writer begins his work in the manner of a storyteller but almost always finishes it as a journalist. A typical example of this is the story "When Hell seems like Paradise".[134] This brief piece conveys directly the author's perceptions, based on feeling rather than speculation, of the essence of the capitalist city with its acute social dissonances. The story begins as an artistic work, describing the room in which a worker's family lives: "A small, bare room ... cold and dark ... the walls were lit only by the feeble illumination of a candle and reflected lights from the street. The hearth was empty, and the wind, entering through the chimney, howled in it."[135]

The story begins at once: the family is waiting for the return of the husband and father from the factory, who will bring coal for heating and cooking. The man arrives empty-handed. He explains to his wife about the situation in the town, where the miners are on strike. This account also forms part of the content of the work. However, the objective narration is frequently interrupted by journalistic digressions by the author, in which he expresses his concern at such a state of affairs, where people go hungry and children die of cold. The story culminates in the death of their child:

The mother rushed over to him, felt his pulse and, biting her lip, called her husband and son to her. Wrapping the child hurriedly in a blanket, she took him in her arms and began kissing him feverishly. But the child was cold, like ice, and as unmoving as the iron of his bed-frame. Neither a blanket nor his mother's warm kisses could return his life to him.[136]

The story-sketch "Over New York's Roofs"[137] is written in something of a similar vein. In it the author invites the reader to look down on the buildings of New York from the top of a skyscraper. Again a rudimentary plot is interrupted by a stream of journalistic utterances by the author, in which, using romantically generalised, symbolised sketches he speaks of the sharp polarisation of the people into rich and poor, into oppressors and oppressed: a small handful of people live in clean and spacious houses, in luxury and leisure, but the majority return every day, following long and exhausting work in mines and pits, to cold and dark slums. Each day, "With the coal there burn also the souls of those men and children who mine in a dreadful darkness".[138] This description has much in common with an extract from a work entitled "New York":

> Your iron womb is barren, your wooden breast is eaten away
> by worms,
> On your copper forehead is a green bloom of oxide and your
> marble mouth has set hard with cold beauty.
> Woe to your sons, woe to those who worship you.
> Woe to you! In your markets, your amusement houses, your banks
> and churches and in your voice is the clanging of gold ...
> Your storehouses hold the world's bounty, your safes are filled with
> treasure,
> Your mansion-houses are the miracle of civilisation ... but your
> shanties are full of destitution and groaning.[139]

The writer comes to a journalistic conclusion: that a society in which there is injustice and deprivation of rights must necessarily undergo social change: "A social system based solely on the disastrous state of its members is a society of injustice and deception. It is so unfit as to need reform, alteration and improvement."[140] Here, as on several previous occasions, Rihani expresses the utopian hope that the solution will take the form of reforms and improvements in moral standards.

Despite the fact that Rihani spent long periods of his life in America, he kept his homeland constantly in mind and always considered himself a son of the Lebanese people and of the whole Arab nation: "I am a Lebanese Arab and want the Americans to know that yesterday, today and tomorrow I was and will remain the son of only one nation. That nation is the Arab people."[141]

An émigré and a wanderer, Rihani loved his long-suffering and humiliated homeland deeply and to an unhealthy degree; he passionately dreamt of seeing it liberated from oppression and slavery, enlightened and blossoming, and fought for its revival in every way he could. Krachkovsky writes: "His homeland – the Lebanon – took first place in all his dreams ... wherever he was, his longings were directed towards the Lebanon."[142]

Rihani created many tales and sketches about life in Lebanon, and specifically of Beirut and its surroundings. In these he clearly and concisely exposes the typical aspects of life for the people of Lebanon ("The cross, or a day in Beirut", "The lofty palace", "From a description of Beirut" and several others). For the author, Beirut represented the homeland, i.e. the Lebanon, as a whole.

Particularly characteristic of Rihani's Beirut sketches is a type of Romantic portrayal in which separate, generalised pictures, filled with specific real detail, build up the everyday life of the city in both its quiet and busy moments.

The fantasy sketch "The Cross, or a Day in Beirut"[143] gives an account of the suffering of the Lebanese, their terrible hunger and the outrages inflicted on them by the Ottoman powers during the First World War. The story is told in the first person, with the narrator witnessing directly all that takes place. He is shocked by what he sees and does not recognise the city of his birth, and nor does anybody recognise him: it is not people that wander in the streets but shadows, afraid to stop and speak; about him lie the corpses of those who have starved, and gallows stand in the squares. Wherever the hero knocks, the door is not opened to him; whoever he asks after is no longer among the living.

> I do not doubt that I am in the city of my birth, but my people – where are my people? Are these really wealthy people who rave in these rags, the people from whom not long ago I took my leave as I departed? Is this really all that remains of those proud, noble and good people? ... are these exhausted and emaciated ghosts those same strong men who used to trade, were involved in education, who wrestled with each other and lived full and happy lives?[144]

The author's shock spills over into his agitated, interrupted speech, full of exclamations and rhetorical questions. It contains pain, grief, despair, horror and indignation:

> O Allah! Who are these skeletons, these ghosts? I saw how they walk, as if their feet were in chains ... And these are the inhabitants of my favourite city, to which I gave a part of my soul! ... Where are my friends? Where are my brothers? Where are they who only yesterday were the best people of this city, the light of our people?[145]

He turns to God: "Forgive, O Lord! I have lost faith in You and deny Your divine disposition and blaspheme against Your name!",[146] and appeals to the people: "My brothers! I looked for you today in the city, but I was brought to you by the dark night, joined by the stars of heaven."[147] At the end of the story, however, Rihani expresses hope that a better future is in store for his people: "My nation is immortal; it will not die so long as there is even a glimmer of hope in its heart. It will not die while its sons become martyrs and die for truth, homeland and freedom!"[148]

The mood of the story is typically a confluence of Realism with the illusory and fantastic. Reality here appears in naturalistic details, and through these the author picks out the realities of Lebanese life all the more sharply:

> Here was a boy, sprawled on the pavement. Hunger had brought him to the ground. When I saw him, I thought that he was dead. Nearby a dog was chewing on a bone. The boy noticed it and crawled towards it on his belly. Reaching the dog, he pulled the bone from its mouth, ignoring its yelp. Then he quickly crawled back, looking about him startled, as though fearing that somebody would take his bounty from him.[149]

"From a Description of Beirut"[150] contains no dramatic scenes or images of violence; its mood is rather elated and exalted. The style of the essay is thickly Romantic. The author aims to recreate the image of Beirut, but does not resort to description. He creates a certain Romantic metaphor for the city on the basis of contrasts. On the one hand, Beirut is the "mother of cities", "the sister of Jerusalem" and "the pearl of the East", while on the other she is the "maidservant of Paris", "a pearl in dirt and dust", "a coral on the beach, where gold is mixed with sand and silver with mud", and so on.

These metaphors characterise all aspects of the city's life, both material and spiritual, its relationship to the West and the state of its cultural development: "Beirut is the pearl of the East, in the copper bezel of the West ... the youth of freedom – and its age ... Beirut is the rostrum of the constitution and its gibbet ... the beauty of order ... [is] noisy anarchy".[151]

The author also uses metaphor to evaluate the role played by Beirut in the transmitting of civilisation from the West to the East: "It is a moon that reflects the light of the West and illuminates the East ... it is a field with good earth in which Europe sows her wheat and her weeds, her roses and her wormwood".[152] Here Rihani emphasises that it is not only the achievements of science and civilisation that are coming from the West to the East, but also its "weeds", that is to say, its shortcomings. At the same time, however, Rihani bitterly comments on the intellectual void of Beirut – the inertness of the intelligentsia, the weak development of literature and the absence of political life: "Dirt, sewage and dust on the streets of Beirut ... and in its literature, and in its politics, and in its religion!"[153]

The style of the essay is not only Romantic; it also reflects the Romantic outlook of the author: the hope of a great future, which will be the result of moral perfection and the correction of man and society under the influence of ethical ideas. The author supposes that this process will be served by "true child-rearing" and "true education", together with progress, patriotism and justice. He writes: "When these virtues become established in the shepherds and the flocks, and in the princes and the people, then the streets of the city will be brought into good repair and the ways of literature, religion and politics will be reformed. Improve life, and power is improved; improve life, and the city is improved."[154]

"The Lofty Palace"[155] is written in a style that is new for Rihani. This work differs from previous stories in having a more exposed plot, in its originality and in its marked ending. The story runs as follows. The author is walking through a valley filled with flowers and vineyards towards Sofar, a suburb of Beirut. He wants to visit the casino and roulette that are situated in the "Lofty Palace", the meeting point for Lebanon's aristocracy and the pride of Sofar. In his modest and dust-covered clothing, the author is not admitted into the building. After much effort, however, and now suitably dressed, he succeeds in entering the restaurant and sees the elite at play. The author checks into the hotel for the night, and in the morning wishes to take a bath. But this proves impossible: the bathroom of the "Lofty Palace", the most luxurious hotel in all Beirut, is out of order. Rihani ironically juxtaposes the pointedly European style of the society dress, the ladies in their décolletée Parisian dress, the ballroom dances, the trained footmen, and the haughtiness and arrogance of the visitors, with the lack of that elementary and essential accessory of a civilised institution – a bathroom.

What is new in this story is a Romantic irony in the contrast of what should be and what in fact is. The constant champion and advocate of the importing of the best achievements of Western civilisation – its culture, technology, science and art – now sees that all this is the wondrous preserve of the privileged society that is to be found at the "Lofty Palace". Thus even the name of the building is given a degree of irony. In Dmitriev's view Romantic irony is the same as Romantic grotesque, being one of the "characteristic stylistic devices of many Romantics, one of the features of their artistic manner".[156]

The beginning of the story is journalistic in style and full of sharp contrasts. It opens with the image of a beautiful valley with vineyards, "whose cheerful greenery concealed the heavy bunches of grapes", and eulogises the hard-working hands that have cultivated the vines. The modest dwellings of the labourers and a small church give the narrator feelings of conciliation and admiration. Yet all this beauty and splendour is in the power of the Jesuits: "We are in the abode, dear reader, the abode of the Jesuit Fathers, in which the law of worldly life, which gives rise to surprise, sorrow and grief, dominates over all."[157]

The author goes on to discuss the hypocrisy, greed and duplicity of the official Church, which preaches one thing while seeking something entirely different: "Be industrious, perfect your labour and strengthen the bonds of solidarity ... be obedient, and you will gain this world and the other! In secret, be who you wish – ... but be dutiful, assiduous, zealous and patient."[158]

Rihani employs themes in "The Lofty Palace" that are characteristic of the Syro-American School: the critique of clerics who distort the true face of religion, and the desire to change life in the homeland for the better with the aid of Western cultural achievements.

Rihani's travel writing occupies a particular place in his prose works and is characterised by his descriptions of everyday life. Let us note that "the Romantics cultivated the everyday-life sketch, which became the middle link between the Enlightenment essay and the 'physiologists', in which elements of realist analysis had already accumulated".[159]

Typical features and details of everyday life are widely included in the fabric of Rihani's tales of his travels. These are particularly concentrated in his depiction of the outward appearance of people – their clothes and manners of behaviour:

> So let us examine the dress of the people of Baghdad ... We will start with the head, or rather with the attire of the head that adorns it: the turban or *sidar* ... The first type of *uqal* that attracts the attention is the large *uqal* that is braided from brown or coffee-coloured wool ... They wear the *uqal* above a dark blue or red headscarf ... From the head let us move down to the body and talk about the *aba* that covers it from above. It may be black with gold, silver or black stitching ... A black *aba* with gold or silver stitching is made in Baghdad from European cloth.[160]

And so on. He also creates picturesque, realistic descriptions of individual streets, alleys, Islamic buildings and domestic animals:

> The mule has a stiff neck and obeys neither the bridle that the rider frequently has to use instead of the knout, nor even the pebbles in the driver's hand. The mule's eyes flare up and break out in red flame at the slightest of provocations. His ears remain alert, as though warning that the mules are about to rebel, and the hoofs obey, with lightning speed, the orders of the eyes and ears; the mule starts to kick with its hind legs, even if there is nothing and nobody behind him. Then he stops in the middle of the road and begins to turn about himself. After this he gallops, until this fit of madness hits upon the first tree or bench to find itself in his path.[161]

Such everyday details and sketches cannot, however, be considered to be Realism. In Rihani's stories of travel they harmonise easily with Romantic style and cohabit on equal terms with the Romantic colouring of the works. For this is the reality of life, whose depiction is innate to both Romanticism and Realism.

Ameen Rihani was a distinctive and original writer whose multifaceted output brought diversity to the range of genres, subject matter and poetics of Arab Romantic literature. His works were strongly pervaded by ideas intrinsic to Romanticism, such as a broad democratism, a pantheistic relationship to nature, a philosophical view of the world, the raising of moral questions, and a sharp critique of bourgeois civilisation. Many of the aesthetic and philosophical positions of the Western Romantics, and in particular of the Transcendentalists, met at a deep level with both the spiritual disposition of Rihani himself and the social questions with which he grappled in his works.

Rihani the Romantic is above all the son of his people and his time, and indissolubly linked to his nation and to Arab reality. Accordingly, in his works Romanticism gains a national character. The originality of Rihani's Romanticism as an Arab writer was also reflected in the particular character of his journalism, which contained vividly expressed artistic traits.

Rihani's artistic output proved a notable phenomenon in the development of the new Arabic literature. His literary legacy not only added depth to the Romantic method but also endowed the next generation of Arab writers with the perceptions and highest attainments of Western Romanticism, which he had thoroughly assimilated.

Chapter 4

Mikhail Naimy and nineteenth-century Russian literature

Introduction

Mikhail Naimy (1889–1988) is one of the most highly reputed of the classic authors in Arabic literature.[1] He was a most progressive, sensitive and gifted son of the Arab intelligentsia who, with immense energy and staggering dedication, joined in the process of creating a new national life, yet in doing so did not forget the uniqueness and wealth of their historical past: humanism, a constant search for truth, moral purity and justice.

Naimy's creative output took a wide range of forms. He was the author of a number of stories and novels (*Memoirs of a Vagrant Soul, Till We Meet, The Book of Mirdad*), plays (*Fathers and Sons, Job*), short story collections (*Once Upon a Time, Grandees, The Man with the Fat Calf*), literary–critical articles (*The Sieve, Press Interviews*), poetry (*Eyelid Whisperings*), aphorisms (*A Vineyard by the Road*), social and political essays (*Beyond Moscow and Washington*) and memoirs (*Seventy*). Many of his articles on social, literary and philosophical topics are also gathered in the collections *Food for the Godward Journey, Threshing Floors, The Idols, Light and Darkness, A Straw in the Wind, Pathways, Marginals* and others.

Mikhail Naimy's early life was linked with Russia, Russian culture and literature.[2] The Lebanese youth found his way to Poltava from his distant Arab homeland by way of the Russian missionary school in Baskinta and the teachers' seminary in Nazareth. In Poltava Naimy encountered the full wealth of classical Russian literature. "While at the seminary I quickly immersed myself in Russian literature", he writes in a biography he later presented to Krachkovsky. "In front of me a truly new world was opening up, full of wonders. I read voraciously. There was hardly a Russian writer, poet or philosopher whom I did not read exhaustively."[3]

The backwardness of Arabic literature in comparison to the Russian, and its isolation from people's real lives, was becoming increasingly evident to him: "The poverty of our literature and the ineptness of its writers, who interest themselves only in the exterior phenomena of the human soul, became increasingly clear to me. Before that time, I had envied some of our writers and poets and tried to imitate them. Now I dreamed of writing as the Russians write."[4] Naimy's period of study in Russia was therefore an important time for his moral and spiritual maturing. From Russia, however, he took not only his indelible impressions of Russian literature, but also the vital spirit of intense and active social and political life and struggle:

123

It is true that I am a guest and a stranger in Russia but, as my life has come to be a part of the life of the country to a great extent, I have come to feel that I am one of its sons, feeling the great pressure to which its people are exposed by the Emperor and his entourage, and the higher classes which cling desperately to their rights, disregarding their duties towards the people.[5]

For taking part in student demonstrations, Naimy was expelled from the seminary for a year. He based his poem "The Dead River" on his impressions of the revolutionary events of 1905; in this poem he compares Russia with a great river that is bound with ice.[6] After passing his final examinations at the Poltava seminary in 1911, Naimy returned to Lebanon.

For the rest of his life Naimy remembered his years in Russia with great gratitude and affection, and likewise the impression he gained from the best examples of classical Russian literature.

The literary stagnation to be found throughout the Arab-speaking world struck me with force when I left Russia. This had an oppressive effect on me and was painful in the extreme for somebody who had been brought up on the fine art of Pushkin, Lermontov and Turgenev, on the laughter-through-tears of Gogol, the captivating realism of Tolstoy, the literary ideals of Belinsky and finally, on the great humanity of the most powerful, deepest, fullest and most moving of all Russian writers, Dostoevsky.[7]

There thus formed, naturally and logically, a link between the Russian and Lebanese literatures, and Naimy's activities were a living example of contact between national literatures.

In this chapter we have set out to expose the influence of Russian literature on Naimy's work, without in any way negating the depth and originality of this talented writer. As Zhirmunsky says, "Comparison does not destroy the specificity (individual, national or historical) of the thing under consideration. On the contrary, it is only through comparison, that is to say through establishing similarity and difference, that it is possible to say in what this specificity consists."[8] In assimilating, or indeed for some reason rejecting one or another of the Russian classics, Naimy always remains an Arab writer; in all details he retains an Eastern flavour that colours the plot, compositional structure, style, imagery and the very character of the life being portrayed. All this is his and reflects national traditions. Given the degree of influence of Vissarion Grigor'evich Belinsky on all of Naimy's work, however, we have considered it necessary to begin this chapter with an analysis of that influence. Naimy's critical and theoretical essays, collected in his book *The Sieve*,[9] are persuasive evidence that he assimilated the principles of Belinsky's aesthetic conception. The fact that Naimy followed Belinsky's critical–aesthetic principles also naturally prefigured, to a certain degree, his interest in the artistic searches of other classical Russian writers.

The influence of Leo Tolstoy on Naimy's world-view pervaded all his work. From his youth Naimy had been particularly interested in moral questions, and found in Tolstoy values close to his own, that addressed his own artistic and aesthetic needs: the call to universal brotherhood and love, to spiritual freedom and to high moral standards. The main ideas in certain of Naimy's works (*Memoirs of a Vagrant Soul*,[10] *The Book of Mirdad*,[11] *The Last Day*[12] and others) are close to some of Tolstoy's social and political writing.*

The influence of Ivan Turgenev on Naimy's output can be seen in parallels between specific works, for example Naimy's play *Fathers and Sons* and Turgenev's novel of the same name. The Realist tendency started by Naimy in his *Fathers and Sons* continues in his early short stories, where the influence of Chekhov can also clearly be seen.

The aesthetics of Belinsky in Naimy's views as a critic

Naimy's critical judgements, which reflect his own literary and aesthetic conceptions, provide important material for understanding his own artistic works. Krachkovsky wrote: "A competent expert on Russian literature who was reared on its classic examples and who has thought through and keenly felt the ideas of Belinsky, he (Naimy) may justifiably be said to be one of the outstanding Arab critics of the present time."[13]

In the 1920s Ignaty Yulianovich Krachkovsky and Klaudia Viktorovna Ode-Vasil'eva (a Palestinian Arab who taught at the Palestinian Society in Nazareth and later at the Institute for Living Oriental Languages in Leningrad) had the idea of creating a reader on contemporary Arabic literature for students of the Oriental Studies Faculty, which would give a brief introduction to the authors. In their search for suitable material they came across an article by Naimy, who at the time was still an unknown critic. Reading the article, the Soviet Arabists "sensed great strength and courage". Krachkovsky remarked, "I was afraid to succumb to my first impression, yet there seemed to me somehow to be all the echoes of Russian critical thought [directed to] the little-known Arabic literature of that time. This impression gained in strength when a collection of his articles appeared in 1923 under the significant title *The Sieve*."[14] In the preface to Naimy's autobiography Krachkovsky remarked: "In his (Naimy's) works, particularly the critical essays, I was aware of traces of the influence of Russian literature, and in particular of Belinsky's school of criticism."[15] Referring to Naimy's statement that the true writer is "the fruit of the feelings and aspirations of

---

* The exchange of ideas and philosophy with Tolstoy was particularly characteristic of Naimy's mature and later periods. For this reason, the present monograph includes analyses of *The Book of Mirdad* (1948) and *The Last Day* (1963), written at a later stage in the development of Arabic literature and in fundamentally different conditions, outside of the Syro-American School and in the context of fervent literary development in the Arab lands. This fact once again proves that Naimy remained influenced by the Russian writer throughout his life and in all his works.

the nation", Dolinina specifically points to Belinsky's article "Literaturnie metania" ("Literary Castings").[16]

Naimy himself recognised that his education was based on Belinsky's literary ideals. "As for Belinsky", he writes, "who was, without doubt, the chief among Russian critics, he showed me the hearth of truthfulness, strength, kindness and beauty in literary activity, and the greatness of the role of the writer, so long as he fulfils it well towards himself, towards the life around him and towards his readers."[17]

Naimy became interested in Russian criticism while still a student at the Poltava seminary. As well as articles by Belinsky, he read the works of other critics and historians of Russian literature, notably Yevgeny Andreevich Solov'yov (1867–1905) and in particular his book *Opyt filosofii russkoy literatury* (*The Philosophical Outcome of Russian Literature*).[18] Russian literature and criticism helped Naimy to feel and understand more deeply the backwardness and stagnation that predominated in his own country. He wrote:

> This was a period of abundant literary harvest, a period in which my thinking came to the boil, a period for me of outbursts of feelings and spiritual growth. And this opened my eyes to the pettinesses with which my country occupied itself, as indeed did all the Arab countries, indeed the whole of the East – particularly in the realm of thought, art and literature.[19]

Under the direct influence of the best examples of classical Russian literature, Naimy's critical attitude towards Arabic literature grew sharper. He wrote in his memoirs:

> My first concern at the start of my literary activity was to declare constant war against hypocrisy in literature. I insisted that truth and sincerity in poetry and prose were more important than sonority of rhythm or the vividness of words and expressions. In my first published article I wrote: "Sincerity!! O if only we had but a little ... a mustard seed!"[20]

It was thus not a coincidence that Naimy's first published literary pieces were critical articles and reviews of works by Arab writers. Particularly noteworthy are his reviews of Gibran's story *Broken Wings*[21] and his collection of prose poems, *A Tear and a Smile*.[22] The émigré poet Nasib 'Arida (1887–1946) remarked in a letter to Naimy on the high professional standard and objectivity shown by the author in the article. At the end of the letter he added, addressing Naimy himself: "I would like to ask you a favour: Read more of the works of the Arab writers, from Yaziji up to our contemporaries. Maybe you will become for us what Belinsky is to the Russians and Sainte-Beuve is to the French."[23] The words of 'Arida proved to be prophetic, for Naimy became one of the first eminent and acknowledged critics of Arabic literature, who viewed artistic works in the context of their organic tie to real life, while also giving importance to the depth of conception of ideas, the form and the artistic language.

The influence of Belinsky can be clearly seen in the articles collected in Naimy's book *al-Ghirbal* (*The Sieve*), which may be considered the writer's aesthetic credo. The title of the book indicates its aim: to filter all the offerings of Arabic literature through the sieve of criticism. The words of Leo Tolstoy spring to mind: "In order to find gold in art it is necessary to collect a lot of material and sift it through the sieve of criticism."[24] It is difficult to say for certain whether Naimy was familiar with this statement by Tolstoy, but there is no doubt that he shared his views on criticism.

The first edition of *The Sieve* was published by the Cairo publishing house al-Matba'a al-'asriyya in 1923, while Naimy was still in New York. It contains all Naimy's articles and criticism, from 1913 to 1922, that had been published in the Arab émigré press, in particular in the magazine *al-Funun* and the newspaper *al-Sa'ih*. The preface[25] to the book was written by the renowned Arab philosopher, poet, prose writer and literary expert 'Abbas Mahmud al-'Aqqad (1889–1964). He speaks highly of Naimy's talent, and his ability to analyse in depth and objectively appraise works of literature, and comments that life was still difficult for those writers who followed the path of innovation and openly spoke out against traditions:

> Truly, I am astonished, in reading this book, at how close it is to that new literary world in which I live. I see a zealous pen that seeks true poetry ... I see that the author grieves on account of the threadbare state of our poetry, which has been left, as he says, without poetry. For poems have been written about practically every occasion of our lives, yet there are no poems that reflect our feelings and thoughts. In the poet Naimy wishes to see a prophet and not an acrobat, and in poetry inspiration and not trickery.[26]

Thus al-'Aqqad hears the echo of the words of Muhyiddin al-Rida, the literary historian and critic: "I knew that *The Sieve* would be received in Egypt like a thunderbolt and would whip up storms."[27]

The article "al-Gharbala" ("Sifting")[28] sets out the author's aims in *The Sieve*. Here Naimy declares his credo as a critic. He believes that "the main task of the literary critic is to distinguish the genuine from the imitation, the beautiful from the ugly and the true from the false".[29] This belief concurs with Belinsky's ideas: "And so, in my opinion, the first and most important question that faces the critic is: is this work really graceful, is this author truly a poet? It is from addressing this question that an answer emerges concerning the quality and importance of the work."[30] What qualities must the critic then have, who undertakes to distinguish the real from the imitation and the deformed from the beautiful? Naimy believes: "There exists only one general attribute, without which the critic cannot proceed. This is an innate capacity to assess the value of things. This quality subsists by its own laws and is not subject to any external rules. It devises certain criteria and measures of its own and does not conform to common criteria and measures."[31] And it was Belinsky who gave particular importance to a sense of aesthetics:

> A fine poetic sensibility and a deep capacity to receive impressions of grace –
> these are what constitute the first condition of the ability to criticise. It is by
> means of these that one can distinguish at first sight imitative from genuine
> inspiration, rhetorical mannerisms from the expression of feeling and fancy
> exercises in form from the breath of aesthetic life.[32]

In line with Belinsky, Naimy does not recognise any fixed or established
standard for beauty.

The task of the critic is to develop taste, and "he penetrates into the
storehouse of the poet's soul and reveals its secrets".[33] By this means the true
critic becomes an educator and mentor to society. Belinsky wrote about this
enlightening mission of the critic thus: "The goal of the Russian critic must
consist not only in widening the range of human understandings of what
is beautiful, but also in spreading within his country the already existing,
settled conceptions on this matter."[34]

Discussing the manner in which works are assessed in Arab criticism,
Naimy remarks that it tends to be arbitrary, momentary and subjective, with
the emphasis on the detail ("al-Maqayis al-adabiyya" ("Literary Criteria")).
At the same time, as a rule, the work as a whole falls out of the critic's field
of vision. "Our problem is not that we do not have criteria. It is that there is
nobody who will occupy himself with their application in literary practice.
Unfortunately for us, the greater part of our literary activity is left to the
newspapers and magazines."[35] Here he cites, with irony, some of the evalu-
ations that the latter give: "a work of genius", "outstanding", "brilliant",
"exceptional" and so on, and states that such "criticism" is disorientating for
the reader and spoils his taste.

In his article "Mihwar al-adab" ("The Crux of Literature")[36] Naimy
argues that the fundamental object of portrayal in literature is the human.

> The most rational and marvellous of all living things ... is the most enigmatic
> of puzzles. From the very moment when he first became conscious of himself,
> right up to the present day, the human being has remained in a constant strug-
> gle with nature ... His spiritual powers are inexhaustible. These are powers that
> place the human above the animal world, that illuminate a path through the
> darkness of existence, that cultivate love within life, which ignite in us a spark
> of hope ... and lead towards the unknown.[37]

The theme of the human as the crown of creation occurs in a series
of other works by Naimy. For example, in the article "Nahnu ahsa, aw
aba'una?" ("Are we Better, or our Fathers?") he writes: "Man, in my view,
is a drop of the divine, containing all powers, all knowledge and all his
descendants. The possibilities for the development of the human self are
unlimited."[38] Naimy holds the deep conviction that the interior world of
man, his feelings, thoughts, life and struggles, his social structure and his
mastery of the powers of nature and so forth are all fertile ground for literary creation. It was precisely this conception of the object of literature that

Belinsky introduced and developed in his critical works: "There is not, for art, a more rewarding and elevated subject than mankind."[39] Not only does literature recreate the experience of life and reproduce life as it is, but it also sifts out much that is irrelevant or, in Naimy's words, "separates the ore from the rock". And it is only he who expresses the thoughts and aspirations of the many, and in whose emotions and experiences the feelings and aspirations of a whole generation are objectively reflected, who may be considered a great artist. "Only those monuments are eternal in which there lives an eternal spirit ..., where human feelings are expressed in the voice of the poet that have not previously been expressed ..., where he reveals in himself what was previously hidden to him and hears that which he was previously unable to hear."[40] These words of Naimy resonate with the oft-cited ideas of Belinsky about the deep interrelationship between the poet and humanity:

> A great poet, when speaking about himself, about his "I", is in fact speaking of the generality, of humanity, because his nature contains everything by which humanity lives. Thus, in his sadness anybody will recognise their own sadness; in his soul anyone will recognise their own, and will see in it *not only the poet but also the man*, his brother in humanity.[41]

Naimy remarks in his theoretical article "al-Maqayis al-adabiyya"[42] that certain of the spiritual values possessed by literature are eternal, not subject to the destructive influence of time or to changing fashions. These are above all the "sphere of the emotions" – such as "hope and despair, triumph and failure, belief and doubt, love and hate, pleasure and pain, sadness and joy and fear and courage."[43] Without doubt, the artistic power of the work depends on the extent to which it satisfies "the requirements of being guided by life".[44] Naimy calls this quality "the light of truth", which literature carries in itself. Finally, the aspiration to beauty is another objective criterion of permanent importance for an artistic work. And naturally the giftedness of the artist is expressed above all in the degree to which he masters the inexhaustible treasury of human speech. Naimy also expects clarity of exposition, good compositional structure and, in poetry, a clear rhythmic system. The ideas expressed in this article by Naimy recur constantly in many works by Belinsky. Belinsky defines the reflection of reality in literature as "the perfect truth of life".[45]

The essence of poetry is discussed in Naimy's article "al-Sha'ir wa al-Shi'r" ("The Poet and Poetry"),[46] in which the critical aims of Belinsky are tangible. Naimy considers poetry to be an inherent human need:

> Poetry has been there with man in all times. From the moment of his appearance in the world it stands beside his cradle and accompanies him in work and rest, in grief and joy, in war and peace and in times of prosperity and in the hour of need. The tailor's needle, the blacksmith's hammer, the bricklayer's plumbline, the sickle of the reaper and the plough of the ploughman – all these are familiar with poetry.[47]

How often, when trying to express our feelings and state, we turn to the works of the great poets, for there we find "the story of life with lively images and an explanation of our feelings and emotions, that which we are not capable of expressing in our own words".[48] This is what Naimy considers to be true poetry, the essence of which, in Belinsky's words, is such that "it gives a bodiless idea a living, sensory and beautiful image",[49] or "expresses the subjective side of man and opens our vision to the *interior* man, and that is why all of it is sense, feeling and music".[50]

Naimy's conclusions about the essence of poetry are natural and profound. "Poetry will always be one of the spiritual necessities of man, since it allows his dreams of beauty, justice, truth and happiness to come true. Poetry creates a picture of life that is understandable to the soul, an understanding that does not require sound or vision. It stands hand in hand with man."[51] He is concerned that Arabic literature has "too many versifiers but very few poets".[52] The main reason for this situation, as Naimy sees it, is that many literary men are still not aware of what constitutes true poetry, which for him is "life itself, that weeps and laughs, that is noisy and silent, that groans and rejoices, that transforms and creates".[53]

So what does an artistic work represent as a form of creation? Is it imagination or fantasy or is it in fact an accurate portrayal of reality?

> You have never created a hill, a forest, a sea, the sun, the sky or a stream. All this you have seen with your own eyes and felt keenly. Yet at the same time you correlated it all, appraised it, discarded what was superfluous and selected what was necessary; then you composed all that you had selected in a way determined by you, and the result was a picture painted in your imagination. You did not alter reality; you did not "create" anything; but rather you took real existing objects and phenomena of nature, discarded the superfluous, increased the necessary and arranged everything in a way that was pleasing to your soul.[54]

Again, this statement by Naimy, on the relationship between existing reality and what is transformed into an image in an artistic work, is in agreement with Belinsky's aesthetic conceptions:

> There is much of beauty in living reality ..., but in order to enjoy this reality, we must first possess it in our understanding ... a landscape created on the canvas of a talented artist is better than any picturesque view in nature. But why is this? – Because it contains nothing by chance and nothing superfluous; all its parts are subordinated to the whole and are all directed towards a single aim, and together form something beautiful, complete and individual, completely and individually. Reality is of course itself beautiful, but it is beautiful by its essence, by its elements and by its content, and not by its form.[55]

Discussing the aim of poetry in his article "al-Sha'ir wa al-Shi'r" ("The Poet and Poetry"), Naimy rejects the idea of art for art's sake and that of the utilitarianism of poetry. In his view, art is intended to answer to the highest spiritual questions: "The poet is a prophet, philosopher, artist, musician and preacher. A prophet, because he sees with his soul what is hidden from others. An artist, because he can embody what he sees and hears of beauty in the forms of words. A musician, because he hears a harmony of sounds where others hear only noise and clatter."[56] He then adds a further definition: "A preacher, because he serves the divine in the form of truth and beauty."[57] It is difficult not to notice that what he says here about what is required of a poet overlaps with Gibran's Romantic conceptions.

The discussion of Arabic poetry continues in the article "al-Hubahib" ("The Firefly"),[58] which is a kind of summary review, broadly similar to the surveys offered by Belinsky to the Russian public. Here we see at once that Naimy severely and even mercilessly criticised Arabic poetry: "Can we reproach our young writers if every day they "treat" us to *qasida*s written "to a formula" or articles that outlive their predecessors?"[59] All of these up to now have been written "for an occasion" and do not depart by a single step from the antiquated canons of panegyrical *qasida*. According to Naimy, in the past a true poet could not give free rein to his talent, but always had to write with an eye to the canon. And for this reason, now even skilled poets are like "sad fireflies that cannot light up the darkness of night." "You must understand, people, the trouble is not that we have a lot of pieces of glass, but rather that we call them diamonds and value them accordingly."[60] Naimy believes that this is because the Arabs are submerged in hibernation and have not yet felt "the beating pulse of the rest of humanity."[61] This sorry picture causes Naimy complete despair, and he declares that in neither the past nor the present could any Arab be named alongside Homer, Virgil, Dante, Shakespeare, Milton, Byron or Tolstoy, completely forgetting the real achievements of Arabic literature. "Our writers lived and died singing the praises of steppe gazelles and the greatness of the elite."[62] In his view, the low standard of contemporary Arabic literature corresponds to the low standard of contemporary criticism. Many critics evade the truth by means of "patriotic" phrases such as "Our country is the cradle of inspiration and humanity and the homeland of the prophets." The sin of remaining silent about the true state of Arabic literature remains on the conscience of the critics. Naimy writes bitterly: "Centuries passed, and still we knock our foreheads on the threshold of churches ... a thick layer of rust has covered our hearts and minds."[63]

Another important cause of the backwardness of Arabic literature is seen by Naimy as a failure to understand the essence of literary language. While ardent in the preservation of its purity and beauty, he is critical of the obsolete dictionaries that have become desk books for many writers, particularly the poets, who take from them archaic words that are no longer understood by their contemporaries. Naimy compares such dictionaries to an old house, "whose inhabitants refuse to change their decor even slightly". He protests against superfluous artistic contrivance in literary language and a lack of taste that can be seen even in the established poets. Naimy believes that observing lexical and structural conventions was not the ultimate criterion for the

continuity of literary traditions. He quotes some lines and verses from contemporary *qasida*s and demonstrates their inner emptiness and their lack of
profundity or true feeling. He ends by calling on poets to renounce archaism
and look more courageously into the face of life, and repeats an optimistic
adage: "Do not despair: after the black clouds the sun will reappear."[64]

Naimy believes that when language no longer evolves, it loses contact
with the historical advance of its people; it becomes stagnant, lifeless, and
ceases to develop.

> Along with the development of humanity came the development of its speech.
> But today's humanity is different from the people who lived centuries ago.
> Likewise, today's languages differ from those that existed before. The secret
> of the mutability in human speech is not in language but in people themselves
> ... it was the developments of humanity that predetermined the changes in its
> language, and not the other way round.[65]

Attaching the greatest importance to the language of artistic works,
Naimy believes that many classics of Arabic literature would not have been
preserved in the memories of his countrymen if their authors had remained
mere imitators and had not moved away from the linguistic canon of their
predecessors. He wrote:

> Had he (al-Mutanabbi) written his poems in the same language as that which
> the writers of *al-Mu'allaqat* used, he would hardly have been noticed in our lan-
> guage, rather than being a living force. This applies to Abu al-'Ala [al-Ma'arri]
> too: if had he written *Ghayru mujdin* in the same language in which he wrote
> his *Epistles*, we would not have had that great poem. If the Andalusian poets
> had tried to compete with the pre-Islamic and *mukhadram* poets, we would not
> have had the *muwashshahat* of Andalusia.[66]

Adherents of tradition, whom Naimy calls "literary frogs" in a stagnant literary swamp, do not see and do not accept as an objective fact the
change in the contemporary Arabic language that is occurring alongside
the changes in contemporary life. "The language with which we understand each other today in our periodicals and papers and which we use in
our speeches, is different from the language of Mudar, Himyar, Tamim and
Quraysh" ("The Croaking of the Frogs").[67] There is nothing new in this,
he goes on to say, for the process of change and development has been influencing our language all through the ages. Naimy stresses a tendency in
Arabic criticism to pay attention not to what is said so much as to the way it
is said. Analysing one or another contemporary work, some critics diligently
seek out those places where the author has sinned against old dictionaries
and grammatical rules. An example of this is the reasoning of an Egyptian
critic on the *qasida* by Gibran entitled *al-Mawakib*.[68] Analysing the verse: *Hal
tahammamta bi 'itrin; Wa tanashshafta bi nurin*[69] (Did you bathe in perfume,
did you dry yourself with light), the critic picks on the use of the fifth form
of the verb *hamma* ("to be hot", "to bathe", "to take a bath", "to heat", etc.)

within the given context. The critic raises the poet's impudent handling of the meaning of the word almost to the level of a crime. His motivation is that the fifth form of the root *hamma* has not been established by Arab lexicographers for this meaning, and that by tradition Gibran should have used, for his intended meaning, the tenth form of the verb, i.e. *istahamma*. Naimy wittily mocks this linguistic purism: "I ask you, gentlemen ... why is it that some obscure Bedouin is allowed to introduce the word *istahamma* into our language, but a poet well known to you and me may not use the word *tahammama*? Especially as you know the intention, you understand the meaning of this word."[70]

Naimy appeals to writers to work on the language, to order it, adding to it with refinements and technical adjustments. But that is not enough. After all, human language is not always capable of representing all the shades, nuances and complexities of human thoughts and feelings. And only an exceptional sensitivity to words on the part of the writer will allow him to put into the text far more than what is written. As Naimy ends his article: "Woe to the writer in whose works there is nothing to read between the lines! And woe to the reader who reads in the words only letters!"[71]

His article "al-Zihafat wa al-'ilal"[72] ("Prosodical Elision and Lengthening") is also a devastating attack. Here Naimy pounces on the classical system of versification, the *'arud*, criticising the scholasticism and restricting character of its use in modern literature:

> My friend al-Khalil (the creator of the *'arud*, classical prosody) died long ago. And yet to this day we are burdened with studying a whole world of concepts such as elisions and erasures (*khabn wa khabl*), adding extra syllables and letters (*tarfil wa tadhyil*), consonantal erasures (*naqs wa waqs*), subtracting and suppressing syllables (*qatf wa kasf*), deleting letters or syllables (*kharm wa thalm*), restrictions and mutilations (*qasr wa batr*) and so on and so forth.[73]

In the heat of polemic Naimy sometimes goes into excess. While justly criticising certain poets for excessive formalism and observance of abstract theoretical propositions, at times he accuses the whole of Arabic poetry of such practice. The Arabs give too much attention to rules, claims Naimy, and have distorted the content and spiritual meaning of poetry: "By giving priority to metre over subject matter, it made of poetry-writing a profession; and, once the rules of it were learned, any dabbler in literature was able to claim the title of poet",[74] he concludes. It is worth noting that Naimy judged the achievements of medieval Arabic literature by the rules of the literature of his own time, and therefore some of his errors as a critic can be explained by this non-historical approach.

At the time of the greatest increase in activity of the Syro-American School, Europe and America were making new discoveries about the Middle Ages. At the same time the Arab East, then at the lowest point in its artistic evolution, was just starting to break with its medieval literature and culture. In this respect the misunderstanding of the Middle Ages by those who thought in the categories so characteristic of the Eurocentrism of Western scholarship can be attributed to the fact that it was precisely at this time that the Arab literary "renovators" were beginning to repeat in their artistic manifestos – almost verbatim – many of the mistakes of nineteenth-century European Oriental studies. Nevertheless, the paradox of the situation was that this false criticism was in fact fruitful for the development of the new Arabic literature, in that it directed attention to the categories of modern culture and facilitated the rejection of traditional aesthetics.

Naimy's frank and polemical articles, with their critical and uncompromising tone – in short, with all his passion – directed against obsolete canons are reminiscent of the style of Belinsky in his works on Aleksandr Bestuzhev-Marlinsky, Vladimir Benediktov, Faddey Bulgarin, Nicholas Gretsch, Mikhail Pogodin and others. Belinsky saw the value of literary works not in terms of a successful form of expression but rather in the degree to which the author fully, objectively and correctly exposes the life of society at a certain stage in its development. He believes that the essence of life is recreated in poetry not by way of syllogisms, reasoning and experiment, but by means of images that embody the substantial, that is to say, by means of reality.

> Poetry is an expression of life or, to put it better, is life itself. More than this: in poetry life is more life than it is in reality itself ... all that is beautiful is contained only in living reality; but in order to enjoy this reality we must first encompass it with our minds, and this is possible only under two conditions: we must grasp it intact, and must do so with serious intent.[75]

As a critic Naimy was concerned not only with the fate of Arabic poetry, but also showed his support on a number of occasions for other literary genres. He wrote a lengthy preface to his play *al-Aba' wa al-banun* (*Fathers and Sons*) discussing questions of dramaturgy. This was included in *al-Ghirbal* under the title "al-Riwaya al-tamthiliyya al-'Arabiyya" ("Arabic Dramaturgy").[76] We should point out that Naimy, like Belinsky, gave great importance to drama in the development of the intellectual life of a society and considered that the formation of the theatre was evidence of the inner maturity of a nation. He had a deep feeling for and understanding of the role of theatre in the life of the people. "In the theatre, the Western viewer lets go, and his soul, tired from work and the cares of life, finds consolation, rest and spiritual nourishment ... the theatre transports him to the world of human passions and shows him the different ways in which they are manifested – from the beautiful to the ugly, from the elevated to the base."[77] Belinsky wrote something akin to this in his article "On Theatre": "Here you live a life that is not your own, suffer sorrows not your own, rejoice in bliss not your own and tremble not for your own safety."[78]

Naimy is troubled not only by the very small number of contemporary national plays in Arab culture that reflect the life of the people, but also by the frivolous and sometimes even disrespectful attitude of the Arab public to theatre in general, it being seen as just a place of amusement. "We still consider the actor as no more than an acrobat, the actress as a prostitute, the theatre as a cafe, and acting as nothing more than a means of amusing ourselves and spending our time",[79] he complains to his writer colleagues, appealing to them to write more material for a national theatre: "Our nation has not yet come to appreciate the importance of the art of acting, as it has not yet seen its own life being reflected on the stage. ... I have no doubt that, sooner or later, we shall see a national theatre in which the different aspects of our national life are reflected."[80]

Naimy also says much about the language of theatrical productions, and gives particular importance to the role of colloquial speech:

> Under the rough cover of this speech is concealed the philosophy of the people, its everyday experience, wisdom and belief. And if one tries to express all this in literary language, the result may sound like a poor foreign translation ... the writer who makes an uneducated *fellah* speak the language of the poetic *diwan*s insults the *fellah*, himself, and his readers and listeners. Furthermore, his char-acters look comic in situations in which comedy was never intended.[81]

Naimy's research articles were devoted to contemporary problems in Arabic literature and were necessary to their time, being progressive and innovative in their substance, though they sometimes suffered from a sub-jective point of view. Part of *The Sieve* is made up of articles that analysed specific literary works by Arab authors. These articles and reviews stand out, because in them Naimy sought to examine the scheme of the ideas of each work in a unity that is organic with its form.

Ahmad Shawqi (Ahmed Shawki, 1868–1932) was one of the gener-ally recognised authorities on Arabic literature whom Naimy was not afraid to "sift" through the sieve of his criticism. In his article "al-Durrat al-Shawqiyya" ("Shawqi's Pearl"),[82] the discussion concerns a little-known *qasida* by the poet. The very title parodies, with heavy irony, the practices of excessive laudation and bombastic epithets which are so common in Arabic poetry. Naimy finds that the poem, with its weak ideas, many contradictions and excessive false emotion, reminds him not so much of the pearl as the empty shell beneath it. In this *qasida* he feels no "pulse of contemporary life". Naimy illustrates his propositions and conclusions with excerpts from the "great poem" and comments on them with great irony. He reproaches Shawqi for continuing to copy the pre-Islamic poets when it is impossible to hold onto the remains of past civilisations without compromising one's own artistic worth.[83]

Nevertheless, Naimy is too severe in his criticism of Shawqi's poetry; his judgements and conclusions are unconditional to a degree that is unfair. It is true that, as Krachkovsky observed, Shawqi "was a typical court poet ... completely frozen in old forms".[84] He was worse than the neo-traditionalist poets "in sincerity of feeling and the lack in many works of their own poeti-cal "'I'."[85] At the same time, however, it must not be denied that the work of this poet "represents an entire phase in the history of Arabic literature and calls for respect from those who love and value traditional classical poetry."[86] For all their conservatism, Shawqi's poems are notable for their social perceptions, patriotic feeling and philosophical reflections, and Naimy bases his rather sweeping generalisations about his work on only one little-known *qasida*. Still, we do not wish to diminish the importance of "Shawqi's Pearl", which openly asserts, giving a specific example, the importance of the form of an artistic work being suited to its content. Similar articles provided lessons in aesthetics and the development of good taste, which were always Belinsky's requirements from literature.

Naimy's attention was drawn to the novel *German Love*, by the German writer Max Müller (1823–1900), in its Arabic translation by the well-known Syrian writer Maryam Ziyada (Mayy, 1895–1941). In an article devoted to analysing this work,[87] Naimy criticises the quality of the translation, but still more the choice by this talented and original writer of such an uninteresting and exaggeratedly sentimental work. "Sentimentalism lends this work a pitiful quality, on top of which it is drenched with hysterics and sobbing, such that one might choke on the sighs and drown in the floods of tears."[88] The article is interesting not so much for its criticism of the translation as for revealing the author's attitude to the Sentimentalist method. After summarising the gist of the novel in all its banality, Naimy concludes that translations of works of this type can only "spoil the taste of the Arab reader".

Naimy also made use of Belinsky's critical perspective when analysing the works of his colleagues. In a review of the manuscript of the *Diwan*[89] by the émigré poet Nasib 'Arida, Naimy sets out his method of examining poetic works:

> The object of my interest is poetry, which I consider to be "the breath of life" ... If I sense that such a breath is present in what I have read, then I understand this to be poetry, but if it is not, then I have read a work devoid of life ... Having satisfied myself that what I have read is true poetry, I give my main attention to the scale, depth and breadth of the design. After this I examine the outward attributes – the structuring of the composition, the musicality of sound, the refinement of style and so on. The last thing I consider is the metre and the observance of the rules of *'arud* and grammar.[90]

Examining 'Arida's poetry, Naimy comments on the individuality of the poems and finds in them a depth of thought that corresponds to the rich imagination, emotional intensity and strength of feeling of the poet himself. This assessment by Naimy agrees with Belinsky's utterance that "poetry comprises depth and power of feeling, lavishness of fantasy, fullness of life and the sharply tangible presence of ideas in artistic form."[91] This article by Naimy is interesting for its attempt to generalise and to reveal universal patterns in poetry. Using the example of 'Arida, he concludes that the maturity of the poet's world-view and his life experience determine the completeness of his poetry.

It is appropriate here to consider Naimy's articles on works by Gibran and Rihani. Belinsky's insights were of particular importance for the analysis of these works; in typological terms the Romantic poetry of their authors was as close to Naimy as, let us say, the poetry of Russian Romanticism was to Belinsky. This does not mean, however, that analogies may not also be found with Belinsky's views on other literary tendencies and methods, such as Critical Realism.

It is unsurprising that the artistic principles of criticism formulated by Belinsky formed the basis of Naimy's responses to Gibran and Rihani. Naimy's analysis of the works of two leading authors of the Syro-American School is also of considerable interest because it offers a view of the literary process from within, through the eyes of its immediate participants and creators. In this respect an overview of Naimy's articles on Gibran and Rihani is necessary to complement the observations already made in the present work in the respective chapters on those authors.

"Al-Rihani fi 'alam al-shi'r" ("Rihani in the World of Poetry")[92] is an article that focuses on the poetry of Ameen Rihani. Naimy singled out immediately the breadth of horizon and variety of genre in the work of his comrade-in-writing: "He is an essayist, sociologist, politician, man of letters, dramatist and poet." Comparing works by Rihani of different genres, Naimy says that Rihani is one of those writers whose works give priority to "clear ideas and iron logic". Because of this, journalism occupies a significant place in relation to other genres. On the basis of this thesis, Naimy considers that the distinguishing characteristic in all the works of *al-Rihaniyyat* was "the capacity and effort to research an idea, to disclose and justify specific phenomena, to subject these to meticulous analysis and break them down into elementary components".[93]

An analogous idea is found in Belinsky's article "A glance at Russian literature of the year 1847", in which he talks of two types of writer. These are the writer-painter, for whom the most important thing is "a feeling for form" and "whose greatest pleasure lies in forever competing with nature in the ability to create",[94] and the writer who is predominated by thought. He ascribes Alexander Herzen to the latter group: "His main strength is not in his creativity or his art, but in his thinking, which is deeply felt and fully realised and developed."[95]

Naimy sees its close link to national traditions as one of the achievements of Rihani's poetry. Even in his English-language works (here Naimy is discussing Rihani's poetry volume *A Chant of Mystics and other Poems*)[96] "a strong Oriental colouring" can be discerned. "The entire collection is impregnated with an Arabic aroma",[97] Naimy comments. Naimy sought in this article to show two principal traits in Rihani's works: the predominance of ideas and thought in his prose, and the presence of a national flavour in his poetry.

One is also reminded of a review[98] by Naimy of two collections by Gibran: *The Madman* (1918) and *The Forerunner* (1920). This is mainly interesting for its historical approach to Gibran's works and to his progress and development. Discussing Gibran's previous works, Naimy notices in them the theme of loneliness: "He criticised, but nobody supported his criticism. He wept, but merely reddened his eyes. He caught fire, but only his heart was consumed. He cried out: 'How absurd is civilisation and how false is everything within it', but civilisation went calmly on its way, paying no attention to his words."[99] In his discussion of *The Madman* and *The Forerunner*, Naimy remarks on Gibran's way of coming close to the people. In his view it is no coincidence that allegorical forms – the parable and the fable – predominate in Gibran's work. By means of these "edifying" forms he aimed to bring his ethical teaching to the public consciousness.

Naimy considers the principal motif of *The Forerunner* to be the continuum of the eternal forward movement of life. Each of us is the "forerunner" for somebody in the future; that on which we stand today will become the basis of our tomorrow. "We sow in this life the grain from an earlier harvest",[100] he concludes.

A substantial contribution to the interpretation of Gibran's works was Naimy's extensive article, "'Asifat al-'Awasif" ("The Storm of *The Tempests*"),[101] on *The Tempests*, a collection published in 1920. Naimy's response is enthusiastic: "Truly Gibran's style, the melodic quality of the poetry and the fineness of description have given us a new understanding of the beauty of composition and exposition. But his brilliant prose poems, created with both inward and outward harmony, have made a uniform rhythm ugly in our eyes."[102]

Naimy concentrates his attention on the subjects of rebellion, subversion and the destruction of formal truths, and on the rejection of deeds and laws that controlled the behaviour of the Arabs down the centuries: "For me Kahlil Gibran is above all a revolution, revolution itself. A 'mutineer' – that is what other people called him and what he called himself."[103] But revolution, in the view of the critic, is not something sudden and unexpected; it is the action of many forces, long lying latent and awaiting the appointed moment. Only a great artist who lives the same life as his people, and who has become their voice and the expression of their inner life, can detect and express their deepest needs and feelings. "And so Gibran", wrote Naimy, "was not only the son of his time, but also the fruit of the feelings and longings of his nation, which had doomed itself or been doomed by fate to what for many centuries could merely speak its language, while its heart would remain silent, squeezed into a clot."[104]

Gibran's books could not but precipitate tumultuous sympathies among the Lebanese: for "many long centuries Lebanon had suffered a gloomy fate of silence, until the hour arrived when it could no longer remain silent and began to speak ... And the first language with which it began to speak was the language of Kahlil Gibran."[105]

We may recall that Belinsky always stressed the indissoluble link between the writer and the life of the people, of society, of humanity:

No poet can be great by himself and through himself, neither by his own suffering nor by his own state of bliss: every great poet is great because the roots of his suffering and his bliss grew deep in the soil of public life and of history, and because he is thus an organ and representative of his society, of his time and of humanity.[106]

Looking back, Gibran, whose soul was, according to Naimy, "a cluster of the subtlest feeling and the most acute perceptions",[107] saw the dark power of the prejudices that stifled the courage, sincerity, creativity and beauty in the hearts of his people. And he rose up, "because his heart was a lyre, and not a moment passed in which life did not touch its strings with its invisible fingertips."[108] Oppressed and forlorn, Lebanon gained in Gibran its voice of protest and hunger for change. The poet's work is linked with indissoluble ties to that time, the destiny of his people and the historical moment. In those years Lebanon, along with the other Arab lands, was awakening to renewal and a new life. And this called for, above all, rebellion against what was obsolete in the arts, in tradition, in morals and in religion. Practically all of Gibran's essays, parables, prose poems and philosophical elegies carry the seeds of the destruction of the obsolete.

The critic's observations of the dualism in Gibran's relationship to the world, which he both cursed and passionately loved, are accurate and profound. Consequently the feeling that prevails in Gibran's works, as Naimy correctly points out, was one of loneliness, of separation from people and a longing for nature, harmony and beauty, to which he always contrasted human life. While Naimy does not say explicitly that Gibran is a Romantic, nevertheless the signs that he observes – the elevated inspiration and emotional style of the writer – effectively define his Romanticism by themselves. In Gibran Naimy finds almost all the qualities that Belinsky considered marks of the Romantic poets.[109]

Naimy also states conclusively that in essence all the characters in Gibran's works, despite their different names, are embodiments of Gibran himself: "Although their names are different, these are the names of one and the same person, and that person is Kahlil Gibran."[110] This is a true observation by Naimy, in that the refusal to objectivise the hero from the personality traits of the artist is a distinguishing characteristic of the Romantics.

> The meaning of existence, in Gibran's opinion, is to seek that which lies beyond its boundaries ... The one whose soul is awake sees that he is surrounded by other souls that are still sound asleep in life's embrace, and he tries to wake them, but they do not wake – and then he finds them strange, reproaches them, comes to hate them and finally rises up against them. At times his hate leads him to recklessly exaggerate his blame and protest.[111]

In Gibran's works Naimy found both the bitterness of disappointment and the enthusiasm of protest. The image of Gibran that he creates can be associated with that of Byron, introduced to him through Belinsky:

The mighty genius on his hill looked ahead into the shimmering distance, but, unable to make out, beyond it, the promised land of the future, he cursed the present and declared an irreconcilable and eternal enmity; carrying in his breast the suffering of millions, he loved humanity, yet despised and hated people, among whom he saw himself alone and outcast with his proud struggle and his undying sorrow.[112]

Naimy's article on Gibran is evidence of his deep penetration into the artistic meaning of the latter's works and his ability to understand and expose the essence and value of Gibran's writings.

All of Naimy's literary activity was directed against stagnant ideas and concepts, false theories and principles, and necessitated the solution of the problems posed to Arabic literature by life in the early twentieth century. His theoretical and critical essays are characterised by searches for new ways of overcoming the old and the obsolete. He was one of the first Arab critics to understand and value the true meaning of new phenomena in literature, whether these be a new tendency or movement, or new genres. For Naimy the most important element in a work was the depth of its ideas and how actively the author related to reality. At the same time, however, he did not lose sight of the importance of artistic merit. Naimy followed new literary talent closely: Nasib 'Arida, Kahlil Gibran, al-Sha'ir al-Qarawi (the pen-name of Rashid al-Khuri, 1887–1984), Ameen Rihani and others. From their first works he considered these to be major artists.

Speaking out against imitation and the mechanical following of traditions, Naimy showed that literature should not serve privileged readers and that art that relies solely on external effects and pompous epithets would be short-lived. In all of this, Belinsky's artistic and aesthetic conceptions can be seen beyond doubt in Naimy's theoretical and active perceptions, as well as in his use of them in his literary practice.

> The defining particularities of Belinsky the critic were his strong adherence to his principles, his implacability towards compromise and his rejection of all inconsistencies. He opposed timid and evasive criticism with that unbounded love of truth that knows no embellishment or omission. Belinsky's creative genius combined social pathos with philosophical reflection, aesthetic feeling with literary talent and the gift of scholarly abstraction with poetical fantasy.[113]

Like Belinsky, Naimy advocated the introduction and propagation of new and progressive outlooks in life, literature and aesthetics. How necessary for Arabic literature, then, in its progression towards the modern, was his voice of theoretically founded criticism, heard there for the first time!

A new collection of critical and literary articles appeared under the name *Fi al-Ghirbal al-jadid* (*The New Sieve*)* in Beirut in 1972. The earliest

* Information on this book was given at the academic conference marking the

piece is dated 1936, the latest 1968, and of the 45 articles contained in the volume, almost half are a type of personalia. They are devoted to the work of both Arab writers of the older generation (Ameen Rihani, Shafiq Ma'aluf, Nasib 'Arida, Iliya Abu Madi and Rashid Ayyub) and foreign writers (Rabindranath Tagore, Friedrich Nietzsche, Walt Whitman and Ralph Waldo Emerson). He also gives attention to the Russian writers Leo Tolstoy, Fyodor Dostoevsky, Alexander Pushkin and Maxim Gorky, and the Ukrainian Taras Shevchenko. A separate article is dedicated to the Academician Ignaty Yulianovich Krachkovsky. The collection also contains prefaces written by Naimy to various books, and letters, and addresses to Arab writers. These include writers of the older generation (Mahmud Taymur, Tawfiq Yusuf 'Awwad, Bishara al-Khuri, Rashid Ma'aluf), and younger writers who became known after the Second World War (Suhayl Idris, Yusuf al-Khal, Tawfiq Sayigh and others).

This volume demonstrates that Naimy keenly observed the literary life of the Arab world (and not only the Arab), and used his authority to play an active part in the forming of contemporary Arabic literature.

The influence of Leo Tolstoy's world-view on Naimy's work

Leo Nikolaevich Tolstoy was one of the world's great artists; his influence as a thinker and artist on the cultural and spiritual life of the world is a universally recognised fact. "All the world, all the Earth looks to him; from China, India and America. From all places there extend towards him living, quivering threads. His soul is for all and for ever",[114] wrote Maxim Gorky. The burning social and human problems he presented in his artistic and journalistic works found an ardent response in the hearts of millions. "With his strong statements and his rejection of all oppressors, regardless of their class or nation, Leo Tolstoy won the attention and sympathy of oppressed people from the various and most distant ends of the earth."[115]

Tolstoy is also widely celebrated in the East: "One of the reasons for the popularity of Tolstoy in the East is the closeness of his humanistic ideals and of his advocacy of universal peace between peoples to the centuries-old moral concepts of the Eastern peoples."[116] The works of Tolstoy have always been a central reference for Arab men of letters[117] and his writings have enjoyed great popularity throughout the Arab world. "The name of Tolstoy is well known to the Arabs, possibly more so than to other inhabitants of the near East",[118] comments Krachkovsky. Many have written about Tolstoy and many have followed his teachings.[119] Arab translators have frequently turned to the work of Tolstoy: "I am firmly convinced that for the Arabs, Leo Tolstoy is the most easily understood of the Russian writers",[120]

centenary of Naimy's birth (Poltava, Ukraine, 24–26 April 1989), in Yu. Kuchubey's paper "Dva Resheta Mikhaila Nuaime" ["Two Sieves by Mikhail Naimy"].

wrote Khalil Baydas, one of the first translators of Tolstoy into Arabic. The well-known Egyptian writer Mahmud Taymur comments: "The heroes of Tolstoy's novels are so close in spirit to us, the people of the East, that they differ only in their names."[121] Also close and accessible to the Arabs were the humanistic pathos of his works and his angry protest against all forms of violence, oppression and rigidity. His speaking out against religious orthodoxy made a deep impression on them, as did, above all, the personality of the writer–philosopher himself. Epithets such as "the great teacher and mentor", "a wise man from among the wise", "wise and knowledgeable" and "the well-known philosopher" have been associated with the name of Tolstoy in the Arab East.

The influence of Tolstoy's philosophical world-view has shown itself especially clearly in the Arab world, in particular his view that the spiritual life takes precedence over the material requirements of man, and also his call to self-perfection and to love. It may be pointed out that Tolstoy himself turned more than once in his works to the thinkers of the ancient East and took an interest in the peoples of the East.

> In reflecting on the historical destinies of humanity and in surveying his contemporary world, in which oppressed peoples were rising up in struggle for a better future, Tolstoy turned his thoughts on a number of occasions to the Arab countries. The Arab peoples, who, at the dawn of mankind, had created one of the richest of civilisations, attracted him still more because there were now struggles in those countries for a renewal of life – for freedom from tyranny and for the triumph of reason over medieval gloom and stagnation.[122]

Tolstoy was particularly interested in ancient Arab culture and Arab folklore. As a child his favourite book was *The Thousand and One Nights*. Later he used certain stories from this series for his own folk tales, though of course transferring them onto Russian soil and giving them Russian colouring. In his memoirs Tolstoy mentions, as his favourites, the stories "Aladdin and the Magic Lamp" and "The Tale of Qamar al-Zaman", while he included two Arab tales in the children's reading-book in the appendix to his Yasnaya Polyana journal: "Ali Baba and the Forty Thieves", under the title "Dunyasha and the Forty Thieves", and "Ali Coglia (Khoja) and the Merchant of Baghdad" with the name "The Unrighteous Court". Tolstoy's *Alphabet* also included other stories from *The Thousand and One Nights*: "The Dervish and the Young Raven" (known in Russian as "Galchonok" ["The Young Jackdaw"]), "A Severe Punishment", "The King and the Shirt" and others. In Tolstoy's stories the didactic was always very clear. He also drew from Arab sources for his stories "Esarhaddon, King of Assyria"[123] and "Ilyas".[124] He included many Arabic proverbs, sayings and aphorisms in his collection *Thoughts of Wise Men*.

The interest in Tolstoy's works among the Arabs and their publication in Arabic translation have always received considerable attention in Soviet Oriental studies, and a number of research works concerning such Arab translations and the distribution of Tolstoy's works in Arab countries have been written by Ignaty Krachkovsky, Anna Dolinina, Alexander Shifman, Pavel Biriyukov and others.[125] No detailed examination of these works is required for our present purpose, which is mainly to trace the extent to which Tolstoy's world-view influenced the works of Mikhail Naimy – a topic that so far has received inadequate attention by Orientalists examining Tolstoy's influence on Arabic literature.

Konstantin Paustovsky remarks that "almost every writer has his own inspirer, his kind genius, who is usually also a writer. He need only read a few lines from a work by this inspirer, and at once is himself ready to write."[126] Examples are given in an article by Andrey V. Fyodorov, "On the question of literary influence", for several writers: for Paustovsky the genius is Stendhal, for Gorky it is Strindberg and for Tolstoy it is Byron.[127] It would seem to us that for Naimy the "inspirer and kind genius" was Leo Tolstoy, whose world-view runs through his entire life.

Naimy first made the acquaintance of Tolstoy's works while still an adolescent at the teachers' seminary in Nazareth.[128] In Poltava, having now learned Russian to a high standard, he turned to Tolstoy again, reading many of his fiction and non-fiction works.[129] In 1908 he wrote in his diary: "I am indebted to you for so many thoughts which filled with light the darkness of my spirit. Your recent works that I read last year were a great source of inspiration which illumined my life. Indeed, you have come to be my teacher and guide, a fact of which you are unaware."[130]

Naimy's acquaintance with Tolstoy's later works was immensely important in the formation of his world-view. These works included *Folk Tales, My Confession, What I Believe, On Life* and "Love One Another". From his youth, when he thought about what he would become and how he would serve people (and for Naimy life and service had the same meaning), he decided to become a writer. "I want to become a writer and to take my deserved place among them ... My highest ideal is to serve people with my pen, honourably and incorruptibly. My aim is to achieve all that is necessary so that my pen can fulfil this service with strength and passion."[131] It is interesting that as a student Naimy was more strongly affected by Tolstoy's works on ideals and morals than by his artistic side. After reading *War and Peace* Naimy notes in his diary certain contradictions of ideals that he discovered in the descriptions of the characters of Kutuzov and Napoleon.

> I've finished *War and Peace* ... I agree with the author's view on Napoleon, because I hate war and those who call to war and lead it. But at the same time I can't help but see a contradiction in the way he talks about Napoleon and about Kutuzov. Napoleon, in his view, was driven not by his own desire but by force of circumstance and the wishes of the peoples. At the same time he gives first place to the wisdom of Kutuzov and his experience and will in his victory over Napoleon and his driving him out of Russia ... It is ludicrous that I should dare to criticise such a great thinker as Tolstoy ... Do forgive me, Leon Nikolaevich.[132]

Through the work of Tolstoy, which reflected "the sober truthfulness of an artistic representation of life, a powerful expression of patriotic feeling, directness and fearlessness in exposing acute social problems, the merciless accusation of exploiters, the passionate defence of the oppressed, an emotional esteem for working people and a deep penetration into the inner world of the human",[133] Naimy came to understand the national elements of Russian literature. He mentions this in various works at different times. For example, in *Beyond Moscow and Washington* he writes: "From the books of Leo Tolstoy I learned that the Russians, in protecting their land, shed rivers of blood, and the hellish suffering that was brought by war, and I believed in the longing of the Russian people for peace."[134] During his time in Poltava the country was preparing to celebrate the eightieth anniversary of Tolstoy's birth. Opposition to the celebrations was led by the Church. Naimy wrote: "It is a disgrace that there are people in Russia who are trying to extinguish this torch which now burns in all countries of the world."[135]

In gradually coming to know Naimy's works, one reaches the conclusion that they coincide in many respects with the world-view of Tolstoy. This is particularly true of his social and political essays, with their confessionary and denunciatory character, in which the designs of the author are stripped of any artistic expression. The idea of moral improvement, the understanding of God as love and all-forgiveness, and the renunciation of carnal impulses for the sake of gaining knowledge of one's spiritual essence – all this had a clear effect on practically all of the ideas found in Naimy's works. The overlap of ideals and philosophy with Tolstoy is particularly characteristic of his mature and late periods, in works such as the story *Liqa' (Till We Meet)*, the novels *Mudhakkarat al-Arqash (Memoirs of a Vagrant Soul)*, *The Book of Mirdad* and *al-Yawm al-akhir (The Last Day)*, and his short stories "Asfar al-nab" ("Yellow Teeth"), "'Abir sabil" ("The Wanderer"), "Qulamat zifr" ("Nail-Paring"), etc. All these works have a philosophical, didactic and exhorting character.

We should mention that the philosophical basis of Naimy's writing was not formed solely from the influence of Tolstoy: he was also affected by Eastern cultural traditions and Eastern philosophy. His tendency towards a genre of preaching and teaching, and to the treatment of the eternal problems of the human essence and the existence of God, are also indisputable evidence of his vital link to the traditions of classical Arabic literature.

What, then, did Naimy take from the moral and religious outlook of Tolstoy? Let us consider Naimy's story "The Wanderer",[136] whose outline is as follows. A girl, sick and paralysed, has a dream in which an old man appears to her and whose face shocks her. On waking, she sketches the face on paper from memory. Her mother recognises the face as that of the Wanderer, who the night before had called at their house and asked to be given shelter for the night, and been refused. The girl is shocked at the cruelty of her parents. She remembers the words that the Wanderer said to her in the dream: "You will be healed of your illness on the day that your parents are healed of theirs."[137] Both mother and daughter entreat the father to bring the Wanderer back, to send a servant out to find him. But the father is both proud and abrupt. He will not lower his dignity. This is his house, and he has the right to offer shelter or refuse it to whom he pleases. Two weeks pass, in which the girl pines and wastes away like a candle. But finally the entreaties of mother and daughter move the father to go out in search of the lost Wanderer. When the mother enters the daughter's room to tell her the good news, she finds her on her feet, happy and healthy: she has been cured.

The didactics of the story are clear: cruelty, selfishness and imperiousness are the vices with which man must constantly struggle. Victory over these is the victory over one's carnal "I", the way to salvation and to eternal life. With agonising effort the father conquers his internal "beast", and his daughter is cured. Children suffer for their parents; it is no coincidence that the girl says to her mother, "The fathers eat sour grapes, but it is the sons whose teeth are set on edge."[138] The Wanderer is of divine origin, possibly an angel or prophet – but this is not made explicit.

This story by Naimy may be compared with one of Tolstoy's folk tales, "The Two Old Men".[139] Two elderly men, Efim and Elias, set out from their village on a long pilgrimage to Jerusalem to pray there at the Holy Sepulchre. Efim is a wealthy man; gathering together a few hundred roubles for the journey is not difficult for him, but Elias has to sell half of his beehives and his spare grain, and still barely gathers one hundred. They go on foot for many days, and come at length to a village near the Volga where the harvest has failed and people are starving. While Efim goes on ahead, Elias stops at the nearest hut to ask for water and sees an old man dying of hunger, and then finds the old woman and their daughter also dying. He decides to stay and begins to take care of them. He helps them obtain food and is able to solve their immediate financial problems using his own money. Realising that he has spent most of his money, however, Elias eventually returns home, not having reached Jerusalem.

Efim, on the other hand, does not wait long for Elias and continues to Jerusalem, where he visits the holy places and zealously makes his prayers. Three times, in the cathedral, he seems to see Elias among the crowds of pilgrims. Then on his journey home he happens to pause at the hut in the village where Elias had previously stopped. Here he is met with kindness, attention and respect. When Efim asks the people why they are so kind and attentive, the woman replies: "We cannot fail to welcome wanderers. From a stranger we learned life ... we would have died, but God sent us somebody just like you, who stayed with us ... and we still don't know whether it was a man or an angel. He loved everybody, he took pity on everybody."[140]

Unfortunately there is no information as to whether Naimy in fact read this particular story by Tolstoy. However, "The Wanderer" shows a fundamentally Tolstoyan philosophy: self-improvement, the struggle with one's demons and passions, and the power of true goodness. Good works performed by man are greater than the outer observance of rituals, dearer and more pleasing to God, and are rewarded. The conflict in Naimy's story completely corresponds to that in Tolstoy's, though the two tales differ in both style and technique. Tolstoy's descriptions show strict realism and restrained, precise detail; the language is very simple and characteristic of a folk tale. In the Naimy work, by contrast, everything is impregnated with mystery; nothing is certain or explained, although there are clear Realist elements such as the girl's impressions and the dialogues between father, mother and daughter. Nevertheless, all aspects of the story are subordinated to its didactic purpose.

Since his youth Naimy had shown an urge towards contemplation, solitude, silence and the forced suppression in himself of even feelings of reciprocated love. Even then he tortured himself with complex questions about the secrets of the universe and human existence. His attention was attracted towards the "inner" world of the man who suppresses natural and sensory phenomena. Thus it is no coincidence that Naimy's first major narrative work was entirely devoted to questions of world-view. Many of the ideas in this work overlap with those of Tolstoy's *My Confession*, his article "What is to be done?" and other sociopolitical pieces. This first large narrative work by Naimy was called *Mudhakkarat al-Arqash* (*Memoirs of a Vagrant Soul*, published Beirut, 1949), which he wrote in New York in 1917. Naimy says of it:

> One night I felt an inflow of strength and sat down to work. Gradually my pen revealed the features of a strange young man. His face carried the scars of smallpox. For this reason I called him Arqash ("pitted-face") and the book "Memoirs of Pitted Face". In his memoirs I revealed all of his inner qualities. I compared his inner world with the world in which he lived.[141]

The story revolves around a diary. It relates how one day the author went into a Lebanese cafe in lower Manhattan, where he heard the tale of a waiter in the cafe who had a pitted face and was called Arqash. The cafe owner explains that he had been a hard-working employee, though extremely silent, but that one fine day he had disappeared without explanation. Arqash's diary is subsequently found among the few items left in his room. It is revealed in the epilogue that Arqash came from a wealthy Arab family, was well educated, and that on his wedding night he had killed his bride and disappeared. He explained his act in a note left at the scene thus: "I slew my love with my own hand, for it was more than my body could feed and less than my soul hungered after."[142]

This plot-line was necessary to Naimy in order to explain how his hero came to be in such an exclusive situation. So also is the love intrigue, which the author touches upon so casually, as though in passing, without any sense of process or any interpretation. It feels as though this was merely a means of separating the hero from other people and situating him in a special world, one in which it is not necessary to live, but sufficient merely to reflect, think and solve philosophical problems.

The plot and denouement of the story effectively form a framework for the narrative, and its kernel is Arqash's diary. The content of the diary is somewhat arbitrary, a non-chronological, sustained exposition of experiences and thoughts, and while to a certain extent these reflect reality, they mostly form a disorderly and chaotic stream of reflections and reasonings on philosophical, moral and occasionally social topics. These thoughts and reflections are set out without any discernible logical links: they neither continue nor complement one another, and they do not develop. An idea suddenly takes hold, is poured out effusively and then, as it were, dies away. So what are these thoughts and reflections about? They are about everything connected with the inner life of a deep, thinking and unhappy man. From the diary one gains the impression of somebody who is very lonely, estranged from people and from everything that is alive and worldly. His only friend, confidant and conversation partner is the page. A few of the writings in the journal might be categorised as sketches and observations of daily life. The hero is depicted as a "human" in a generalised sense: there is no detailed biography, no social milieu, no homeland and no date of birth. It is no surprise that Arqash calls himself a "son of the world": "People do not trouble me about where I was born and of whom. I have no homeland. I am the son of the limitless world."[143] Arqash does not recognise any human or social bonds – family, marriage, homeland or friendship – although he expresses hatred and scorn towards racial and national discords and religious enmity. He is entirely concentrated on realising the essence of existence in general and that of the individual existence in particular, that is to say, his own "I". Arqash notes in his diary: "That which is transient is not eternal, but what is constant never disappears."[144] In other words, the inner essence of man is eternal and constant, as is his soul and his desire for union with God.

In *Memoirs of a Vagrant Soul* Arqash formulates his understanding of human life: "Life is a sacred school that is concerned with divine education. Leave earthly life behind and you enter the divine."[145] In his view, life for the overwhelming majority of people consists solely in their realising their vain and carnal principle, unaware of the truth. "People need to know that property does not improve the basis of life",[146] Arqash comments. It is from this misunderstanding, in his view, that all disappointment and suffering arises.

Arqash is profoundly engaged in coming to know the truth of existence: what is the purpose of man's life, what is he and what is his relationship to the world? The knowledge of the world is possible by knowing oneself, and the complete mastery of oneself is the key to mastery of all secrets of the world: "He who wants to know nature must first know himself. And he who wants to become lord of nature must become lord of himself."[147]

Various social institutions and attributes are subjected by Arqash to reappraisal and criticism: the authorities, the courts, war, religion and so forth. "People say: he wasn't born where you were born, he doesn't speak your language, he doesn't eat what you eat, he doesn't wear what you wear, so he is your enemy ... I repudiate such enmity, and my view is far from the views of the people."[148] He castigates the hypocrisy of the Church that gives its blessing to war and to national and religious strife: "If people knew God, they would not split themselves into Jews, Christians and Muslims, and man would not shed the blood of man."[149] These utterances are close to the corresponding views of Tolstoy in his *My Confession*, where he writes:

> At that time Russia was at war. And Russians, in the name of Christian love, began to kill their fellow men. It was impossible not to think about this, and not to see that killing is an evil repugnant to the first principles of any faith. Yet prayers were said in the churches for the success of our arms, and the teachers of the Faith acknowledged killing to be an act resulting from the Faith ... And I took note of all that is done by men who profess Christianity, and I was horrified.[150]

The same thoughts occur to the Russian writer in his letter to Mahatma Gandhi of 7 September 1910: "the life of the Christian nations presents a greater contradiction between what they believe and the principle on which their lives are built: a contradiction between the love which should pre scribe [*sic*] the law of conduct, and the employment of force, recognised under various forms – such as governments, courts of justice, and armies, which are accepted as necessary and esteemed."[151]

The influence of Tolstoy's ideals can also be clearly seen in those parts of Naimy's story where he calls upon people to join together in peaceful labour for the common good: "Why do people have to fight each other, when what they need is to join the hands, thoughts and hearts of all people in common work. And then the results of this work should be divided equally among all."[152]

In his book *What is to be Done?* of 1882, written in response to the famine that had broken out in Russia, Tolstoy writes: "To execute that eternal and certain law of mankind: to labour with all of one's being, without being ashamed of any kind of work, and to struggle with nature to maintain one's own life and that of others."[153]

The hero of *Memoirs of a Vagrant Soul* thirsts for truth and true being, which are achieved by mastering one's intellect, will and passions. "O Arqash, if all the secrets of the universe could be revealed for you ... if I could tell every person that his eyes are closed and his ears are closed, and that through reflection and silence he could see what the eyes do not see, and could hear what the ears do not hear."[154] He considers man to be the divine principle. "Each of them is a king and on the head of each is a divine crown."[155] Arqash's discourse on the understanding of truth through the knowledge of the self is close to the propositions set out by Tolstoy in his book of essays, *On Life*, which deals with the idea of the essence of happy human existence. In Tolstoy's view, "the renunciation of the benefits of the animal self is the law of human life";[156] only then can man overcome his own animal principle and submit himself to the law of universal love, and thus gain for himself eternity:

Rational consciousness always shows man that the gratification of the demands of his animal self cannot be to his good, and thus his life, and it leads him irrepressibly to that good, and thus to that life, that is his true nature and that is too large to fit into his animal self ... The renunciation of the good of the self is not a merit, nor is it an act of heroism, but rather an inescapable condition of human life.[157]

And according to the convictions of Arqash, each man's reason must overcome his passions and he must love not himself but others.

The hero of Naimy's story also speaks out his views on social inequality and on the rights of man. Arqash asks: "Why is work not divided out among people equally, as food is distributed in the army? How can people justify competition, hatred, envy and fighting among themselves?"[158] Here he approaches Tolstoy in his understanding of the essence of human life and human "being".

A well-researched monograph on Naimy[159] expresses the idea that the spiritual searching and insights of the hero of *Memoirs of a Vagrant Soul* are the distillation of the immense dissatisfaction, inner conflicts and new thoughts and experiences that impacted upon the author when he came to New York. The writer of the monograph, Nadeem Naimy, suggests that this quintessentially materialistic city, which, as it were, embodied all the errors and vices of humanity, and in which everything was subordinated to serving the animal principle in man, made an immense impression on Mikhail Naimy. In New York the deepest contradictions were vividly enacted between that which Naimy valued in the human and recognised as most important and what he directly witnessed in this city that boiled with passions, struggle and suffering.

Nadeem Naimy observes a certain similarity between *Memoirs of a Vagrant Soul* and Fyodor Dostoevsky's novel *Crime and Punishment*, alleging that there are common elements between the motive for the murder by Arqash of his bride and that for the murder committed by Raskolnikov. We would question the validity of this suggestion, however, since the only common factor in the two works is the actual murder. All other aspects – the motives and the type of murder, as well as the surrounding circumstances – are quite different.

In Naimy's novel the cause of murder is the split personality of Arqash. He is a man of intense spiritual searching and the love he experiences is higher than that known by ordinary people. At the same time, his greatest earthly love is in conflict with his longing for the elevated spiritual life that was the aim of his existence. To resolve the situation Arqash decides on murder. All of his subsequent ascetic life, all his self-absorption, silence and spiritual wakefulness bear the marks of it.

Raskolnikov was incited to murder by two things: the social "dead end" and, even more, by the desire to verify himself – whether he is "a miserable creature, or has rights". His desire to "verify himself" arises from a highly individualistic theory whereby all people are divided, from birth, into two unequal groups: those who are doomed to humiliation and obedience, and those who have the right to live according to their will, and who set the laws and restrictions for the remaining "miserable creatures". For Raskolnikov the classical example of self-will was Napoleon. "And now I know, Sonya," said Raskolnikov, "that he who is strong and powerful in mind and spirit is lord over them!"[160] Or: "I guessed then, Sonya ... that power is given only to him who dares to bend forward and take it ... I ... I wanted to *dare*, and killed ...".[161] The proud and ambitious pauper, placed by circumstances on the furthest and lowest rung of the social ladder, an individualist and a loner, dreams of power over all "miserable creatures and over the entire ant-hill!"[162]

If we compare the motives for the two murders, we see that Arqash committed murder for the sake of complete power over his own soul and his inner "I", while Raskolnikov had the aim of gaining power over others, over all "miserable creatures". The difference is substantial.

One might also wonder whether *Memoirs of a Vagrant Soul* is a reflection of the episode in Tolstoy's *The Kreutzer Sonata* in which Pozdnyshev murders his wife. We can see that to a certain degree both stories are united by the theme of wrestling with the body and by the utopian conclusion that the ideal human life is obtained through complete asceticism and celibacy. However, the motives for murder and the basic ideas of the two works are not comparable. The fundamental idea in Tolstoy's story is the decay of the family in bourgeois society, in which the wife is made into a slave and the husband into a depraved slave-owner. They come together, and then exist side-by-side without spiritual union. Pozdnyshev kills his wife out of feelings of jealousy towards the violinist Trukhachevsky. This jealousy has formed out of unceasing and growing hatred and mutual irritation. As Pozdnyshev says, "We were like two galley-slaves fastened to the same ball, cursing each other, poisoning each other's existence, and trying to shake each other off."[163] In this story Tolstoy does not individualise the main characters: neither Pozdnyshev, nor his wife, nor the presumed lover. All that is drawn out are the generalised features, which he seeks here to typify, of a senseless marriage that ties together two entirely incompatible and mutually hostile people who are not bonded by any common endeavour, shared concerns or interests that might engender a sense of closeness or kinship. Thus it can be seen that neither the causes, motives or situations of the three murders have anything in common.

In terms of subject matter Naimy's novel *The Book of Mirdad*,[164] published in 1948, might seem to be a sort of sequel to *Memoirs of a Vagrant Soul*. This similarity does not relate to the plot and thematic content but to the recurrence of certain ideas. Like *Memoirs of a Vagrant Soul*, *The Book of Mirdad* poses and tries to resolve the "eternal problems" of man and God. However, in *Mirdad* they assume a complete philosophical conception. Through his unceasing movement towards perfection the principal character of the novel, Mirdad, approaches the person of a Messiah or prophet.

The novel was well-received widely. The Cairo newspaper *al-Misri* printed a rapturous review by the well-known writer and public figure 'Abd al-Rahman al-Hamsi (1920–87), in which he wrote:

> If all of the East may take pride in its thinkers, philosophers, poets and writers, then we, the sons of the Arab nation, are entitled to consider Mikhail Naimy the principal object of our pride in contemporary literature and intellectual life. Naimy personifies the sole humanist school of its kind, which is the purest and most disinterested of all the most rewarding of tendencies in human thought.[165]

The Book of Mirdad has much in common with Gibran's *The Prophet*, although it is considerably more complex in its plot and a larger work. The basic ideas of each are comparable, and each represents a form of addressing and exhorting the people, telling them how they should best live, how to save themselves from delusion and how to realise the meaning of their lives and become merged with God. Like al-Mustafa, Mirdad speaks in terms of everyday precepts, explaining the truth by means of the light of everyday life.

The foundation of the story is the Biblical legend of Noah and the Flood. Noah's son Shem builds an ark at the summit of a mountain, and a group of priests come to live there. Soon, however, the priests begin to neglect the covenant of Noah and the ascetic way of life it calls for. One day Mirdad climbs the mountain and enters the ark, with the intention of calling the priests back to the true path. One of the priests writes down Mirdad's teachings, and the result is *The Book of Mirdad*. As in previous works by Naimy, the main character expresses the "I" of the author. The name Mirdad itself is symbolic, meaning "the one who is returning" in Arabic and carrying the sense of a messiah who has returned to save mankind once more from the sin, lies and hypocrisy into which it has sunk. Both the hero's name and what it stands for suggest that the book contains teaching and exhortation, and this is indeed the case. The work is a corpus of the philosophical, religious, moral, ethical and, to a certain extent, social views of the author. Much in the book can be seen to reflect the teachings of Tolstoy in his last years.

The novel comprises two independent sections. The first, entitled "History of the Book", describes in a mystical–romantic manner how the narrator–hero ascended the mountain to reach the ark, which is surrounded by various legends. On the way, which is difficult and dangerous, he encounters a number of obstacles and mysterious meetings with symbolic figures: a goatherd with goats, an old woman with a naked girl, an old man and an old woman, and others. They pose him difficult riddles and questions. Finally, however, he reaches the ark, where a priest tells him about Mirdad. The priest hands him the sacred book of Mirdad, but himself turns to stone. The main content of this holy book is the sermons given by Mirdad, in which can be heard "the call to the highest level of human development".

The second section is called "The Book of Mirdad" and contains Mirdad's teachings, which are a concentration of the philosophical, religious and social outlook of Naimy himself.

One of the key themes of the novel is the conception of God. For Naimy, as for Tolstoy, God is Love. Since every person contains the divine principle, then love of God manifests itself through love of man for man. It follows that to love God is to love all people. Love is the most active and most universal law of human life. "God's oneness, my companions, is the only law of being. Another name for it is Love. To know it and abide by it is to abide in Life."[166] We might mention an utterance by Tolstoy that is close to this sentiment: "To love means to give oneself up to God and to do what God desires; but God is love, i.e. he desires the good of all [mankind]."[167] Like Tolstoy, Mirdad absolutely rejects the mediation of any kind of priesthood between man and God. Prayer does not require the help of words and rites, but rather the heart and one's actions. The way to the truth lies through silent contemplation, quiet prayer and asceticism. The logical consequence is the complete rejection of any specific religion, and in its place a kind of religious universalism.

Naimy believes that God is neither Allah, Jesus or the Buddha, but an eternal moral law. Tolstoy also understood the generality of all religions as a certain generality beyond any dependence on their names. In his reply to a letter from a Persian youth who had expressed indignation at the "heathenism" of the Christians and the absurdity of the Christian dogmatists, Tolstoy advises him to look to other religions and seek out only that which answered the needs of his soul, saying that he himself also adheres to such a principle.[168] Tolstoy understood belief as a comprehension of truth that engaged all of a person's spiritual powers. He wholly repudiated and caustically ridiculed outward ritual and the observance of obligatory church canons. This view is also a basic idea in Naimy's book: "Nor have you any need for temples to pray in. Whoever cannot find a temple in his heart, the same can never find his heart in any temple."[169] The influence of Tolstoyan teaching on Naimy's anticlerical stance is confirmed by Naimy himself in a letter to Ignaty Krachkovsky: "My inner agitation against the Church and its arid dogmas has forced me to seek and find support in the late works of Tolstoy."[170]

As in *Memoirs of a Vagrant Soul*, in *The Book of Mirdad* the entire system of human relations and social institutions is fundamentally criticised. Again the social utopia has an abstract character that transcends class. In Mirdad's preaching all material life is reviewed critically: state boundaries are repudiated, as are all penal and controlling systems in society such as the courts, prisons, money, the administrative organs and religious and national belonging. Mirdad's positive ideal is asceticism, the love of neighbours and the rejection of wealth and power. He disavows property, considering it one of the primary origins of evil and vices: people are enslaved by things. He calls for religious abodes and churches to be liberated from their assets. Money is for him the source of violence, offence and oppression. "For what were money but the sweat and blood of men coined by the crafty into mites and shekels wherewith to shackle men? ... Woe and woe again onto them who burn away their minds and hearts and slay their nights and days in storing riches! For they know not what they store."[171] We may recall Tolstoy's invective against property:

> Property is the root of all evil; the distribution and provision of property occupies practically the whole world ... No sooner does man call his property that which is not his body, but that which he would desire, to subordinate that to his will, than he has made a mistake and brings on himself disappointment and suffering and becomes obligated to force suffering on others.[172]

Mirdad considers self-perfection the only possible route to universal harmony: "In truth, man struggles only with his own soul ... And never shall the balance [of vacillating human states caused by passions] be adjusted till men have learned to knead all their desires in the kneading trough of Love and bake of them the bread of Holy Understanding."[173] In his view, each person must master and govern his own "I"; only then will he become "mightier than Time, and much more spacious than Space". In his *My Confession* and in *What is to be Done?*, Tolstoy calls people to wrestle and overcome their passions, vices and evil: "Woe unto them that call evil good, and good evil; that put darkness for light, and light for darkness; that put bitter for sweet, and sweet for bitter!"[174]

The Book of Mirdad is the moral and ethical testament of Naimy himself, in which his philosophical, religious and artistic ideas are interwoven. It is the author's credo. In particular, Naimy's novel draws on Tolstoy's idea of religious "salvation". The novel's characteristic motifs include the criticism of materialism, a call for the purification of religion from empty ritual and the aim of uniting people with ideas of universal love, which again resonate with the teaching of Tolstoy. Also common to both writers is a path of renewal for man and mankind, which they saw as the moral development of the individual. As is well known, Tolstoy linked his social views with moral and religious philosophy, and in *Mirdad* social conflicts are portrayed in the form of moral conflicts. We would add that a Sufi influence can be discerned in *The Book of Mirdad*, and also ideas from the Arab Enlightenment.

Naimy's novel *al-Yawm al-akhir* (*The Last Day*) is a summary work of the author's world-view. It is, as it were, the final confession of the author, revealed through the mouth of its hero. This hero is a teacher of philosophy, a man who thinks in philosophical categories; his confession, immensely concentrated and pouring forth as an unbroken stream, effectively forms a complete philosophical system. The theme of the novel is the self-examination of his life, looking at it as if there remained only 24 hours to live, and that is what the hero, Musa al-'Askari, does. The novel is structured to this end, with 24 chapters, each corresponding to one of the remaining hours of Musa's life. In each of these hours he reviews not only his own life, but that of human society as a whole, reassessing many conditions and categories of human consciousness.

The primary task that the hero sets himself is formulated in Musa's monologue: "Today I want to know what until today I did not want to know. I want to know what connects me to the son of Hisham and his wife. I want to know everything in my life that links me to people and events."[175]

This last day of his life, filled with reflections and answers, creates a different Musa al-'Askari, quite unlike the one that existed up to this day. Now he has a quite different attitude towards people, to the world, to God, to human values and to social institutions. To re-evaluate is to criticise and to drop previous opinions and understandings, and that is what happens in *The Last Day*: everything that Musa considers during this single day he sees from a new perspective, as though scales have fallen from his eyes. Among these things he sees many of society's institutions in an ugly light: the army, the courts, prisons and so on. Sometimes what Musa says addresses social questions:

> In the courts I see people invested in the mantle of lords of the law, and I see men and women who expect from them justice and mercy in the name of the law. I see the mercy and justice that knock diligently at the door of the courts. However, those doors are not opened up and they are not permitted entry.[176]

> In the prisons I see thousands of those whom the law has sentenced to live within gloomy and severe walls, shut away from the life-giving sun, the air that invigorates and the cleanliness that revives.[177]

He speaks of the army thus:

> In the barracks I see people who have been made by human laws into puppets, toys, whom the devil, taking the name of a state or nation, has offered for sacrifice. These puppets have no other function than blind or dumb obedience. They have no right to cry out, to groan or to complain, whatever requirements are imposed upon them. They exist in order, when necessary, to sow or reap death.[178]

His comments correspond to Tolstoy's view of the Tsarist army as quintessentially an instrument of violence:

> The first means of human enslavement, by direct violence and the threat of death by the sword, has never disappeared and will not disappear for so long as there continues, in one form or another, the enslavement by people of other people, since this is the very basis of all enslavement ... We forget but one small fact – about those hundreds of millions in the standing army, without which not one state can exist, and whose disappearance would mean the inevitable collapse of the economic structure of every state. But what are these millions of soldiers, if they are not the personal slaves of those who control them?[179]

In his reflections Musa passes definitive sentence on the things that man worships: wealth, power, religion, property and so on. Before Musa's eyes there sail ships, symbolically representing the accumulation of things of worth to man: ships of power, of wealth, of science and so on. Musa is filled with indignation at mankind's worship of material existence. He says: "In the shops I see shopkeepers who lie in wait for their customers as a spider waits for flies. All of them hang ensnared in the spider's web, from which they are unable to escape. This web is the god of charm, the insidious, omnipotent, whose name is Dinar."[180] And Tolstoy wrote about money as follows:

> The man who has money can buy up all the bread, and so starve the next man, and enslave him completely for bread. And this happens before our eyes on an enormous scale ... The oppressor does not need money for exchange – he can take what he needs without exchange – but only for the convenience of the violence that consists in the harbouring of money, and it is easiest to hold money by enslaving as many people as possible.[181]

The same ideas form the basis of Naimy's book of essays entitled *al-Awthan* (*The Idols*), written in the 1950s, in which one can detect a consonance with the main themes of Tolstoy's book *On Life* and other of his sociopolitical writings. In this book Naimy reflects on the fact that in the course of their lives people venerate the idols they have created themselves: "Idolatry is something created by man, and it is that which he worships as though it truly possesses the absolute capacity to make man happy, to heal him and to provide for his needs, including his material needs."[182]

The author reveals a living scene that shows the substance, origin and effect of the "idols": money, power, strength, public opinion, nationalism, science and the like. Here is his discourse about the essence of wealth and money:

> And as regards the *fils* [a small denomination of currency], it has done what neither the devils nor the angels could do ... it has put one [man] in the place of thousands, and sometimes of millions.
> Here is the secret. This is the trap, the place where one can slip. Here it is, that immense source of hatred, envy and conflict between people.
> The invention in hell of the *fils* led to the situation in which one man gained the ability to appropriate to himself the portions of the common good of thousands of people, while thousands of people were left without the share of even one.
> The result of this was the oppression of man by man, the submission of the masses to one individual and the exploitation of those to whom the *fils* did not take a liking by those whom it sought out as its companions.[183]

The anticlerical element of Naimy's work can also be clearly seen in *The Last Day*: as Musa says, "In the churches I see incense and burning candles, foreheads beating the ground, hands raised high, fingers making the sign of the cross and lips whispering prayers, psalms and supplications."[184]

In *The Last Day* Naimy continues to seek the true meaning of existence, and finds it, as also in *Memoirs of a Vagrant Soul* and *The Book of Mirdad*, in the knowledge and study of one's own self: "He [man] will not find the way to God if he does not find the way to his own self. Man is the path from man to man. What could be more foolish than trying to find God and oneself outside of one's own 'I'?"[185] So Musa reasons, affirming a meaning for human existence only in the knowledge of one's own self and in the exaltation of man's spiritual powers. Naimy's deep grasp of the essence of the human self had already found expression in his earlier works:

> Man, in my view, is a seed of the divine (may the fault-finders forgive my resorting to metaphor). This seed contains all the powers of supremacy – from the knowledge of all things to ability in all things, from existence in all times to existence in all places – just as the seed of a plant contains all the specifics of the plant that grew it. The possibilities for his growth are without limit.
>
> "Are we Better, or our Fathers?"[186]

The same ideas also appear in his aphorisms: "The ocean has its shore, the dry land has its boundaries and the planets have their unceasing paths. But where are the shores and boundaries of man, and who knows his path?' (*A Vineyard by the Road*).[187]

In conception, *The Last Day* to a certain degree parallels the theme of Tolstoy's story *The Death of Ivan Il'ich* (or *Ilyich*).[188] Ivan Il'ich Golovin is an important functionary who has lived, like many of those around him, a life of falsity and deceit. Shortly before his death he sees reality in a new and piercing light: now he perceives his wife, his colleagues, his son and the peasants who wait on him differently, and realises that his service up to now, and his relations with his wife, colleagues and comrades, have all been false and insincere. His former "respectable, jolly and pleasant life", as it appears before Ivan Il'ich's death, is a greater horror even than the horror of his imminent death. With great artistic power and psychological insight, Tolstoy portrays the moral rebirth of a man in the face of approaching death; in the face of death everything is revealed to him anew, as though the veil of the flesh that had previously covered the essence of life has been lifted. And Ivan is horrified. But Tolstoy, as the great realist, links these complex intellectual foresights with the real and specific circumstances that surrounded him. Thus it is illness that exacerbates the sensitivity of Ivan's soul and the acuteness with which he comprehends the falsity that surrounded him, and that exposes to him the essence of things. This theme has not been developed in Naimy's novel.

The Last Day is written from a Romantic standpoint, and from wishful and imaginary perspectives: a contrived life, eccentric situations, hyperbolised feelings, impossible heroes and abstract reasoning. One may speak of closeness to the Tolstoy work only in the sense that in both works the self-analysis of the heroes is the primary device, and in particular that both heroes are trying to understand the lives they have passed as they stand on the boundary of life and death.

Naimy's novel shows certain direct coincidences in imagery with certain works by Tolstoy. One example is Musa's dream, which he remembers perfectly on waking; in the dream he finds himself swimming against the current of the "river of life", which symbolises existence. All people, however, submit to the current and do not row their ships against it. Musa says:

> I am on the bank of a deep, wide river ... It flows, and yet somehow does not flow. Having reached the place where I stand, it enters a dark tunnel, where it can no longer be seen or heard ... On the surface of the river, as far as the eye can see, there jostle countless ships and boats of different shapes, sizes and colours. All of them sail down the river towards the tunnel, and disappear into it.[189]

Small boats and great ships sail past, each symbolising, for example, wealth, power, religion, art, the military, science, etc.; they reach the tunnel and disappear inside it. When Musa asks why he is being shown this, he is answered by the "black-and-white man": "My purpose, as I have already said, is to show you the perpetual procession. Everything that flows along the river of time must finish its journey in the tunnel of darkness. Everything that does not point to its own true condition is doomed to oblivion."[190] When Musa asks who can save himself, he is given this reply: only the one who rows against the current. "Yes, if you row against the current of the river, which is time, until you reach its source, then you will arrive where there is no time or space, and Essence, which has no beginning, can have no end."[191]

Suddenly Musa notices a small boat emerging from the mouth of the tunnel: "The boat moved against the current of the river. The two men in the boat rowed with great zeal, and their movements showed no wavering, weakness or fear."[192] These men were on their way to immortality. It is interesting to compare this passage with an extract from Tolstoy's *My Confession*:

> What happened to me was something like this: I was put into a boat (I do not remember when) and pushed off from an unknown shore, shown the direction of the opposite shore, had oars put into my unpractised hands, and was left alone. I rowed as best I could and moved forward; but the further I advanced towards the middle of the stream the more rapid grew the current bearing me away from my goal and the more frequently did I encounter others, like myself, borne away by the stream. There were a few rowers who continued to row, there were others who had abandoned their oars; there were large boats and immense vessels full of people. Some struggled against the current, others yielded to it. And the further I went the more, seeing the progress down the current of all those who were adrift, I forgot the direction given me. In the very centre of the stream, amid the crowd of boats and vessels which were being borne down stream, I quite lost my direction and abandoned my oars. Around me on all sides, with mirth and rejoicing, people with sails and oars were borne down the stream, assuring me and each other that no other direction was possible. And I believed them and floated with them. And I was carried far; so far that I heard the roar of the rapids in which I must be shattered, and I saw boats shattered

in them. And I recollected myself. I was long unable to understand what had happened to me. I saw before me nothing but destruction, towards which I was rushing and which I feared. I saw no safety anywhere and did not know what to do; but, looking back, I perceived innumerable boats which unceasingly and strenuously pushed across the stream, and I remembered about the shore, the oars, and the direction, and began to pull back upwards against the stream and towards the shore.

That shore was God; that direction was tradition; the oars were the freedom given me to pull for the shore and unite with God. And so the force of life was renewed in me and I again began to live.[193]

The symbolic elements that unite the two writers are the image of the river with its fast current, to which practically everybody submits, the current itself, which draws boats away towards their destruction (for Naimy, in the tunnel; for Tolstoy, on the rapids) and the sole means of salvation, which is to row against the current. In *The Last Day* can be seen the influence of Tolstoy's moral–religious outlook, his uncompromising criticism of the structure of human society, and his quest for the religious ideal and for self-knowledge.

As with the other works by Naimy mentioned earlier, this novel contains no natural development of life and no living interaction between people. The main character has been removed from his natural setting and placed in a rarefied situation. He discusses, learns and reveals only eternal truths, incomprehensible to ordinary people. Typical features of this type of text in Naimy include the recounting of prophetic dreams, prophecies and presentiments, and the appearance of angels, prophets and divine envoys.

One should not expect from this group of Naimy's works (*Memoirs of a Vagrant Soul*, *The Book of Mirdad* and *The Last Day*), with their philosophical and parable-like substance, an accurate portrayal of real Lebanese life. Nevertheless, they are an objective reflection of reality. The moral outlooks of Naimy's heroes and his views on many contemporary problems were typical of many Arab writers, and they excited and continue to excite his contemporaries.

Fathers and Sons: Naimy's play and Turgenev's novel

The name *Fathers and Sons* is common to two works, one by the Lebanese writer and one by the Russian, and has inevitably attracted the attention of Soviet scholars of the new Arabic literature to Naimy's play.

Krachkovsky calls this play "one of the dramas of the new school",[194] remarking that he finds in it "reminiscences of Russian literature".[195] Ode-Vasil'eva asserts that Naimy's drama carries "onto Arab soil and into the Arab milieu the ideas and images of the well-known Russian author's novel of the same name".[196] This view is also shared by Dolinina, who notes that "this supposition may indeed have an entirely real basis, since

Naimy, the 'Poltava seminarist', was, as he says himself, raised on Russian literature".[197]

It is difficult not to take into account Naimy's assertion that the main idea of Turgenev's novel *Fathers and Sons* was merely his "point of departure". The problems around which the dramatic conflict is based, the basic images of the "fathers" and "sons", the setting, circumstances, surroundings and characters, as well as the development of the plot, the ending and additional sub-plots, are nevertheless entirely specific to the reality of Lebanese life in the early twentieth century, a time of great social change. The appearance of common factors in the portrayals by different writers of the pressing problems of their day, though they may be far apart in time and place, is an interesting and widely encountered phenomenon in world literature. On the basis of such similarities there emerges a response to the questions of the time, which is bounded by specific social and historical needs for social development, and also the natural process of interaction between world literatures.

Naimy's play *Fathers and Sons* is not merely a stage adaptation of Turgenev's novel, with a changed plot-line and names of characters, and re-situated in the Lebanon. Inter-generational conflict was as topical a problem for the Arab East in the early twentieth century as it had been for Russia in the mid-nineteenth. As V.Yu. Troitsky justly remarks,

> it was probably not a coincidence that Bazarov attracted the attention of all thinking people ... of course such an attitude was not by chance, and Turgenev's novel contained questions of relevance to all countries, and characters like Bazarov were appearing in different countries at the time of collapse of the obsolete forms; Bazarov was "familiar" to many.[198]

There is little doubt that Naimy had read the Russian author's novel. He mentions in his autobiography that, like Pushkin and Lermontov, he considered Turgenev his literary teacher.[199] On the link between the play and the novel he writes:

> I wrote the drama *Fathers and Sons* in three weeks. In choosing the title I was fully aware that it was already the name of an acclaimed novel by the Russian writer Turgenev. I see nothing wrong in this. After all, the title is not original; on the contrary, it is perhaps the first thought that comes into the mind of any writer who wants to examine the conflict between two generations. This title is not unlike, say, "Poetry and Poets", "East and West", "Life and Death" and so on. In such situations, where the titles and ideas are similar, what is required is a different approach to the theme. And my approach to the struggle between fathers and sons is entirely different to that of Turgenev in terms of the events, the heroes and the dialogues.[200]

Naimy's play was written in 1916 and first published in parts in the émigré newspaper *al-Funun/Funoon* (*The Arts*), but in 1918 it was printed in book form in New York and became Naimy's first published literary work. "The first of my books to be printed was the play *Fathers and Sons*, published in 1918",[201] he wrote.

Fathers and Sons may be considered as an attempt by Naimy to embody artistically the aesthetic principles and demands that he proclaims in his works of criticism. The basic idea of *Fathers and Sons* is a social conflict between two generations. On the one side are the fathers, who strictly adhere to their traditional convictions, jealously and fanatically preserving the ancient customs and the old way of life, convinced that this approach to life is the only acceptable one and that their children must be brought up in the same spirit. On the other are the sons, who, influenced by new trends, avidly imbibe all that is modern and try to escape the narrow confines of the outdated canons that no longer satisfy them, and strive to create the new with their own hands.

Before analysing Naimy's play, let us recall the main substance of Turgenev's novel. In *Fathers and Sons* Turgenev portrays with great artistic force the struggle between Russian democratic thinking and Russian liberalism, and reflects one of the main social phenomena of late nineteenth-century Russia: the growing self-awareness of the peasant masses and their fermenting hatred of the nobility and bureaucracy. G.A. Bialy comments that: "In developing the burning issues of his time, he (Turgenev) created the image of a great country full of inexhaustible possibilities and moral forces ... This picture of Russia, painted by a great realist, enriched the artistic consciousness of all humanity."[202] Additionally Turgenev had occasion to reflect substantial elements in his works of the revolutionary–democratic movement of the 1860s.

> Turgenev's literary activity was deeply influenced by the emancipation movement that was developing in Russia in the mid and late nineteenth century. At the same time, his works were in fact a significant factor in that movement. Turgenev's works played a major role in developing social awareness and in overcoming delusions, prejudices and misconceptions in the struggle against social ills.[203]

However, as with all notable works by great artists, the value and importance of the novel is not limited to the topical content of its period and the resulting portrayal of typical scenes that in their turn reveal certain patterns of Russian life. The novel is broad in its artistic scope. The specific aspects of life with which it deals are revealed with such depth and artistic power that the temporal elements, which belong to a certain moment in the nation's history, take on a universal significance and help to bring to light various aspects of universal progress. "The novel overstepped the boundaries of a specific literary phenomenon to become a 'document' of immense social and political significance."[204]

To illustrate this, here is an extract by the American writer Sinclair Lewis from the preface he wrote to a new translation (1943) of the novel into English:[205]

'Turgenev's novel has not gone out of date ... the story of Bazarov is just as moving in 1943 as it was in 1862, ... because it tells of those difficult searches for
ways in life that always disturb people. Bazarov called himself a "nihilist." Call
him a communist, a surrealist or a biopsychologist, give him cigarettes instead
of roll-ups and a fast car instead of the post-carriage in which he hurried to
see his beloved Anna Sergeyevna, and then the burning in his heart and the
rebelliousness in his mind will not seem old-fashioned to anybody. His name is
one of the few in literature that is alive.[206]

Here Sinclair Lewis captures what is most striking in the character Bazarov:
"the burning in his heart and the rebelliousness in his mind". In Bazarov,
Turgenev succeeded in expressing the eternal daring of youth and its desire
to re-examine and shake up all that is old and outdated, and to express that
nihilism towards the older generation and its achievements which is particular to one at that stage of adolescent youth, a stage which is not yet entirely
formed and has not grasped the full measure of things.

What matters here is not whether the portrayal of Bazarov is positive or
negative or the degree of accuracy with which he reflects the leading figures
of his time. What is entirely clear is that Bazarov, who is drawn in graphic
and tangible detail, personifies a Russia awakening, on the threshold of revolution and of renouncing for ever the old social system and all its countless
ramifications. At the universal level, however, Bazarov represents a generic
young shaker and rebel; it is no coincidence that Turgenev declared Bazarov
to be akin to the entire line of Russian rejectionists, beginning with Belinsky. It may be noted that at that time the idea of a "rejectionist" was sacro-
sanct, and referred to a person who passionately protested against all violence, rigid routines, stagnancy and injustice. Guy de Maupassant observed
that "Turgenev ... was the first to turn his attention to that new state among
the leading intellects ... to that unknown and hitherto unnoticed political
and philosophical fermentation that was to shake Russia."[207]

The heroes of Turgenev's other works – such as Insarov (*On the Eve*),
Nezhdanov (*Virgin Soil*) and Rudin (*Rudin*) – similarly depict leading figures
whose convictions and aspirations are always contrary to the values of the
lives that surround them. As G.A. Bialy comments, "The successive heroes
of Turgenev's novels, who each represented one or another generation of
ideas, created in the mind of the Russian reader and of readers throughout
the world the typical image of a thinking Russian person who realised that
his personal destiny was inseparably linked to the fate of his country."[208]

At the start of the twentieth century the mood among Arab writers
and intellectuals, including Naimy, coincided with the awakening of national self-consciousness in the countries of the East. The transition of the
Arab countries to capitalism took place against the backdrop of a national
freedom struggle against the expansionist policies of the European powers.
The late nineteenth and early twentieth centuries were marked in the Arab
lands (particularly Syria and Egypt) as the era of Enlightenment, the era
of the Arab Renaissance. The demand for more widespread education of

the masses, and a mood of protest against outdated conventions and prejudices, against the power of religion, fanaticism and violence – these were
the general feelings most characteristic of the leading Arab intelligentsia at
that time. As a result of the growth of national self-consciousness in the sociopolitical and cultural spheres of Arab society, an ideological battle raged
between the old and the new, between the conservatives and the supporters
of reform.

The events described in Naimy's play take place in a small Lebanese
town at the start of the twentieth century and concern an apparently happy,
well-to-do and distinguished family. Umm Ilyas, the widow of the deceased
Butrus Bek Samaha, tries with all her strength to maintain order in her
family and controls the destiny of her children as she wishes, relying on the
canons established by centuries of tradition. "Children should honour their
parents" is Umm Ilyas' fundamental motto. She prepares to give her daughter in marriage to the dissolute and frivolous Nasif Bek, solely because he
and his father Musa Bek Arkush are of noble stock and carry the title "Bek"
(bey, beg). By means of this marriage Umm Ilyas dreams of becoming
related to a traditionally respected noble line.

Her eldest son Ilyas Samaha is an educated young man with progressive views. However, he does not have the power to oppose his mother. In
the family circle Ilyas comes up against the severe and outdated traditions
that are manifest in his mother's despotic power. Ilyas is convinced that
the old puts down roots that are too deep in the consciousness of people.
He reflects on this, and is overcome by a mood of pessimism. In vain he
seeks a way out of the contradictions between the traditions and values of
conservative Oriental society and the modern mode of thinking that was
introduced to him by his education. He feels too alone, and the forces of
evil that oppose him are unflinching. Consequently, Ilyas does not believe
it possible to act with determination and defend his freedom and that of his
sister. The only solution he can find to this increasingly complex situation
is suicide.

But then Ilyas' friend, the schoolteacher Da'ud Salama, comes to his
mother's house on a visit. His appearance interrupts the normal course of
life in the family of Butrus Bek Samaha. Da'ud's arrival breathes new life
into the household, and he tries to instil in Ilyas and his sister a belief in a
better future and to dispel their joyless thoughts.

As Dolinina correctly observes, "the plot of Naimy's drama bears a re-
semblance to that of Turgenev's novel."[209] The distinctive mark of Turgenev
the novelist is the fact that the plots of all his novels begin immediately
the main hero is introduced. Moreover, this hero is placed by the author
straight into dramatic conflict, be this psychological or of ideas, with the
other characters. Thus Rudin first appears in the background of a salon
held by the lady and landowner Dar'ya Lasunskaya; Lavretsky (*A Nest of
Gentlefolk*) bumps into the successful functionary and Westerniser, Vladimir
Panshin, and the Bulgarian Insarov is at once juxtaposed with the liberals

Bersenev and Shubin. Bazarov is quickly introduced to all three Kirsanovs. This is the psychological and ideological basis of the plot.

The plot of Naimy's play thus begins with the appearance of the major positive character, Da'ud Salama, at the house of Umm Ilyas Samaha, who clings on to the most bigoted and hardened traditional ways. Da'ud has come to visit his long-standing friend Ilyas. Da'ud is thirty years old and not from a noble background; he lives on the meagre means of a teacher, but is an optimist (in complete contrast to Bazarov) and full of dignity. He is tolerant and always ready to help people; he believes in the power of reason to direct and improve the condition of society. Da'ud does not accept life as he finds it. In his view, the purpose of man is to fight for the way life ought to be: "Is it not so that all life is a struggle? If our life were a constant fight against ignorance, injustice, poverty, weakness and servility, then there would be more freedom, which we have to revive. For we do not love life the way it is, but rather life the way we want it to become."[210]

One of the main problems with which the play deals is introduced from the first scene: respect for one's elders and obedience to them. When Ilyas complains that his mother demands his unquestioning obedience to her every whim, Da'ud, while agreeing in principle with this ancient patriarchal position, makes a sound modification: "They say: 'Respect your father and your mother.' But they do not say 'Obey your father and your mother even when they are mistaken.'"[211] He appeals to the use of reason and logic, while not rejecting universal ethical rules. If absurdity and nonsense come even from one's mother, one should resist them "with all one's strength". By marrying his sweetheart Zinat, however, Da'ud gains the blessing of her mother for the wedding in accordance with the old customs, may call her "Mother", and goes to live in her house. As we can see, he has little of Bazarov in him or of his arrogant nihilistic pride towards all that is traditional and his desire to destroy. It is true that Da'ud speaks words to Ilyas that might be ambiguous: "There dwell hand in hand inside me a passion to destroy and a passion to create." But he says this in passing, without attaching these passions to "destroy and create" to any specific words or actions.

The one thing that is clear from all his appearances is that he considers the idea of complete obedience to one's elders to be prejudiced, and is indignant at religious intolerance and its external ritual. He himself does not believe in God, but carries Him in his heart. It is implied as a logical conclusion that Da'ud stands for enlightenment (he is after all a teacher) and for a position of dignity for women in society. Thus his struggle against obscure prejudices, religious intolerance and external Church religiosity, and for the education of the people and an improved position for women, is the very moderate agenda of an Arab enlightener of the early twentieth century, and far from active protest or demands for radical change.

Da'ud also has a very modest view of his own strengths and opportunities. In the final monologue, addressed to his future mother-in-law, he describes himself thus: "You think of me as poor, but I am not poor. I have

firm resolve, love, strength, a sense of my own dignity and some intelligence
... My pedigree is here before you: myself."[212] This monologue characterises
Da'ud's human dignity: modesty, honesty, belief in himself and also a belief
in the triumph of good forces in life. "Yes, this is the life we have in this
East", he says to his sister. "But it will change, without fail it will change.
It will change because the present generation was born in a different world
that is not like the one in which their parents were born."[213] But when? For
what reason? What circumstances will cause "this Eastern life" to change?
Not one word is spoken about this in the entire play. Even Da'ud's remarks
– and he is the main representative of the new directions – come over as
modest, calm and as though waiting for something. Here are none of the
storms or passions of a Bazarov.

It is also worth noting that the role of Da'ud in the structure of the play
is modest. In the novel, Bazarov is a necessary and key participant in the
action throughout the story. All the other characters are grouped around
him, and the development of events can only take place through him.
Da'ud, on the other hand, is only an important character in the first act.
In the second act he does no more than declare his love to Zinat – who in
any case has all but openly declared her love to him already. In the third act
Da'ud appears in the tenth and final scene, where he is subjected to a brutal
insult. He is accused of cohabiting with his sister with the aim of polygamy.
In response to the accusations Da'ud merely exclaims, "Thieves, bandits!"
When he is ejected by force from the room, he leaves obediently. On top of
this, the episode nearly costs his beloved Zinat her life; in despair at what
has taken place she drinks poison. And the fourth, concluding act does not
involve Da'ud at all.

Overall, we may conclude that the representation of Da'ud is sketchy,
somewhat one-dimensional and rational. His actual actions in the play are
very few, and his inner world and convictions are revealed only in his monologues, where he acts to a large degree as a mouthpiece for the positive
ideas of the author. All this is indicative of the fact that in creating the
character of Da'ud Naimy made use of Enlightenment Realist methods.
It is generally the case for Enlightenment writers that their characters are
poorly defined in terms of specific social circumstances, by which we mean
not only the plausibility of specific details but also a broad and trustwor-
thy portrayal of the social situation, morals and customs of the country.
Enlightenment Realists do not fully reveal the essence of life itself and the
social relations that define all other factors. Therefore, the positive hero in
Enlightenment works almost always appears as a philosophiser or preacher,
and not a flesh-and-blood person. Little is revealed of Da'ud as a person, as
an individual with feelings and a self. We hear only his monologues, with
which he appeals solely to the listener's reason, logic and understanding.

Nevertheless, we should realise that in even creating the character of
Da'ud Naimy was a reformer of Arab literature, standing far ahead of the
literary milieu in which he moved (that of the émigré Arabs in the USA),

which, by force of historical circumstance, had at that time only begun to adopt Romanticism (in particular that of Kahlil Gibran, Ameen Rihani and others) while European literature had already been engaged with Critical Realism for a number of decades.

Other figures in the play are, however, portrayed in greater depth and are more persuasive, revealing a Critical Realist approach by the author.

A certain degree of sketchiness is also evident in the unfolding of the action. This is based on the relationships of two couples: between Da'ud and Zinat, sister of his friend Ilyas, and between Shahida, sister of Da'ud, and Ilyas. The plot develops in such a way that Da'ud "saves" Zinat, while his sister Shahida "saves" the weak-willed and disillusioned pessimist Ilyas. All is concluded in the best possible way, with both pairs joined by happy marital ties.

More artistically convincing is the character of Ilyas. He is an educated, sensitive, but emotionally depressed man. He holds the same progressive views as his friend Da'ud. However, he sees around him an insurmountable wall of darkness, ignorance and powerful ancient prejudices, and is driven to despair by his sense of powerlessness against them. Naturally, this hatred of the evil around him is coupled with his sense of the pointlessness of struggle, and causes him to be disillusioned with life. At his first meeting with Da'ud, Ilyas says: "I'm on the verge of choking, Da'ud, choking in this world which lives in the past, which sees neither the present nor the future. Life has become a heavy burden, and my presence in this world is the drop that causes the cup to overflow."[214] He compares his sister somewhat poetically to "a precious stone in the hands of a blind merchant", that is to say in the hands of his mother, who is forcing her to marry the ungifted versifier Nasif Bek, who, it transpires, is bankrupt and is sent off to the debtors' prison at the end of the play. To Da'ud's question "Have you tried to talk sense to your mother?", Ilyas replies:

> You are talking nonsense, my friend. And this is no surprise, for you don't know my mother's character. You don't know my sister. I tell you, for me this house has become a burial vault, and life has become hellish. Do not hold it against me if somebody tells you tomorrow that your friend Ilyas Samaha has hanged himself from one of the oaks in the grove outside the entrance to the city.[215]

With his aversion to everything around him, Ilyas does not lift a finger to make even the smallest change in his surroundings. One of Da'ud's merits is that he reawakens in his friend the will and belief, which had been suppressed by his mother, in the possibility of altering reality.

Ilyas cannot of course be compared to Arkady Kirsanov in Turgenev's novel, a man with an unusual lack of distinctiveness or originality, who is forever falling under the influence of stronger personalities – first Bazarov and then Ekaterina Odintsova. Ilyas, by contrast, has views and ideas of his own and is an attentive and subtle observer of life. One may nevertheless reproach him for lacking the necessary will to be faithful to his principles.

For example, he describes his mother accurately and at length to Da'ud:

> Don't forget, my friend, that Umm Ilyas does not only represent her own
> generation; the convictions, prejudices and illusions of many generations have
> put down their roots in her soul and are firmly anchored in its earth. And by
> no means is it easy to pull out these roots. You do not have to overcome her,
> probably the reverse. Be reasonable, Da'ud. Tear out one root, and a thousand
> will grow in its place.[216]

From this it would seem that Ilyas thinks more deeply and soberly than
does Da'ud. He makes a witty comparison: the chances of bringing Umm
Ilyas round to a new point of view on any matter would be like that of
scooping out the ocean with the cap of an acorn. And ultimately it is he who
turns out to be right, not Da'ud: Umm Ilyas gives in not because she has
been convinced by some point of view contrary to her own, and not because
her only daughter has poisoned herself and almost died. Even after her
daughter's attempted suicide she goes again to discuss the shady deal with
the father of the presumed groom, who has offered to marry them without
Zinat's consent. It is only the news that this "groom" has been jailed for his
debts that causes her to agree to her daughter's marriage to Da'ud. Ilyas is
right: his mother is an inflexible person whose mind is so callous and en-
crusted that it is impossible to get through to her by any logical reasoning
or example.

Ilyas is capable of faithful and unselfish love, and this is the manner in
which he loves his sister Zinat. He is overcome with joy and rapture on
hearing of Da'ud's love for her and his intention of marrying her: "My
God, if this is so, then my wildest dream has come true." Therefore Ilyas
evaluates the circumstances and recognises Da'ud as the possible husband
of his sister.

Towards the end of the play Ilyas undergoes a sea change, becoming
more active, showing more joy in life and referring to himself as a blind
man whose sight has been restored: "Shahida! ... You are everything to me
in this life", he says to his bride. "Shahida! I was blind but my sight has
been restored. Your love has become the light in my eyes! ... Shahida! How
beautiful life is!"[217] And the reader is left in no doubt that Ilyas will be a
deserving member of the new generation. One is given to believe that this
complete change in Ilyas is the result of Shahida's love and that it was her
that instilled resolve, courage and certainty in him, since Ilyas had always
asserted that life is meaningless and ugly, and had been ready to end his.
Having fallen in love, however, he becomes a conscious supporter of the
"sons", the representatives of the new.

The characters of the two young women in *Fathers and Sons*, Zinat and
Shahida, add much to the success of the work. The person of Zinat is particularly appealing. Despite her meekness and femininity, she exhibits a strong
character. She submits to her mother out of her own conviction, if one may
say such a thing. Having deeply absorbed the old truth, fed to her every

year of her life, that the first debt of the child is to obey her parents, Zinat consciously serves her mother and trusts her, although she has no feeling whatsoever for the fiancé intended for her. The love that is awoken in her towards Da'ud gives her strength and resolve, and the capacity to act. Going against her mother's prohibition, she goes to Da'ud and tells him of her love; when it seems to her that they will never be together, she takes poison. She is akin to those women who are capable of undertaking heroic deeds and dying for their moral principles. The entire description of Zinat is convincing: gentle, tender, submissive, restrained in her words and loyal in her love.

Shahida, Da'ud's sister, has a very different nature. Her spiritual kinship with her brother and her hard-working, independent life lend a sense of certainty, self-respect and courage to her actions. She speaks a good deal and confidently, without circumspection or half-tones. In the play she is also highly active. She responds quickly to whatever her brother does, supporting him. Her unselfish care, concern and night vigils save Zinat's life. With her active energy, persistence and strength of will Shahida succeeds in winning Ilyas and instils in him optimism and faith. She is in love with life and capable of embracing all its beautiful manifestations. "I am envious of myself because I live in this world and am grateful with all my soul to the creator. All physical ailments, difficulties of the soul and trials of the heart are no more than a small white cloud in a summer sky. Life is beautiful!"[218] Also noteworthy in her character is a thirst for action. At her first meeting with Ilyas she expresses amazement at his lack of action when her sister is about to be given in marriage by force. "How strange that a young man like you, who seeks the meaning of his existence, watches in silence while his sister is coerced to marry someone she does not love and who is unfit to be even her servant. And you have not tried to save your sister."[219]

While recognising Naimy's creative triumph in these two characters, we find no common ground between them and the female characters of Turgenev's novel, Odintsova and her sister.

The character of Khalil, Ilyas' younger brother, is necessary both to the composition of the play and as an addition to the general portrayal of the morals and way of life in a Lebanese town in the early twentieth century. It is through Khalil that both the main characters and the audience gain essential information about the comical poetaster and ne'er-do-well Nasif Bek. Nasif is a close chum of Khalil and can be found at every gathering or occasion for merrymaking. Khalil is openly cynical and primitive, and not prone to excess scruples: for the sake of gossip, effect and a good life not only does he maintain his friendship with Nasif but also feels no pity for his own sister. And so, without thinking, he blurts out to his mother everything he knows about Nasif. And it is Khalil who thus brings her the breaking news about his arrest and the auctioning of his father's house. Here his role is natural and vital for the action to proceed. For these are the circumstances that finally persuade the unbending Umm Ilyas that her daughter's marriage to Nasif does not bear thinking about.

The negative characters of Naimy's play, the "fathers", are also artistically persuasive, representing stagnated and obsolete opinions and militantly
guarding the truth as they see it. The principal such character is Umm Ilyas,
the mother of Ilyas, Khalil and Zinat. She is a wealthy widow who considers
herself the sovereign ruler of her family. The other character that personifies all the negative qualities of the archaic generation is Musa Bek Arkush,
a former bailiff and the father of Nasif Bek. What is particularly interesting is that despite the fact that their views on morals and the preservation
of the old ways are entirely in agreement, they are very different people.
Despite her imperiousness, obstinacy and bellicosity in standing for the old
order, Umm Ilyas is unsophisticated, gullible and sincere. Nowhere is she
a hypocrite, nor does she act against her conscience, so firm is her conviction that passion and persistence will see her through. Her code of everyday
moral conduct is extremely primitive. Her model of a man is her deceased
husband, who used to cut off the heads of Muslims, both Sunnis and Druze,
with a sword, and who carefully attended every church service. For her, the
most important thing in a person is his breeding. No matter if Nasif Bek is a
drunkard and a loafer; he is a "Bek", and for Umm Ilyas that says it all. Her
superior court is "what they will say in town, and the neighbours". When
Musa Bek persuades her to let him marry her daughter to his son by force,
she expresses this reserve: "But what if Zinat dies? What will people say
then?" As for children, in her view their most important virtue is absolute
and unquestioning obedience. She herself relates crudely and ignorantly
to her children, and she deals with any trace of rebelliousness by swearing,
cursing and the cane. Even religion, which she values so zealously, is alien
to her in its moral principles. Everything boils down, for her, to external
ritual: to go to church, when this is prescribed, to light candles and repeat
the prescribed prayers.

Umm Ilyas is not particularly intelligent. She takes everything that the
sly and resourceful Musa Bek tells her at face value, without thinking for
a moment about what he is saying. Her favourite son is Khalil, because
he never opposes her; she forgives him the fact that he is an idle gossip
and hypocrite with no principles. Her elder son Ilyas remains a mystery
to her, and most significantly she is not in any way perturbed by the pain,
despair and confusion he experiences; she believes that he puts this on "to
spite her". As she says of him, "He is a loafer and an ignoramus ... he needs
neither God nor the devil, and he does not care what is heaven and what is
hell. Now he talks about hanging or shooting himself, and now suddenly he
wants to become a ploughman, to sow and reap."[220]

It has never occurred to Umm Ilyas to think of what her daughter represents. While the latter serves her without demur, everything remains calm
and in its place. When her daughter starts to stand up to her, Zinat at once
becomes in her mother's eyes a "vile creature", a "she-devil", "ungodly" and
a "whore without shame or conscience". Here one should remember that
Umm Ilyas, having grown accustomed to the unquestioned obedience of all

those in her power, is incapable of showing any restraint or self-control, or of thinking through the consequences of her actions.

Yet in front of Musa and Nasif Bek she is wholly meek and gentle, her tone towards them respectful to the point of ingratiating. This is not because she wants something from them, but simply because these are "Beks", and she finds it flattering to associate with them. This woman, who understands nothing in life, who thinks nothing through, and who is deaf and blind to everything that is forever accepted on what in reality is a foundation of conventions and prejudices, surely comes over as barbaric. And the fate of her children would seem still more tragic, for they are far more intelligent, complex and delicate than their mother. After all, it is only chance that saves both Ilyas and Zinat from the deaths wished upon them by her blind and unreasoning force.

In the character of Umm Ilyas, Naimy has formed a cogent summary of an obtuse fanatic who blindly persecutes all that does not conform to her ideas of what is acceptable or "correct". For Umm Ilyas, the "correct" is determined by the system in which children are brought up and by religious ministry. She represents a broad artistic generalisation by Naimy of this personality type.

The author does not, however, abandon the inner truth of even this character, causing Umm Ilyas' heart to soften and be filled with gratitude towards Shahida for selflessly saving the life of her daughter after she had taken the poison. She even dares to object to Musa Bek Arkush himself: "And I should tell you, Musa Bek, I have seen plenty of girls in my life, but have never seen and never will see another like this. ... She sat at the head of Zinat's bed like an angel. She had nothing to eat or drink for two or three days, and did not sleep for a minute ... Finally my heart trembled".[21] By revealing this human element in such an impenitent and stern personality as Umm Ilyas, Naimy underlines still more strongly the terrible power of prejudice, stagnation and habitual thinking. After all, it turns out that even Umm Ilyas could have been a different person, had it not been for that setting, that environment, which made her what she is.

Musa Bek Arkush, the other figure in the play who represents the "fathers" of the older generation, is a clerk of the court. He plays an active part in the pettifoggery, extortion and humiliation by the lawyers of ordinary people. Being a court official, however, he has learned to maintain a good exterior appearance, behind which he hides the basest thoughts and feelings. Like Umm Ilyas, he will not argue, nor will he express his true motives. Everything is hidden behind the mask of a seemingly reserved, respectable, quiet and polite individual. He is clever and cunning, and adroitly manipulates the people he needs. Musa understands Umm Ilyas completely; he is aware of her stupidity, gullibility and reverence towards him. He is a "Bek", and is thus able to play the accompaniment to her recitatives of outrage about the younger generation: "But this is the younger generation, Umm Ilyas! Oh, God forbid. When did we or our ancestors ever hear about a daughter being able to disobey her father or mother? And heaven knows what else you might hear – have you seen, they want to marry only out of love, without priests, and divorce whenever they like!"[222]

From Musa's words one can see how far the breakdown of the old values has proceeded, and that society has inevitably split into two camps. In front of Umm Ilyas he does not hint at his real reasons for wanting to marry his son Nasif to her daughter. Hypocritically he reminds her of his friendship with her deceased husband, adding that he is captivated by Zinat's superb upbringing and beauty, and that his ultimate motivation is his respect for Umm Ilyas herself. Musa lies even to Nasif. He is concerned less about his son than about himself, for while they are both used to a life of idleness and luxury, playing cards and spending their time in coffee houses, he is now threatened with complete bankruptcy. As he says to Nasif:

> Do you think that I want to have her wealth for myself? My days are numbered, but what will you live on in future? ... If you let go of these spoils, who will give you money to eat, drink and buy clothes? How will you repay your debts? My vineyards have been sold. My mulberry groves have been sold. My land has been sold. The horse has been sold. The house has been mortgaged.[223]

Musa teaches his son how to be successful in arranging his marriage: first he should eliminate (that is, kill) the rival, then pretend to be in love with, and all-forgiving towards Zinat and also attract her younger brother Khalil onto his side, well aware of the latter's lack of principles. And so, in the scene with Da'ud, Musa, while pretending to be polite, tolerant and understanding, strikes him outright with an abominable slander. He delivers this in his habitually reserved and respectable tone of voice: "I have one more thing to ask you. If you marry this noble young lady, then what do you propose to do with your current wife? Divorce her?" Musa Bek does not react to Da'ud's angry puzzlement, but continues to defame him: "Well, you can't fool me. I'm talking about the woman who lives with you whom you pass off as your sister. But I and everybody around you know that this is no sister, but your wife."[224] As if thunderstruck, Da'ud is at a loss at such effrontery. But Musa takes advantage of the general confusion to eject Da'ud from the room. At that moment Zinat decides to take poison.

Musa's hypocrisy and cold calculation are astonishing. After sending his supposed new daughter-in-law almost to her grave, no sooner has she begun to recover than he goes to Umm Ilyas to enquire about her daughter's health:

> Believe me, from the first day of the girl's illness I could neither eat nor drink. Even in my sleep I thought only of her ... But you should have seen Nasif. He would not eat or drink, and the name Zinat did not pass his lips. Where didn't he go, to avoid saying "Zinat, Zinat, Zinat ...". He even said that if Zinat should die, God forbid, of course, then he himself would not go on living.[225]

He can lie so impudently only to the dim and naive Umm Ilyas. But Musa Bek understands her perfectly well, just as he understands all the other members of the Samaha family: Zinat, Khalil and the elder brother Ilyas. He tries to flatter Ilyas, feigning sympathy with him. When his enraged mother rushes at him with a stick, Musa plays the peacemaker, addressing the woman thus:

> Respected Umm Ilyas! Enough. Get over it! Ilyas is a little out of balance at the moment. Would you be so kind as to let me have a word with him? (*To Ilyas:*) Ilyas! I understand that you're concerned about the welfare of your sister, although you don't realise what will make her happy. But all the same, you're a good lad. I'm very pleased for you.[226]

When all prospects for Musa's hoped-for marriage are almost lost, he resorts to his final dirty trick, proposing to call a priest to come and take the couple unawares, reading the matrimonial prayer and thereby, as it were, sealing the rite of marriage. Thanks to the stupidity and moral dullness of Umm Ilyas this plan almost succeeds, but for the sudden news, brought by Khalil, of Musa's total ruin and his son's arrest.

Generally, the "father" characters are considerably more persuasive and successful. The two of them are quite different and individually drawn. To a large extent this has also allowed them to have individual manners of speech. The crude, undisciplined, self-willed and imperious language of Umm Ilyas, full of swearing, cursing and folk expressions, is indicative not only of her delight in unbridled power, but also of a lack in her of any power of observation, intelligence or understanding of other people. Musa Arkush has altogether different speech; indeed, he modifies it to suit the situation and the person to whom he is speaking. With Zinat he is insinuating, smooth-tongued and courteous, while with Umm Ilyas he is dashing, hypocritical and servile; he talks to his son persuasively, using reason and logic, and to Ilyas nobly and with reserve, appealing to his feelings.

Turgenev portrays the struggle of two generations in the form of a socio-psychological novel, one that represents the highest achievement in the evolution of Critical Realism. Naimy, on the other hand, exposes the conflict in his play using a didactic approach – that is, in a genre that is most accessible and best adapted to a declaratory exposition of the main and general ideas of the author himself. This method was typical of Enlightenment literature.

Naimy gave great importance to the language used in *Fathers and Sons*, considering this to be one of the most important problems for the development of the genre. The language of the play must be accessible and understandable to a broad mass audience. Thus, the language of drama should be rich in folk dialects, idioms and free use of colloquial speech. In this, Naimy departed from the Russian viewpoint. By no means, however, did this indicate that he should neglect the traditions and norms of literary Arabic, which he valued highly. He wrote of the conundrum – and his solution to it – in the preface to the play as follows:

Of all literary forms, drama is the one that cannot dispense with the colloquial language, but this raises the problem that, if we follow the rule, we should have to write all our plays in colloquial, as there is none amongst us who speaks pre-Islamic or early Islamic Arabic. And that means the dying-out of classical Arabic – a national calamity which we are far from desiring to bring about ... All I could do, after much reflection, was to make the educated characters in my play speak literary Arabic, and the uneducated speak colloquial. But I sincerely admit that this does not solve the fundamental problem.[227]

His solution was thus a skilful and creative combination of the two language groups that succeeded in revealing both the wealth of the language and the vital pulse of its spoken form. The educated characters of *Fathers and Sons* are given literary speech, while the uneducated speak in dialect. For example, Umm Ilyas uses words and phrases normally found in everyday situations. The monologues of Ilyas, Da'ud and Shahida are saturated with peculiar folk expressions and turns of phrase. Nevertheless, they conform to the grammatical structure of the literary language. The author acknowledges that his method is still far from a complete solution to the complex problem of language for stage works. As he says, "What then is the way out? I have tried in vain to find a solution for this problem. It needs more than one mind for its solution."[228]

We conclude, from our analysis of Naimy's *Fathers and Sons*, that it is an independent and distinctive work whose ideas reflect the burning issues and problems that affected Lebanon in a certain historical period. In his preface to the play the author himself comments that the basic idea of Turgenev's novel has a "universal character", posing a problem that is characteristic of all periods of change. "In it [the play] I have tried to touch on an aspect of a major topic in the lives of all the peoples of the world, and in particular of the East. This theme is the eternal conflict between fathers and their sons, the unending contradiction between the old and the new."[229] In his play Naimy also draws on this "general idea" of the struggles between two generations, between the old and the young, or between two stages of social development. For Naimy the new generation expresses the progressive ideas of the Arab Enlightenment period, and is opposed to the archaic, feudal ways of life in the East. For Turgenev the "sons" are the activists of the 1860s who took their stand against the liberalism of the nobility, the "fathers". And this unites them. The compositional device of opposition is also natural: the main hero and those who support him are placed in opposition to the bearers of the opposing view and their supporters. Everything else, meanwhile – the genres, the images of the main characters, their milieu and the entire backdrop of life, the action, and the development of the plot and the ending – are all of an entirely different character, one that reflects the difference between the two countries, their historical eras and their level of literary development.

Naimy's short stories and the Chekhovian tradition

The short story occupies an important part of the work of Naimy, who was one of the first in Arabic literature to adopt the method of Critical Realism. His first story was published in the USA, and despite this "it became famous throughout the Arab world, because it was written in pure literary Arabic and was organic to the spiritual world of the Arabs."[230] The Lebanese critic Na'im Hasan al-Yafi comments: "Undoubtedly, first place goes to Naimy as regards the short story. He is the first short story writer to understand the particularities of literary forms so deeply, and for half a century has been enriching the treasure house of our art with his works."[231] Discussing Naimy's contribution to the formation of Realism in Arabic prose, the well-known critic Muhammad Yusuf Najm writes: "He [Naimy] is the most talented short story writer in our literature for his study and analysis of the human soul and his ability to convey it to the reader in ways that correspond to real life."[232]

As a writer of stories, Naimy had come under two influences: the classics of Russian literature (especially the short stories of Anton Chekhov) and Arab émigré literature (in particular the work of Gibran). Certain Arab authors before Naimy had also read Chekhov,[233] but did so through the small number of translated editions, whereas Naimy knew Chekhov in the original Russian.

Naimy's stories were gathered into three collections: *Kana ma kan* (*Once upon a Time*, Beirut, 1937), *Akabir* (*Grandees*, Beirut, 1953) and *Abu Batta* (*The Man with the Fat Calf*, Beirut, 1959). Some stories were also included in collections of his articles, such as *Sawt al-'Alam* (*The Voice of the World*, Cairo, 1948), *al-Nur wa al-Dayjur* (*Light and Darkness*, Beirut, 1959), and *Durub* (*Pathways*, Beirut, 1954).[234] It is not our aim in the present work to carry out a complete comparative analysis of the works of Naimy and Chekhov; this would be the subject of separate research. Here we shall attempt rather to outline that common factor in the methods of the two writers that allows one to speak of Naimy as being a follower of the Chekhovian school. We also aim to reveal what in his Realism was particular to him, to demonstrate that he remained a distinct artist in his own right, able to flexibly adapt the Chekhovian form to the national traditions and requirements of Arab life.

It is widely known that Chekhov's works summed up many of the achievements of nineteenth-century Russian Realism. His stories and tales combined the simplicity, preciseness and laconism of Pushkin, the laughter through tears of Gogol, Turgenev's lyricism, the raucous laugh of Saltykov-Shchedrin and Tolstoy's ability to penetrate the interior world of the human being. He inherited what had been formed by his predecessors, yet was himself an innovator. For "this great artist, in drawing on what was available to him from his forerunners and contemporaries, did not merely 'improve' it, but rather combined it with new elements that he had developed himself to create a new quality, in which the familiar took on a fundamentally fresh meaning."[235]

As a student of Chekhov, Naimy inherited from him many features of Russian Realist literature, but it was in the short story in particular that he was able to convey his understanding and vision of contemporary Arab life.

It should be remembered that the degree of artistic comprehension and endeavour were not commensurate for Naimy and Chekhov; there is also a typological divergence between the two writers. Naimy began to write at a time when Arabic literature had only begun to assimilate Realist methods, whereas Chekhov the story-writer had learned his art on the fertile soil of a fully established Critical Realism. The breadth with which reality is comprehended in Chekhov's Realism is also well known, whereas Naimy was only able to depict certain aspects of Arab reality.

The close relationship of Naimy's short stories to those of Chekhov can be clearly seen with the naked eye and is frequently postulated in research on his works. This is reinforced by his own remarks, by the observations of his contemporaries, and by the opinions of Soviet Arabists. "His [Naimy's] little stories, which date back to 1914–1919 but were not published in a separate book until 1937, give a clear indication of the importance of Russian writers in his works",[236] wrote Krachkovsky. Elsewhere he added: "In his psychological stories Mikhail Naimy devotes much attention to deep analysis, and not without the influence of nineteenth-century Russian literature."[237] Muhammad Yusuf Najm, the Arab critic, shares his view: "He [Naimy] received a Russian literary education and knew the works of masters such as Andreev, Gogol, Turgenev, Dostoevsky, Chekhov and others ... Without doubt, by reading the work of these writers Naimy gained a good mastery of the short story genre."[238] He sees the influence of Chekhov particularly in Naimy's ability to reveal the psychology of people and their complex inner contradictions.

Nevertheless, in most cases these assertions suffer from a certain declarative quality, since a detailed analysis and comparison of the material is often lacking. Within the framework of the present research we shall try to bring together certain significant aspects of the methods of both writers. A similar approach would allow the path to be mapped out for further comparative and poetological analysis, which could prove extremely productive for research on the problems of Realism in Oriental literature.

Generally speaking, the Chekhovian school is most evident in Naimy in the sharp social orientation of his stories, their realism and striking humanism, and their love and compassion for the human being. Naimy's stories are canvases of the everyday life, morals, relationships, occupations and psychology of primarily simple people. They create vivid characters that belong to a certain setting and time. In portraying the life of the people, their troubles and needs, and the injustice of the social systems, he created a persuasive archetype of the Arab labourer. His stories bring to the reader images of poor peasants who naively believe in the kindness of landowners, and city low-life, artisans and the powerful in this world. "The reader may encounter the heroes of Naimy's stories anywhere: among the regulars of the cafes and the shepherds in the fields; the gossips who have come to chatter with dilettantes; little boys destroying birds' nests, and lovers of nature; idlers and the unhappy wanderers who roam the streets in the wind and rain, and so on."[239]

The legacy of Chekhov is reflected particularly in Naimy's adoption of one of Chekhov's main principles of reflecting reality: laconism, with the slogan "The shorter, the better."[240] It is well known that Chekhov considered long-windedness to be a sign of lack of talent, and he considered that excessive detail merely obscured the main elements of the story. He advised beginning writers to dispense with the definitions of most verbs and nouns and to strive for precision and keenness in their use of language. He extended the use of simplicity and naturalness to his plots and conflicts; complexity and tragedy, beauty and ugliness appear in his stories in their everyday garb, shorn of outer effects. These aesthetic principles are the source of the particular poetics of Chekhov's stories: brevity of exposition, swiftness of plot, speed of development and unexpectedness of outcome.

"The short story has its own aesthetic objective and laws of construction. Most frequently the short story has been constructed as a way of suspending a single moment – a meeting, a scene, a dialogue."[241] Naimy understood these requirements. "The basis of the story", he wrote, "is laconism in describing the events and people and the dynamics of the dialogue; the story must be grasped directly and with ease, and should leave in the memory of the reader those impressions that the author hoped for."[242] In Naimy's view, brevity should aid the reader in grasping as effectively as possible the message of the work and its aesthetic point.

Naimy's stories are themselves compact: usually brief and cleverly constructed. The effect of this laconism is reached through purely compositional techniques: a short exposition that often consists of only a single phrase, a momentary opening to the plot, fast development of the action, aided by dialogue, and a quick, unexpected denouement. Unlike in Chekhov, however, whose endings often have a tragicomic element ("The Death of a Civil Servant", "The Chameleon", "Fat and Thin" and others), Naimy tends rather towards the tragic, or indeed – frequently – melodramatic ending. His story "Hadiyya" ("The Gift") finishes with the words, barely audible, of the dying Mas'ud: "Doctors, doctors ...", while "Sadiq" concludes with a suicide note: "Woe to the world that has no room for the Truth!" The last words of the dying girl in "Shahidat al-shahd" ("Martyred for Honey") strike a tragic note: "Give this to Nu'man ..." (referring to honey she has obtained for her brother Nu'man from wild bees, and for which she pays with her life).

In the manner of Chekhov, Naimy uses a principle of dynamic exposition to pitch the reader into the story right away. Thus "Martyred for Honey" begins: "Khayziran decided to run away from home and die, so unbearable had life with her mother become"; and "Dhanab al-himar" ("The Tail of the Donkey"): "Handing the rein of his chestnut donkey, al-Ashqar, to the unknown buyer, Barakat was so stricken as to arouse the curiosity of those around him." The story "Bakaluriya" ("The Bachelor's Degree") has a like-wise dynamic opening: "When Abu Shahin had received the money due to him and shaken his customer's hand, he was suddenly seized with deep remorse." The stories "Akabir" ("Grandees"), "The Stroke of the Hammer" and others are similar in this respect.

The straightforwardness of the opening in the Chekhovian short story and the naturalness of the writer's presence in the life of his characters is closely related to Chekhov's aesthetic of the everyday. "It is generally accepted that what is real for Chekhov is to be found in the form of the everyday and wears the garb of the habitual and the institutionalised. The everyday relationships of common human life are the only possible aesthetic reality for Chekhov",[243] comments I.A. Gurvich. The typification of the eve-ryday leads to Chekhovian symbolism, in which the artist "takes a micro-scopically small yet typical fact from the sphere of everyday life and draws from it the entire system of human relations throughout the world."[244]

We see a constant attempt at this kind of typification and generalisation in Naimy too. An example of this approach may be drawn from "Grandees", one of his vivid stories of country life.[245] The plot is extremely simple. The peasant Abu Rashid, like all the inhabitants of his village, rents a strip of land from a big landowner. He is obliged to give a large part of his harvest to his landlord. The harvest is poor, however, and the reasons for this are low-grade seed, drought and a lack of modern implements. Abu Rashid has a wife and a son, but the liveliest things in their household are a cock and a goat kid, with whom the boy likes to play. One day the landlord and his family arrive to collect their share of the harvest. Traditionally, they should be treated by the tenants as their guests. However, Abu Rashid is in no posi-tion to receive them in the required manner, and the only food he can offer is baked eggs and a few vegetables. All else in his wretched hovel is ruled by emptiness. Yet the "educated" landowners shy away from entering Abu Rashid's house and sharing his poor meal, which amounts to an indelible insult to the peasant. However, the landowner's young daughter decides that she likes the cock and the kid and wants these "playthings" for herself. The family has no choice but to let her have them. Abu Rashid's son then runs after the landowners' car as it takes away his beloved playmates, "as fast as his little legs could carry him", crying loudly. "The sky heard his cries, and the mountains replied with a great echo."[246]

This story exhibits a bareness of plot, a generality of character and an extreme meagreness in the means of portrayal that add to the dynamism of the narrative. All description is functional and laconic. The house is de-scribed thus: "a wretched hovel built from the branches and twigs of trees"; as for utensils, "there are none, except for a few tin plates, a clay jug and a pair of wooden spoons". Two words [in Arabic] sum up the harvest: "half of last year's". No further description is used. Yet there is in Naimy's story a broad social generalisation beyond the individual predicament it describes, rather as "behind the depiction of individual characters' lives there is always in Chekhov something more important than their individual destinies".[247]

Let us also highlight the economy and precision of detail in "Martyred for Honey".[248] This tells of the death of a peasant girl, her life exhausted by her severe and commanding mother. The author does not explain anything that is not directly relevant to the narrative. Khayziran's mother is a widow, but we do not know how she became widowed, nor how she is treated by the neighbours, how she dresses, what conditions were like in the home, what friends the girl has, whether she loves her mother or what she longs for. There is not the slightest divergence from the lightning-fast develop-ment of the conflict. The mother demands honey, free of charge, for her sick brother. Tearing herself from the hands of her mother as she beats her, the girl runs to a gorge. There she finds a nest of wild bees and decides to obtain the "free honey" her mother wants. Hardly has she managed to break off the honeycomb than she is attacked by the swarm. The girl runs home, collapses on the threshold and, as she dies there, utters only the words, "Give this to Nuʿman". In this little story the author has managed to create the characters of both an unhappy girl and a cruel, authoritarian mother who is fixated on the idea of harbouring money.

In Chekhov's stories the action is almost always moved forward by dia-logue, and exceptions to this rule are few. In Naimy's stories, by contrast, there is little dialogue, and the author himself is, as it were, included in the world he portrays. He gives an identity to the main character and has him perform certain actions. It would seem that Naimy did not adopt this method of narrative development by chance. Chekhov frequently charac-terised one or another social phenomenon in a satirical vein: servility in "Fat and Thin", crude violence and boorishness in "Sergeant Prishibaev", fear of authority in "Death of a Civil Servant" and opportunism by of-ficials in "The Chameleon", etc. Because of this, Chekhov considered the most effective and economical means of portraying his characters to be dialogue. His characters' speech was also a means of reinforcing the traits he typified.

Naimy, however, did not aim to satirise individual aspects of social behav-iour, but rather to show the character as a whole, with all its complexities. In so doing he sought also to reflect a broader picture of life, morals and circumstances. In a number of stories (e.g. "'Ulbat al-kibrit" ("The Box of Matches"), "The Stroke of the Hammer", "Sadiq") the author addresses the reader directly: "It is impossible to tell you, dear reader, everything the poor boy endured. He was hit on the cheeks by a peasant, who trod on him and showered him with abusive language. Sadiq's soul was nearly parted from his body".[249]

In his early stories Chekhov noted the beauty of nature, talent and spir-ituality of ordinary people ("The Huntsman", "A Day in the Country",

"Art", "Panikhida" ("The Requiem")). In general, however, the attempt to create a type of "positive, beautiful person" was strange to him. "His refusal to idealise allowed Chekhov to make his contribution to such complex tasks of critical realist art as creating the image of a positive hero."[250]

As regards Naimy's positive hero, it is precisely on idealism that this is founded. As a rule, his positive hero is a man of the people, a peasant or labourer. For him, working is as natural as breathing, eating, walking and sleeping. He patiently bears life's adversities and tolerates the dependency of his position on the wealthy and the powers that be, yet never loses his sense of human dignity or honour (as he traditionally understands this), nor his love for life.

Unlike Chekhov (for example, in his stories "Peasants" and "The New Villa"), Naimy does not emphasise savagery, ignorance and obscurity in his peasant heroes. If he sometimes still portrays women as cantankerous, full of prejudice and sanctimony, and blinded by the pursuit of wealth, then Naimy portrays male peasants and small craftsmen as submissive and uncomplaining; he paints their complete obedience to fate, to the landowner and to God. They show no protest, no anger or complaint, but rather silent and unquestioning submission. In Naimy one does not encounter peasants who are cunning, crude, greedy or on the make. As a rule the peasant is his positive hero – hard-working, straightforward, honest, considerate, sensitive and capable of deep and pure feeling. Such are Mas'ud from "The Gift", Barakat from "The Tail of the Donkey", Abu Shahin from "The Bachelor's Degree", and Abu Rashid and Umm Rashid from "Grandees".

While clearly idealising his old-style heroes, a contrast is essential for the author to depict the gravity and injustice of the social order. And so Naimy's positive hero is almost always placed in opposition to members of the upper classes, aristocrats or the wealthy, who are generally sketched in a highly unattractive manner. These people are evil, crude, imperious and mercenary. Naimy strives to emphasise their haughtiness and heartlessness and their awareness of their right to wield power over others, and to insult them. It is unsurprising that Naimy's portrayals of the "elite" are almost always sketchy and one-dimensional. Thus, in "The Bracelet"[251] the wealthy Farid Sarsur reprimands his fellow university student, Fu'ad, who has always helped him to pass his examinations. Fu'ad's mother has fallen ill; he needs medicine for her and has asked Farid for money. "'What does the son of a laundress need a degree for?', scoffed Farid with indignation. 'Go and work ... and don't try to climb above your station.'"[252]

The meanness and stinginess of the elite is given exaggerated treatment in "The Box of Matches".[253] The character in question is the owner of a hotel in which the hero of the story has stayed for two years, becoming almost a member of the family, and who on leaving has given costly gifts. As he leaves, having settled his final bill, the owner stops his car with a shout and reminds him that he has forgotten to include the cost of a box of matches on the bill.

In many stories Naimy creates a system based on the opposition of "old" times to the "new", that is, of the patriarchal orders opposed to bourgeois morals. The reason for this arises from the history of the Arab countries. The Arab émigré intelligentsia had seen the dark side of life in the capitalist countries of Europe and America, and as a result tended to idealise their own countries' pasts, contrasting the values of patriarchal antiquity with the pressure of bourgeois development. In doing so they dispersed the illusions of bourgeois democratism and humanism, and received Western influences, particularly in their homelands, with an advance warning. It should be added that the way of life of the Arab bourgeoisie also gave grounds for accusations of losing touch with the people and the labouring masses, and for betraying the patriarchal traditions. One inevitably comes to the conclusion that the ways of the old world were dear to Naimy; of these, he tries to observe only the ideal elements: humaneness, kindness and unsophistication. He cautions that the "new" that has come to take the place of tradition will be far worse, more savage and inhuman.

Some of Naimy's stories stand out for their psychological approach. The author achieves this by various methods: for example, when he wishes to portray the vortex of changing feelings and moods in a person, he introduces an interior monologue:

> All you have got ahead of you, Sadiq, is ending your life. You're already twenty years old, and you haven't been able to hold down a single one of the jobs you've had so far, even though other people keep their first job for the rest of their lives. You're not feeble-minded; you don't make up stories, like the widow said about you; you're not idle or a thief, or a liar or a gossip; and you aren't rude or bad-tempered. So why do other people shun you? Why does happiness never smile on you? You strive to procure your sustenance, but it escapes you. If you had your rightful place in life, like other people, then it would already be time for you to know your place and be guided to it. But there is no place for you, you are a parasite, you are nothing amongst people. And anybody who found themselves in such a situation as you, Sadiq, would do away with himself, as the only way to escape such a life.[254]

It is true that sometimes, in conveying the experiences of his characters, the author substitutes a psychological analysis for the naturalistic, "physiological" description. For example, in "Auntie Marsha"[255] the heroine is the childless aunt Marsha, who is well known for her bitterness and dislike of children. One day, to calm a crying child that has been left in her care by a neighbour, she gives him her empty breast.

> The child was immediately silent, and fell greedily to the breast and started to suck with pleasure. At the same instant, the rage that had been storming in the blood of Auntie Marsha calmed down, and she was overcome by the sweetness of a feeling of well-being and bliss. It seemed to her that her empty breast had filled again, and the child was receiving real milk ... It even seemed to her that she could see real milk froth on his lips and could hear the milk gurgling down

his throat. It seemed to emanate from every pore of her body and to flow in every blood vessel, to run in her eyes and ears and from every hair on her head, and from the depths of her heart and the soles of her feet.[256]

The mood with which nature is depicted harmonises in many of Naimy's stories with the internal state of the characters, and the landscape serves, as it were, to introduce an emotional colouring into the narrative. The story "Sanatuha al-jadida" ("Her New Year")[257] is set on a cold, dark New Year's Eve, with the wail of a raging storm: "But what was this? The roar of the wind, beating on the windows of the house and dying away like a drawn-out, agonising moan? Or a dog's howling, carried on the wind? Or was it a human voice, released from a breast rent with pain? The storm cried out, the sky wept."[258] At this moment the wife of the shaykh Abu Nasif was giving birth to her seventh child – but would it be a boy or a girl? The hoped-for boy would be "the crown of all his hopes, his life's dream and his support in old age, the inheritor of his riches and the successor of his line" – but what if it was a girl? These excruciating worries are reinforced by the portrayal of the stormy night; the shaykh's condition is like the storm itself. "His ears were ringing, strange shadows passed in front of his eyes, his head was flushed and thunder roared in his chest ... his breathing slowed, his head grew heavy and the light died in his eyes. He was sinking ... Oh Jesus."[259]

The landscape plays a different role in "The Bracelet": "The night was full of the breath of spring, moonlight and calm. On such a night the heart beats more strongly, and especially the hearts of those in love."[260] One would expect such a portrait to be followed by a love scene; instead, however, it precedes the description of the internal state of a youth who confesses to his girl that he is a thief, and that this causes him burning shame and despair. In this case, then, the landscape provides a vivid contrast.

In Naimy's stories the details and circumstances of everyday life and the relationships between people of different social stations create a realistic picture of life in the working village. He describes the work of the donkey driver, the burden carrier, the sheep farmer and the stone-breaker:

> Every morning he started work where he had left off the previous evening. He sat down on a pile of gravel, placed his legs in front of him, took a stone, placed it between his legs and hit it with his hammer until it broke into pieces. Then he took another stone, then a third, and continued until sunset. As the day progressed a long mound of fine gravel formed behind him.
>
> "The Stroke of the Hammer"[261]

At times his heroes almost become merged with the tools of their labour, or with their houses, huts or farms (for example, "The Bachelor's Degree", "The Gift").

The little story "al-Yubil al-almasi" ("The Diamond Wedding")[262] reveals a new face to Naimy's talent – a soft, melancholy, lyric humour that is a match for Chekhov. Certain elements of the story are even reminiscent of

Chekhov's humoresque "The Jubilee". The story goes as follows. On the eve of publication, the chief editor of the *al-Nur* newspaper is up to his ears with hundreds of pressing tasks, when a half-deaf old woman of 90 years, Fitna, comes into his office with an urgent request. The conversation is filled with comedy. At first they do not understand each other, so far apart are their interests and concerns.

> She did not speak clearly, and she lisped; there was not a single tooth in her mouth ...
>
> "I am Fitna."
>
> "You do us an honour ... What has Fitna come to tempt us with?"*
>
> "I'm sorry, I can't hear very well. Can you speak up a little?"
>
> "You do us an honour!", the chief editor shouted. "What can I do for you?"
>
> "I am Fitna, wife of Ya'qub."
>
> "Alaykum as-salam ... What does Fitna the wife of Ya'qub desire of the editor of *al-Nur*?"[263]

The conversation continues in the same humorous mode until the editor realises that Fitna's husband Ya'qub worked in the printing shop of the newspaper for fifty years. Today is the seventieth anniversary of their marriage, and Fitna has come to ask the editor to mark their diamond wedding by including a picture of Ya'qub and a suitable caption in the new edition of the paper. This was to be her anniversary gift to her husband. The editor finally understands, laughs cheerfully and promises Fitna that he will fulfil her request.

> In that day's newspaper not a line was written about the elections! Instead there was a long article by the editor about his meeting with the old Fitna ... [He] got carried away and gave an inspired description about the hard work that goes on in the printing shop that nobody knows about. He eulogised Ya'qub's long and remarkable life – over a hundred years – that was filled with wisdom and selflessness and hidden meaning.[264]

However, unlike Chekhov, Naimy does not turn the comical situation into a satire, but retains a lyrical intonation, laced with humour.

In outlining and underlining the innovation in Naimy's short stories as he moved towards Critical Realism, we must not ignore the literary environment and traditions in which his artistry was formed. He was linked to that environment by many personal, social and artistic threads. Naimy was writing his stories at exactly the time when Romanticism was becoming widespread in Arabic literature and actively displacing the medieval forms and traditions.

---

* In Arabic the name Fitna means "temptation", so here the author is making a friendly and humorous play on words.

Naturally, then, there can be found in Naimy's stories not only a Chekhovian Realism but also elements of Romanticism and even Sentimentalism. Good examples are "The Bracelet", "Sadiq" and "The Box of Matches", which have in common the contrasting of different social groups, with no nuances or shades, and an idealisation of patriarchal relations, excessive sensitivity and hyperbolised feelings.

An example of this Romanticism is Fu'ad's monologue in "The Bachelor's Degree", in which he expresses the storm of indignation and the chaos of his thoughts and feelings following the insult to his dignity by his friend:

> When I left him, a volcano was raging inside me, I was seething with anger. If at that moment I could have destroyed the earth, the sky and the whole world, I would have done it ... What good can there be in a life in which the *sursur** is an eagle, and the eagle is a nobody? ... Fu'ad has toppled from the summit to the abyss ... he will die, having just risen up against everything that is base, decaying and decomposing, against injustice and meanness.[265]

These mutinous words are followed by a short epilogue which states that Fu'ad has been imprisoned for distributing revolutionary leaflets.

Romantic and Sentimentalist elements can be clearly seen in "al-'Aqir" ("The Barren Woman").[266] The subject of the story is the tragic suicide of a young woman. At first, everything in her life is happy: she has married a man whom she loves deeply, and the days of their first year together are joyful and bright with the attention, love and tenderness of her husband and of all around them. But gradually the relationship of everybody towards her, and particularly of her husband, begins to change. This is because she is unable to bear a child. Her husband begins to hate her and her relatives to despise her. Jamila endures deep moral anguish. Her human dignity, her love and understanding of life, and all her feminine feelings are crushed and violated. Her own character changes. Everything loses value in her eyes. All that is left is her passionate yearning for the love of her husband, which is lost. But then a miracle occurs: she becomes pregnant. And everything changes, as if in a magical dream: again there is love, tenderness and care. But one day her husband 'Aziz finds her not at home. Eventually he finds, in their bedroom, a note she has left for him, which says that he will find her in their favourite nook under the old oak tree. 'Aziz hurries there and finds ... her dead body. On her breast he finds a letter explaining that the child is not his, and that it was not her that was barren, but him.

The letter is long and detailed, and Jamila writes of her great love for her husband and her moral anguish and violated dignity. She decided to end her life because she could not endure her unhappiness in love with her husband:

> You do not know how much hurt my injured heart suffered! And the first wound you inflicted on me was when I realised that your love had never been love for

---

* A *sursur* is a cricket.

me myself, as a person, with a character and qualities of her own. What you loved in me was the future mother of your children, the female function, that before it died would leave you your descendants.[267]

This highly melodramatic story shows distinct traits of Sentimentalism in its hyperbolisation of feelings and experience, in the behaviour of the heroine Jamila and in the contents of her letter, in which she examines her thoughts, feelings and suffering. This is no letter, but rather an acknow-ledgement that is also accusatory and that touches on complex questions of love, the dignity of women and social injustice. Its style is passionate and moving.

The ending of the story is melodramatic:

Jamila lay on the ground in front of him. She had on her wedding dress, the dress in which, eleven years earlier, she had stood beside him at the altar in front of Bulos the priest. On her head was a wreath, and her silky hair lay in disarray about her shoulders. She was lying on her side, with her hand under her cheek ... He bent over her, still hoping that she was asleep. But, raising her head a little, he cried out and recoiled in horror. His little lamb was a lifeless corpse.[268]

In outlining the basic Realist tendency of Naimy's stories, we have also pointed out certain elements of Romanticism and Sentimentalism. It would seem appropriate also to observe a link between Naimy's stories and the national traditions that give particular colouring to his writing manner. This is most prominent in the extensive range of epithets, hyperbole, and figures of words, and the aphoristic character of his language. His stories contain many solemn forms of address: "O friend!", "O my brother!", "O my love!" and so on, and hyperbole: "The entire horde of evil spirits had established themselves in this woman" ("Auntie Marsha"), and "With the passion of one in love he threw himself to kiss his beloved donkey" ("The Tail of the Donkey"). Then there are aphorisms: "Each of my son's tears is dearer to me than all of his [the landowner's] wealth", "Honour is more precious than all the riches in the world" ("Grandees"), and "Children are insatiable leeches that suck the blood of their parents" ("Auntie Marsha"). The stories also contain a degree of sententiousness, and a tendency to make rational argument: "You start reading a book with its title", "A crowded house has room for a thousand friends", "Children are like the fruit of the locust tree", "Tiredness is like dirt, and it is easy to remove with a short sleep" and "Idle hands are the devil's spoon and the scourge of happiness, but hands that work are the hammer of God and the key to happiness", etc. All Naimy's stories reflect the characteristic features of Arab reality. They are national not only in their topic and content but also in their very spirit.

All this shows that Naimy was a wholly original and distinctive artist. Chekhov's work enabled Naimy to create, with typical subjects, a true picture of Lebanese realities at the start of the twentieth century. Each of these writers was a brightly individual and creative person, whose work was in complete accordance with the requirements of their time and the needs of their people, and was closely tied to the roots of their national cultural and literary traditions.

Conclusion

The appearance of the special literary school that became known as the Syro-American School was a response to the needs of an awakening nation at a new stage in its historical development. The work of the principal exponents of this school, Kahlil Gibran, Ameen Rihani and Mikhail Naimy, significantly broadened the scope of social issues and themes in the reality reflected by literature. The search for ideas by these émigré writers naturally led them to seek new artistic forms and methods. In the course of their literary development they progressed through and beyond the methods of Enlightenment Didacticism and Sentimentalism to assimilate the poetics of Romanticism and Critical Realism.

Parallel to this was a renewal of the genres. Development was particularly strong for the smaller forms: the sketch, the essay and the short story, which were best adapted to a rapid response to the needs of the times. There was, however, also progress in the medium formats such as the longer story and the play. The prose poem (*al-shi'r al-mansur*), created by Gibran and Rihani, also gained a foothold and proved to be of immense importance for the period examined here; it subsequently became established as a traditional lyric genre in Arabic romantic prose.

The Syro-American School created a new literary style. As far as was possible, its members sought to liberate Arabic literary style from archaisms, ponderous syntactical constructions and the excesses of artificial rhetorical embellishment. At the same time, however, they maintained an attitude of respect towards the Arabic classics.

Gibran, Rihani and Naimy all felt the need to familiarise themselves closely with the best of Western culture and literature, which gave them the new ideas and forms that were so necessary to them if they were to adequately reflect the historical reality with which they sought to interact.

The examples of the work of the Syro-American School that have been examined in the present study corroborate links between the Arab writers and the English Lake School, the work of the American Transcendentalists and the Critical Realism of Russian literature. In each of the three instances a particular combination of ideas and methods was observed, peculiar to the tendencies of each, and the specific method of each individual creative form for the adoption of the respective artistic method was discussed.

Each of the three writers gained his own command of the arsenal of ethical and artistic values laid down in his method, and developed and adapted them to his own artistic practice. Gibran and Rihani turned to Western Romanticism. However, unlike the Egyptian Romantic poets, these writers did not merely imitate the external attributes of Romanticism, but rather took it on as an artistic method, that is, as a new point of view which allowed them to express their relationship to the demands of Arab

reality. They were the first to break out of the tight confines of Enlightenment and make a definitive breakthrough to Romanticism. In the work
of Gibran and Rihani the Romantic tendency is not merely adopted, but
enriched and made more complex. This was possible partly thanks to the
intricate synthesis of Arab literary tradition and the lessons of Western Romanticism, but also because of the personal contribution of both artists. As a
result, they were able to reach a point where they could formulate universal
questions, and where they were no longer merely participants who enjoyed
equal rights with others in the world literary process, but could now champion new artistic values in world literature.

The familiarity of the Arab writers with the English and American
Romantics can be seen in both their subject matter and style. The very
spirit of English Romanticism resonated deeply with their own world-view:
a rebellion against social levelling and cheerless functionalism. Despite the
general spirit of mutiny and protest that is typical of the Arab writers' work,
and particularly of Gibran's prose, however, there is a lack of that universality of apprehending the problems in question and the appeals for their
radical solution that are so typical of the English Romantics.

The entire system of ethical ideas present in the poetry of Gibran and
Rihani – the demand for the complete emancipation of the human, their
hatred of slavery, the ideas of the interdependence and interconnectedness
of the phenomena of life and of human acts and deeds, and the ideas of love
and the belief in primordial human goodness and justice – corresponds to
the philosophical conception and ideological basis of the Romanticism of
the Transcendentalists.

The Arab authors gained their perspective of the moral principle, interpreted *in abstracto* and extra-socially, together with the concept of the
perfection of the individual and a pantheistic attitude towards nature, from
the American Romantics, in particular from Ralph Waldo Emerson, Walt
Whitman and Henry Thoreau. Romanticism also posed the question of the
civic duty of the writer and his role in society, and proposed its own interpretation of the meaning of the poet, and this all found a deep resonance in
the work of the Arab writers.

Gibran's creative activity spanned a little over 20 years. His methods
underwent significant changes from when he reached creative maturity,
and this evolution in his world-view can be seen in the transition from the
Sentimentalism of his early prose through to Romanticism.

For a considerable time, however, the traces of Sentimentalism and Romanticism coexisted in Gibran's output. His collection *A Tear and a Smile*
(1914), containing pieces written between 1903 and 1908, the collections
Nymphs of the Valley (1907) and *Spirits Rebellious* (1908), and particularly the
story *Broken Wings* (1912), reveal vacillations between the domination of
Sentimentalism and his emerging Romanticism.

Sentimentalism prevails in several stories ("Marta al-Baniya" and "Warda
al-Hani", for example) and particularly in *Broken Wings*. Characteristically,

the author gives attention in all these works to the question of the emancipation of the Oriental woman, approaching the problem not from a social and political perspective but purely in terms of protecting the feelings of women and defending their rights within the family.

In "Marta al-Baniya" and "Warda al-Hani" the author concentrates entirely on the changing fortunes of the heroes, and of their elevated feelings and intimate experiences. The Sentimentalist style can be seen both in the long monologues, in which the characters tell of their unsuccessful lives, and in the voice of the author in the narration itself. Generally, the characters are artistically poor, sketchy and revealed only to the extent required by the ideas they embody.

The substance and idea of *Broken Wings* are confined to the disclosure of the internal worlds of the heroes and their elevated feelings and experiences. The spirit of the story and its plot-line are subordinated to the main objective, the self-expression of the author–narrator. The melodramatic ending and the fate of the heroes – sadness, submission to destiny and bitter disappointment (albeit without dramatic despair or outbursts of anger) – bear the hallmarks of Sentimentalism.

The lyricism and confessional nature of *Broken Wings*, and its tendency to monologue, demand a constant appeal to the personal experience of the narrator. The entire story is cemented by the person of the author, and this reveals one of the basic principles in the construction of the Romantic image. The strongest evidence for the Romantic world-view emerging here is the description of the heroines as having exclusive natures that strive for liberation and freedom; but this end is also served by the hyperbolised feelings, and by the landscape, which is often mysterious and symbolic. *Broken Wings* remains an example of Sentimentalism that is visibly evolving towards Romanticism. In addition to anticipating the development of the Romantic method in Arabic literature, with this story Gibran also consolidated two principal themes for it: women and anticlericalism.

If Gibran's narrative prose is marked by a Sentimentalist tendency, then the genres represented in *A Tear and a Smile*, essays and prose poems, could not be better suited to the Romantic mode. *A Tear and a Smile* reveals how Gibran began to assimilate Romanticism. It includes a number of Romantic themes that prior to Gibran had never been made so distinct (the poet and his role in society, the greatness and omnipotence of the human individual, love and beauty, nature and its deep connection to man, and so on). Much in both the style and content of many of Gibran's works reveals the influence on him of works by the English and American Romantics.

One of the principal themes in the collection, that of the poet (e.g. "The Poet's Death is his Life", "Night", "A Poet's Voice"), gives clear evidence of the influence on Gibran of the American Transcendentalists, particularly Emerson. For Gibran, the theme of the poet is always attended by ethical and aesthetic problems, and, as with the Transcendentalists, an artistic solution to these problems is frequently replaced by moralising and didactics.

The ideal of beauty and humaneness was also always the prerogative of the Romantic artist. In contrast to the Enlighteners, the Romantic poet apprehends the world creatively and with inspiration; he tears the mantle of ordinariness from things and phenomena and reveals the beauty within. Like the Western Romantics, Gibran also assigns the highest place in the system of spiritual values to beauty, defining it as something universal and ideal, such as the eternal and highest truth and the quintessence of life (for example, "The Life of Love", "Beauty", "Before the Throne of Beauty", "The Queen of Fantasy" and "Song of Beauty"). For him, beauty is inseparable from moral and spiritual ideas. Gibran regards the poet as a "mediator of beauty" whose task is to draw the attention of people, distracted by everyday concerns, towards beauty as the "prototype of truth".

A further aspect of the theme of the poet in Gibran's work is the exaltation of the Romantic self ("The City of the Past", "The Blind Force", "Under the Sun", "Song of Happiness" and others). The image of the human that stubbornly moves forward towards infinite knowledge, to the "city of the future" and to the "society of the future", and the theme of his eternal striving for physical and moral perfection, is consonant with Western Romantic poetry, in particular that of Whitman and Blake.

The favourite theme in Gibran's poetry is the exaltation of nature in all its guises: the forests and plains, the seas and mountains, the wind and rain. All these aspects attract his attention and provide themes for his songs ("Song of the Wind", "O Earth", "O Wind", etc.). For him, nature is the world of desired being, in which the depository of the human soul may be uncovered. Like many Western Romantics, Gibran was a pantheist and considered man to be an organic part of nature, and that in nature man finds the pledge of eternal life of the soul. In many of his poems, as also in Emerson, Shelley and Coleridge, the kinship of man with the rule of nature, and their common origin, are highlighted. Singing of the beauty and grandeur of nature, Gibran, like Byron and Wordsworth, hints at the negative effect of urbanism and bourgeois civilisation on human life ("Lament of the Field" and "History and the Nation", for example).

In *A Tear and a Smile* Gibran turned to the genre of the prose poem. These are small essays that capture scattered thoughts and impressions from the author's philosophical reflections. His prose poems are elegant, musical and have a fine, aphoristic language. They are highly expressive, and feature rhetorical questions and exclamations.

By the start of the 1920s Romanticism had become established as Gibran's primary artistic method. *The Tempests* (1920) reveals a qualitatively different Romanticism – stormy, mutinous, bearing the marks of that of Byron, Shelley and Blake. Practically every piece in the collection is coloured by characteristically Romantic sentiments: rebellion, disdain for the world, the thirst for solitude, a deep disappointment in, and criticism of, civilised society, the rejection of the Church and its rites, a passionate inclination towards nature as the sole refuge for the offended spirit, and a proud calling to God.

In this collection Gibran's output also becomes more diverse in genre terms. As well as prose poems, *The Tempests* contains stories, essays and psychological studies. The sum of the ideas, themes and motifs gathered here further confirms that Gibran was now influenced by the Romantic legacy of the Lake School. This tells not so much in individual motifs and situations as in the general spirit of mutiny and protest that is typical of his prose.

Gibran's freedom-loving Romantic hero (for example, Yusuf al-Fakhri from the story "The Storm"), who runs from people and civilisation to the bosom of nature, recalls analogies with the heroes of European Romantic works: Byron's Childe Harold, Hugo's outcasts, the heroes of Chateaubriand who are unable to find their place in life, and indeed those of Shelley, thrown into worlds that are foreign to them. In this work and a number of others, Gibran's hero is a dreamer who has taken refuge in his interior world, and is not a warrior in search of grand deeds. His individualism does not take the form of rebellion; instead, his opposition to reality takes the form of proud solitude. In his sanctuary in nature he finds above all "a life of the spirit and the heart, of thought and of the flesh", and senses an awakening to, and longing for, self-knowledge. Gibran's attitude to his Romantic hero is somewhat peculiar. His heroes do not contemplate complete separation from society or eternal disappointment in life; they are not prone to a sense of superiority over the crowd. In dealing with the problem of the self and society, he avoids the Romantic extremism and subjectivistic anthropocentricism of the Western European Romantics.

In comparing Gibran with the English Romantics we have mentioned in various connections that the Romantic pathos, the white heat of feelings, and the hatred and passion, are in his case somewhat tempered. Perhaps the exception to this is his anticlericalism, which appears with extreme sharpness and emotion. This harsh criticism of the Christian Church can be found in the story "Satan", a philosophical examination of the inescapable coexistence of two absolute principles: good and evil. Like Shelley, Gibran considers the Church to be a symbol of human weakness and religion a collection of nonsensical superstitions. As a subtext, the story includes God as a character. This God is estranged from man and exists in the form of an unquestionable truth and eternal power that forces the believer to submit to and obey it, which enchains the creative and freedom-loving spirit of man. On this point the story resonates with Shelley's play *Prometheus Unbound*, Byron's drama *Manfred* and Blake's *Prophetic Books*.

Some stories and essays from the collection *The Tempests* (including "The Gravedigger", "Slavery" and "The Captive Ruler") would seem to contain the quintessence of the Romantic world-view. In some cases their symbolism is complex ("The Gravedigger"). On the whole, the tone of these works is of desperation, hopelessness and sadness; they express one of the aspects of Gibran's Romanticism – his conviction that man has the calling to a spiritual life and strives for moral perfection. This brings him close to the Transcendentalists.

At this stage Gibran was also influenced by certain aspects of the prophetic and messianic style of Nietzsche. His ideas were close to those of the German philosopher in regard to the Church and to social institutions. However, as in other situations, in Gibran the Nietzschian doctrine of contempt and hatred for the "masses", and his opposition of the "masses" to the "chosen one", is tempered and does not appear in such an extreme form.

The Prophet (1923) signifies the final stage of development in Gibran's artistic method. In this book he tackles a series of universal problems (freedom, life and death, good and evil, and the essence and meaning of human existence), and calls man to the way of self-knowledge and moral perfection. The character of al-Mustafa as prophet, teacher and visionary is a response to Gibran's strictly Romantic views on the poet. His Prophet, like the Poet of the Transcendentalist Romantics, is charged with vocalising all that which ordinary people also experience intuitively but are themselves incapable of expressing. The postulations of the Prophet almost completely coincide with the points of departure of the Transcendentalists on human existence and the exaltation of man as the centre and substance of the universe.

What is particular about Gibran the Romantic is that the heroes of his works are far more human than are the classical Romantic heroes. Al-Mustafa, unlike the traditional Romantic figure, not only fails to oppose himself to "the masses", but, as it were, merges with them. Rather as many European writers saw their ideal of the chosen individual in Christ (Milton, Ernest Renan and Romain Rolland), Gibran embodied his ethical ideal in the character of the Prophet.

The work of Ameen Rihani, which absorbed ideas from the Arab Enlightenment and was influenced by Western Romanticism, generally followed the course of the new Arabic literature. His work bears the mark of his following the principles of the American Transcendentalists and of his attention to universal ethical problems.

Rihani's poetry, prose and journalism broadly reflected many characteristically Romantic ideas, such as the pantheistic approach to nature, a philosophical interpretation of reality and the posing of ethical questions. He gave equal importance, however, to national issues such as the goal of uniting the people in their struggle for independence, the importance of the historical past of the Arab nation and the struggle for education.

Much attention is given by Rihani to the theme of nature. This is of course a general trait among Romantics. However, in most cases the relationship to nature is coloured by the author's individualism. As it concerns Rihani, apart from the fact that nature is the source of beauty and inspiration and of eternal and all-embracing truths, it is a direct influence on the harmony of relations between man and society. In nature Rihani seeks the spiritual and moral principle of existence and a refuge from intractable contradictions, and from misfortune and regret.

As a follower of Transcendentalism, Rihani's perception of nature draws out the idea of the unity of Man, God and Nature. This Trinity is eternal, indissoluble and perfectly embodies the meaning of existence. Rihani is in agreement with Thoreau's postulate that "Man comprehends God in the contemplation of nature" ("My Temple in the Valley", "The Call of the Valleys", "The Valley of Frayki, or a return to nature", "At the Cot of Spring", "Hymns of the Valleys" ("Goddess of the Valley! Heal me!"), etc.). The Romantic conception of nature in Rihani, as with Gibran, is opposed to the theme of loneliness. For the Transcendentalists, the loneliness of the Romantic self is closely tied to the experience of "union with nature" (Thoreau). In Rihani we also encounter images of nature hostile to man, which symbolise society's incomprehension and the futility of all efforts by the lyric hero to have an impact on his surroundings ("A Branch of Roses").

Pivotal to the philosophy in Rihani's poetry are such universal problems as the essence of existence, the predestination of man in the world, the relationship between man and God, and categories of good and evil and of time and space, as likewise is his understanding of the essence of life as love and mercy (for example, "The Naj'wa" and "The Simoom Wind"). This aligns Rihani with the Transcendentalists. He saw progress itself primarily as the comprehensive development of man and his moral perfection. This is the basis of his interest in the problem of the individual, since for him the improvement of society begins with the improvement of the individual.

For Rihani, the problem of morals is directly linked to the understanding of religion as a "moral feeling". He considers God to be the highest moral law ("Seeds for the Sower", "The Wisdom of the Creator", etc.).

The idea of freedom gained particular importance in the system of Romantic symbolism, and this can be clearly seen in Rihani's philosophical lyric poetry. He understands freedom extremely broadly: the freedom of the self, creative freedom and the freedom of the people from oppression. While constantly speaking of "freedom", however, he almost never links these ideas to specific social or historical situations. Once more following the Transcendentalists, Rihani links the perfection of the social structure with the "correction of morals" (Emerson) and with education and reform. A true Romantic, Rihani also created "the utopia of the ideal revolution" in his poem "The Stones of Paris".

Rihani regarded his artistic work as a service to society. It is also no coincidence that his works frequently include themes and ideas that touch on his longing for the renewal of his homeland and on ways towards that renewal. The idealisation of the national past, which called for the renewal and unification of the nation, was a theme of importance in Enlightenment literature, and was adopted and developed by Rihani. He sought in the past a harmonious and free individual; his Romantic pathos, like that of Whitman, is associated both with ideas of national traditions in the struggle for independence and with the cult of enlightenment. This was a further facet of his Romantic outlook. The idealisation of the Arab past, which Rihani presents as a community of interests, is conditioned by national character and lends his Romanticism originality and a particular colouring. Neither struggle, conflict, oppression nor social demarcation are heeded; he speaks of the nation as a whole, one that in the past experienced a period of prosperity and greatness ("The Arabian Eagle", "I am the East", "On Revisiting the Valley", etc.).

In the poem "To Gibran" (1931), new aspects of Rihani's Romanticism can be seen, typified by a deeper grasp of reality. It is Rihani's view that Gibran expressed in his work an awakening to self-awareness for the Arab people. In the poem Gibran appears as a typical Romantic hero, an elevated and inspired individual and a person who gives himself wholly to his art. Overall, "To Gibran" is wholly Romantic both in its outlook and its methods. It contains much agitation and tension of feeling, and its hero is a singular individual. Creativity is portrayed as an unfathomable, intuitive and secret process. In the Romantic spirit, this elevated individual is juxtaposed with the capitalistic city. At the same time, however, Rihani is also looking for new means by which to reflect reality: there are many specific and lifelike details as well as typical generalisations. The Romantic landscape cohabits with the Realist one. All this is evidence of a certain tendency in Rihani's Romantic method towards a Realist outlook.

In his prose works Rihani's Romanticism assumes a special character. He gained many positive ideas from the legacy of the Arab Enlightenment. Thus, he continued to develop one of the cardinal Enlightenment themes: the emancipation of the Oriental woman from centuries of oppression (*The Lily of Ghore* (1910) and *Jahan* (1917)). This theme is fully and persuasively developed in the long narrative *Jahan*, in which the reader is captivated by the emotional saturation and vividness of the characters, the acute and contemporary nature of the problems it poses and its complex design. The main idea of the work is the struggle of woman for freedom from the powers of dark prejudice, which humiliate her as a person and trample her human dignity.

The Romantic quality of this work consists not only in the pathos of the love of freedom and social protest, and not only in the exclusiveness of the heroine, but also in the very manner in which the plot unfolds. The story contains no descriptions of everyday life and no recording of places or situations. There are no sideward steps, no tokens of ordinary life, and no detail is given to the heroine's surroundings. The entire story-line and all dramatic conflicts are concentrated on the heroine and her collisions with the other characters, while everything else is mere background whose sole purpose is to give emphasis to the exceptional character of the heroine. The Romantic element is also to be found in the tense lyricism of the narration, the descriptions of nature and the character portraits, and in the elated and emotional style of the work.

Rihani felt himself to be not only a writer but also a patriot and a fighter. All his interests and designs brought him to the centre of the sociopolitical and intellectual life of his people. This explains his natural affinity with political journalism. His short stories, pamphlets, essays and sketches are all filled with journalistic pathos; their figurative artistic elements are closely interwoven with straight journalistic writing, and indeed Rihani often begins his works in the manner of a storyteller but ends them as a journalist. Typical examples are "When Hell seems like Paradise" and "Over New York's Roofs".

Rihani created many tales and sketches about life in Beirut and its environs; for him these places served to represent the homeland, that is, Lebanon as a whole ("The Cross, or a Day in Beirut" and "From a Description of Beirut", for instance). Particularly characteristic of Rihani's Beirut sketches is a type of Romantic portrayal in which separate, generalised outlines, filled with specific real detail, build up the everyday life of the city in both its quiet and busy moments. His story "The Lofty Palace" stands out with its more distinct plot-line, more focused events and more expressed finale, revealing a new aspect of Rihani's artistic method: Romantic irony.

The artistic methods of both Gibran and Rihani evolved naturally and underwent qualitative changes, which allowed each to master new artistic means for portraying reality. As their Romanticism began to mature, both writers found themselves moving towards a more Realist world-view.

Arab émigré literature was, however, truly enriched by a Realist tendency in the work of Mikhail Naimy. Naimy started out with a thorough grounding in the Russian literary classics to create a critical view of life in Lebanese society at this new stage in its historical development.

Naimy was not only a major writer and innovator, but also a respected critic and theoretician of Arabic literature. His critical perspective was decisively influenced by the artistic and aesthetic views of Vissarion Belinsky. The theoretical and scholarly articles of Naimy, collected in *The Sieve* (1923), characterised by searches for new ways to overcome the old and the obsolete, are visibly tinged with the lessons he learned from the Russian critic. Belinsky's particular influence on Naimy was not contained in any single view or statement, but in his overall aesthetic conception. His idea that "art is ... thought in images" appears throughout Naimy's theoretical articles (for example, "Sifting", "Literary Criteria", and "The Crux of Literature"). Naimy's utterances on Arabic poetry ("The Poet and Poetry", "The Firefly", "Prosodic Elision and Lengthening"), with their frank, polemical tone and lack of compromise, and their criticism of obsolete canons, are in passionate agreement with the positions set out by Belinsky in his articles "The division of poetry into classes and types", "The poems of Mikhail Lermontov", and others.

The critical attitudes formulated by Belinsky in his articles "A Glance at Russian Literature in 1847", "The Works of Gibran", "The Complete Collected Works of A. Marlinsky" and "Russian Literature in 1842" formed the basis of Naimy's estimations of Gibran and Rihani. This is further evidence that the poetry of the Arab writers was typologically close to

European Romantic poetry and also to that of the Russian Romantics that were Belinsky's subject.

In many respects the world-view of Naimy coincides with the teachings of Leo Tolstoy. Tolstoy was for Naimy, as for many thinkers of the East, not so much a great Realist artist as a teacher of beliefs, whose philosophy and humanistic ideals met with their own ideas and aspirations. Ideas such as moral perfection, love and all-forgivingness, and the sublimation of the flesh for the sake of spiritual knowledge, all had a marked effect on the content of Naimy's works.

This commonality of ideas with Tolstoy remained throughout Naimy's creative life, from his early works through to his mature and late periods (the novels *The Book of Mirdad* and *The Last Day*, the long story *Memoirs of a Vagrant Soul*, and short stories including "Yellow Teeth", "Nail-Paring", "The Wanderer" and a few others). The ideas contained in "The Wanderer" (a teaching about God as the symbol of love and unity among people, and the approach to God through love and service to people) are almost identical to those of Tolstoy's story "The Two Old Men".

In *Memoirs of a Vagrant Soul* (1918) Naimy addresses the cardinal questions of human existence and the meaning of life. Its hero, Arqash, thirsts for the truth and wants to master his destiny, believing that this can be achieved when a person is able to control his intellect and his will by his own strength, and to conquer his passions. This story provides a critique of social institutions and the hypocrisy prevalent in the Church, and expresses pacifist themes. Its basic ideas reveal a closeness to Tolstoy's *My Confession* and his articles "On Life" and "What is to be Done?". The call to peaceful labour for the common good also acquires here a Tolstoyan colouring.

The Book of Mirdad (1948) continues to develop the ideas of the above work. This work is a corpus of the author's philosophical, religious, moral, ethical and, to a certain extent, social views. In particular, the novel draws on Tolstoy's idea of religious "salvation". The novel's characteristic motifs include the criticism of spiritual impoverishment, the demand that religion be purged of empty ritual, and the desire of uniting people with ideas of universal love, and these again bring Naimy close to Tolstoy's teachings. Both writers also saw in the moral improvement of the individual a path of renewal for man and for mankind as a whole. The idea of God as love also coincides with Tolstoy's article "Love One Another". Following Tolstoy, Naimy bases his social views on moral and religious philosophy, and social conflicts are portrayed in the form of moral conflicts.

Naimy's novel *The Last Day* (1963) is, in terms of his world-view, the author's summary work. It is influenced by Tolstoy's moral and religious views and his uncompromising criticism of the structures of human society, and points towards a search for the religious ideal and for self-knowledge. The desire of the hero of *The Last Day* to re-examine life and to understand, in the last few hours remaining to him, what it means to be human, brings the pathos of the work close to Tolstoy's *The Death of Ivan Il'ich*.

But Tolstoy, as a Realist artist, links his hero's intellectual and moral foresights with the specific realities of real life and his surroundings, whereas *The Last Day* is characteristically philosophical and parabolic in substance, and remains abstracted and alienated from immediate life. It is similar to Tolstoy's story only in so far as both works concentrate on the self-analysis of the leading characters and their efforts to understand the lives they have lived. There is, however, a direct coincidence of images in the novel with Tolstoy's *My Confession*: the boats and ships, the rivers and the banks, as seen in Musa's dream and experienced by the hero of *My Confession*.

Naimy's play *Fathers and Sons* (1918) is based upon the idea of the conflict of two generations. The hero, Da'ud Salama, becomes the mouthpiece of the progressive ideas of the Arab Enlighteners, and is opposed to the archaic norms of the medieval East. Drawing on the idea of Turgenev's novel of the same name, which concerns inter-generational conflict and is primarily structured on the clash of the principal hero and his friends with those who hold opposing views, Naimy practically reflected the Enlightenment aesthetic ideal in the plot, the treatment of the conflicts and the placement of the characters. However, in creating his characters Naimy was a Critical Realist, and this ultimately defined his role as the innovator of the genre of Realist drama in Arabic literature. It is in the Realist portrayal of the life of his heroes, in the precise emphasising of the substantial and the incidental, and in the ability, in a single episode of the hero's life, to reveal a characteristic moment in the history of the country, that Russian literature in general, and the work of Turgenev in particular, can be seen.

An important element of Naimy's work is the short story. His creativity in this field was strongly influenced by that of Anton Chekhov. Naimy's stories are mostly gathered into three collections: *Once upon a Time* (1937), *Grandees* (1953) and *The Man with the Fat Calf* (1959). It should be remembered that the degree of artistic comprehension and endeavour were not commensurate for Naimy and Chekhov; there is also a typological divergence between the two writers. However, the Chekhovian school can be seen in Naimy in the sharply social orientation of his stories, their striking humanism and their love and compassion for the human being. Naimy's adherence to Chekhov is also evident in his adoption of important principles of the Chekhovian method of reflecting reality, such as a laconic prose style.

In outlining and underlining the innovation in Naimy's short stories as he moved towards Critical Realism, we must not ignore the literary environment and traditions in which his artistry was formed. Naimy was writing his stories at exactly the time when Romanticism was becoming widespread in Arabic literature. It is therefore natural that, along with a Chekhovian Realism, Naimy's stories also contain Romantic and Sentimentalist elements.

To conclude, then, each of our three authors – Khalil Gibran, Ameen Rihani and Mikhail Naimy – perceived and transformed, in their many-sided artistic ventures, the achievements of European and American literature, and organically synthesised the values of these with the best of their own national artistic traditions. In their case, their mastery of the artistic experience of foreign literatures had an artistic character and met the demands and tasks of the arts in their own country, which allowed them to preserve both the specifics of their nation and a unique national colouring.

Although the three influencing tendencies discussed here – English and American Romanticism and Russian Critical Realism – were not coincident in time, each of the three Arab writers was ready and able to undertake his chosen direction. In each case they acquired a certain set of ideas and devices characteristic of that direction, and each developed a personal mode of approach to the mastery of his artistic method. And finally, each of the three authors was able, in his own way, to master the arsenal of ethical and artistic values inherent in that method and to develop and apply them in their artistic practice.

It is possible that the literary contacts and the apperception of the ideas of the Western schools were facilitated by the fact that all three writers shared a link to these influences by their being Christian. This would have made it relatively easy for them to overcome the barrier of ideological rejection of the values of Western culture and to find an adequate means of affirming those values on the basis of universal and humanistic ideals, which had always been familiar to the cultures of the Eastern peoples.

The Syro-American School paved the way for a host of successors, not only in Arab literature but also in the literatures of other Eastern countries. This can be attributed, to a large extent, to the fact that much of what they wrote was in English. The works of the members of the Syro-American School therefore occupied a position far beyond the framework of their own national literature alone, and took their deserved place in world literature. This literary activity served, as it were, that channel of communication that enabled Western and Eastern literatures to exchange their intellectual achievements.

Kahlil Gibran, Ameen Rihani and Mikhail Naimy thus raised Arabic literature to a new level and gave it access to the best of world literature, including that of the great Russian tradition. Because of this, the mission fell to the Arab writers of further widening the horizons of twentieth-century Arabic literature, introducing greater variety to its thematic repertoire and range of genres, and creating new forms of artistic expression.

It would hardly be an exaggeration to assert that it was thanks to the work of these writers that twentieth-century Arabic literature was able to move beyond the limits of a regional literature and make its inherent and inalienable contribution to the process of world literature.

Endnotes

Common Russian bibliographical terms in the notes

Works = *Sochinenia*

Selected Works = *Izbrannoe*; *Izbrannie proizvedenia* (*Izbr. proizv.*);
Izbrannie sochinenia (*Izbr. soch.*); *Sobrannie sochinenia* (*Sobr. soch.*)

Complete Collected Works = *Polnoe sobrannie sochinenia* (*Poln. sobr. soch.*)

Notes to Introduction

1. Lutsky, V.B., *Novaya istoria arabskikh stran*, Moscow, 1966, pp.33–54.

2. Krachkovsky, I.Yu., "Arabskaya literatura v XX veke", in Krachkovsky, *Izbr. soch.*, vol. 3, Moscow and Leningrad, 1956, p.92.

3. Cited in Krymsky, A.E., *Istoria novoy arabskoy literatury: XIX–nachalo XX veka*, Moscow, 1971, p.253.

4. For details, see Sarraj, Nadira Jamil, *Shu'ara al-Rabita al-Qalamiyya'*, Cairo, 1955, pp.36–8.

5. See Dolinina, A.A., *Ocherki istorii arabskoy literatury novogo vremeni: Egipet i Siria*, Moscow, 1973, pp.23–5.

6. Dima, A., *Printsipy sravnitel'nogo literaturovedenia* (Russ. trans. from Romanian), Moscow, 1977, p.142. See also Neupokoeva, I.G., *Istoria vsemirnoy literatury: Problemy sistemnogo i sravnitel'nogo analiza*, Moscow, 1976. In Neupokoeva's words, "truly national literature can appear and develop only within fruitful interrelationships with the literatures of other peoples" (ibid. p.256).

7. Krachkovsky, I.Yu., "Arabskaya literatura v XX veke", in Krachkovsky, *Izbr. soch.*, vol. 3, pp.18–19.

8. Krachkovsky, I.Yu., "Arabskaya literatura v Amerike (1895–1915)", *Izvestia LGU*, vol. 1, Leningrad, 1928, pp.2–12; see also his "Arabskaya literatura v XX veke", pp.17–21.

9. Krachkovsky, I.Yu., "Introduction to *Ameen Rihani*", *Izbr. proizv.* (Russ. trans. with notes by I.Yu. Krachkovsky), Petrograd, 1917, in Krachkovsky, *Izbr. soch.*, vol. 3, pp.137–45; also his Introduction to *Ameen Rihani: Stikhotvorenia v proze*, 1922, *Izbr. soch.*, vol. 3, pp.146–7; his "Filosof doliny Fureyki", in *Nad arabskimi rukopisyami*, Moscow, 1965, pp.60–7; his "al-Ma'arri, Rihani i Leningrad", *Izbr. soch.*, vol. 3, pp.261–3; and his "Listky vospominaniy o knigakh i lyudyakh", *Izbr. soch.*, vol. 1, Moscow and Leningrad, 1955, pp.46–9.

10. Krachkovsky, I.Yu., "Arabskaya literatura v Amerike (1895–1915)", pp.18–23; also his "Ocherki novo-arabskoy literatury", *Izbr. soch.*, vol. 3, pp.65–71; and his introduction to Ode-Vasil'eva, K.V., *Obraztsy novo-arabskoy literatury*, *Izbr. soch.*, vol. 3, pp.47–64, 115–20.

11. Krachkovsky, I.Yu., "O knige M. Nuayme o Dzhebrane" (1941), *Izbr. soch.*, vol. 3, pp.348–52; also his "Avtobiografia Mikhaila Nuayme" (1931), *Izbr. soch.*, vol. 3, pp.223–9.

12. In Rihani, A., *Izbr. proizv.*; *Sovremennaya arabskaya proza*, Leningrad, 1961, pp.21–35, 55–82; *Arabskaya romanticheskaya proza XIX–XX vv*, Leningrad, 1981,

pp.87–97, 184–200; Gibran, K., *Izbrannoe*, Moscow and Leningrad, 1986, pp.118–50; Rihani, A., *Izbrannoe*, Leningrad, 1988, pp.32–42, 164–209, 215–42.

13. See Dolinina, A.A., "Neopublikovannie perevody iz arabskoy literatury v arkhive I.Yu. Krachkovskogo", in *Pis'mennye pamyatniki i problemy istorii kul'tury narodov Vostoka*, Moscow, 1977.

14. Krachkovsky, I.Yu., Preface to Ode-Vasil'eva, *Obraztsy novo-arabskoy literatury*, *Izbr. soch.*, vol. 3, pp.57–8. See also Krachkovsky, I.Yu., "Arabskaya literatura v XX veke", p.93, and his "Preface to *Ameen Rihani*", *Izbr. proizv.*, p.17.

15. Krachkovsky, I.Yu., "Arabskaya literatura v Amerike (1895–1915)", p.10.

16. See Krachkovsky, I.Yu., *Izbr. soch.*, vol. 3, "Novo-arabskaya literatura", p.75; "Arabskaya literatura v XX veke", p.94; "Avtobiografia Mikhaila Nuayme", pp.223–8; "Russko-arabskie literaturnie svyazi", pp.274–5; "Chekhov v arabskoy literature", pp.312–13; "Basni Krylova v arabskikh perevodakh", p.325; also his *Nad arabskimi rukopisyami*, pp.78–90.

17. Ode-Vasil'eva, K.V., *Obraztsy novo-arabskoy literatury (1880–1925)*, Moscow, 1928; also her *Obraztsy novo-arabskoy literatury (1880–1947)*, Moscow, 1949.

18. Ode-Vasil'eva, K.V., Preface to *Rasskazy pisateley Livana*, Moscow, 1958, pp.5–9.

19. Ode-Vasil'eva, K.V., "Mikhail Nuayme", in *Livanskie novelly*, Moscow, 1958, pp.5–8.

20. Dolinina, A.A., Preface to *Sovremennaya arabskaya proza*, Moscow and Leningrad, 1961, pp.6–11; also her "Iz istorii russko-arabskikh literaturnikh svyazey ('Otsy i deti' M. Nuayme)", in *Vestnik LGU, seria istorii, yazyka i literatury*, 1963, no. 20, issue 4, pp.89–95; also her "Iz predystorii realizma v novoy arabksoy literature", in collection *Problemy stanovlenia realizma v literature Vostoka*, Moscow, 1964, pp.278–92; also her Afterword to Naimy, M., *Moi sem'desyat let* (Russ. trans. from Arabic by S. Batsieva), Moscow, 1980, pp.222–36; also her Preface to *Arabskaya romanticheskaya proza XIX–XX vv.*, Leningrad, 1981, pp.5–22; [and] "Ameen Rihani", in Rihani, A., *Izbrannoe*, Leningrad, 1988, pp.3–23.

21. See *Sovremennaya arabskaya proza*, pp.39–82, 241–8, 268–90; Gibran, K., *Izbrannoe*, pp.260–73, 306–16; Rihani, A., *Izbrannoe*, pp.27–32, 301–419.

22. Kutelia, M.V., *Mirovozzrenie Dzhebran Khalila Dzhebrana*, candidate philological dissertation, Baku, 1978.

23. Markov, V.V., Preface to "Dzhebran Khalil Dzhebran", *Izbrannoe*, Leningrad, 1986; also his *Filosofskaya antropologia Dzh. Kh. Dzhebrana*, author's abstract of candidate philosophy dissertation, Leningrad, 1987.

24. Levin, Z.I., *Filosof iz Fureyki*, Moscow, Nauka, 1965.

25. Levin, Z.I., *Razvitie osnovnykh techeniy obshchestvenno-politicheskoy mysli v Sirii i Egipte*, Moscow, 1972, pp.203–7.

26. Tazetdinova, L.A., *Poezia Amina Rihani*, candidate dissertation in philology, Leningrad, 1986.

27. Imangulieva, A.N., *Literaturnoe ob"edinenie "Assosiatsia pera" i Mikhail Nuayme*, candidate dissertation in philology, Baku, 1966; Imangulieva, A.N., *"Assosiatsia pera" i Mikhail Nuayme*, Moscow, 1975; Muminov, H.K., *Mikhail Nuayme kak teoretik kriticheskogo realizma v arabskoy literature*, candidate dissertation in philology, Tashkent, 1975; Bilyk, I.E., *Tvorchesky metod Mikhaila Nuayme*, candidate dissertation in philology, Moscow, 1984; Nikolaeva, M.V., *Kharakter otrazhenia religioznogo mirovozzrenia v tvorchestve sovremennykh livanskikh romanistov (1950–70gg)*, candidate dissertation in philology, Moscow, 1984. In this work only two works by Naimy are examined (*My Seventy Years*, part 1, and *The Last Day*) within the general course of the development of religious and philosophical themes in the Lebanese novel. The

same topic is explored in Nikolaeva, M.V., "Religioznaya kontseptsia mira i cheloveka v romanakh Mikhaila Nuayme", in *Khudozhestvennie traditsii literatur Vostoka i sovremennost': traditsionalizm na sovremennom etape*, Moscow, 1986, pp.190–215.

28. Muminov, H.K., dissertation cited above, p.129.

29. Bilyk, I.E., dissertation cited above, p.179.

30. al-Badawi, Mulaththam, *al-Natiqun bi al-dad Amirika al-Janubiyya* (*Arab writers in South America*), Cairo, 1956; *Leading figures of Arabic literature in exile*, Amman, 1956 [Arabic not found]; *The newspaper al-Huda in Arabic and Lebanese emigrants in the USA, 1856–1968*, New York, 1966 [Arabic not found]; Jad Hasan, Hasan, *al-Adab al-'Arabi fi al-mahjar* (*Arabic literature in exile*), Cairo, 1962; Qindilchi, Amir Ibrahim, *al-'Arab fi al-mahjar al-Amriki* (*Arab emigrants in the USA*), Baghdad, 1977; Qunsul, Ilyas, *Adab al-mughtaribin* (*Arab émigré literature*), Damascus, 1963; Sarraj, Nadira Jamil, *Nasib 'Arida, al-Sha'ir al-katib al-suhufi* (*The poets of the "Pen League"*), Cairo, 1955; Saydah, George, *Adabuna wa udaba'una fi al-mahajir al-Amirikiyya* (*Our literature and our men of letters in American exile*), Beirut, 1964; Tomeh, George, *al-Mughtaribun al-'Arab fi Amrika al-shamaliyya* (*Arab emigrants in North America*), Damascus, 1965; al-Khuri, Alfred, *al-Kalima al-'Arabiyya fi al-mahjar* (*The Arabic word in exile*), Beirut, 1960.

31. 'Abbas, Ihsan, and Najm, Muhammad Yusuf, *al-Shi'r al-'Arabi fi al-mahjar* (*Arabic poetry in exile in North America*), Beirut, 1957; 'Abd al-Ghani Hasan, Muhammad, *al-Shi'r al-'Arabi fi al-mahjar* (*Arabic poetry in exile*), Cairo, 1962; Ashtar, 'Abd al-Karim, *al-Nathr al-mahjari* (*Émigré prose: the writers of the "Pen League"*), Cairo, 1960–61, in 2 parts; Dib, Wadi' Amin, *Arabic poetry in America* (*al-Shi'r al-'Arabi fi al-mahjar al-Amriki*), Beirut, 1955; Maridan, 'Aziza, *al-Qawmiyya wa al-insaniyya fi shi'r al-mahjar al-janubi* (*National and human tendencies in South American exile poetry*), Cairo, 1966; Anas, Da'ud, *al-Tajdid fi shi'r al-mahjar* (*Innovation in the poetry of exile*), Cairo, 1968; Haddara, Muhammad Mustafa, *Dirasat fi al-shi'r al-'Arabi* (*Studies in Arabic poetry*), Cairo, 1975.

32. Marun, 'Abbud, *Judad wa qudama'* (*Innovators and traditionalists*), Beirut, 1963, pp.81–175; Jabr, Jamil, *Jubrān, sīratuhu, adabuhu, falsafatuhu wa rasmuhu* (*Gibran: his biography, his literature, philosophy and art*), Beirut, 1958; Jabr, Jamil, *Mayy wa Jubran* (*Mayy and Gibran*), Cairo, 1961; Mas'ud, Habib, *Jubrān hayyan wa mayyitan* (*Gibran living and dead*), Beirut, 1966, 2nd edn; Naimy, Mikhail, *Jubrān Khalīl Jubrān, hayātuhu, mawtuhu, adabuhu fannuhu* (*Gibran Kahlil Gibran: his life and death and literary and artistic works*), Beirut, 1936; Naimy, Mikhail, *Nabi'a Lubnan Jubran Khalil Jubran* (*Lebanon's genius Gibran: problems of his life and the drama of his death*), Cairo, 1958; Sayigh, Tawfiq, *Adwa' jadida 'ala Jubran* (*Gibran in a new interpretation*), Beirut, 1966; Talisi, Khalifa Muhammad, *al-Shabbi wa Jubran* (*al-Shabbi and Gibran*), Tripoli, 1957; Hawi, Khalil, *Kahlil Gibran: his background, character and works*, Beirut, 1963.

33. Marun, 'Abbud, *Amin al-Rihani*, Cairo, 1952; Jabr, Jamil, *Amin al-Rayhani: al-rajul wa al-adib* (*Ameen Rihani, man and writer*), Beirut, 1947; al-Kiyali, Sami, *Amin al-Rihani*, Aleppo, 1948; Musa, Muhammad 'Ali, *Amin al-Rayhani* (*Ameen Rihani: his life and works*), Beirut, 1961; Nashashibi, Is'af, *al-Lughat al-'Arabiyya wa al-Rayhani* (*The Arabic language and Rihani*), Cairo, 1928; Rawi, Haris Taha, *Amin al-Rayhani: jawanib shakhsiyyatih wa-atharih fi nahdat al-'Arab* (*Ameen Rihani and his influence on the Arabic revival*), Beirut, 1958; Reyhani, Albert, *Amin al-Rihani*, Beirut, 1941; Rafi'i, Tawfiq, *Amin al-Rihani: a biography*, Cairo, 1922; Khuri, Ra'if, *Amin al-Rihani*, Beirut, 1948.

34. Abu Shabaka, Ilyas, *Dirasat wa dhikrayat* (*Collected articles and memoirs on Mikhail Naimy*), Beirut, 1948; Ma'luf, Shafiq, *Habbat zumurrud* (*A granule of emerald: contemporary Arabic literature*), Damascus, 1966, pp.121–5; Malhas, Thurayya, *Mikha'il Nu'ayma al-adib al-sufi* (*Mikhail Naimy: a Sufi writer*), Beirut, 1964; Naimy, Nadeem,

Mikhail Naimy: an introduction, Beirut, 1967 (in English); Khuri, Alfred, *Gibran and Naimy*, Beirut, 1960; Khuri, Yuhanna, *Radd 'ala Mikha'il Nu'ayma fi Mirdad* (*Naimy's Book of Mirdad*), Sayda, 1956; Shafiq, Muhammad, *Falsafa Mikha'il Nu'ayma* (*The philosophy of Mikhail Naimy*), Beirut, 1979.

35. 'Abbas, Ihsan, and Najm, Muhammad Yusuf, *al-Shi'r al-'Arabi fi al-mahjar*, Beirut, 1957.

36. Ibid. p.42.

37. Ibid.

38. Ibid. p.43.

39. 'Abbas, Ihsan, and Najm, Muhammad Yusuf, *al-Shi'r al-'Arabi fi al-mahjar*, p.44.

40. Krachkovsky, I.Yu., "Arabskaya literatura v Amerike (1895–1915)", p.10.

41. 'Abbas, Ihsan, and Najm, Muhammad Yusuf, *al-Shi'r al-'Arabi fi al-mahjar*, p.250.

42. Ibid. pp.109–16.

43. Ibid. p.114.

44. Hawi, Khalil, *Kahlil Gibran: his background, character and works*, Beirut, 1963.

45. Naimy, Nadeem, *Mikhail Naimy: an introduction*.

46. Hawi, Khalil, *Kahlil Gibran, his background, character and works*, p.167.

47. Naimy, Nadeem, *Mikhail Naimy: an introduction*, p.327.

48. Brockelmann, C., *Geschichte der arabischen Literatur*, suppl. III, Leiden, 1942.

49. Kampffmeyer, G., "Arabische Dichter der Gegenwart", *MSOS*, 29, 2. Abt, 1926; XXXI, 2. Abt, 1928; "Index zur neueren arabischen Literatur", *MSOS*, 31, 2. Abt, 1928.

50. Khemiri, T., and Kampffmeyer, G., *Leaders in contemporary Arabic literature: a book of reference*, part 1, London, 1930.

51. Gibb, H.A.R., "Studies in contemporary Arabic literature", in *Bulletin of the School of Oriental Studies*, vol. 4, 1927–28, vol. 5, 1929.

52. Najib, Ullah, *Islamic literature*, New York, 1963, pp.107–10.

53. Ghougassian, Joseph P., *Kahlil Gibran: wings of thought – the people's philosopher*, New York, 1973; Gibran, Jean, and Gibran, Kahlil, *Kahlil Gibran: his life and world*, Boston, 1974; Otto, Annie Salem, *The parables of Kahlil Gibran: an interpretation of his writings and art*, New York, 1967.

54. Ibid. p.56.

55. Ibid. p.57.

56. Gibran, Jean, and Gibran, Kahlil, *Kahlil Gibran: his life and world*.

Notes to Chapter 1

1. See Krymsky, A.E., *Istoria novoy arabskoy literatury: XIX–nachalo XX veka*, Moscow, 1971, pp.95–138.

2. See al-Khalil, Mustafa, and Farruh, Omar, *Missionery i imperializm v arabskikh stranakh*, Moscow, 1961.

3. Levin, Z.I., *Razvitie osnovnykh techeniy obshchestvenno-politicheskoy mysli v Sirii i Egipte*, Moscow, 1972, p.37.

4. Hitti, Philip, *Ta'rikh Suriyya wa Lubnan wa Falastin*, part 2, Beirut, 1959, pp.352–6.

5. Krachkovsky, I.Yu., "Arabsky perevod 'Istorii Petra Velikogo' i 'Istorii Karla XII, korolya Shvetsii' Vol'tera", *Izbr. soch.*, vol. 3, Moscow and Leningrad, 1956, p.367.

6. See Kotlov, L.N., *Stanovlenie natsional'no-osvoboditel'nogo dvizhenia na Arabskom Vostoke*, Moscow, 1975, pp.274–85.

7. Levin, Z.I., *Razvitie osnovnykh techeniy obshchestvenno-politicheskoy mysli v Sirii i Egipte*, pp.32–3.

8. Ibid. p.33.

9. See Kudelin, A.B., "O putyakh razvitia novoy arabskoy poezii", in *Vzaimosvyazi afrikanskikh literatur i literatur mira*, Moscow, 1975, p.18.

10. See Taymur, Mahmud, *Fi al-adab al-'Arabi al-hadith*, Beirut, 1954, p.30.

11. Usmanov, N.K., "Literatura arabskikh stran", in *Literatura Vostoka v novoe vremya*, Moscow, 1975, p.52.

12. Hitti, Philip, *Ta'rikh Suriyya wa Lubnan wa Falastin*, part 2, p.358.

13. For details see Dolinina, A.A., *Ocherki istorii arabskoy literatury novogo vremeni: Egipet i Siria*, Moscow, 1968, pp.13–18; al-Rifa'i, Shams al-Din, *Ta'rikh al-sihafa al-Suriyya: fi al-'ahd al-'Uthmani (1800–1917)*, Cairo, 1969.

14. Lutsky, V.B., "Pod"em natsional'no-osvoboditel'nogo dvizhenia v arabskikh stranakh v period pervoy russkoy revolyutsii, 1905–1907gg", in *Pervaya russkaya revolyutsia i mezhdunarodnoe revolyutsionnoe dvizhenie*, part 2, Moscow, 1956, pp.426–8; Lazarev, M.S., *Krushenie turetskogo gospodstva na Arabskom Vostoke*, Moscow, 1960, p.31.

15. See Petrosyan, Yu.A., *Mladoturetskoe dvizhenie (vtoraya polovina XIX–nachalo XX v)*, Moscow, 1971.

16. Lutsky, V.B., *Novaya istoria arabskikh stran*, Moscow, 1965, p.300.

17. Ibid. pp.118–19; Similyanskaya, I.M., *Krest'yanskoe dvizhenie v Livane v pervoy polovine XIX v.*, Moscow, 1965, pp.203–4; Kurd Ali, Muhammad, *Ghutat Dimashq*, Damascus, 1952, p.141.

18. Marx, K., "Sobytia v Sirii: Angliyskaya parlamentskaya sessia: Sostoyanie britanskoy torgovli", in Marx, K., and Engels, F., *Sochinenia*, 2nd edn, vol. 15, p.102.

19. Krachkovsky, I.Yu., "Novoarabskaya literatura", *Izbr. soch.*, vol. 3, p.70. See Dolinina, A.A., *Ocherki istorii arabskoy literatury novogo vremeni*, 1968, pp.5–6, 13–18.

20. Krachkovsky, I.Yu., "Arabskaya literatura v XX veke.", *Izbr. soch.*, vol. 3, p.22.

21. Hidda, Hasan, *Ta'rikh al-mughtaribin al-'Arab fi al-'alam*, Damascus, 1974, pp.217–29.

22. Krachkovsky, I.Yu., "Arabskaya literatura v Amerike (1895–1915)", *Izvestia LGU*, vol. 1, Leningrad, 1928, p.2.

23. Ruppin, Artur, *Sovremennaya Siria i Palestina* (Russ. trans. from German, ed. A.O. Zaydenman), Petrograd, 1919, p.19; Hidda, Hasan, *Ta'rikh al-mughtaribin al-'Arab fi al-'alam*, pp.219–21.

24. Saydah, George, *Adabuna wa udaba'una fi al-mahajir al-Amirikiyya*, Beirut, 1964, p.226.

25. Qindilchi, Amir Ibrahim, *al-'Arab fi al-mahjar al-Amriki*, Cairo, 1977, p.15.

26. Krachkovsky, I.Yu., "Arabskaya literatura v Amerike (1895–1915)", p.1.

27. Naimy, M., *Moi sem'desyat let* (Russ. trans. of autobiography *Sab'un* by S. Batsievaya), Moscow, 1980, p.14.

28. Hasan, Jad Hasan, *Adab al-'Arabi fi al-mahjar*, Beirut, 1962, pp.67–9.

29. Qunsul, Ilyas, *Adab al-mughtaribin*, Damascus, 1963, p.21.

30. Tarazi, Filipp, *Ta'rikh al-sihafa al-'Arabiyya*, vol. 4, Beirut, 1933, p.407.

31. Tomeh, George, *al-Mughtaribun al-'Arab fi Amrika al-shamaliyya*, Damascus, 1965, pp.68–9.

32. Ibid. p.71.

33. For details, see Imangulieva, A.N., *"Assosiatsia pera" i Mikhail Nuayme*, Moscow, 1975, pp.9–26.

34. Krachkovsky, I.Yu., "Preface to *Ameen Reyhani*", *Izbr. proizv.*, p.17.

35. Krachkovsky, I.Yu., "Arabskaya literatura v XX veke", p.22.

36. Sarraj, Nadira Jamil, *Shu'ara al-Rabita al-Qalamiyya*, Cairo, 1955, p.309.

37. Dolinina, A.A., Preface to *Arabskaya romanticheskaya proza XIX–XX vekov*, Leningrad, 1981, p.13.

38. See Gerasimova, A.S., *Literatura Afganistana*, p.82.

39. Rawi, Haris Taha, "al-Thawra al-fikriyya fi adab al-mahjar", in *al-Adab*, 5, Beirut, 1954, p.51.

40. Najm, Muhammad Yusuf, *al-Kissa fi al-adab al-'Arabi al-hadith*, Cairo, 1952, pp.25–6.

41. Nawri, 'Isa, *Adab al-mahjar*, Cairo, 1959, p.62.

42. Cited in Borisov, V.M., *Sovremennaya egipetskaya proza*, Moscow, 1961, pp.30–1.

43. Krachkovsky, I.Yu., "Arabskaya literatura v XX veke", p.24.

44. Meletinsky, Ye.M., "Literatura Blizhnego Vostoka i Sredney Azii (vvedenie)", in *Istoria vsemirnoy literatury*, vol. 2, Moscow, 1984, p.210.

45. Chelyshev, Ye.P., "Teoreticheskie i metodologicheskie aspekty izuchenia vzaimodeystvia kul'tur Vostoka i Zapada", in *Vzaimodeystvie kul'tur Vostoka i Zapada*, Moscow, 1987, p.3.

46. Mikhaylov, A.D., Introduction to *Istoria vsemirnoy literatury*, vol. 2, Moscow, 1984, p.12.

47. Nikiforova, I.D., Preface to *Vzaimosvyazi afrikanskikh literatur i literatur mira*, Moscow, 1975, p.3.

48. Neupokoeva, I.G., *Istoria vsemirnoy literatury: Problemy sistemnogo i sravnitel'nogo analiza*, Moscow, 1976, p.254.

49. Zhirmunsky, V.M., "Problemy sravnitel'no-istoricheskogo izuchenia literatur", in Zhirmunsky, *Sravnitel'noe literaturovedenie*, Leningrad, 1979, p.74.

50. Neupokoeva, I.G., "Nekotorie voprosy izuchenia vzaimosvyazey i vzaimodeystvia natsional'nykh literatur", in *Vzaimosvyaz' i vzaimodeystvia natsional'nykh literatur*, Moscow, 1961, pp.28–9.

51. See Chelyshev, Ye.P., "Teoreticheskie i metodologicheskie aspekty izuchenia vzaimodeystvia kul'tur Vostoka i Zapada", in *Vzaimodeystvie kul'tur Vostoka i Zapada*, pp.3–20.

52. See Dolinina, A.A., *Ocherki istorii arabskoy literatury novogo vremeni*, 1973, pp.25–32.

53. For details see Dolinina, A.A., "Fridrikh Ryukert kak perevodchik 'Makam' al-Khariri", in *Vzaimodeystvie kul'tur Vostoka i Zapada*, pp.70–9.

54. Goethe, Johann Wolfgang von, *Zapadno-vostochny divan*, p.5.

55. Ivbulis, V.Ya., "Romantizm i traditsionnaya indiyskaya mysl", in *Vzaimodeystvie kul'tur Vostoka i Zapada*, p.31.

56. Zykova, Ye.P., "Vostok v tvorchestve poetov 'ozernoy shkoly'", in *Vzaimodeystvie kul'tur Vostoka i Zapada*, p.49.

57. Ibid. p.45.

58. Konrad, N.I., "Problemy realizma i literatury Vostoka", in Konrad, *Zapad i vostok*, Moscow, 1972, p.347.

59. Bushmin, A.S., *Preemstvennost' v razvitii literatury*, Leningrad, 1978, pp.61–2.

60. Cited in Kirpichenko, V., *Sovremennaya egipetskaya proza (60–70-e gody)*, Moscow, 1986, p.13.

61. See Ali-zade, E.A., *Egipetskaya novella*, Moscow, 1974, pp.47–69.

62. See Khodzhaeva, R.U., *Ocherki razvitia egipetskoy poezii*, Tashkent, 1985, pp.12–58.

63. Volkov, I.F., *Tvorcheskie metody i khudozhestvennie sistemy*, Moscow, 1978, p.128.

64. Konrad, N.I., "Problemy realizma i literatury Vostoka", in Konrad, *Zapad i Vostok*, p.348.

65. Volkov, I.F., *Tvorcheskie metody i khudozhestvennie sistemy*, p.130.

66. Ivbulis, V.Ya., *Literaturno-khudozhestvennoe tvorchestvo Rabindranata Tagora*, Riga, 1981, p.39.

67. Dmitriev, A.S., "Teoria zapanoevropeyskogo romantizma", in *Literaturnie manifesty zapadnoevropeyskikh romantikov*, Moscow, 1980, p.7.

68. Ibid. p.8.

69. Ibid. p.9.

70. Ivbulis, V.Ya., *Literaturno-khudozhestvennoe tvorchestvo Rabindranata Tagora*, p.36.

71. See Dolinina, A.A., *Ocherki istorii arabskoy literatury novogo vremeni*, 1968, pp.3–37.

72. Introduction to *Razvitie literatury v epokhu formirovania natsii v stranakh tsentralnoy i yugo-vostochnoy Evropy*, p.7.

73. Dolinina, A.A., Preface to *Arabskaya romanticheskaya proza XIX–XX vekov*, p.7.

74. Moreh, S., *Modern Arabic poetry (1800–1970): the development of its forms and themes under the influence of Western literature*, Leiden, 1976, p.58.

75. Iezuitova, R.V., *Istoria russkoy poezii*, Leningrad, 1968, vol. 1, p.231.

76. Abu Shadi, A.Z., *Atyaf al-rabi': Muqaddima*, Cairo, 1933, p."xa".

77. Badawi, M.M., *A critical introduction to modern Arabic poetry*, Cambridge, 1973, p.115.

78. Dolinina, A.A., Preface to *Arabskaya romanticheskaya proza XIX–XX vekov*, p.12.

79. Nikolyukin, A.N., *Estetika amerikanskogo romantizma*, Moscow, 1977, p.17.

80. Bauers, David, "Demokraticheskie dali", in *Literaturnaya istoria Soedinennikh Shtatov Ameriki*, vol. 1, Moscow, 1977, p.423.

81. Zhirmunsky, V.M., "Problemy sravnitel'no-istoricheskogo izuchenia literatur", in Zhirmunsky, *Sravnitel'noe literaturovedenie*, p.74.

82. Hawi, Khalil S., *Kahlil Gibran: his background, character and works*, Beirut, 1963, p.97.

83. Gibran, K., "Ibn Sina wa qasidatuhu", in Gibran, K., *al-Majmu'a al-kamila li mu'allafat Jibran Khalil Jibran* [Complete Collected Works, organised and introduced by Mikhail Naimy], Beirut, 1961, pp.532–5.

84. Gibran, K., *al-Majmu'a al-kamila li mu'allafat*, pp.532, 535.

85. Gibran, K., "Mustaqbal al-lugha al-'arabiyya", in *al-Majmu'a al-kamila li mu'allafat*, pp.544–52.

86. Gibran, K., "al-Huruf al-nariyya", in *al-Majmu'a al-kamila li mu'allafat*, pp.252–3.

87. Rihani, Ameen, *Muluk al-'Arab*, Beirut, 1924, part 1, p.6.

88. For details, see Imangulieva, A.N., "Istoki arabsko-russkikh kul'turnikh i literaturnykh svyazey", in anthology *Blizhny i Sredny Vostok*, Baku, 1986, pp.147–72.

89. *Imperatorskoe Pravoslavnoe Palestinskoe obshchestvo i yego deyatel'nost' (1882–1907gg)*, Istoricheskaya zapiska [historical records], St Petersburg, 1907, p.117.

90. Semyonov, D.V., "Russkoe Palestinskoe obshchestvo i yego deyatel'nost' do voyny 1914 g", in *Novy Vostok*, 1925, Nos. 8–9, p.210.

91. Seventh report of Imperatorskogo Pravoslavnogo Palestinskogo obshchestva (for years 1889–1890), St Petersburg, 1891, Appendix 1.

92. Krachkovsky, I.Yu., *Nad arabskimi rukopisyami*, Moscow, 1965, pp.75–6.

93. Cited in article by Merenz, D., "Chelovek, kotory poznakomil arabov s Rossiey", in *Literaturnaya gazeta*, 1946, 27 April.

94. Naimy, M., *Moi sem'desyat let*, p.60.

95. Dmitrievsky, A.A., *Russkaya literatura v arabskikh perevodakh*, Petrograd, 1915, p.4.

96. See Krachkovsky, I.Yu., "Literaturnie kharakteristiki", *Izbr. soch.*, vol. 3, p.226, note 1.

97. Krymsky, A.E., *Istoria novoy arabskoy literatury: XIX–nachalo XX veka*, p.314.

98. Krachkovsky, I.Yu., "Basni Krylova v arabskikh perevodakh", *Izbr. soch.*, vol. 3, p.319.

99. For details see, Dolinina, A.A., *Russkaya literatura XIX veka v arabskikh stranakh*, Candidate diploma dissertation, Leningrad, 1953; Cherkassky, L.Ye., *Russkaya literatura na Vostoke (Teoria i praktika perevoda)*, Moscow, 1987.

100. Krachkovsky, I.Yu., "Russko-arabskie literaturnie svyazi", *Izbr. soch.*, vol. 3, p.274.

101. Cherkassky, L.Ye., *Russkaya literatura na Vostoke (Teoria i praktika perevoda)*, Moscow, 1987, p.8.

102. Kirpichenko, V., *Sovremennaya egipetskaya proza (60–70-e gody)*, p.261.

103. Konrad, N.I., "Problemy realizma i literatury Vostoka", in Konrad, *Zapad i Vostok*, p.352.

104. Konrad, N.I., "Problema realizma v literaturakh Vostoka", in *Problemy stanovlenia realizma v literaturakh Vostoka*, Moscow, 1964, p.16.

105. *Problemy realizma v mirovoy literature*, Moscow, 1959, p.304.

106. Dyurishin, D., *Teoria sravnitel'nogo izuchenia literatur* (trans. from Slovak), Moscow, 1979, p.78.

107. Neupokoeva, I.G., "Nekotorie voprosy izuchenia vzaimosvyazey i vzaimodeystvia natsional'nykh literatur", in *Vzaimosvyaz' i vzaimodeystvia natsional'nykh literatur*, p.38.

Notes to Chapter 2

[Editor's note: *Izbrannoe* is a Russian-language edition of Gibran's *Selected Works*, and *CCW* (1961 and 1964) is an edition of his *Complete Collected Works* containing pieces in the original language in which he wrote them (Arabic or English).]

1. On the life and creative path of Kahlil Gibran, see Imangulieva, A.N., *Cübran Xelil Cübran*, Baku, 1975.

2. al-Ida, Yamni, *Adab Jubran bayn al wa'y wa al-waqi'a, al-Tariq*, Beirut, 1970, no. 2, p.107.

3. Gibran, K., "Khafnatun min rimal al-shatt" (from collection *al-Bada'i' wa al-Tara'if* [*The New and the Marvellous*]), in Gibran, K., *al-Majmu'a al-kamila li mu'allafat (Complete Collected Works* [hereafter *CCW*]), Beirut, 1961, pp.491–2. (Further citations from works by Gibran are taken from this edition and the 1964 edition, which also contains works translated from the English. [Editor's note: as far as can be ascertained, in the citations that follow the 1961 edition is being referred to unless otherwise specified.])

4. Gibran, K, "Madinat al-madi" (from collection *Dam'a wa ibtisama*), *CCW*, p.290.

5. Belinsky, V.G., "Sochinenia Pushkina", *Izbr. soch.*, Moscow, 1946, p.503. [Editor's note: Nikolay Mikhailovich Karamzin (1766–1826), Russian Sentimentalist poet and historian.]

6. See Dolinina, A.A., "Iz predystoriya realizma v novoy arabskoy literature", in *Problemy stanovlenia realizma v literaturakh Vostoka*, Moscow, 1964, pp.278–92.

7. Naimy, M., "Ibtisama wa dumu'", in *al-Ghirbal*, Beirut, 1964, p.182.

8. Belinsky, V.G., "Russkaya literatura v 1845 godu", *Izbr. soch.*, p.789 [Editor's note: Lizin prud, formerly a pond on the land of the Simonova (Uspensky) monastery in Moscow, was the setting of Karamzin's Sentimental story *Poor Liza* (1792). The heroine of the story drowns herself in the pond out of unrequited love.]

9. Dolinina, A.A., Preface to *Arabskaya romanticheskaya proza XIX–XX vv*, Leningrad, 1981, p.14.

10. Najm, Muhammad Yusuf, *al-Shi'r al-'Arabi fi al-mahjar*, Beirut, 1957, p.42; Ghougassian, Joseph P., *Kahlil Gibran: wings of thought – the people's philosopher*, New York, 1973, p.92.

11. Krachkovsky, I.Yu., "Arabskaya literatura v Amerike (1895–1915)", *Izvestia LGU*, vol. 1, Leningrad, 1928, p.20.

12. Gibran, K., "Marta al-baniyya", *CCW*, pp.56–66. (Russ. trans. from Arabic by Z. Levina, in Ode-Vasil'eva K.V., *Rasskazy pisateley Livana*, Moscow, 1958, pp.24–33.)

13. Gibran, K., "Warda al-Haniyya", *CCW*, pp.81–95. (Russ. trans. from Arabic by A. Gorodetskaya, in Ode-Vasil'eva K.V., *Rasskazy pisateley Livana*, pp.33–47.)

14. Gibran K., *al-Ajniha al-mutakassira*, *CCW*, pp.163–226. (Russ. trans. from Arabic by V. Volosatova, in Gibran, K., *Izbrannoe*, Leningrad, 1986, pp.24–72.)

15. On this, see Krachkovsky, I.Yu., "Preface to *Kasim Amin: Novaya zhenshchina*", *Izbr. soch.*, vol. 3, Moscow and Leningrad, 1956, pp.123–36; Ode-Vasil'eva K.V., *Otrazhenie byta sovremennoy arabskoy zhenshchiny v novelle*, Zapiski kollegi vostokovedov, 1930, vol. 5, pp.293–306; Dolinina, A.A., *Ocherki istorii arabskoy literatury novogo vremeni*, 1968, pp.69–84; Levin, Z.I., *Razvitie osnovnykh techeniy obshchestvenno-politicheskoy mysli v Sirii i Egipte*, Moscow, 1972, pp.213–19; Usmanov, N.K., "Razvitie prosvetitel'skikh idey na arabskom Vostoke v XIX v", in *Prosvetitel'stvo v literaturakh Vostoka*, Moscow, 1973, pp.48–67.

16. Cited in al-Talisi, Khalifa Muhammad, *al-Shabbi wa Jubran*, Beirut, 1957, pp.99–100. [Editor's note: see also *A Third Treasury of Kahlil Gibran*, ed. Andrew Sherfan, London 1993, p.181.]

17. Dolinina, A.A., "Iz predystorii realizma v novoy arabskoy literature", *in Problemy stanovlenia realizma v literaturakh Vostoka*, p.283.

18. Ode-Vasil'eva K.V., *Rasskazy pisateley Livana*, pp.24–6.

19. Ibid. p.33.

20. Gibran, K., Letter to Mary Elizabeth Haskell, New York, 6 May 1912, *Izbrannoe*, p.467.

21. Gibran, K., *Izbrannoe*, pp.32–3.

22. Karamzin, N.M., *Pis'ma russkogo puteshestvennika*, Povesti, Moscow, 1980, p.535.

23. Gibran, K., *Izbrannoe*, pp.34–5.

24. Ibid. p.39.

25. Ibid. p.55.

26. Ibid. p.45.

27. Ibid. pp.58–9.

28. Ibid. p.57.

29. Ibid. p.61.

30. Ibid. p.46.

31. Dolinina, A.A., "Iz predystorii realizma v novoy arabskoy literature", in *Problemy stanovlenia realizma v literaturakh Vostoka*, p.256.

32. Belinsky, V.G., "Russkaya literatura v 1841 godu", in *Izbr. soch.*, p.324.

33. Gibran, K., *Izbrannoe*, p.45.

34. Ibid. p.54.
35. Ibid. p.53.
36. Ibid. p.56.
37. Ibid. p.44.
38. Gibran, K., *Dam'a wa ibtisama*, *CCW*, pp.236–339.
39. Gibran, K., "Zayrat al-hikma", *CCW*, pp.266–7. (Russ. trans. from Arabic by I.Yu. Krachkovsky, in Gibran, K., *Izbrannoe*, pp.129–30.)
40. Krachkovsky, I.Yu., "Arabskaya literatura v Amerike (1895–1915)", p.20.
41. Gibran, K., "Bayna al-kukh wa-l qasr", *CCW*, pp.274–5.
42. Ibid. p.274.
43. Ibid. p.275.
44. Ibid.
45. Gibran, K., "Ibtisama wa dam'a", *CCW*, pp.248–9.
46. Gibran, K., "al-Mujrim", *CCW*, p.286.
47. Ibid.
48. Ibid.
49. Gibran, K, "al-Hayawan al-abkam", *CCW*, pp.304–5.
50. Ibid. p.306.
51. Gibran, K., *CCW*, p.249.
52. Markov, V.V., Preface to *Izbrannoe*, pp.10–11. [Editor's note: Vladimir Markov was the translator of much of Gibran from English into Russian, including *Izbrannoe* (*Selected Works*).]
53. English critical texts, Delhi, 1979, p.175. [Editor's note: Preface to *Lyrical Ballads* by William Wordsworth and Samuel Taylor Coleridge].
54. Quoted in article by Robert E. Spiller, "Ralph Waldo Emerson", in *Literaturnaya istoria SShA*, vol. 1, Moscow, 1977, p.450.
55. Gibran, K., "Mawt al-sha'ir hayatuhu", *CCW*, pp.243–4.
56. Gibran, K., "al-Sha'ir", *CCW*, p.307.
57. Gibran, K., "Zaklyuchenie" [Conclusion]. (Russ. trans. from Arabic by I.Yu. Krachkovsky, in Gibran, K., *Izbrannoe*, p.154.)
58. Gibran, K., "Ayyuha al-layl", in collection *al-'Awasif* [*The Tempests*], *CCW*, p.373.
59. Gibran, K., *Sand and Foam* [*Ramal wa zabat*] (written in English; trans. into Arabic by the Beirut Archimandrite Antonius Bashir), *CCW*, 1964, p.162.
60. Ibid. pp.162–3.
61. Cited in article by M.O. Mendelson, "Ya s vami, lyudi drugikh pokoleniy", in Whitman, W., *List'ya travy* [*Leaves of Grass*], *Izbr. proizv.*, Moscow, 1970, p.6. [Editor's note: Maurice Mendelson was one of Whitman's biographers in Russian.]
62. Whitman, W., "Pesnya o sebe" ["Song of Myself"], *Izbr. proizv.*, p.50.
63. Gibran, K., "Sawt al-sha'ir", *CCW*, pp.334–8. (Russ. trans. from Arabic by A.A. Dolinina, in Gibran, K., *Izbrannoe*, pp.150–3.)
64. Gibran, K., *CCW*, p.334.
65. Mendelson, M.O., "Ya s vami, lyudi drugikh pokoleniy", p.6.
66. Whitman, W., "U beregov golubogo Ontario" ["By Blue Ontario's Shore"], *Izbr. proizv.*, p.233.
67. Gibran, K., "Nafsi mushakkalatun bi asmarihi" (from *al-Bada'i' wa al-Tara'if* [*The New and the Marvellous*]), *CCW*, p.490.
68. Ghougassian, Joseph P., *Kahlil Gibran: wings of thought*, pp.56–7.
69. Gibran, K., *al-Sulban*, *CCW*, p.457. (Russ. trans. from Arabic by A.A. Dolinina, in *Sovremennaya arabskaya proza*, Moscow and Leningrad, 1961, pp.43–54.)

70. Gibran, K., *CCW*, p.244.

71. Quoted in Urnov, D.M., "Zhivoe plamya slova", in *Poezia angliyskogo romantizma*, Moscow, 1975, p.18.

72. *Poezia angliyskogo romantizma*, pp.498–9.

73. Gibran, K., "Uniyat al-jamal", *CCW*, p.330. (Russ. trans. from Arabic by I.Yu. Krachovsky, in Gibran, K., *Izbrannoe*, p.147.)

74. Gibran, K., "al-Jamal", *CCW*, p.251. (Russ. trans. from Arabic by I.Yu. Krachkovsky, in Gibran, K., *Izbrannoe*, pp.124–5.)

75. Gibran, K., *Izbrannoe*, p.125.

76. Ibid.

77. Spiller, Robert E., "Ralph Waldo Emerson", in *Literaturnaya istoria SShA*, vol. 1, p.450.

78. Gibran, K., "Malakat al-khayal", *CCW*, p.280.

79. Volkov, Ivan F., "Osnovnie problemy izuchenia romantizma", in *K istorii russkogo romantizma*, Moscow, 1973, p.20.

80. Gibran, K., "al-Quwwa al-amya'", *CCW*, pp.296–7.

81. Whitman, W., *List'ya travy*, Moscow, 1982, p.95.

82. Gibran, K., "Tahta al-shams", *CCW*, p.270.

83. Ecclesiastes i, 14.

84. Gibran, K., "Tahta al-shams", *CCW*, p.279.

85. Gibran, K., "Madinat al-madi", *CCW*, p.290.

86. Blake, W., "Vechnosushchee evangelie" ["The Everlasting Gospel"], in *Poezia angliyskogo romantizma*, p.121.

87. Whitman, W., 'Pesnia o sebe', in *List'ya travy*, p.93.

88. Rossiyanov, O.K., "Romantizm v vengerskoy literature", in *Razvitie literatury v epokhe formirovania natsiy v strankakh Tsentral'noy i Yugo-Vostochnoy Evropy*, p.57. [Editor's note: O.K. Rossiyanov was a Soviet scholar specialising in Hungarian literature.]

89. Gibran, K., *Izbrannoe*, p.154.

90. Gibran, K., *CCW*, 1964, p.157.

91. Ibid. p.155.

92. Whitman, W., *List'ya travy*, p.238.

93. Gibran, K., "Yawm mawlidi", *CCW*, p.310. (Russ. trans. from Arabic by I.Yu. Krachkovsky, in *Izbrannoe*, pp.135–9.)

94. Gibran, K., "al-Yaqza al-akhira", *CCW*, 1964, p.74. (Russ. trans. from English by I. Ivanova, in *Izbrannoe*, p.188.)

95. D'yakonova, N.Ya., *Angliysky romantizm: Problemy estetiki*, Moscow, 1978, p.59.

96. Gibran, K., "Nazara ila al-ati", *CCW*, pp.279–80. (Russ. trans. from Arabic by I.Yu. Krachkovsky, in *Izbrannoe*, pp.132–3.)

97. Gibran, K., "Aghani", *CCW*, pp.328–33. (Russ. trans. from Arabic by I.Yu. Krachkovsky, in *Izbrannoe*, pp.145–50.)

98. Gibran, K., *Izbrannoe*, pp.146–7.

99. Gibran, K., "Amama 'arsh al-jamal", *CCW*, p.265. (Russ. trans. from Arabic by I.Yu. Krachovsky, in *Izbrannoe*, pp.127–9.)

100. Cited in article by Robert E. Spiller, "Ralph Waldo Emerson", in *Literaturnaya istoria SShA*, vol. 1, p.428.

101. Ashtar, 'Abd al-Karim, *al-Nathr al-mahjari*, Cairo, 1969, p.88.

102. Gibran, K., "Ayyatuha al-ard", in *al-Bada'i' wa al-Tara'if* [*The New and the Marvellous*], *CCW*, p.526.

103. Neupokoeva, I.G., *Revolyutsionny romantizm Shelli*, Moscow, 1959, p.51.

104. Shelley, P.B., *Izbr. proizv.* (Russ. trans. from English by Boris Pasternak), Moscow, 1962, p.75.

105. Coleridge, S.T., "Gimn Zemle Gekzametry", in *Poezia angliystkogo romantizma*, p.211.

106. Whitman, W., "My dvoe, kak dolgo my byli obmanuti", in *List'ya travy*, p.113.

107. Gibran, K., "Ayyatuha al-rih", *CCW*, p.319.

108. Ibid. p.319.

109. Shelley, P.B., *Izbr. proizv.*, p.58.

110. Gibran, K., "Hayat al-hubb", *CCW*, p.236.

111. Ibid.

112. *Poezia angliyskogo romantizma*, p.513.

113. Urnov, D.M., "Zhivoe plamya slova", in *Poezia angliyskogo romantizma*, p.13.

114. Elistratova, A.A., *Nasledie angliyskogo romantizma i sovremennost'*, Moscow, 1960, p.110.

115. Ibid. p.107. [Editor's note: see "William Wordsworth's Letter to John Wilson, 1802: a corrected version", ed. John Hayden, *TWC* [*The Wordsworth Circle*], XVIII, 1987, pp.33–8.]

116. *Rasskazy pisateley Livana*, p.26.

117. Gibran, K., "al-Dahr wa al-umma", *CCW*, pp.263–4.

118. Ibid. p.263.

119. Gibran, K., "al-'Asifa", *CCW*, pp.427–8. (Russ. trans. from Arabic by G. Bogolyubova, in Gibran, K., *Izbrannoe*, pp.221–32.)

120. *Iskusstvo romanticheskoy epokhi*, Materialy nauchnoy konferentsii (1968), Moscow, 1969, p.9.

121. Suchkov, B.L., *Istoricheskie sud'by realizma*, Moscow, 1967, p.71.

122. *Iskusstvo romanticheskoy epokhi*, pp.53–4.

123. Dmitriev, A.S., "Teoria zapadnoevropeyskogo romantizma", in *Literaturnie manifesty zapadnoevropeyskikh romantikov*, Moscow, 1980, p.12.

124. Byron, G.G., "Lara", in *Sochinenia*, vol. 1, Moscow, 1974, p.399. [Editor's note: *Lara*, canto II, part VII.]

125. Gibran, K., *Izbrannoe*, p. 221.

126. Ibid. p.224.

127. Ibid. p.226.

128. Ibid.

129. Byron, G.G., "Palomnichestvo Chaylda Garol'da, Pesn' II", in *Sochinenia*, vol. 1, p.184. [Editor's note: *Childe Harold's Pilgrimage*, canto II, part XXV].

130. Byron, G.G., "Poslaniya Avguste" ["Epistle to Augusta"], in *Poezia angliyskogo romantizma*, p.417.

131. Byron, G.G., "Kogda b ya mog v moryakh pustynnykh", in *Poezia angliyskogo romantizma*, p.375.

132. Gibran, K., *Izbrannoe*, p.229.

133. Ibid. p.231.

134. Gibran, K., *CCW*, pp.439–49.

135. Ibid. p.442.

136. Ibid. p.447.

137. Ibid, pp.447–8.

138. Cited in Elistratova, A.A., *Nasledie angliyskogo romantizma i sovremennost'*, p.78.

139. Ibid. p.99.

140. Neupokoeva, I.G., *Revolyutsionny romantizm Shelli*, p. 87.

141. Gibran, K., "Yuhanna al-majnun", *CCW*, pp.67–78.

142. Ibid. p.77.

143. Gibran, K., "Khalil al-kafir", *CCW*, pp.116–59. (Russ. trans. from Arabic by G. Tregulova, in *Sovremennaya arabskaya novella*, Moscow, 1963, pp.87–132.)

144. *Sovremennaya arabskaya novella*, p.117.

145. Gibran, K., "Haffar al-qubur", *CCW*. (Russ. trans. from Arabic by G. Bogoly-ubova, in *Arabskaya romanticheskaya proza XIX–XX vv*, p.201–5.)

146. Ibid. p.202.

147. Gibran, K., "al-'Ubudiyya", *CCW*, pp.362–4. (Russ. trans. from Arabic by A. Samorodnitsky, in Gibran, K., *Izbrannoe*, pp.196–8.)

148. Ibid. p.196.

149. Ibid.

150. Ibid. p.197.

151. Ibid. p.198.

152. Dolinina, A.A., Preface to *Arabskaya romanticheskaya proza XIX–XX vv*, p.15.

153. Kutelia, M.V., *Mirovozzrenie Dzhebrana* (candidate dissertation), Baku, 1978, pp.68–76; Jabr, Jamil, *Jubran, siratuhu adabuhu falsafatuhu rasmuhu*, Beirut, 1958, pp.206–7; Naimy, Mikhail, *Jubran Khalil Jubran: Hayatuhu wa mawtuhu, adabuhu wa fannuhu*, Beirut, 1951, p.153; Ghougassian, Joseph P., *Kahlil Gibran: wings of thought*, pp.52–3.

154. Prigarina, N.I., *Poezia Muhammada Ikbala (1900–1924)*, Moscow, 1972, pp.110, 127–8.

155. Ghougassian, Joseph P., *Kahlil Gibran: wings of thought*, p.52.

156. Ibid.

157. Oduev, S.F., *Reaktsionnaya sushchnost' nitssheanstva*, Moscow, 1959, pp.149, 156, 165; also his *Tropami Zaratustry*, Moscow, 1971, p.63.

158. Gibran, K., *Izbrannoe*, p.170.

159. Gibran, K., "al-Banafsaj al-tamuh", from *al-'Awasif*, *CCW*, p.473. (Russ. trans. in Gibran, K., *Izbrannoe*, pp.235–8.)

160. Gibran, K., *Izbrannoe*, p.236.

161. Ibid. p.238.

162. Bashir, Antonius, Mulhaqa bi kitab [Appendix] to *al-Nabi li Jubran Khalil Jubran*, Beirut, 1936, p.5.

163. Ibid. p.68.

164. Jubran Khalil Jubran, *al-Nabi*, Beirut, 1956. This work was included in the complete collection of the author's writings (Beirut, 1964, pp.84–148). A Russian translation was made from the English by V.V. Markov, in Gibran, K., *Izbrannoe*, pp.344–83.

165. Gibran, K., Letter to Mayy, New York, 9 November 1919, in *Izbrannoe*, p.479.

166. Gibran, K., Letter to Mayy, New York, 3 December 1923, in *Izbrannoe*, p.484.

167. Gibran, K., *Izbrannoe*, p.383.

168. Emerson, R.W., "Poet" (Russ. trans. from English by A.M. Zvereza), in *Estetika amerikanskogo romantizma*, Moscow, 1977, p.306.

169. Gibran, K., *Izbrannoe*, p.378.

170. Gibran, K., Letter to Mayy, New York, 3 December 1923, in *Izbrannoe*, p.485.

171. Gibran, K., *Izbrannoe*, p.362.

172. Ibid. p.353.

173. Ibid.

174. Ibid. p.359.

175. *Literaturnaya istoria SShA*, vol. 1, p.421.

176. Gibran, K., *Izbrannoe*, p.381.

177. Ibid. p.370.
178. Ibid. p.357.
179. Ibid. p.375.
180. Ibid. p.374.
181. Ibid. p.357.
182. Ibid. p.358.
183. Ibid. p.350.
184. Ibid. p.378.
185. Ibid. p.379.
186. Ibid.
187. Gibran, K., "Masa' al-'id", *CCW*, pp.412–14.
188. Gibran, K., "Yasu' ibn al-insan", *CCW*, pp.367–9.
189. Ibid., 1964, pp.203–64. (Russ. trans. from English by V.V. Markov, in Gibran, K., *Izbrannoe*, pp.400–14.)
190. Ashtar, 'Abd al-Karim, *al-Nathr al-mahjari*, p.40.
191. Gibran, K., *CCW*, p.368.
192. Ibid.
193. Ibid.
194. Ibid. p.369.
195. Gibran, K., *Hadiqat al-nabi*, *CCW*, 1964, pp.449–84. (Russ. trans. from English by V.V. Markov, in Gibran, K., *Izbrannoe*, pp.384–99.)
196. Gibran, K., *Izbrannoe*, p.398.

Notes to Chapter 3

1. Konrad, N.I., "Problema realizma v literaturakh Vostoka", in *Problemy stanovlenia realizma v literaturakh Vostoka*, Moscow, 1964, p.18.
2. Krachkovsky, I.Yu., "Preface to *Ameen Rihani: Stikhotvorenia v proze*", in Krachkovsky, *Izbr. soch.*, vol. 3, Moscow and Leningrad, 1956, p.146.
3. Levin, Z.I., *Razvitie osnovnykh techeniy obshchestvenno-politicheskoy mysli v Sirii i Egipte*, Moscow, 1972, p.182.
4. Krachkovsky, I.Yu., "Translator's note in *Ameen Rihani*", *Izbr. proizv.* (Russ. trans. with notes by I.Yu. Krachkovsky), Petrograd, 1917, p.11.
5. Levin, Z.I., *Filosof iz Fureyki*, Moscow, 1965, p.53.
6. Krachkovsky, I.Yu., "Preface to *Ameen Rihani*", *Izbr. proizv.*, in Krachkovsky, *Izbr. soch.*, vol. 3, p.140.
7. For more detail on Rihani's world-view, see Levin, Z.I., *Filosof iz Fureyki*, and also his *Razvitie osnovnykh techeniy obshchestvenno-politicheskoy mysli v Sirii i Egipte*, pp.203–7.
8. Dolinina, A.A., Preface to *Arabskaya romanticheskaya proza XIX–XX vv*, Leningrad, 1981, p.16.
9. Rihani, A., "Comfort in misfortune and misfortune in comfort". (Russ. trans. by I.Yu. Krachkovsky, in *Sovremennaya arabskaya proza*, Moscow and Leningrad, 1961, p.68.)
10. Krachkovsky, I.Yu., "Preface to *Ameen Rihani*", *Izbr. proizv.*, in Krachkovsky, *Izbr. soch.*, vol. 3, p.142.
11. Rihani, A., "Ma'badi fi al-wadi", in *Hutaf al-awdiya*, Beirut, 1955, pp.46–9.
12. Ibid. p.47.

13. *Poezia SShA*, Moscow, 1982, p.121.

14. Spiller, Robert E., "Ralph Waldo Emerson", in *Literaturnaya istoria SShA*, vol. 1, Moscow, 1977, p.440.

15. Rihani, A., *Izbr. proizv.*, pp.30–1.

16. Dmitriev, A.S., "Teoria zapadnoevropeyskogo romantizma", in *Literaturnie manifesty zapadnoevropeyskikh romantikov*, Moscow, 1980, p.12.

17. *Poezia SShA*, p.246.

18. Rihani, A., "Wadi al-Furayki aw al-'awd ila al-tabi'a", in *Rihaniyyat*, vol. 1, Beirut, 1910, pp.5–20. (Russ. trans. from Arabic by I.Yu. Krachkovsky, in Rihani, A., *Izbr. proizv.*, pp.29–42.)

19. Dolinina, A.A., "Ameen Rihani" (introductory article), in *Ameen Rihani, Izbrannoe* (Russ. trans. from Arabic and English), Leningrad, 1988, p.16.

20. Rihani, A., *Izbr. proizv.*, p.29.

21. Ibid. p.38.

22. Rihani, A., *Hutaf al-awdiya*, p.46.

23. Cited in Robert E. Spiller, "Ralph Waldo Emerson", in *Literaturnaya istoria SShA*, vol. 1, p.434.

24. Rihani, A., *Izbr. proizv.*, p.33.

25. Thoreau, H.D., *Walden*, Moscow, 1979, p.367.

26. Rihani, A., *Izbr. proizv.*, p.34.

27. Ibid. p.35.

28. Dolinina, A.A., "Ameen Rihani", in *Ameen Rihani, Izbrannoe*, p.17.

29. Rihani, A., *Izbr. proizv.*, p.39.

30. Whitman, W., "Pesnya radostey" ["A Song of Joys"], in *List'ya travy* [*Leaves of Grass*], Moscow, 1982, p.165.

31. Rihani, A., *Izbr. proizv.*, p.115.

32. Rihani, A., "Fi al-'uzlati", in *Rihaniyyat*, vol. 1, Beirut, 1956, p.119.

33. Rihani, A., "Bulbul wa riyah", in *Hutaf al-awdiya*, p.72.

34. Rihani, A., "'Inda mahd al-rabi'i", in *Hutaf al-awdiya*, pp.26–35. (This poem was written in 1907, on the death of the writer's nephew.)

35. Ibid. pp.26–7.

36. Rihani, A., "Ghusn ward", in *Hutaf al-awdiya*, pp.41–5.

37. Ibid. p.41.

38. Ibid.

39. Rihani, A., *Izbr. proizv.*, pp.116–17.

40. Ibid.

41. Canby, Henry Seidel, "Walt Whitman", in *Literaturnaya istoria SShA*, vol. 1, p.558.

42. Whitman, Walt, "Pesnya o sebe", in *List'ya travy*, pp.62–5.

43. Cited in Canby, Henry Seidel, "Walt Whitman", in *Literaturnaya istoria SShA*, vol. 1, p.573.

44. Dmitriev, A.S., "Teoria zapadnoevropeyskogo romantizma", in *Literaturnie manifesty zapadnoevropeyskikh romantikov*, p.11.

45. Rihani, A., "al-Naj'wa", in *Hutaf al-awdiya*, p.103.

46. Rihani, A., "Rih simum", in *Hutaf al-awdiya*, pp.11–15.

47. Ibid. p.15.

48. Cited in Spiller, Robert E., "Ralph Waldo Emerson", in *Literaturnaya istoria SShA*, vol. 1, p.444.

49. Ibid.

50. Levin, Z.I., *Filosof iz Fureyki*, pp.30–1.

51. Rihani, A., *Rihaniyyat*, vol. 1, Beirut, 1922 reprint, p.217.

52. Rihani, A., *Rihaniyyat*, vol. 1, Beirut, 1956 reprint, p.166.

53. Ibid. p.8.

54. Rihani, A., "al-Naj'wa", in *Hutaf al-awdiya*, pp.102–4.

55. Ibid. p.103.

56. Ibid.

57. Ibid. pp.103–4.

58. Dmitriev, A.S., "Teoria zapadnoevropeyskogo romantizma", in *Literaturnie manifesty zapadnoevropeyskikh romantikov*, pp.11–12.

59. Ibid. p.12.

60. Rihani, A., "Rih simum", in *Hutaf al-awdiya*, pp.11–15.

61. Ibid. p.15.

62. Cited in Venidiktova, T.D., *Poezia Ualta Uitmena*, Moscow, 1982, p.17.

63. Rihani, A., *Rihaniyyat*, vol. 1, Beirut, 1922 reprint, p.119.

64. Terteryan, I.A., "Romantizm kak tselostnoe yavlenie", in *Voprosy literatury*, 1983, no. 4, p.171.

65. Whitman, Walt, "Tebe, demokratiya", in *Poezia SShA*, p.231.

66. Pulsifer, Harold T., "The Harvest of Time". (Russ. trans. by A. Rihani, as "Hasd al-zaman", in *Hutaf al-awdiya*, pp.137–8.)

67. Rihani, A., "al-Baʿth", in *Hutaf al-awdiya*, pp.139–40. Both poems were printed in the New York weekly newspaper *The Saturday Review of Literature*, April 1933, no. 1.

68. Rihani, A., *Hutaf al-awdiya*, pp.137–8.

69. Ibid. pp.139–40.

70. Terteryan, I.A., "Romantizm kak tselostnoe yavlenie", in *Voprosy literatury*, 1983, no. 4, p.171.

71. Rihani, A., "Hawla al-musawat" in *Rihaniyyat*, vol. 2, Beirut, 1910, pp.92–6. (Russ. trans. by I.Yu. Krachkovsky, in Rihani, A., *Izbr. proizv.*, pp.81–5.)

72. Rihani, A., "al-Sawra", in *Rihaniyyat*, vol. 2, pp.183–5. The poem has been translated into Russian (by I.Yu. Krachkovsky, in *Vostok*, 1922, I, pp.49–50), and Ukrainian (by A. Kovalevsky, in *Ameen Rihani: Revolutsia*, Kharkov, 1932).

73. Krachkovsky, I.Yu., "Otzvuki revolyutsii 1905 goda v arabskoy khudozhestvennoy literature", in *Sovietskoe vostokovedenie*, Moscow and Leningrad 1945, III, p.14.

74. Cited in Krachkovsky's translation in *Arabskaya romanticheskaya proza XIX–XX vv*, p.87.

75. *Arabskaya romanticheskaya proza XIX–XX vv*, p.89.

76. Levin, Z.I., *Razvitie osnovnykh techeniy obshchestvenno-politicheskoy mysli v Sirii i Egipte*, p.189.

77. Rihani, A., *Izbr. proizv.*, p.83.

78. Rihani, A., "Hijarat Baris", in *Hutaf al-awdiya*, pp.119–22.

79. Ibid. p.119.

80. Ibid. p.122.

81. Dmitriev, A.S., "Teoria zapadnoevropeyskogo romantizma", in *Literaturnie manifesty zapadnoevropeyskikh romantikov*, p.13.

82. Rihani, A., "Rafiqati", in *Hutaf al-awdiya*, pp.110–14.

83. Ibid. pp.112–13.

84. Ibid. pp.113–14.

85. Terteryan, I.A., "Romantizm kak tselostnoe yavlenie", in *Voprosy literatury*, 1983, no. 4, p.181.

86. Cherkassky, L.Ye., *Novaya kitayskaya poezia (20–30-e gody)*, Moscow, 1972, p.132.

87. Rihani, A., "al-Nasr al-'Arabi", in *Hutaf al-awdiya*, pp.141–7.

88. Ibid. p.141.

89. Rihani, A., "Ana al-sharq", in *Hutaf al-awdiya*, pp.84–91.

90. Ibid. pp.84–5.

91. Ibid. pp.86–7.

92. Ibid. p.90.

93. Ibid. p.91.

94. Rihani, A., "al-'Awd ila al-wadi", in *Hutaf al-awdiya*, pp.115–18.

95. Ibid. p.118.

96. Rihani, A., "Ila Jubran", in *Hutaf al-awdiya*, pp.123–6.

97. Ibid. p.127.

98. Ibid. pp.131–2.

99. Gibran, K., Letter to Mayy from New York, 11 June 1919, in Gibran, K., *Izbrannoe*, Leningrad, 1986, p.478.

100. Rihani, A., "Ila Jubran", in *Hutaf al-awdiya*, pp.130–1.

101. Ibid. pp.127–8.

102. Ibid. pp.124–5.

103. Ibid. p.124.

104. Ibid. p.132.

105. Ibid.

106. Rihani, A., *Kharij al-harim aw Jahan*, New York, 1917. (Russ. trans. from Arabic by M. Derdirov, in *Arabskaya romanticheskaya proza XIX–XX vv*, pp.98–174.)

107. Ibid. p.98.

108. Ibid. p.126.

109. Zalesskaya, L.I., *O romanticheskom techenii v sovetskoy literature*, Moscow, 1973, p.16.

110. Maymin, E.A., *O russkom romantizme*, Leningrad, 1975, p.9.

111. Rihani, A., *Kharij al-harim aw Jahan*, in *Arabskaya romanticheskaya proza XIX–XX vv*, p.126.

112. Ibid. p.150.

113. Cited in Maymin, E.A., *O russkom romantizme*, p.9.

114. Rihani, A., *Kharij al-harim aw Jahan*, in *Arabskaya romanticheskaya proza XIX–XX vv*, p.130.

115. Ibid. p.128.

116. Ibid. p.156.

117. Ibid. p.102.

118. Dolinina, A.A., Preface to *Arabskaya romanticheskaya proza XIX–XX vv*, p.18.

119. Rihani, A., *Kharij al-harim aw Jahan*, in *Arabskaya romanticheskaya proza XIX–XX vv*, pp.100–1.

120. Ibid. p.100.

121. Ibid. p.101.

122. Ibid. p.127.

123. Ibid. p.100.

124. Ibid. p.166.

125. Ibid. p.99.

126. Ibid. p.100.

127. Ibid. p.98.

128. Ibid. p.101.

129. Ibid. p.161.

130. Ibid. p.172.

131. Ibid. p.165.

132. Dolinina. A.A., Preface to *Arabskaya romanticheskaya proza XIX–XX vv*, p.19.

133. Naimy, M., "Rihani fi 'alam al-shi'r", in collection *al-Girbal*, Beirut, 1964, p.163.

134. Rihani, A., "Wa fi mithli hadha al-yawm tabat jahannam", in *Rihaniyyat*, vol. 1, Beirut, 1910, pp. 68–73. (Russ. trans. by A. Krachkovsky, in *Sovremennaya arabskaya proza*, Moscow and Leningrad, 1961, pp.64–7.)

135. *Sovremennaya arabskaya proza*, p.64.

136. Ibid. pp.65–6.

137. Rihani, A., "Fawqa sutuhi Nyu York", in *Rihaniyyat*, vol. 1, Beirut, 1910, pp.63–6.

138. Ibid. p.65.

139. *Rihaniyyat*, vol. 4, pp.15–19.

140. Ibid. vol. 1, p.66.

141. Cited in Jundi, Anwar, *al-Muhafaza wa al-tajdid fi al-nathr al-'Arabi al-mu'asir fi mi'at 'am*, Cairo, 1961, p.501.

142. Krachkovsky, I.Yu., "Preface to *Ameen Rihani*", *Izbr. proizv.*, in Krachkovsky, *Izbr. soch.*, vol. 3, p.142.

143. Rihani, A., "al-Salib aw yawm fi Bayrut", in *Rihaniyyat*, vol. 4, Beirut, 1924. (Russ. trans. by S. Kuz'min, in *Rasskazy pisateley Livana*, Moscow, 1958, pp.19–24.)

144. Ibid. pp.19–20.

145. Ibid. pp.20–2.

146. Ibid. p.23.

147. Ibid.

148. Ibid.

149. Ibid. p.22.

150. Russian trans. from Arabic by I.Yu. Krachkovsky, in *Sovremennaya arabskaya proza*, pp. 61–3.

151. *Sovremennaya arabskaya proza*, p.61.

152. Ibid. p.62.

153. Ibid. p.63.

154. Ibid.

155. Translated from Arabic by Z. Levin, in *Rasskazy pisateley Livana*, pp.11–18.

156. Dmitriev, A.S., "Teoria zapadnoevropeyskogo romantizma", in *Literaturnie manifesty zapadnoevropeyskikh romantikov*, p.23.

157. *Rasskazy pisateley Livana*, p.12.

158. Ibid.

159. Terteryan, I.A., "Romantizm kak tselostnoe yavlenie", in *Voprosy literatury*, 1983, no. 4, p.153.

160. Rihani, A., from his book *Qalb al-'Iraq* [*The Heart of Iraq*]. (Russ. trans. from Arabic by A.A. Dolinina, in *Ameen Rihani, Izbrannoe*, Leningrad, 1988, pp.326–7.)

161. Ibid. p.340.

Notes to Chapter 4

1. For more detail on Naimy's life and creative path, see Imangulieva, A.N., *"Assosiatsia pera" i Mikhail Nuayme*, Moscow, 1975, pp.51–102. [Editor's note: Naimy may also be spelt Nuaime, Nu'ayme or Nu'ayma.]

2. For more detail on this period of the writer's life, see Nuaime, M., *Moi sem'desyat let* (trans. from the Arabic *Sab'un* [*Seventy*] by S.M. Batsevaya), Moscow, 1980.

3. "Avtobiografia Mikhaila Nuayme", in Krachkovsky, I.Yu., *Izbr. soch.*, vol. 3, Moscow and Leningrad, 1956, p.226.

4. Naimy, M., *Ab'ad min Musku wa min Washintan* [*Beyond Moscow and Washington*], Beirut, 1957, p.29.

5. Naimy, M., *Sab'un* [*Seventy*], *Hikayat 'umr*, vol. 1, Beirut, 1959, p.253.

6. A photo-manuscript of this poem in Russian, entitled "Mertvaya reka" ["The Dead River"], was first included in Naimy's album issued to celebrate the 90th anniversary of his birth (Naimy, M., *Tariq al-dhat ila al-dhat* [*The Way to the Greater Self*], Beirut, 1978, pp.16–17). After the Russian Revolution of 1917, Naimy translated the poem into Arabic and called it "al-Nahr al-mutajammida" ["The Frozen River"]. Soviet Arabists have since referred to the poem under this name, which in Russian is "Zastyvshaya reka".

7. "Avtobiografia Mikhaila Nuayme", in Krachkovsky, I.Yu., *Izbr. soch.*, vol. 3, pp.224–5.

8. Zhirmunsky, V.M., *Sravnitel'noe literaturovedenie*, Moscow, 1979, p.67.

9. Naimy, Mikhail, *al-Ghirbal*, Cairo, 1923.

10. Naimy, Mikhail, *Mudhakkarat al-Arqash* [also known as *Memoirs of Pitted Face*], Beirut, 1949.

11. Naimy, Mikhail, *Kitab Mirdad*, Beirut, 1948.

12. Naimy, Mikhail, *al-Yawm al-akhir*, Beirut, 1963.

13. Krachkovsky, I.Yu., "Arabskaya literatura v XX v.", *Izbr. soch.*, vol. 3, p.94.

14. Krachkovsky, I.Yu., *Nad arabskimi rukopisyami*, Moscow, 1965, p.78.

15. "Avtobiografia Mikhaila Nuaime", in Krachkovsky, I.Yu., *Izbr. soch.*, vol. 3, p.223.

16. Dolinina, A.A., Preface to *Arabskaya romanticheskaya proza XIX–XX vv*, p.19.

17. Naimy, Mikhail, *Ab'ad min Musku wa min Washintan*, p.73.

18. Naimy, Mikhail, *Sab'un, Hikayat 'umr*, 5th edn, Beirut, 1977, p.231.

19. Ibid. p.273.

20. Ibid. p.80.

21. Naimy, Mikhail, "Fajar al-amal ba'd laylat al-ya's" ["The dawn of hope after a night of despair"], in *al-Funun*, New York, 1913. See Naimy, Mikhail, *Jubran Khalil Jubran, hayatuhu, mawtuhu, adabuhu, fannuhu*, Beirut, 1934, pp.135–7.

22. Naimy, Mikhail, "al-Akhmas wa al-asdas" [lit. "Fifths and Sixths"], in *as-Sa'ih*, New York, October 1915.

23. Naimy, Mikhail, *Sab'un*, Beirut, 1960, p.34.

24. Quoted in Sukhotna-Tolstaya, T.L., *Vospominania*, Moscow, 1980, p.416.

25. al-'Aqqad, 'Abbas Mahmud, "Muqaddima", in Naimy, Mikhail, *al-Ghirbal*, 7th edn, Beirut, 1964, pp.5–6. (Note that subsequent *al-Ghirbal* citations are from this edition.)

26. Ibid. p.6.

27. Cited in Naimy, Mikhail, *Sab'un*, Beirut, 1960, vol. 2, p.201.

28. Naimy, Mikhail, "al-Gharbala", in *al-Ghirbal*, pp.13–23.

29. Ibid. p.15.

30. Belinsky, V.G., "O russkoy povesti i povestiakh g. Gogolia", *Izbr. soch.*, Moscow and Leningrad, 1946, p.66. (Further citations are from this edition; the article and page are indicated.)

31. Naimy, Mikhail, *al-Ghirbal*, p.17.

32. Belinsky, V.G., "Stikhotvorenia Vladimira Benediktova", *Izbr. soch.*, p.80.

33. Naimy, Mikhail, *al-Ghirbal*, p.20.

34. Belinsky, V.G., "O russkoy povesti i povestiakh g. Gogolia", *Izbr. soch.*, p.66.

35. Naimy, Mikhail, *al-Ghirbal*, p.73.

36. Naimy, Mikhail, "Mihwar al-adab", in *al-Ghirbal*, pp.23–8.

37. Ibid. pp.23–5.

38. Naimy, Mikhail, "Nahnu ahsa aw aba'una?", in *Sawt al-'Alam [The Voice of the World]*, Beirut, 1961, p.134.

39. Belinsky, V.G., "Obshchaya ideia narodnoy poezii", *Izbr. soch.*, p.293.

40. Naimy, Mikhail, *al-Ghirbal*, pp.26–7.

41. Belinsky, V.G., "Stikhotvorenia M. Lermontova", *Izbr. soch.*, p.210.

42. Naimy, Mikhail, "al-Maqayis al-adabiyya", in *al-Ghirbal*, pp.65–74.

43. Ibid. p.65.

44. Ibid. p.70.

45. Belinsky, V.G., "O russkoy povesti i povestiakh g. Gogolia", *Izbr. soch.*, p.70; see also "Razdelenie poezii na rody i vidy", *Izbr. soch.*, p.224.

46. Naimy, Mikhail, "al-Sha'ir wa al-Shi'r", in *al-Ghirbal*, pp.75–89.

47. Ibid. p.77.

48. Ibid. p.79.

49. Belinsky, V.G., "Sochinenia Derzhavina", *Izbr. soch.*, p.435.

50. Belinsky, V.G., "Gore ot uma", *Izbr. soch.*, p.96.

51. Naimy, Mikhail, *al-Ghirbal*, p.80.

52. Ibid. p.76.

53. Ibid. p.77.

54. Ibid. p.82.

55. Belinsky, V.G., "Stikhotvorenia M. Lermontova", *Izbr. soch.*, pp.194–5.

56. Naimy, Mikhail, *al-Ghirbal*, p.84.

57. Ibid. p.85.

58. Naimy, Mikhail, "al-Hubahib", in *al-Ghirbal*, pp.37–64.

59. Ibid. p.38.

60. Ibid. p.44.

61. Ibid. p.46.

62. Ibid. p.48.

63. Ibid. p.52.

64. Ibid. p.64.

65. Ibid. p.93.

66. Ibid. p.95.

67. Naimy, Mikhail, "Naqiq ad-dafadi'", in *al-Ghirbal*, pp.95–6.

68. Ibid. pp.97–8.

69. Gibran, Kahlil, *al-Mawakib [The Processions,* long poems in dialogue form, 1919], *Poln. sobr. soch. [CCW]*, p.353.

70. Naimy, Mikhail, *al-Ghirbal*, pp.97–8.

71. Ibid. p.106.

72. Naimy, Mikhail, "al-Zihafat wa al-'ilal", in *al-Ghirbal*, pp.107–25. The terms "al-zihaf" and "al-'ilal" refer to a deviation from the poetic metre allowed by the *'arud* theory in classical Arabic poetry, thus a change to its basic model. *Zihaf* is an artificial

shortening of a syllable in pronunciation, in order to align it with the corresponding syllable of the metre of the poem; '*ilal* is an artificial lengthening of a syllable in
pronunciation.

73. Naimy, Mikhail, *al-Ghirbal*, p.108.

74. Ibid. p.118.

75. Belinsky, V.G., "Stikhotvorenia M. Lermontova", *Izbr. soch.*, p.194.

76. Naimy, Mikhail, "al-Riwaya al-tamthiliyya al-'Arabiyya", in *al-Ghirbal*, pp.29–36.

77. Ibid. p.31.

78. Belinsky, V.G., *O teatre*, Moscow, 1982, p.21.

79. Naimy, Mikhail, *al-Ghirbal*, p.32.

80. Ibid. p.36.

81. Ibid. pp.32, 34.

82. Naimy, Mikhail, "al-Durrat al-Shawqiyya", in *al-Ghirbal*, pp.145–54.

83. Ibid. p.148.

84. Krachkovsky, I.Yu., "Novoarabskaya literatura", *Izbr. soch.*, vol. 3, p.72.

85. Khodzhaeva, R.U., *Ocherki razvitia egipetskoy poezii*, Tashkent, 1985, p.29.

86. Ibid. pp.33–4.

87. Naimy, Mikhail, "Ibtisamat wa dumu'" ["Smiles and Tears"], in *al-Ghirbal*, pp.178–84.

88. Ibid. p.182.

89. *al-Arwah al-ha'ira*, New York, 1946. This collection of 'Arida's poems was published posthumously.

90. Naimy, Mikhail, *al-Ghirbal*, p.129.

91. Belinsky, V.G., "Geroy nashego vremeni", *Izbr. soch.*, p.147.

92. Naimy, Mikhail, "Al-Rihani fi 'alam al-shi'r", in *al-Ghirbal*, pp.163–9.

93. Ibid. p.164.

94. Belinsky, V.G., "Vzglyad na russkuyu literaturu 1847 g.", *Izbr. soch.*, p.944.

95. Ibid.

96. Rihani, Ameen, *A chant of mystics and other poems*, New York, 1921.

97. Naimy, Mikhail, *al-Ghirbal*, p.168.

98. Naimy, Mikhail, "al-Sabiq" ["The Forerunner"], in *al-Ghirbal*, pp.170–7.

99. Ibid. p.170.

100. Ibid. p.176.

101. Naimy, Mikhail, "'Asifat al-'Awasif", in *al-Ghirbal*, pp.218–43. (Russ. trans. from Arabic by T. Demina, in *Arabskaya romanticheskaya proza XIX–XX vv*, pp.257–74.)

102. Ibid. p.260.

103. Ibid. p.261.

104. Ibid.

105. Ibid. p.262.

106. Belinsky, V.G., "Sochinenia Derzhavina", *Izbr. soch.*, p.432.

107. *Arabskaya romanticheskaya proza XIX–XX vv*, p.262.

108. Ibid. p.263.

109. See Belinsky, V.G., "Polnoe sobranie sochineniy A. Marlinskogo", *Izbr. soch.*, p.140.

110. *Arabskaya romanticheskaya proza XIX–XX vv*, p.268.

111. Ibid. p.270.

112. Belinsky, V.G., "Russkaya literatura v 1842 g.", *Izbr. soch.*, p.414.

113. Lavretsky, A., *V.G. Belinsky*, vol. 1, Moscow, 1962, p.508.

114. Gorky, Maxim, *Sobranie sochineniy v 30–ti tomakh*, vol. 14, Moscow, 1951, p.280.

115. Biryukov, P.I., "Tolstoy i Vostok", in *Novy Vostok*, Moscow, 1924, no. 6, p.393.

116. Shifman, A.I., "Lev Tolstoy i narody Vostoka", in *Azia i Afrika segonya*, Moscow, 1979, no. 9, p.40.

117. See Krymsky, A.E., *Istoria novoy arabskoy literatury*, Moscow, 1971, pp.314–15, 643.

118. Krachkovsky, I.Yu., "Russkie pisateli v arabskoy literature", *Izbr. soch.*, vol. 3, p.267.

119. Rihani, A., "Tolstoy" (trans. from Arabic by I.Yu. Krachkovsky, in Rihani, A., *Izbr. proizv.*, Petrograd, 1917, pp.60–5); al-Manfaluti, M., "Tolstomu" (trans. from Arabic by L. Petrova, in *Arabskaya romanticheskaya proza XIX–XX vv*, pp.80–4); see also Shifman, A.I., "Tolstoy i arabskie strany", in *Lev Tolstoy i Vostok*, Moscow, 1971, pp.397–408.

120. Cited in Merenz, D., "Chelovek, kotory poznakomil arabov s Rossiey", in *Literaturnaya gazeta*, 27 April 1946.

121. Cited in "Arabskie pisateli o russkoy i sovetskoy literature", in *Sovremenny Vostok*, 1958, no. 9, pp.65–6.

122. Shifman, A.I., *Lev Tolstoy i Vostok*, p.381.

123. Tolstoy, L.N., "Povesti i rasskazy 1903–1910", *Sobr. soch.*, vol. 14, Moscow, 1983, pp.17–21.

124. Tolstoy, L.N., "Povesti i rasskazy 1872–1886", *Sobr. soch.*, vol. 10, Moscow, 1982, p.261.

125. See Dmitrievsky, A.A., *Russkaya literatura v arabskikh perevodakh*, Petrograd, 1915, pp.12–13; Biryukov, P.I., "Tolstoy i Vostok", in *Novy Vostok*, Moscow, 1924, no. 6, p.3; Krachkovsky, I.Yu., "Russko-arabskie literaturnie svyazi", *Izbr. soch.*, vol. 3, pp.267–332; Dolinina, A.A., "Russkaya literatura XIX veka v arabskikh stranakh" (author's abstract of Candidate degree thesis in philology), Leningrad, 1953, pp.13–16; Dolinina, A.A., "Russkaya literatura XIX veka v arabskikh stranakh", in *Russkaya literatura*, 1960, no. 1, pp.202–10; Dolinina, A.A., "Arabsky perevod *Kreytserovoy sonaty* L. Tolstogo (Cairo, 1904)", in *Voprosy filologii stran Azii i Afriki*, 2nd edn, Leningrad, 1973, pp.116–23; Shifman, A.I., "Tolstoy i arabskie strany", in *Lev Tolstoy i Vostok*, pp.381–408; Cherkassky, L.Ye., *Russkaya literatura na Vostoke (Teoria i praktika perevoda)*, Moscow, 1987, pp.7, 26–8; Chukov, B.V., "Irakskaya khudozhestvennaya proza i russkaya literatura", in *Narody Azii i Afriki*, 1975, no. 6, p.102.

126. Paustovsky, K.G., *Sobr. soch.*, vol. 2, Moscow, 1957, p.595.

127. Fyodorov, A.V., "K voprosu o literaturnom vlianii", in *Vzaimosvyazi i vzaimodeystvie natsional'nykh literatur*, Moscow, 1961, pp.301–2.

128. Naimy, Mikhail, *Sab'un*, 5th edn, p.142.

129. Ibid. pp.181, 184, 187, 212, 269, 270.

130. Ibid. p.187.

131. Ibid. pp.209, 222–3.

132. Ibid. p.187.

133. Motyleva, T.L., *O mirovom znachenii L.N. Tolstogo*, Moscow, 1957, p.3.

134. Naimy, Mikhail, *Ab'ad min Musku wa min Washintan*, p.72.

135. Naimy, Mikhail, *Sab'un*, 5th edn, p.212.

136. Naimy, Mikhail, "'Abir sabil", in *Akabir*, Beirut, 1963, pp.43–51.

137. Ibid. p.47.

138. Ibid. p.48.

139. Tolstoy, L.N., "Povesti i rasskazy 1872–1886", *Sobr. soch.*, vol. 10, Moscow, 1982, pp.291–308.

140. Ibid. p.306.

141. Naimy, Mikhail, *Sab'un*, Beirut, 1960, p.76.

142. Naimy, Mikhail, *Mudhakkarat al-Arqash*, 3rd edn, Beirut, 1962, p.134. (Further citations are from this edition.)

143. Ibid. p.29.

144. Ibid. p.50.

145. Ibid. p.51.

146. Ibid. p.41.

147. Ibid. p.80.

148. Ibid. pp.32–3.

149. Ibid. p.26.

150. Tolstoy, L.N., "Ispoved'", *Sobr. soch.*, vol. 16, Moscow, 1983, pp.161–2.

151. *Literaturnoe nasledie*, vols. 37–8, Moscow, 1939, pp.350–1.

152. Naimy, Mikhail, *Mudhakkarat al-Arqash*, pp.112–13.

153. Tolstoy, L.N., "Chto zhe nam delat'?", *Sobr. soch.*, vol. 16, p.377.

154. Naimy, Mikhail, *Mudhakkarat al-Arqash*, pp.22, 92.

155. Ibid. p.65.

156. Tolstoy, L.N., "O zhizni", *Sobr. soch.*, vol. 17, Publitsisticheskie proizvedenia (1886–1908), Moscow, 1984, p.58.

157. Ibid. p.59.

158. Naimy, Mikhail, *Mudhakkarat al-Arqash*, p.113.

159. Naimy, Nadeem, *Mikhail Naimy: an introduction*, Beirut, 1967.

160. Ibid. pp.176–7.

161. Dostoevsky, F.M., *Sobr. soch.*, vol. 5, Moscow, 1957, p.436.

162. Ibid.

163. Tolstoy, L.N., "Povesty i rasskazy 1885–1902", *Sobr. soch.*, vol. 12, Moscow, 1982, p.162.

164. *The Book of Mirdad* appeared in English in Beirut in 1948. Soon afterwards, an order was placed by a Mumbai library for 1000 copies. In 1954 a Gujarati translation was published in Mumbai. A Dutch edition, *Het Boek van Mirdad*, was published in 1960. It appeared in London bookshops in 1962 and a Portuguese edition was released in Brazil in 1965 (*O Livro de Mirdad*, São Paulo). In 1968 a German edition was published in Harlem, *Das Buch von Mirdad*, and an Italian edition was issued from Rome in 1977.

165. Cited in Naimy, Mikhail, *Sab'un*, vol. 3, Beirut, 1960, p.221.

166. Naimy, Mikhail, *Kitab Mirdad*, Beirut, 1959, p.103. (Further citations are from this edition.)

167. Tolstoy, L.N., "Lyubite drug druga", *Poln. sobr. soch.*, vol. 37, Moscow, 1956, p.61.

168. Cited in Bryukov, P.I., "Tolstoy i Vostok", in *Novy Vostok*, 1924, no. 6, p.398.

169. Naimy, Mikhail, *Kitab Mirdad*, p.127.

170. "Avtobiografia Mikhail Nuaime", in Krachkovsky, I.Yu., *Izbr. soch.*, vol. 3, p.226.

171. Naimy, Mikhail, *Kitab Mirdad*, p.147.

172. Tolstoy, L.N., "Tak chto zhe nam delat'?", *Sobr. soch.*, vol. 16, pp.382–3.

173. Naimy, Mikhail, *Kitab Mirdad*, pp.69, 313.

174. Tolstoy, L.N., "Tak chto zhe nam delat'?", *Sobr. soch.*, vol. 16, p.297.

175. Naimy, Mikhail, *al-Yawm al-akhir*, Beirut, 1963, p.114. (Further citations are from this edition.)

176. Ibid. p.54.

177. Ibid. p.55.

178. Ibid. p.54.
179. Tolstoy, L.N., "Tak chto zhe nam delat'?", *Sobr. soch.*, vol. 16, p.263.
180. Naimy, Mikhail, *al-Yawm al-ahkir*, p.53.
181. Tolstoy, L.N., "Tak chto zhe nam delat'?", *Sobr. soch.*, vol. 16, p.254.
182. Naimy, Mikhail, *al-Awthan*, Beirut, 1962, p.1.
183. Ibid. pp.15–16.
184. Naimy, Mikhail, *al-Yawm al-akhir*, p.53.
185. Ibid. p.187.
186. Naimy, Mikhail, "Nahnu ahsa, aw aba'una?", in *Sawt al-'alam*, Beirut, 1961, pp.134–5.
187. Naimy, Mikhail, *Karm 'ala darb*, Beirut, 1962, p.72.
188. Tolstoy, L.N., *Sobr. soch.*, vol. 12, Moscow, 1982, pp.54–107.
189. Naimy, Mikhail, *al-Yawm al-akhir*, p.261.
190. Ibid. p.267.
191. Ibid. pp.267–8.
192. Ibid. p.268.
193. Tolstoy, L.N., "Ispoved'", *Sobr. soch.*, vol. 16, pp.152–3.
194. Krachkovsky, I.Yu., Preface to "Obraztsy novoarabskoy literatury (1888–1925): Ode-Vasil'evoy K.V.", *Izbr. soch.*, vol. 3, p.50.
195. Krachkovsky, I.Yu., *Nad arabskimi rukopisyami*, p.78.
196. Ode-Vasil'eva, K.V., Preface to Naimy, Mikhail, *Livanskie novelly*, Moscow, 1959, p.7.
197. Dolinina, A.A., "Iz istorii russko-arabskikh literaturnikh svyazey ("Otsy i deti" Mikhaila Nuaime)", in Vestnik LGU [Leningrad State University Bulletin] History, Languages and Literature Series, 1963, no. 20, issue 4, p.89.
198. Troitsky, V.Yu., *Kniga pokoleniy: O romane I.S. Turgeneva "Otsi i deti"*, Moscow, 1979, p.86.
199. "Avtobiografia Mikhaila Nuaime", in Krachkovsky, I.Yu., *Izbr. soch.*, vol. 3, p.224.
200. Naimy, Mikhail, *Sab'un*, vol. 2, Beirut, 1960, p.62.
201. Ibid. p.64.
202. Bialy, G.A., *Turgenev i russky realizm*, Moscow and Leningrad, 1962, p.246.
203. Khrapchenko, M.B., *Tvorcheskaya individual'nost' pisatelia i razvitie literatury*, 3rd edn, Moscow, 1975, p.332.
204. Batyuto, A.I., *Turgenev-romanist*, Leningrad, 1972, p.13.
205. Turgenev, I., *Fathers and Sons*, New York, 1943. Preface by Sinclair Lewis.
206. "Sinkler L'yuis o Turgeneve", in *Voprosy literatury*, 1958, no. 9, p.90.
207. Maupassant, Guy de, *Sobr. soch. v 12 tomakh*, vol. 3, Moscow, 1956, p.64.
208. Bialy, G.A., *Turgenev i russky realism*, p.245.
209. Dolinina, A.A., "Iz istorii russko-arabskikh literaturnykh sviazey", p.90.
210. Naimy, Mikhail, *al-Aba' wa al-banun* [*Fathers and Sons*], Beirut, 1953, p.34. (Further citations are from this edition.)
211. Ibid.
212. Ibid. p.136.
213. Ibid. p.61.
214. Ibid. p.25.
215. Ibid. p.27.
216. Ibid. p.35.
217. Ibid. p.132.
218. Ibid. p.51.
219. Ibid. p.52.

220. Ibid. p.90.

221. Ibid. p.117.

222. Ibid. p.95.

223. Ibid. p.83.

224. Ibid. pp.109–10.

225. Ibid. p.114.

226. Ibid. pp.107–8.

227. Naimy, Mikhail, from Preface to *al-Aba' wa-l banun*. (Trans. T. Khemiri and G. Kampffmeyer, *Leaders in Contemporary Arabic literature*, Berlin, 1930, p.31.)

228. Ibid.

229. Ibid. p.36.

230. *al-Adib*, Beirut, 1965, no. 2, p.29.

231. Ibid.

232. Najm, Muhammad Yusuf, *al-Qissa fi al-adab al-'Arabi al-hadith*, 2nd edn, Beirut, 1961, p.287.

233. See "Arabskie pisateli o russkoy i sovetskoy literature", in *Sovremenny Vostok*, 1958, no. 9, p.65; Kirpichenko, V.N., "Chekhovskoe zvuchanie rannikh rasskazov Yusefa Idrisa", in *Literatura Vostoka*, Moscow, 1969, pp.3–9; Chukov, B.V., "O rasprostranenii russkoy klassiki v Irake", in *Russkaya klassika v stranakh Vostoka*, Moscow, 1982, p.90; al-Shazli, Mahmud M.E., "Ideynoe i khudozhestvennoe vlianie russkoy i sovetskoy literatury na egipetsky roman" (abstract of Candidate dissertation in philology), Moscow, 1973, p.7; Cherkassky, L.Ye., *Russkaya literatura na Vostoke (teoria i praktika perevoda)*, pp.46–7.

234. For a detailed discussion, see "Novellistika Mikhaila Nuaime", in Imangulieva, A.N., *"Assosiatsia pera" i Mikhail Nuayme*, pp.103–28.

235. Chudakov, A.P., *Mir Chekhova*, Moscow, 1986, p.8.

236. Krachkovsky, I.Yu., "Arabskaya literatura v XX v", *Izbr. soch.*, vol. 3, p.94.

237. Krachkovsky, I.Yu., "Novoarabskaya literatura", *Izbr. soch.*, vol. 3, p.75.

238. Najm, M.Yu., *al-Qissa fi al-adab al-'Arabi al-hadith*, p.278.

239. al-Khuri, Ibrahim, *Tahta al-majhar*, Beirut, 1960, p.2.

240. Chekhov, A.P., *Sobr. soch.*, vol. 12, Moscow, 1956, p.56.

241. Elizarova, M.E., *Tvorchestvo Chekhova i voprosy realizma kontsa XIX veka*, Moscow, 1958, p.180.

242. *al-Adib*, Beirut, 1965, no. 2, p.30.

243. Gurvich, I.A., *Proza Chekhova (Chelovek i deystvitel'nost')*, Moscow, 1970, p.20.

244. Bialy, G.A., "Chekhov", in *Istoria russkoy literatury*, vol. 9, part 2, Moscow and Leningrad, 1956, p.399.

245. Naimy, Mikhail, "Akabir", in *Akabir*, pp.7–16. (Russ. trans. ("Vysshie") from Arabic by V. Krasnovsky, in Mikhail Nuaime, *Livanskie novelly*, Moscow, 1959, pp.53–8.)

246. *Livanskie novelly*, p.58.

247. Elizarova, M.E., *Tvorchestvo Chekhova i voprosy realizma kontsa XIX veka*, p.179.

248. Naimy, Mikhail, "Shahidat al-shahd", in *Abu Batta*, Beirut, 1959, pp.63–70. (Russ. trans. ("Zhertva meda") by A. Rashkovskaya, in *Livanskie novelly*, pp.27–31.)

249. Naimy, Mikhail, "Sadiq", in *Akabir*, pp.73–80. (Russ. trans. ("Sadyk") by T. Kezma, in *Livanskie novelly*, pp.15–20.)

250. Berdnikov, G.P., *A.P. Chekhov: Ideynie i tvorcheskie iskania*, 3rd edn, Moscow, 1984, p.490.

251. This story was originally called "Tha'iran" ("Two Rebels'); in *Abu Batta*, Beirut, 1959, pp.106–16. (Russ. trans. ("Braslet") by A. Rashkovskaya, in *Livanskie novelly*, pp.21–6.)

252. *Livanskie novelly*, p.25.

253. Naimy, Mikhail, "'Ulbat al-kibrit", in *Akabir*, pp.106–12. (Russ. trans. ("Korobka spichek") by T. Kezma, in *Livanskie novelly*, pp.37–41.)

254. *Livanskie novelly*, p.18.

255. The original Arabic title of this story is "Umm wa laysat bi-umm" ("Mother and Not Mother"); in *Akabir*, pp.34–42. (Russ. trans. ("Tetushka Marsha") by L. Stepanov, in *Livanskie novelly*, pp.59–64.)

256. *Livanskie novelly*, p.61.

257. Naimy, Mikhail, "Sanatuha al-jadida", in *Kana ma kana*, Beirut, 1966, pp.39–51. (Russ. trans. ("Ee novy god") by T. Kezma, in *Livanskie novelly*, pp.65–73.)

258. *Livanskie novelly*, p.68.

259. Ibid. pp.69–70.

260. Ibid. p.21.

261. This was originally called "Kusar al-hasa" ["Gravel Debris"]; in *Akabir*, pp.26–33. (Russ. trans. ("Stuk molotka") by R. Aytuganov, in *Livanskie novelly*, pp.32–6.

262. Originally called "al-Yubil al-almasi"; in *Abu Batta*, Beirut, 1959. (Russ. trans. ("Almaznaya svad'ba") by V. Shagal', in *Sovremennaya arabskaya novella*, Moscow, 1963, pp.263–7.)

263. *Sovremennaya arabskaya novella*, p.265.

264. Ibid. p.268.

265. *Livanskie novelly*, pp.25–6.

266. Naimy, Mikhail, "al-'Aqir", in *Kana ma kana*, pp.52–83. (Russ. trans. ("Besplodnaya") by V. Ushakov, in *Rasskazy pisateley Livana*, Moscow, 1958, pp.47–65.)

267. *Rasskazy pisateley Livana*, p.64.

268. Ibid. p.62.

Bibliography

'Abbas, Ihsan, and Najm, Muhammad Yusuf, *al-Shi'r al-'Arabi fi al-mahjar*, Beirut, 1957.
'Abd al-Ghani Hasan, Muhammad, *al-Shi'r al-'Arabi fi al-mahjar*, Cairo, 1962.
Abd el-Jalil, Jean-Mohammed, *Brève Histoire de la Littérature Arabe*, Paris, 1946.
Abramovich, G.L., *Vvedenie v literaturovedenie*, Moscow, 1970.
Abu Shabaka, Ilyas, *Dirasat wa dhikrayat*, Beirut, 1948.
Abu Shadi, Ahmad Zaki, *Atyaf al-rabi': muqaddima*, Cairo, 1933.
Aghani, Sulayman, *al-Adab al-'Arabi wa ta'rikhuh*, Cairo, 1955.
Ali-zade, E.A., *Egipetskaya novella*, Moscow, 1974.
——, *Mahmud Taymur*, Moscow, 1983.
Anthologie de la Littérature Arabe Contemporaine, ed. Jacques Berque et al., Paris, 1964.
Amin, Ahmad, *al-Naqd al-adabi*, Cairo, 1957.
Anas, Da'ud, *al-Tabi'at fi shi'r al-mahjar*, Cairo, 1966.
——, *al-Tajdid fi shi'r al-mahjar*, Cairo, 1968.
al-'Aqqad, 'Abbas Mahmud, "Muqaddima", in Naimy, Mikhail, *al-Ghirbal*, 7th edn, Beirut, 1964.
Arabskaya romanticheskaya proza XIX-XX v., Leningrad, 1981.
"Arabskie pisateli o russkoy i sovetskoy literature", *Sovremenny Vostok*, 9, 1958.
'Arida, Nasib, *al-Arwah al-ha'ira*, New York, 1946.
Ashtar, 'Abd al-Karim, *al-Nathr al-mahjari*, 2 vols., Cairo, 1960–61 and 1969.
al-Badawi, Mulaththam, *al-Natiqun bi al-dad fi Amirika al-Janubiyya*, Cairo, 1956.
Badawi, M.M., *A critical introduction to modern Arabic poetry*, Cambridge, 1973.
Bashir, Antonius, *Mulhaqa bi kitab "al-Nabi" li Jubran Khalil Jubran*, Beirut, 1936.
Batyuto, A.I., *Turgenev-romanist*, Leningrad, 1972.
Bauers, David, "Demokraticheskie dali", in *Literaturnaya istoria SShA*, vol. 1, Moscow, 1977.
Belinsky, V.G., *Izbrannoe sochinenia*, Moscow and Leningrad, 1946.
——, *O teatre*, Moscow, 1982.
Belyaev, I.P., "Vmeste so vsemi pisatelyami Azii i Afriki", in *Sovremenny Vostok*, 9, 1958.
Berdnikov, G.P., *A.P. Chekhov: ideynie i tvorcheskie iskania*, Moscow, 1984.
Berkovsky, N.Ya., *Romantizm v Germanii*, Leningrad, 1973.
Bertel's, E.A., "Sufizm i sufiyskaya literatura", in *Izbr. trudy*, vol. 3, Moscow, 1965.
Bialy, G.A., "Chekhov", in *Istoria russkoy literatury*, vol. 9, Moscow and Leningrad, 1956.
——, *Turgenev i russky realizm*, Moscow and Leningrad, 1962.
Bielawski, J., *Historia literatury arabskiej*, Warsaw, 1968.
Bilyk, I.E., *Tvorchesky metod Mikhaila Nuayme* [candidate dissertation in philology], Moscow, 1984.
Biryukov, P.I., "Tolstoy i Vostok", *Novy Vostok*, 6, Moscow, 1924.
Blagoy, D.D., "Dialektika literaturnoy preemstvennosti", in *Voprosy literatury*, 2, 1962.
Blake, William, "Vechnosushchee evangelie" ["The Everlasting Gospel"], in *Poezia angliyskogo romantizma*, Moscow, 1975.

Borisov, V.M., "Arabskaya literatura posle vtoroy mirovoy voyny", in *Voprosy literatury*, 8, 1958.
——, *Sovremennaya egipetskaya proza*, Moscow, 1961.
Braginsky, I.S., "Zametky o realisticheskikh traditsiakh v literaturakh Vostoka", in *Sovremenny Vostok*, 9, 1958.
——, "K obsuzhdeniu voprosa ob internatsional'nom i natsional'nom v literaturakh Vostoka", in *International'noe i natsional'noe v literaturakh Vostoka* (*Tezisy k soveshchaniu*), Moscow, 1972.
——, "Zapadno-vostochny sintez v "Divane" Gete", in Goethe, *Zapadno-vostochny divan "Moganin-name"* (*Kniga pevtsa*), Moscow, 1988.
Brockelmann, C., *Geschichte der arabischen Literatur*, Suppl. III, Leiden, 1942.
Bushmin, A.S., *Preemstvennost' v razvitii literatury*, Leningrad, 1978.
Bustani, Karam, *al-Qisas al-Lubnaniyya*, Beirut, 1961.
Byron, George Gordon, "Lara" and "Palomnichestvo Chaylda Garol'da", *Sochinenia*, vol. 1, Moscow, 1974.
——, "Kogda b ya mog v moryakh pustynnykh" and "Poslania Avguste", in *Poezia angliyskogo romantizma*, Moscow, 1975.
Canby, Henry Seidel, "Walt Whitman", in *Literaturnaya istoria SShA*, vol. 1, Moscow, 1977.
Chekhov, A.P., *Sobranie sochineniy* (in 12 vols), Moscow, 1954–7.
Chelyshev, Ye.P., "Lev Tolstoy i indiyskaya literatura", in *Russkaya klassika v stranakh Vostoka*, Moscow, 1982.
——, "O natsional'nom i internatsional'nom v indiyskoy literature", in *International'noe i natsional'noe v literaturakh Vostoka*, Moscow, 1972.
——, "Teoreticheskie i metodologicheskie aspekty izuchenia vzaimodeystvia kul'tur Vostoka i Zapada", in *Vzaimodeystvie kul'tur Vostoka i Zapada*, Moscow, 1987.
——, "Traditsii literatur Vostoka i ideologicheskaya bor'ba (Vmesto zaklyuchenia)", in *Khudozhestvennie traditsii literatur Vostoka i sovremennost': traditsionalizm na sovremennom etape*, Moscow, 1986.
Cherkassky, L.Ye., *Novaya kitayskaya poezia (20–30-e gody)*, Moscow, 1972.
——, *Russkaya klassika na Vostoke*. Ekstra- i sotsiolingvisticheskie aspekty perevoda, in *Vzaimodeystvie kul'tur Vostoka i Zapada*, Moscow, 1987.
——, *Russkaya literatura na Vostoke* (*Teoria i praktika perevoda*), Moscow, 1987.
Chudakov, A.P., *Mir Chekhova*, Moscow, 1986.
Chukov, B.V., "Irakskaya khudozhestvennaya proza i russkaya literatura", in *Narody Azii i Afriki*, 6, 1975.
——, "Literatura Livana", in *Literatura Vostoka v noveyshee vremya*, Moscow, 1977.
——, "O rasprostranenii russkoy klassiki v Irake", in *Russkaya klassika v stranakh Vostoka*, Moscow, 1982.
Chukovsky, K., "Uolt Uitmen", preface to Whitman, W., *List'ya travy*, Moscow, 1955.
Coleridge, Samuel Taylor, "Gimn Zemle geksametry", in *Poezia angliyskogo romantizma*, Moscow, 1975.
Dasuqi, 'Abd al-'Aziz, *Jama'at Apullu*, Cairo, 1965.
Dasuqi, 'Umar, *Fi al-adab al-hadith*, Cairo, 1954.
Dib, Wadi' Amin, *al-Shi'r al-'Arabi fi al-mahjar al-Amiriki*, Beirut, 1955.
Dima, A., *Printsipy sravnitel'nogo literaturovedenia*, Moscow, 1977.
Dmitriev, A.S., "Teoria zapanoevropeyskogo romantizma", in *Literaturnie manifesty zapadnoevropeyskikh romantikov*, Moscow, 1980.

Dmitrievsky, A.A., *Russkaya literatura v arabskikh perevodakh*, Petrograd, 1915.

Dolin, A.A., "Yaponskaya proza na Zapade: perevod, stilizatsia, adaptatsia", in *Vzaimodeystvie kul'tur Vostoka i Zapada*, Moscow, 1987.

Dolinina, A.A., "Ameen al-Rihani", in al-Rihani, A., *Izbrannoe*, Leningrad, 1988.

——, "Arabsky perevod Kreytserovoy sonaty L. Tolstogo (Cairo, 1904)", in *Voprosy filologii stran Azii i Afriki*, 2nd edn, Leningrad, 1973.

——, "*Arap Petr Velikogo* i *Baryshnya-krest'yanka* Pushkina na arabskom yazyke", in *Pamyati akademika I.Yu. Krachkovskogo*, Leningrad, 1958.

——, "Fridrikh Ryukert kak perevodchik 'Makam' al-Khariri", in *Vzaimodeystvie kul'tur Vostoka i Zapada*, Moscow, 1987.

——, "Gogol' v arabskoy literature", in *Gogol': stati i materialy*, Leningrad, 1954.

——, "Iz istorii russko-arabskikh literaturnikh svyazey ("Otsy i deti" Mikhaila Nuaime)", in *Vestnik LGU, History, Languages and Literature Series*, 20/4, 1963.

——, "Iz predystorii realizma v novoy arabskoy literature", *Problemy stanovlenia realizma v literaturakh Vostoka*, Moscow, 1964.

——, "Neopublikovannie perevody iz arabskoy literatury v arkhive I.Yu. Krachkovskogo", in *Pis'mennye pamyatniki i problemy istorii kul'tury narodov Vostoka*, Moscow, 1977.

——, *Ocherki istorii arabskoy literatury novogo vremeni: Egipet i Siria. Publitsistika (1870–1914)*, Moscow, 1968.

——, *Ocherki istorii arabskoy literatury novogo vremeni: Egipet i Siria*, Moscow, 1973.

——, "O nekotorykh kharakternykh chertakh prosveshchcnia na Arabskom Vostoke", in *Trudy mezhvuzovskoy nauchnoy konferentsii po istorii literatur zarubezhnogo Vostoka*, Moscow, 1970.

——, "Pervy arabsky perevod Dostoevskogo", in *Russkaya klassika v stranakh Vostoka*, Moscow, 1982.

——, "Pervy sbornik proizvedeniy M. Gor'kogo na arabskom yazyke", in *Gor'ky i literatura zarubezhnogo Vostoka*, Moscow, 1968.

——, "Pushkin v arabskoy literature", in *Pushkin v stranakh zarubezhnogo Vostoka*, Moscow, 1979.

——, Preface to *Arabskaya romanticheskaya proza XIX–XX vv*, Leningrad, 1981.

——, Preface to Naimy, M, *Moi sem'desyat let*, Moscow, 1980.

——, Preface to *Sovremennaya arabskaya proza*, Moscow and Leningrad, 1961.

——, *Russkaya literatura XIX veka v arabskikh stranakh* [candidate diploma dissertation], Leningrad, 1953.

——, "Russkaya literatura XIX veka v arabskikh stranakh", in *Russkaya literatura*, 1, 1960.

Dostoevsky, F.M., *Sobranie sochineniy* (in 10 vols.), vol. 5, Moscow, 1957.

Drelov, A., "Romanticheskaya tipizatsia", in Ameen al-Rihani, *Izbrannoe*, Leningrad, 1988.

D'yakonova, N.Ya., *Angliysky romantizm: problemy estetiki*, Moscow, 1978.

Dyurishin, D., *Teoria sravnitel'nogo izuchenia literatury*, Moscow, 1979.

Elistratova, A.A., *Nasledie angliyskogo romantizima i sovremennost'*, Moscow, 1960.

——, "Poemy i lirika Kolridzha", in *Kolridzh Samuel' Teylor, Stikhi*, Moscow, 1974.

Elizarova, M.E., *Tvorchestvo Chekhova i voprosy realizma kontsa XIX veka*, Moscow, 1958.

Emerson, Ralph Waldo, "Poet" (Russ. trans. A.M. Zverev), in *Estetika amerikanskogo romantizma*, Moscow, 1977.

——, "O literaturnoy morali" (Russ. trans. A.M. Zverev), in *Estetika amerikanskogo romantizma*, Moscow, 1977.

——, "Priroda" (Russ. trans. A.M. Zverev), in *Estetika amerikanskogo romantizma*, Moscow, 1977.

Eyshiskina, N.M., *Trantsendentalizm*, in *KLE*, vol.7, Moscow, 1972.

Fahuri, Hanna, *Ta'rikh al-adab al-'Arabi*, Beirut, 1960.

Filosofskaya entsiklopedia: metod, vol. 3, Moscow, 1964.

Filosofskoe nasledie narodov Vostoka i sovremennost', Moscow, 1983.

Filshtinsky, I.M., *Istoria arabskoy literatury*, Moscow, 1985.

Fokht, U.R., "Formy literaturnykh vzaimodeystviy i metodika ikh izuchenia", in *Vzaimosvyazi i vzaimodeystvie natsional'nykh literatur*, Moscow, 1961.

——, "Nekotorie voprosy teorii romantizma (zamechania i gipotezy)", in *Problemy romantizma*, Moscow, 1967.

Fuller, M., "Amerikanskaya literatura: ee sostoyanie v nastoyashchee vremya i perspektivy na budushchee" (Russ. trans. from Engl. A.M. Zverev), in *Estetika amerikanskogo romantizma*, Moscow, 1977.

Fyodorov, A.V., "K voprosu o literaturnom vlianii", in *Vzaimosvyazi i vzaimodeystvie natsional'nykh literatur*, Moscow, 1961.

Gabrieli, F., *La Letteratura Araba*, Florence, 1967.

——, "Mikhail Naimy, an autobiography", in *Islam and its Cultural Divergence*, ed. G. Tikku, Urbana, IL, 1971.

Gerasimova, A.S., *Literatura Afganistana*, Moscow, 1986.

Gey, N.K., "Stil' L. Tolstogo i romanticheskaya poetika", in *K istorii russkogo romantizma*, Moscow, 1973.

Ghougassian, Joseph P., *Khalil Gibran: wings of thought – the people's philosopher*, New York, 1973.

Gibb, H.A.R., *Arabskaya literatura*, Moscow, 1960.

——, "Studies in contemporary Arabic literature", in *Bulletin of the School of Oriental Studies*, vol. 4, 1927–28, vol. 5, 1929.

Gibran, Jean, and Gibran, Khalil, *Khalil Gibran: his life and world*, Boston, 1974.

Gibran, Kahlil, (Dzhebran, Khalil), *Izbrannoe*, Leningrad, 1986 and 1988.

——, *Jesus Son of Man*, New York, 1930.

——, *Kalimat*, Cairo, 1950.

——, (Jubran, Khalil), *al-Majmu'a al-kamila li mu'allafat*, Beirut, 1961; 2nd edn., Beirut, 1964.

——, *al-Nabi*, Beirut, 1956.

——, *Raml wa zabad*, Beirut, 1962.

——, *Sleza i ulybka* (Russ. trans. V. Volosatova), Moscow, 1976.

——, *Slomannie krylya* (Russ. trans. V. Volosatova), Moscow, 1962.

Goethe (Gete), Johann Wolfgang von, *Zapadno-vostochny divan*, Moscow, 1988.

Gorky, Maxim, *Sobranie sochineniy* (in 30 vols.), vol. 14, Moscow, 1951.

Grunebaum, G.E., "Esteticheskie osnovy arabskoy literatury", in *Osnovnye cherty arabo-musul'manskoy kul'tury*, Moscow, 1981.

Gurevich, A.M., "O tipologicheskikh osobennostyakh russkogo romantizma", in *K istorii russkogo romantizma*, Mosow, 1973.

Gurvic, I.A., *Proza Chekhova (Chelovek i deystvitel'nost')*, Moscow, 1970.

Haddara, Muhammad Mustafa, *Ittijahat al-shi'r al-'Arabi fi al-qarn al-thani al-hijri*, Cairo, 1963.

——, *al-Tajdid fi shi'r al-mahjari*, Cairo, 1957.

Hanna, Jurj, "O literature Livana", in *Sovremennaya arabskaya literatura*, Moscow, 1960.

Harakat al-tajdid fi al-adab al-'Arabi, Cairo, 1976.

Hasan, Jad Hasan, *Adab al-'Arabi fi al-mahjar*, Beirut, 1962.

Hawi, Khalil S., *Khalil Gibran: his background, character and works*, Beirut, 1963.

Hidda, Hasan, *Ta'rikh al-mughtaribin al-'Arab fi al-'alam*, Damascus, 1974.

Hitti, Philip, *The Syrians in America*, New York, 1930.

——, *Ta'rikh Suriyya wa Lubnan wa Falastin*, part 2, Beirut, 1959.

Horvat, K., "Romanticheskoe vozzrenie na prirodu", in *Evropeysky romantizm*, Moscow, 1973.

Huart, Clement, *A History of Arabic Literature*, London 1903, and Beirut, 1966.

Husayn, Taha, et al., *Al-Muntakhab fi al-adab al-'Arab*, Cairo, 1934.

Huwayk, Yusuf, *Dhikrayati ma'a Jubran*, Beirut, 1959.

al-Ida, Yamni, "Adab Jubran bayn al wa'y wa al-waqi'a", *al-Tariq*, 2, Beirut, 1970.

Idei gumanizma v literaturakh Vostoka (collected articles), Moscow, 1967.

Ideologicheskaya bor'ba i sovremennie literatury zarubezhnogo Vostoka (collected articles), Moscow, 1977.

Iezuitova, R.V., *Istoria russkoy poezii*, Leningrad, 1968.

Imangulieva, A.N., *"Assosiatsia pera" i Mikhail Nuayme*, Moscow, 1975.

——, *Imperatorskoe Pravoslavnoe Palestinskoe obshchestvo i yego deyatel'nost' (1882–1907gg)*, Istoricheskaya zapiska [historical records], St Petersburg, 1907.

——, "Istoki arabsko-russkikh kul'turnikh i literaturnykh svyazey", in *Blizhny i Sredny Vostok*, Baku, 1986.

——, *Jubran Khalil Jubran* (in Azeri), Baku, 1975.

——, *Literaturnoe ob'edinenie Mikhail Nuayme i "Assosiatsia pera"* [candidate dissertation in philology], Baku, 1966.

——, "Priroda v tvorchestve Amina ar-Rihani", in *Blizhny i Sredny Vostok*, Baku, 1986.

——, "Romantizm ar-Rihani v povesti *Vne sten garema* i malykh prozaicheskikh zhanrakh", in *Problemy zarubezhnogo Vostoka: istoria i sovremennost'*, Baku, 1988.

——, "Russkaya literaturno-kriticheskaya mysl' i tvorchestvo M. Nuayme", in *Voprosy vostochnoy filologii*, Baku, 1986.

International'noe i natsional'noe v literaturakh Vostoka (collected articles), Moscow, 1972.

Iskusstvo romanticheskoy epokhi (Materialy nauchnoy konferentsii, 1968), Moscow, 1972.

Isma'il, Adham, "Mikha'il Nu'ayma", *Majallat al-Hadith*, 6, 1944.

Istoria russkoy literatury, vol. 9/2, Moscow and Leningrad, 1956.

Istoria vsemirnoy literatury, vol. 2, Moscow, 1984.

Istoria zarubezhnoy literatury IX v., Moscow, 1982.

Ivanov, V.V., *Temy i stili Vostoka v poezii Zapada*, Moscow, 1987.

Ivbulis, V.Ya., *Literaturno-khudozhestvennoe tvorchestvo Rabindranata Tagora*, Riga, 1981.

——, "Romantizm i traditsionnaya indiyskaya mysl'", in *Vzaimodeystvie kul'tur Vostoka i Zapada*, Moscow, 1987.

Jabbar, Muhammed Yunis, *L.N. Tolstoy i sovremennaya literatura arabskogo Vostoka* [candidate dissertation in philology], Moscow, 1978.

Jabr, Jamil, *Amin al-Rayhani: al-rajul wa al-adib*, Beirut, 1947.

——, *Jubran, siratuhu, adabuhu, falsafatuhu wa rasmuhu*, Beirut, 1958.

——, *Mayy wa Jubran*, Cairo, 1961.

Jad Hasan, Hasan, *al-Adab al-'Arabi fi al-mahjar*, Cairo, 1962.

Jamati, Habib, "al-Mir'at ... fi hayat Jubran", *Majallat al-Hilal*, 2, 1947.

Jundi, Anwar, *al-Kitab al-mu'asirun, adwa 'ala hayatihim*, Cairo, 1955.

——, *Mu'allim al-adab al-'Arabi al-mu'asir*, Cairo, 1964.

——, *al-Muhafaza wa al-tajdid fi al-nathr al-'Arabi al-mu'asir fi mi'at 'am*, Cairo, 1961.

Kafi, Muhammad, *'Arab fi al-mahjar al-shimali*, Cairo, 1954.

al-Kaiyali, Mawahib, "O sovremennoy arabskoy literature", in *Sovremennaya arabskaya literatura*, Moscow, 1960.

Kampffmeyer, G., "Arabische Dichter der Gegenwart", *MSOS*, 29/2, 1926; 31/2, 1928.

——, "Index zur neueren arabischen Literatur", *MSOS*, 31/2, 1928.

Karamzin, N.M., *Pis'ma russkogo puteshestvennika*, Povesti, Moscow, 1980.

Kasimkhodzhaev, A.S., *Bor'ba idey v literaturnoy zhizni Egipeta (1875–1975 gg)*, Tashkent, 1983.

Kessel, L.M., *Gete i "Zapadno-vostochny divan"*, Moscow, 1973

al-Khalil, Mustafa, and Farrukh, Omar, *Missionery i imperializm v arabskikh stranakh* (Russ. trans. from Arabic), Moscow, 1961.

Khemiri, T., and Kampffmeyer, G., *Leaders in contemporary Arabic literature*, London, 1930.

Khodzhaeva, R.U., *Ocherki razvitia egipetskoy poezii*, Tashkent, 1985.

Khrapchenko, M.B., *Tvorcheskaya individual'nost' pisatelia i razvitie literatury*, Moscow, 1975.

Khrestomatia po teorii literatury, Moscow, 1982.

Khudozhestvennie traditsii literatur Vostoka i sovremennost': traditsionalizm na sovremennom etape, Moscow, 1986.

al-Khuri, Alfred (Farid), *Jubran Khalil Jubran wa Mikha'il Nu'ayma*, Beirut, 1960.

——, *al-Kalima al-'Arabiyya fi al-mahjar*, Beirut, 1960.

al-Khuri, Ibrahim, *Tahta al-majhar*, Beirut, 1960.

al-Khuri al-Muqaddas, Anis, *al-Ittijahat al-adabiyya fi al-'alam al-'Arabi al-hadith*, Beirut, 1961.

——, *Tatawwur al-asalib al-nathriyya fi al-adab al-'Arabi*, Beirut, 1960.

Khuri, Ra'if, *Amin al-Rihani*, Beirut, 1948.

Khuri, Yuhanna, *Radd 'ala Mikha'il Nu'ayma fi Mirdad*, Sayda, 1956.

Kirpichenko, V.N., "Chekhovskoe zvuchanie rannikh rasskazov Yusefa Idrisa", in *Literatura Vostoka*, Moscow, 1969.

——, "O putyakh razvitia realizma v egipetskoy proze", in *Narody Azii i Afriki*, no.5, 1976.

——, *Sovremennaya egipetskaya proza (60–70-e gody)*, Moscow, 1986.

al-Kiyali, Sami, *Amin al-Rihani*, Aleppo, 1948.

Kiyko, E.I., *V.G. Belinsky*, Moscow, 1972.

Klimenko, E.I., *Angliyskaya literatura pervoy poloviny XIX veka*, Leningrad, 1971.

Klyashtorina, V.B., *"Novaya poezia" v Irane*, Moscow, 1975.

Konrad, N.I., "Problema realizma i literatury Vostoka", in *Problemy stanovlenia realizma v literaturakh Vostoka*, Moscow, 1964.

——, "Problemy sovremennogo sravitel'nogo literaturovedenia", in *Izvestia AN SSSR, OLYa*, vol. 18/4, 1959.

——, *Zapad i vostok*, Moscow, 1972.

Kotlov, L.N., *Stanovlenie natsional'no-osvoboditel'nogo dvizhenia na Arabskom Vostoke*, Moscow, 1975.

Kotsarev, N.K., *Pisateli Egipta, XX veka: materialy k bibliografii*, Moscow, 1976.

Krachkovsky, I.Yu., "Arabskaya literatura v Amerike (1895–1915)", *Izvestia LGU*, vol. 1, Leningrad, 1928.

——, *Arabskaya literatura v XX veke*, Leningrad, 1946.

——, "Arabskaya zarubezhnaya literatura", in *Izbrannie sochinenia*, vol. 3, Moscow and Leningrad, 1956.

——, "Arabsky perevod *Istorii Petra Velikogo* i *Istoria Karla XII, korolya Shvetsii* Vol'tera*" (1947), in *Izbrannie sochinenia*, vol. 3, Moscow and Leningrad, 1956.

——, "Avtobiografia Mikhaila Nuaime" (1931), in *Izbrannie sochinenia*, vol. 3, Moscow and Leningrad, 1956.

——, "Filosof doliny Fureyki", in *Nad arabskimi rukopisyami*, Moscow, 1965.

——, "Listky vospominaniy o knigakh i lyudyakh", in *Izbrannoe sochinenia*, vol. I, Moscow and Leningrad, 1955.

——, "al-Maari, ar-Rihani i Leningrad" (1944), in *Izbrannie sochinenia*, vol. 3, Moscow and Leningrad, 1956.

——, "Novoarabskaya literatura" (1935), in *Izbrannie sochinenia*, vol. 3, Moscow and Leningrad, 1956.

——, "O knige Mikhaila Nuaime o Dzhebrane" (1941), in *Izbrannie sochinenia*, vol. 3, Moscow and Leningrad, 1956.

——, "Ot perevodchika" [Translator's note], in *Amin Rihani: Izbr. proizvedenia*, Petrograd, 1917.

——, "Otzvuki revolyutsii 1905 goda v arabskoy khudozhestvennoy literature", in *Sovietskoe vostokovedenie*, vol. 3, Moscow and Leningrad 1945.

——, Preface to *Amin Rihani: Izbr. proizvedenia* (1917), in *Izbrannie sochinenia*, vol. 3, Moscow and Leningrad, 1956.

——, Preface to *Amin Rihani: Stikhotvorenia v proze* (1922), *Izbrannie sochinenia*, vol. 3, Moscow and Leningrad, 1956.

——, Preface to *Qasim Amin: Novaya zhenshchina* (1912), in *Izbrannie sochinenia*, vol. 3, Moscow and Leningrad, 1956.

——, Preface to Ode-Vasil'eva, K.V., *Obraztsy novoarabskoy literatury* (1928), in *Izbrannie sochinenia*, vol. 3, Moscow and Leningrad, 1956.

——, "Russko-arabskie literaturnie svyazi", in *Izbrannie sochinenia*, vol. 3, Moscow and Leningrad, 1956.

Krymsky, A.E., *Istoria novoy arabskoy literatury (XIX–nachalo XX veka)*, Moscow, 1971.

Kudelin, A.B., "O putyakh razvitia novoy arabskoy poezii", in *Vzaimosvyazi afrikanskikh literatur i literatur mira*, Moscow, 1975.

——, *Srednevekovaya arabskaya poetika (vtoraya polovina VIII–XI vv.)*, Moscow, 1983.

Kurd Ali, Muhammad, *Ghara'ib al-gharb*, Damascus 1910.

——, *Ghutat Dimashq*, Damascus, 1952.

Kurlyanskaya, G.B., *Turgenev i russkaya literatura*, Moscow, 1980.

Kuteliya, M.Ya., *Mirovozzrenie Dzhebrana* [candidate dissertation in philology], Baku, 1978.

Lavretsky, A., *V.G. Belinsky*, vol. 1, Moscow, 1962.

Lazarev, M.S., *Krushenie turetskogo gospodstva na Arabskom Vostoke*, Moscow, 1960.

Levin, Z.I., *Filosof iz Fureyki*, Moscow, 1965.

——, *Razvitie arabskoy obshchestvennoy mysli 1917–1945 gg*, Moscow, 1979.

——, *Razvitie osnovnykh techeniy obshchestvenno-politicheskoy mysli v Sirii i Egipte*, Moscow, 1972.

——, "Zapad v tvorchestve ar-Rihani (1876–1940)", in *Kratkie soobshchenia Instituta narodov Azii AN SSSP*, 45, Moscow, 1979.

Lewis, Sinclair, "O Turgeneve", in *Voprosy literatury*, 9, 1958.

Lifanov, N.V., "Livan", in *Sovremennaya Azia*, Moscow, 1977.

Likhachev, D.S., *Literatura, real'nost', literatura*, Leningrad, 1984.

Literatura stran zarubezhnogo Vostoka 70-x godov (collected articles), Moscow, 1982.

Literatura Vostoka (collected articles), Moscow, 1969.

Literatura Vostoka v novoe vremya, Moscow, 1975.

Literatura Vostoka v noveyshee vremya (1917–1945), Moscow, 1977.

Literatura Vostoka v srednie veka, vol. 2, Moscow, 1970.

Literatura zarubezhnoy Azii v sovremennuyu epokhu, Moscow, 1975.

Literaturnaya istoria SShA, vol. 1, Moscow, 1977.

Literaturnoe nasledie, vol. 1, "Tolstoy i zarubezhny mir", bk. 1, Moscow, 1965.

Literaturnoe nasledie, vols. 37–8, Moscow, 1939.

Lutsky, V.B., *Novaya istoria arabskikh stran*, Moscow, 1966.

——, "Pod"em natsional'no-osvoboditel'nogo dvizhenia v arabskikh stranakh v period pervoy russkoy revolyutsii, 1905–1907gg", in *Pervaya russkaya revolyutsia i mezhdunarodnoe revolyutsionnoe dvizhenie*, pt. 2, Moscow, 1956.

Majmu'at al-Rabita al-Qalamiyya, Beirut, 1964.

Malhas, Thurayya, *Mikha'il Nu'ayma al-adib al-sufi*, Beirut, 1964.

Ma'aluf, Shafiq, *Habbat zumurrud*, Damascus, 1966.

Mandur, Muhammad, *Fi al-adab wa al-naqd*, Cairo, 1952.

——, *al-Naqd wa al-nuqqad al-mu'asirun*, Cairo, 1963.

al-Manfaluti, Mustafa, "Tolstomu" (Russ. trans. from Arabic L. Petrova), in *Arabskaya romanticheskaya proza XIX–XX vv*, Leningrad, 1981.

Mann, Yu.V., *Poetika russkogo romantizma*, Moscow, 1976.

Maridan, 'Aziza, *al-Qawmiyya wa al-insaniyya fi shi'r al-mahjar al-janubi*, Cairo, 1966.

Markov, V.V., *Dzhebran Khalil Dzhebran, Izbrannoe*, Leningrad, 1986.

——, *Filosofskaya antropologia Dzh. Kh. Dzhebrana* [author's abstract of candidate philosophy dissertation], Leningrad, 1987.

Marun, 'Abbud, *Adab al-'Arab*, Beirut, 1960.

——, *Amin al-Rihani*, Cairo, 1952.

——, *Fi al-mukhtabar*, Harisa, 1952.

——, *Judad wa qudama'*, Beirut, 1963.

——, *Mujaddidun wa mujtarrun*, Beirut, 1948.

Marw, Adib, *al-Sihafa al-'Arabiyya, nash'atuha wa tatawwuruha*, Beirut, 1961.

Mas'ud, Habib, *Jubran hayyan wa mayyitan*, Beirut, 1966.

Maupassant, Guy de, *Sobranie sochineniy* (in 12 vols.), vol. 3, Moscow, 1956.

Maymin, E.A., *O russkom romantizme*, Leningrad, 1975.

Meletinsky, Ye.M., "Literatura Blizhnego Vostoka i Sredney Azii (vvedenie)", in *Istoria vsemirnoy literatury*, vol. 2, Moscow, 1984.

Melikov, T.D., *Nazim hikmeti novaya poezia turtsii*, Moscow, 1987.

Mendelson, Maurice, "Ya s vami, lyudi drugikh pokoleniy", in Whitman, W., *Izbrannie proizvedenia*, Moscow, 1970.

——, *Zhisn'i tvorchestvo Uitmena*, Moscow, 1967.

Merenz, D., "Chelovek, kotory poznakomil arabov s Rossiey", in *Literaturnaya gazeta*, 27 April, 1946.

Mets, A., *Musul'mansky Renessans*, Moscow, 1966.

Mikhaylov, A.D., Introduction to *Istoria vsemirnoy literatury*, vol. 2, Moscow, 1964.

Monteil, V., *Les grands courants de la littérature arabe contemporaine*, Beirut, 1976.

Moreh, S., *Modern Arabic poetry (1800–1970): the development of its forms and themes under the influence of Western literature*, Leiden, 1976.

Motyleva, T.L., *O mirovom znachenii L.N. Tolstogo*, Moscow, 1957.

——, "Tolstoy i sovremennie zarubezhnie pisateli", in *Literaturnoe nasledstvo*, 69/1, Moscow, 1961.

Muhsin, Jamal al-din, *al-'Iraq fi al-shi'r al-'Arabi wa al-mahjari*, Baghdad, 1966.

Muminov, H.K., *Mikhail Nuayme kak teoretik kriticheskogo realizma v arabskoy literature* [candidate dissertation in philology], Tashkent, 1975.

Musa, Muhammad 'Ali, *Amin al-Rayhani*, Beirut, 1961.

Naimy, Mikhail, *al-Aba' wa-l banun*, trans. T. Khemiri and G. Kampffmeyer, in *Leaders in contemporary Arabic literature*, Berlin, 1930.

——, (Nu'ayma, Mikha'il), *Ab'ad min Musku wa min Washintan*, Beirut, 1957.

——, *Abu Batta*, Beirut, 1959.

——, *Ahadith ma'a al-sahafa*, Beirut, 1973.

——, *Akabir*, Beirut, 1963.

——, "al-Akhmas wa al-asdas", in *as-Sa'ih*, New York, October 1915.

——, *al-Awthan*, Beirut, 1962.

——, *Ayyub*, Beirut, 1967.

——, "Fajar al-amal ba'd laylat al-ya's", in *al-Funun*, New York, 1913.

——, *Fi al-adab al-'Arabi al-hadith*, Beirut, 1954.

——, *al-Ghirbal*, Cairo, 1923, and Beirut, 1964.

——, *Jubran Khalil Jubran, hayatuhu, mawtuhu, adabuhu, fannuhu*, Beirut, 1934 and 1951.

——, *Kana ma kana*, Beirut, 1966.

——, *Karm 'ala darb*, Beirut, 1962.

——, *Khudozhestvennie traditsii literatur Vostoka i sovremennost': traditsionalizm na sovremennom etape*, Moscow, 1986.

——, *Kitab Mirdad* [*The Book of Mirdad*], Beirut, 1948 and 1959.

——, *Liqa'*, Beirut, 1958.

——, *Livanskie novelly*, Moscow, 1959 (Russ. trans. from Arabic).

——, *al-Marahil*, Beirut, 1950.

——, *Mudhakkarat al-Arqash*, Beirut, 1949 and 1962.

——, *al-Mukhtarat min Mikha'il Nu'ayma*, Beirut, 1955.

——, *Nabi'a Lubnan Jubran Khalil Jubran*, Cairo, 1958.

——, *Najwa al-ghurub*, Beirut, 1973.

——, *Sab'un*, Beirut, 1930, 1959 and 1960 (Russ. trans. by S.M. Batsevaya as *Moi sem'desyat let*, Moscow, 1980).

——, *Sawt al-'alam*, Beirut, 1961.

——, *Tariq al-dhat ila al-dhat*, Beirut, 1978.

——, *al-Yawm al-akhir*, Beirut, 1963.

Naimy, Nadeem, *Mikhail Naimy: an introduction*, Beirut, 1967.

——, *The Lebanese Prophets of New York*, Beirut, 1985.

Najib Ullah, *Islamic Literature*, New York 1963.

Najm, Muhammad Yusuf, *Fann al-qissa*, Beirut, 1955.

——, *al-Qissa fi al-adab al-'Arabi al-hadith*, Cairo, 1952 and 1961.

Nalivayko, D., "Romantizm kak esteticheskaya sistema", in *Voprosy literatury*, 11, 1982.

——, *al-Shi'r al-'Arabi fi al-mahjar*, Beirut, 1957.

Nashashibi, Is'af, *al-Lughat al-'Arabiyya wa al-Rayhani*, Cairo, 1928.

Nawri, 'Isa, *Adab al-mahjar*, Cairo, 1959.

——, *Udaba' min al-Sharq wa al-Gharb*, Beirut, 1966.

Neupokoeva, I.G., *Istoria vsemirnoy literatury: problemy sistemnogo i sravnitel'nogo analiza*, Moscow, 1976.

——, "Nekotorie voprosy izuchenia vzaimosvyazey i vzaimodeystvia natsional'nykh literatur", in *Vzaimosvyaz' i vzaimodeystvia national'nykh literatur*, Moscow, 1961.

——, *Problema vzaimodeystviya sovremennykh literatur*, Moscow, 1963.

——, *Revolyutsionno-romanticheskaya poema pervoy poloviny XIX veka*, Moscow, 1971.

——, *Revolyutsionny romantizm Shelli*, Moscow, 1959.

Nicholson, R.A., *A Literary History of the Arabs*, Cambridge, 1945.

Nikiforova, I.D., Introduction to *Vzaimosvyazi afrikanskikh literatur i literatur mira*, Moscow, 1975.

Nikolaev, P.A., *Realizm kak tvorchesky metod*, Moscow, 1975.

Nikolaeva, M.V., *Kharakter otrazhenia religioznogo mirovozzrenia v tvorchestve sovremennykh livanskikh romanistov (1950–70gg)* [candidate dissertation in philology], Moscow, 1984.

——, 'Religioznaya kontseptsia mira i cheloveka v romanakh Mikhaila Nuayme', *Hudojestvennie traditsii literatur vostoka i sovremennost'*, Moscow, 1986.

Nikol'sky, S.E., "Tvorcheskoe vospriatie khudozhestvennogo opyta drugoy literatury", in *Vaimosvyazi i vzaimodeystvie natsional'nykh literatur*, Moscow, 1961.

Nikolyukin, A.N., *Estetika amerikanskogo romantizma*, Moscow, 1977.

Noveyshaya istoria arabskikh stran (1917–1966), Moscow, 1968.

Ode-Vasil'eva, K.V., 'Mikhail Nuayme', in Naimy, M., *Livanskie novelly*, Moscow, 1959.

——, *Obraztsy novo-arabskoy literatury (1880–1925)*, Moscow, 1928; *(1880–1947)*, Moscow, 1949.

——, *Otrazhenie byta sovremennoy arabskoy zhenshchiny v novelle*, *Zapiski kollegi vostokovedov*, vol. 5, 1930.

——, *Rasskazy pisateley Livana*, Moscow, 1958.

Oduev, S.F., *Reaktsionnaya sushchnost' nitssheanstva*, Moscow, 1959.

——, *Tropami Zaratustry*, Moscow, 1971.

Otto, Annie Salem, *The parables of Khalil Gibran: an interpretation of his writings and art*, New York, 1967.

Paustovsky, K.G., *Sobranie sochineniy*, Moscow, 1957.

Petrosyan, Yu.A., *Mladoturetskoe dvizhenie (vtoraya polovina XIX–nachalo XX v)*, Moscow, 1971.

Poezia angliyskogo romantizma, Moscow, 1975.

Poezia SShA, Moscow, 1982.

Pospelov, G.N., *Teoria literatury*, Moscow, 1978.

Prigarina, N.I., *Poezia Muhammada Ikbala (1900–1924)*, Moscow, 1972.

Problemy arabskoy kul'tury (collected articles in memory of Academician I.Yu. Krachkovsky), Moscow, 1987.

Problemy istorii literatury SShA, Moscow, 1964.

Problemy realizma v mirovoy literature (collected articles), Moscow, 1959.

Problemy romantizma (collected articles), Moscow, 1967.

Problemy stanovlenia realizma v literaturakh Vostoka (collected articles), Moscow, 1964.

Prosvetitel'stvo v literaturakh Vostoka (collected articles), Moscow, 1973.

Prozhogina, S.V., *Rubezh epokh – rubezh kul'tur: problemy tipologii literatur na frantsuzskom yazyke v stranakh Severnoy Afriki, 40-80-e gody*, Moscow, 1984.

Pustovoyt, P.G., *Roman I.S. Turgeneva "Otsy i deti" i ideynaya bor'ba 60-x godov XIX veka*, Moscow, 1965.

Qindilchi, Amir Ibrahim, *al-'Arab fi al-mahjar al-Amriki*, Cairo, 1977.

al-Qisas al-Lubananiyya, mukhtarat, Beirut, 1948.

Qunsul, Ilyas, *Adab al-mughtaribin*, Damascus, 1963.

Qutb, Sayyid, *al-Naqd al-adabi*, Cairo, 1954.

Rafi'i, Tawfiq, *Amin al-Rihani: A Biography*, Cairo, 1922.

Ra'i, 'Ali, "Mihka'il Nu'ayma wa masrahiyya al-ra'ida 'Al-Aba' wa al-banun'", *Majallat al-'Arabi*, 239, 1979.

Rasa'il Amin al-Rihani, Beirut, 1950.

Rasa'il Jubran, Beirut, 1951.

Rasskazy pisateley Livana (Russ. trans. from Arabic), Moscow, 1958.

Rawi, Haris Taha, *Amin al-Rayhani*, Beirut, 1958.

——, "al-Thawra al-fikriyya fi adab al-mahjar", *al-Adab*, 5, Beirut, 1954.

Razvitie literatury v epokhu formirovania natsiy v stranakh Tsentral'noy i Yugo-vostochnoy Evropy (collected articles), Moscow, 1983.

Reyhani, Albert, *Amin al-Rihani*, Beirut, 1941.

al-Rifa'i, Shams al-Din, *Ta'rikh al-sihafa al-Suriyya: fi al-'ahd al-'Uthmani (1800–1917)*, Cairo, 1969.

Rihani, Ameen, *A Chant of Mystics and other Poems*, New York, 1921.

——, (al-Rayhani, Amin), *Adab wa fann*, Beirut, 1958.

——, *Haqiqat al-dimukratiyya al-Amirikiyya*, Beirut, 1948.

——, *Hutaf al-awdiya*, Beirut, 1955.

——, *Izbrannie proizvedenia*, Petrograd, 1917, and Leningrad, 1988.

——, *Kharij al-harim aw Jahan*, New York, 1917, and Beirut, 1943.

——, *Muluk al-'Arab*, Beirut, 1924.

——, *al-Rihaniyyat*, 1–4, Beirut, 1910, 1922, 1924, 1956.

Rossiyanov, O.K., "Romantizm v vengerskoy literature", in *Razvitie literatury v epokhe formirovania natsiy v stranakh Tsentral'noy i Yugo-Vostochnoy Evropy*, Moscow, 1983.

Ruppin, Artur, *Sovremennaya Siria i Palestina* (trans. from German, ed. A.O. Zaydenman), Petrograd, 1919.

Russkaya klassika v stranakh Vostoka (collected articles), Moscow, 1982.

Russko-evropeyskie literaturnie svyazi (collected articles), Moscow, 1966.

Safronov, V.V., "K zarozhdeniu romanticheskogo napravlenia v egipetskoy proze XX veka", in *Vestnik Moskovskogo gosudarstvennogo universiteta*, series 13, *Vostokovedenie*, 1, 1987.

Sa'ib Sa'd, *Shu'ara' min Amrika al-Janubiyya*, Baghdad, 1974.

Sarraj, Nadira Jamil, *Shu'ara al-Rabita al-Qalamiyya*, Cairo, 1955.
——, and 'Arida, Nasib, *al-Sha'ir al-katib al-suhufi*, Cairo, 1955.
Saydah, George, *Adabuna wa udaba'una fi al-mahajir al-Amirikiyya*, Beirut, 1964.
Sayigh, Tawfiq, *Adwa' jadida 'ala Jubran*, Beirut, 1966.
Schiller, Friedrich, *Istoria zapadnoevropeyskoy literatury novogo vremeni*, vol. 1, Moscow, 1936.
Semyonov, D.V., "Russkoe Palestinskoe obshchestvo i yego deyatel'nost' do voyny 1914 g", in *Novy Vostok*, 8–9, 1925.
Shafiq, Muhammad, *Falsafa Mikha'il Nu'ayma*, Beirut, 1979.
Shafrutdinova, R.Sh., "Russko-arabskie kul'turnie svyazi na Blizhnem Vostoke", in *Palestinsky sbornik*, 26 (89), Leningrad, 1978.
al-Shahal, Ridwan, "Progressivnie realisticheskie techenia v sovremennoy arabskoy literature", in *Sovremennaya arabskaya literatura*, Moscow, 1960.
Sharabi, Hisham, *Arab Intellectuals and the West: the formative years (1887–1914)*, Baltimore/London, 1970.
al-Shazli, Mahmud M.E., "Ideynoe i khudozhestvennoe vlianie russkoy i sovetskoy literatury na egipetsky roman" [abstract of candidate dissertation in philology], Moscow, 1973.
Sharbatov, G.Sh., "Arabskaya novella", in *Sovremenny Vostok*, 9, 1958.
Shelley, Percy Bysshe, *Izbrannie proizvedenia* (trans. by Boris Pasternak), Moscow, 1962.
Shidfar, B.Ya., *Obraznaya sistema arabskoy klassicheskoy literatury (VI–VII vv)*, Moscow, 1974.
Shifman, A.I., "Lev Tolstoy i narody Vostoka", in *Narody Azii i Afriki*, Moscow, 1979, No. 9.
——, "Tolstoy i arabskie strany", in *Lev Tolstoy i Vostok*, Moscow, 1971.
Smilyanskaya, I.M., *Krest'yanskoe dvizhenie v Livane v pervoy polovine XIX v.*, Moscow, 1965.
Solov'ev, V., Fil'shtinsky, I. and Yusupov, D., *Arabskaya literatura: kratky ocherk*, Moscow, 1964.
Sovremennaya arabskaya literatura, Moscow, 1960.
Sovremennaya arabskaya novella, Moscow, 1963.
Sovremennaya arabskaya proza, Moscow and Leningrad, 1961.
Spiller, Robert E., "Ralph Waldo Emerson", in *Literaturnaya istoria SShA*, vol. 1, Moscow, 1977.
Stalknecht, N., et al., *Comparative Literature: method and perspective*, Carbondale, IL, 1971.
Startsev, L.I., "Genri Toro i ego Uolden", in Thoreau, Henry David, *Uolden ili Zhizn' v lesu*, Moscow, 1979.
Suchkov, B.L., *Istoricheskie sud'by realizma*, Moscow, 1967.
Suhayl, Idris, "Zaydan wa Jubran wa Nu'ayma: ruwwad al-qissa fi Lubnan", *Majallat al-Adib*, 3/5, 1958.
Sukhotina-Tolstaya, T.L., *Vospominania*, Moscow, 1980.
Surovtsev, Yu.I., "Natsional'noe svoeobrazie i natsional'ny kharakter: metodologicheskie zametki", in *International'noe i natsional'noe v literaturakh Vostoka*, Moscow, 1972.
Talisi, Khalifa Muhammad, *al-Shabbi wa Jubran*, Tripoli, 1957, and Beirut, 1967.
Tarazi, Filipp, *Ta'rikh al-sihafa al-'Arabiyya*, vol. 4, Beirut, 1933.

Ta'rikh al-adab al-'Arabi al-hadith, Baghdad, 1971.

Ta'rikh jarida al-Huda wa al-jawwali al-Lubnaniyya fi Amrika, New York, 1968.

Taymur, Mahmud, *Fi al-adab al-'Arabi al-hadith*, Beirut, 1954.

Tazetdinova, L.A., *Poezia Amina al-Rihani* [candidate dissertation in philology], Leningrad, 1986.

Teoria literaturnykh stiley: sovremennie aspekty izuchenia (collected articles), Moscow, 1982.

Terteryan, I.A., "Romantizm kak tselostnoe yavlenie", in *Voprosy literatury*, 1983, 4.

Thoreau, Henry David, *Walden*, Moscow, 1979.

Timofeev, L.I., "O ponyatii khudozhestvennogo metoda", in *Tvorchsky metod*, Moscow, 1960.

——, *Osnovy teorii literatury*, Moscow, 1976.

Tipologia i vzaimosvyazi srednevekovykh literatur Vostoka i Zapada (collected articles), Moscow, 1974.

Tolstoy, L.N., "Chto takoe religia i v chem ee sushchnost'?", *Poln. sobr. soch. (yubileynoe)*, vol. 35, Moscow and Leningrad, 1956.

——, "Lyubite drug druga", *Poln. sobr. soch.*, vol. 37, Moscow, 1956.

——, *Sobranie sochineniy*, vols. 10 and 12, Moscow, 1982; vols. 14 and 16, Moscow, 1983; vol. 17, Moscow, 1984.

Tomeh, George, *al-Mughtaribun al-'Arab fi Amrika al-shamaliyya*, Damascus, 1965.

Troitsky, V.Yu., *Kniga pokoleniy: o romane I.S. Turgeneva "Otsi i deti"*, Moscow, 1979.

Turgenev, I., *Fathers and Sons*, New York, 1943.

——, *Sobrannie sochineniy*, Moscow, 1954.

Tvorchesky metod (collected articles), Moscow, 1960.

Urnov, D.M., "Zhivoe plamya slova", in *Poezia angliyskogo romantizma*, Moscow, 1975.

Usmanov, N.K., "Literatura arabskikh stran" and "Osobennosti arabskogo prosveshchenia", in *Literatura Vostoka v novoe vremya*, Moscow, 1975.

——, "Razvitie prosvetitel'skikh idey na arabskom Vostoke v XIX v", in *Prosvetitel'stvo v literaturakh Vostoka*, Moscow, 1973.

V moem gorode idet dozhd' (*novelly pisateley Sirii, Livana, Iordana*) (Russ. trans. from Arabic), Moscow, 1966.

Vanslov, V.V., *Estetika romantizma*, Moscow, 1966.

Venidiktova, T.D., *Poezia Uolta Uitmena*, Moscow, 1982.

Vertsman, I., Preface to Rousseau, J.J., *Izbr. soch.*, vol. 1, Moscow, 1961.

Volkov, I.F., "Osnovnie problemy izuchenia romantizma", in *K istorii russkogo romantizma*, Moscow, 1973.

——, *Tvorcheskie metody i khudozhestvennie sistemy*, Moscow, 1978.

Volosatov, V.A., Preface to Gibran, K., *Sleza i ulybka*, Moscow, 1976.

——, Preface to Gibran, K., *Slomannie krylya*, Mosocw, 1962.

Voprosy romantizma i realizma v zarubezhnoy literature (collected articles), Dnetropetrovsk, 1969.

Vostochnie motivy: stikhotvorenia i poemy, Moscow, 1975.

Vostochny al'manakh: osen' v gorakh. 7, Moscow, 1979.

Vzaimodeystvie kul'tur Vostoka i Zapada (collected articles), Moscow, 1987.

Vzaimosvyazi afrikanskikh literatur i literatura mira (collected articles), Moscow, 1975.

Vzaimosvyazi i vzaimodeystvie national'nykh literatur (materialy diskussii, 1960 g.), Moscow, 1961.

Weisstein, U., *Comparative Literature and Literary Theory*, Bloomington, IL, and London, 1973.

Whitman, Walt, *Izbrannie proizvedenia*, Moscow, 1970.

——, *List'ya travy*, Moscow, 1982.

Young, Barbara, *This Man from Lebanon*, New York, 1956.

Yunis, Adel, "The Arab who follows Columbus in the Arab World", *The Arab Information Center*, 6/12, 1966.

Zalesskaya, L.I., *O romanticheskom techenii v sovetskoy literature*, Moscow, 1973.

Zhirmunsky, V.M., *Sravnitel'noe literaturovedenie*, Leningrad, 1979.

——, "Problemy sravnitel'no-istoricheskogo izuchenia literatur", in *Vzaimosvyazi i vzaimodeystvie natsional'nykh literatur*, Moscow, 1961.

Zykova, Ye.P., "Vostok v tvorchestve poetov 'ozernoy shkoly'", in *Vzaimodeystvie kul'tur Vostoka i Zapada*, Moscow, 1987.

Index

Kahlil Gibran, Ameen Rihani and Mikhail Naimy are not indexed in their individual chapters